Cognitive Neuroscience of Memory

Lars-Göran Nilsson
Hans J. Markowitsch
(Editors)

# Cognitive Neuroscience of Memory

 Hogrefe & Huber Publishers
Seattle · Toronto · Bern · Göttingen

**Library of Congress Cataloging-in-Publication Data**

is available via the Library of Congress Marc Database under the
**LC Catalog Card Number 99-71722**


**Canadian Cataloguing in Publication Data**

Main entry under title:
Cognitive neuroscience of memory

Based on a conference entitled Cognitive neuroscience and memory, held in
Lidingo, Stockholm, Sweden, June 13–15, 1997.
Includes index.
ISBN 0-88937-213-6
1. Memory – Congresses.  2. Cognitive neuroscience – Congresses.
I. Nilsson, Lars-Göran, 1944–    . II. Markowitsch, Hans J., 1949–    .
QP406.C63              1999            612.8'2            C99-930606-5

© Copyright 1999 by Hogrefe & Huber Publishers
USA:                    P.O. Box 2487, Kirkland, WA 98083-2487
                        Phone (425) 820-1500, Fax (425) 823-8324
CANADA:                 12 Bruce Park Avenue, Toronto, Ontario M4P 2S3
                        Phone (416) 482-6339
SWITZERLAND:            Länggass-Strasse 76, CH-3000 Bern 9
                        Phone (031) 300-4500, Fax (031) 300-4590
GERMANY:                Rohnsweg 25, D-37085 Göttingen
                        Phone (0551) 49609-0, Fax (0551) 49609-88

Printed and bound in Germany
ISBN 0-88937-213-6

# Foreword

Cognitive neuroscience is one of the most exciting areas of scientific research at the present time. The new techniques of functional neuroimaging have literally revolutionized the study of the neural correlates of perception, memory, language, and thinking, enabling cognitive and brain scientists to work within a common framework. The present book – focusing on the cognitive neuroscience of memory – captures this excitement and interdisciplinary stimulation extremely well. The chapters are written by European investigators, and this gives the volume a fresh and interesting perspective. The authors draw on ideas and findings from neuroanatomy, neurology, psychiatry, cognitive psychology, neuropharmacology, and other disciplines to present a set of views that fit together surprisingly well given the complexity of the phenomena under investigation. Individual chapters give state-of-the-art accounts of work using PET imaging, case studies of memory impairments following both brain lesions and environmental stress, computational modelling, genetic markers, animal studies of learning, and much else. The roles of the hippocampus, frontal lobes and other brain regions are explored, discussed, and integrated into speculative but plausible frameworks. It is abundantly clear that "memory" is not one monolithic entity, and this collection shows how the different memory systems perform different functions, and are mediated by different brain regions and by different neurochemical systems.

The editors make the interesting comment that brain researchers at the turn of the century *did* take anatomy, physiology, psychology, and clinical data into account in formulating their theories, but that later generations of scientists became progressively more specialized. Cognitive neuroscience has once again brought these various perspectives together, and the resulting interactions are exciting indeed. This volume does an excellent job of conveying the flavor of ongoing research into the neural correlates of memory and learning. Although the topic is a complex one – nothing less than the integration of mind and brain – the present collection provides a comprehensive account of current concepts and data, and also conveys a satisfying sense that real advances in our understanding are being made.

Fergus Craik, University of Toronto

# Preface

The exploration of human memory has been an area of considerable research interest for more than a century now. During most of this period the scientific study of memory has largely followed two separate traditions, with relatively little interaction between them. One tradition has its roots in the important discoveries made by the German experimental psychologist, Hermann Ebbinghaus (1850–1909), whereas the other tradition has its origin in the French experimental and clinical psychologist, Théodule Ribot (1839–1916).

Although Ebbinghaus and Ribot were both experimental psychologists, the traditions emerging from their work developed quite differently. Ebbinghaus was the first to demonstrate that learning and memory can be measured. In his ground-breaking 1885 book, *Über das Gedächtnis*, he described how he, as the constructor of the study materials, the experimenter, and the sole subject, spent several hours each day over a 2-year period learning these materials and testing himself on how much he remembered. Although the work of Ebbinghaus was heavily criticized, it also did much to convince the skeptical that quantitative methods could be applied to the study of higher mental processes such as memory. At the risk of making an oversimplification, it is probably fair to say that the vast majority of memory researchers ever since have worked within an Ebbinghaus tradition, at least those memory researchers who had their training in experimental psychology.

Ribot's main contribution to our understanding of memory was detailed in a book he published in 1881, *Les Maladies de la Mémoire*, in which he put forward a theory of the progressive loss of memory brought about by brain diseases. Ribot's book was very soon translated into English as *Diseases of Memory* (1882) and came to have an important impact on researchers interested in clinical and biological aspects of memory all over the world.

Important contributions were made within both the experimental Ebbinghaus tradition focusing on functional aspects of memory and the clinically and biologically oriented Ribot tradition, which soon came to focus on brain lesions and the role of various brain structures for memory. With few exceptions, memory researchers within these two traditions developed their respective fields in isolation, with little or no influence from the parallel developments in the other field. However, as knowledge accumulated within each of these two areas of memory research, some brave scholars in the middle of the 20th century crossed the border to obtain fresh new inspiration. This cross-fertilization of the two traditions soon took on new dimensions with the arrival of technological developments such as equipment for brain imaging. As students of memory have learnt more and more about the basics of the two traditions of memory research, a new scientific discipline has begun to emerge, that of cognitive neuroscience. This new discipline combines cognitive psychology, neuropsychology, behavioral neurology, neuroanatomy, neurophysiology, genetics, psychopharmacology, and computational modeling.

It was in the context of a new scientific discipline in the process of being formed that a conference on "Cognitive Neuroscience and Memory" took place at the Södergarn Conference Center, Lidingö, Stockholm, Sweden, on June 13–15, 1997. The prime objective of the conference was to assemble prominent scientists actively working in the area of cognitive neuroscience and memory to discuss and develop a common ground for research in this field. During these few sunny days and bright nights in splendid surroundings, the participants listened to and discussed many excellent papers. In addition to regular presentations, considerable time was devoted to discussions. The speakers and a small group of graduate students and colleagues from Swedish universities seemed to enjoy the whole event. When the speakers agreed to publish the ideas that were presented and discussed, to let the rest of the world know about what had emerged, we were encouraged to think that a more appropriate title of the book would be *Cognitive Neuroscience of Memory*, rather than the more modest title of the conference.

The conference was made possible by financial support from the Swedish Council for Research in the Humanities and Social Sciences, who also provided support for the publication of this book. This support is gratefully acknowledged. All practical arrangements related to the conference and the publication of this book ran very efficiently. For this, we are indebted to graduate students from the Department of Psychology at Stockholm University: Carola Åberg, Farah Moniri, Julie Yonker, and, most of all, to Susanne Eliasson, who took the main responsibility for the smooth arrangements.

*Lars-Göran Nilsson, Hans J. Markowitsch*

## References

Ebbinghaus, H. (1885). *Über das Gedächtnis* [On memory]. Leipzig: Duncker & Humbolt.

Ribot, T. (1882). *Diseases of memory*. New York: D. Appleton and Co. [French original: Ribot, T. (1881). *Les maladies de la mémoire*. Paris. German translation, cited after Kalberlah (1904): Ribot, T. (1882). *Das Gedächtnis und seine Störungen*. Hamburg, Leipzig].

# Contents

Fergus Craik:
Foreword . . . . . . . . . . . . . . . . . . . . . . . . . . . . . . . .   v

Lars-Göran Nilsson & Hans J. Markowitsch:
Preface . . . . . . . . . . . . . . . . . . . . . . . . . . . . . . . .  vii

List of Contributors . . . . . . . . . . . . . . . . . . . . . . . . .  xi

Chapter 1
Lars-Göran Nilsson & Hans J. Markowitsch:
Cognitive Neuroscience of Memory . . . . . . . . . . . . . .   1

Chapter 2
Endel Tulving:
On the Uniqueness of Episodic Memory . . . . . . . . . . . .  11

Chapter 3
Lars Nyberg:
Functional Neuroanatomy of Component Processes
of Episodic Memory Retrieval . . . . . . . . . . . . . . . . . .  43

Chapter 4
Daniela Perani:
The Functional Basis of Memory: PET Mapping of the
Memory Systems in Humans . . . . . . . . . . . . . . . . . . .  55

Chapter 5
Katharina Henke:
The Roles of the Hippocampus in Memory . . . . . . . . . . .  79

Chapter 6
Shu-Chen Li & Ulman Lindenberger:
Cross-Level Unification: A Computational Exploration
of the Link Between Deterioration of Neurotransmitter
Systems and Dedifferentiation of Cognitive Abilities
in Old Age . . . . . . . . . . . . . . . . . . . . . . . . . . . 103

Chapter 7
Lars-Göran Nilsson:
Aging, Dementia, and Memory . . . . . . . . . . . . . . . . 147

Chapter 8
Gianfranco Dalla Barba:
Confabulation and Temporality . . . . . . . . . . . . . . . . 163

Chapter 9
Hans J. Markowitsch:
Stress-Related Memory Disorders . . . . . . . . . . . . . . 193

Chapter 10
Giovanni A. Carlesimo:
Perceptual and Conceptual Components of Repetition
Priming in Anterograde Amnesia . . . . . . . . . . . . . . . 213

Chapter 11
Jean Delacour:
The Memory System and Brain Organization:
From Animal to Human Studies . . . . . . . . . . . . . . . 239

Chapter 12
Hans J. Markowitsch & Lars-Göran Nilsson:
Memory and Brain: Unresolved Issues . . . . . . . . . . . . 271

Author Index . . . . . . . . . . . . . . . . . . . . . . . . . . 277

Subject Index . . . . . . . . . . . . . . . . . . . . . . . . . . 295

# List of Contributors

Giovanni A. Carlesimo
IRCCS S. Lucia
Via Ardeatina 306
I-00179 Rome
Italy

Gianfranco Dalla Barba
U324 INSERM Centre Paul Broca
2 ter, rue d'Alésia
F-75014 Paris
France

Jean Delacour
Université Paris 7
Laboratoire de psychophysiologie
63 rue des Bruyeres
F-92310 Sevres
France

Katharina Henke
Neuropsychologische Abteilung
Neurologische Universitätsklinik
Zurich
Frauenklinikstrasse 26
CH-8091 Zurich
Switzerland

Shu-Chen Li
Max Planck Institute for
Human Development
Centre for Lifespan Development
Lentzealle 94
D-14195 Berlin
Germany

Hans J. Markowitsch
Physiological Psychology
University of Bielefeld
PO Box 100131
D-33501 Bielefeld
Germany

Lars-Göran Nilsson
Department of Psychology
Stockholm University
S-10691 Stockholm
Sweden

Lars Nyberg
Psykologiska Institutionen
Umeå Universitiet
S-90187 Umeå
Sweden

Daniela Perani
Consiglio Nazionale delle Richerche
Istituto di Neuroscienze e
Bioimmagini
Via Olgettina 60
I-20131 Milan
Italy

Endel Tulving
Rotman Research Institute of
Baycrest Centre
3560 Bathurst Street
North York, Ontario
M6A 2E1
Canada

# Cognitive Neuroscience of Memory

*Lars-Göran Nilsson and Hans J. Markowitsch*

Memory research constitutes one of the most progressive and dynamic fields of study at the present time. There is more than one reason for this. The nature of memory itself is obviously one reason. The ability to retain information from one occasion to the next is essential for all living organisms. For less developed animals it is crucial for survival. For humans it is indispensable for a meaningful intelligent life; without it the individual lacks history and critical anchor points to others in society at large. Recent technological developments have made it possible to study the nature of memory from a cognitive neuroscience perspective as never before.

The growing interest in memory functions is also based on more pragmatic concerns in relation to various kinds of memory disorders. The understanding of memory decline in old age is an example of this. Memory and other cognitive problems, including those accompanying Alzheimer's disease and other progressive brain diseases, are going to increase with the increasing populations of the elderly. This realization has contributed to the dramatic increase of research in this field. As the number of elderly people keeps increasing in most countries in the world, there is a growing concern to understand what the reasons for this memory decline are, and whether there is any cure or remediation.

Moreover, the unexpected discoveries about the high degree of selectivity in the impairment of memory functions of brain damaged clinical patients, who for a long time had been assumed to be globally amnesic, have contributed to the interest that memory holds for scientists in many fields. This is reflected in the emergence of a new scientific discipline under the name of cognitive neuroscience. It combines cognitive psychology, neuropsychology, behavioral neurology, neuroanatomy, neurophysiology, genetics, psychopharmacology, and computational modelling.

The discoveries of specificity in the impairment of memory functions in humans have set the stage for increased research activity in learning and memory of other animals. The discovery of long-term potentiation and long-term depression, and the realization of the possibility that the cellular and molecular mechanisms might provide the long sought-after substrate of learning and memory have broadened the scope of the field, thereby also contributing to the expansive nature of memory research.

As a result of all these developments, research on memory has undergone a dramatic change during the last couple of decades. Most research in this field was previously done with little or no interaction between different disciplines. Such a strategy is now more or less abandoned; a more interactive and interdisciplinary approach is presently underway, with the ambition to integrate current knowledge about the brain with knowledge about the functional aspects of memory.

The recent development of neuroimaging methods such as positron emission tomography (PET) and functional magnetic resonance imaging techniques (fMRI) has brought new impulses to the study of memory and new insights to the understanding of memory. As we will see in several chapters of this volume, the development of these methods has extended the field of enquiry in many ways. For one thing, many students of memory were satisfied for a long time with merely using the experimental methods developed in cognitive psychology for studying memory. This is not the case any more. Today, cognitive psychologists have become as much aware of the physiological and neurobiological advances in the study of learning and memory as neurobiologists have become aware of the nature of the paramount issues of learning and memory—those concerning human memory. Even orthodox experimentalists working in the field of cognitive psychology some two or three decades ago are now using PET or fMRI to extend their knowledge of memory beyond the psychological aspects of remembering. Moreover, these new neuroimaging methods have made it possible to explore the mind-brain relationship without having to rely on lesion studies in brain damaged people.

The twelve chapters of the present book deal with different aspects of neuroscience and memory. Following this introductory chapter, Endel Tulving argues in Chapter 2 for the uniqueness of episodic memory. As known all along since Tulving (1972), episodic memory is the form of memory that makes it possible for people to consciously recollect personally experienced events as experienced. In his chapter, Tulving notes that scientists and lay persons alike seldom appreciate uniqueness of episodic memory in evolution, probably because of its ubiquity in the human species. He also thinks that people seldom appreciate its uniqueness among the large family of memory forms that human beings possess, because they simply take for granted the ability to remember previously experienced events. The thesis of Tulving's chapter is that episodic memory is truly unique in that it exists only in mature healthy human beings. It does not exist, at least in the same form, in other animals and in young children, and it is greatly impaired in a number of neurological disease states and in brain damage. Although the absence of episodic memory in non-human animals and in young children cannot be proven, the argument rests on the absence of evidence for the presence of episodic memory in these populations. The argument is also based on the presence of a good deal of evidence that many memory achievements of which non-human animals and young children are capable do not require autonoetic conscious recollection of the past. In his chapter, Tulving also presents an interesting refinement and extension of the HERA model (Tulving, Kapur, Craik, Moscovitch, & Houle, 1994).

In Chapter 3, Lars Nyberg presents a review of PET studies on memory with the purpose of identifying functional neuroanatomical correlates of three components in retrieval from episodic memory. The first component, referred to by Nyberg as retrieval mode, is based on processes involved in attempting to retrieve memories of previously experienced events. Several studies reported in the literature have found increased activity in a right medial anterior prefrontal region of cortex to be associated with the initializing and maintaining a given mental set, that the person has experienced before. The second component is called ecphory, which is a term that Richard Semon coined long ago (Semon, 1909) to mean activation of a latent engram. Tulving (1976) later revitalized this term and it has ever since been seen as a principal component of episodic memory retrieval (e. g., Tulving, 1983; Schacter & Tulving, 1994). This process of recovering stored information has been associated with increased activity in hippocampal regions as well as in some lateral temporal and medial neocortical areas. The third component, referred to by Nyberg as recollective experience, reflects processes involved in assessing ecphoric information as veridical. Nyberg reports that there is some evidence linking this component to bilateral prefrontal activation. The component analysis by Nyberg summarizing these converging findings provide a promising first step towards the understanding of the functional neuroanatomy of episodic memory retrieval. Important future steps will be to characterize the nature and timing of interactions between neural regions that underlie different component processes.

Daniela Perani presents an instructive review in Chapter 4 about the functional basis of memory on the basis of PET mapping studies of various memory systems in humans. First, PET studies in steady-state conditions are described in the context of a model of pathological memory. Special emphasis is given to global amnesia, Alzheimer's disease, and multiple sclerosis. In amnesic patients there is a significant reduction of metabolism in a network of interconnected brain regions involving temporal mesial cortex, thalamus, cingulate gyrus and frontal basal cortex. For Alzheimer patients, Perani reports the results from a multiple regression analysis of test scores with metabolic data. For short-term memory and semantic memory there are strong correlations to the left perisylvian language areas. For procedural learning there is a correlation to a network involving cerebellum, the basal ganglia, and the dorsolateral frontal cortex. The association between episodic memory and the structures of Papez's circuit is also reported to be confirmed in these analyses. In another section of the chapter Perani presents a review of in vivo mapping of memory systems in normal subjects by means of PET activation. Emphasis in this section is given to studies on short-term memory/working memory and declarative memory with some important highlights on PET studies of semantic memory. Interestingly, Perani points out that the results from PET neuroimaging studies reported in this latter section could not have been predicted from neuropsychological investigations in amnesic patients. Thus, it is concluded "that PET data has more than a simple confirmatory role of the results of lesion-based neuropsychological investigations" (Perani, this volume).

In Chapter 5, Katharina Henke provides an interesting review of what is known about the roles of the hippocampus in memory. Henke starts out by describing a very mixed picture concerning the role of the hippocampal formation in declarative memory. Results from lesion studies in both animals and humans show the role of the hippocampus to be far from clear. This is also the case for results from studies on epilepsy surgery and functional neuroimaging. Some of the different roles of the hippocampus are summarized in Henke's chapter. One role is to memorize and recall spatial information (O'Keefe & Nadel, 1978), another role is to assess novelty (Tulving, Markowitsch, Kapur, Habib, & Houle, 1994; Tulving, Markowitsch, Craik, Habib, & Houle, 1996; Knight, 1996), still another is to consolidate information from short-term memory to long-term memory (Squire, 1992; Squire & Alvarez, 1995), and a further role is to bind different aspects of a learning episode in memory and to allow for a flexible retrieval (Cohen & Eichenbaum, 1993). Henke reports in her chapter of a PET study of her own (Henke, Buck, Weber, & Wieser, 1997), that was designed to test these hypotheses. It is concluded on the basis of this study that binding aspects of a learning event in memory is probably the most basic and crucial role of hippocampus.

Shu-Chen Li and Ulman Lindenberger present an interesting computational exploration of the link between aging-induced degeneration in neurotransmitter systems and the dedifferentiation of cognitive abilities in old age in Chapter 6. They take developmental theories of intelligence as the point of departure for their discussion. These theories offer a continuum from differentiation to dedifferentiation to reflect the ontogeny of the structure of intelligence across the life span. As children develop, their intellectual abilities become more differentiated, whereas for old people the intellectual abilities dedifferentiate. This dedifferentiation of cognitive abilities in old people expresses itself empirically as an increasing correlation between performances in different cognitive tasks. Li and Lindenberger argue that recent findings by Baltes and Lindenberger (1997) showing a strong link between cognitive and sensory functioning provide strong support for the dedifferentiation hypothesis. When the brain ages with its efficacy attenuated, performances in different cognitive tasks become more related to each other because the effects from task-specific processes are overshadowed by the overwhelming common effect of general brain aging. Neural network simulations are used to explore the possibility of a general factor leading to the dedifferentiation of performances in different tasks. Age-induced changes in brain efficacy is modeled by manipulating a gain parameter of the activation function of the network. The gain parameter affects the slope of the activation function in ways that are analogous to the modulatory effects of dopamine. Reducing gain, simulating a defective dopaminergic system, leads to low responsivity of the network's processing units and high internal noise. Samples of networks are constructed and trained to perform different memory and categorization tasks. Correlations between performances in different tasks are then computed across networks. The results show that performances of the networks with reduced gain are intercorrelated more highly to each other. Li and Lindenberger conclude that they demonstrate computationally that a single general factor which decreases the responsivity of a system and, at the same time, increases its internal noise can lead to the dedifferentiation of the performances of the system.

In Chapter 7, Lars-Göran Nilsson describes a longitudinal study on memory, health and aging. The study is in many ways unique; it is based on the participation of a large number of subjects who are randomly sampled from the population of one city in Sweden, ten different age cohorts are followed across three different waves of data collection, four different samples are used to differentiate the effects of chronological age, cohort and time of measurement with the possibility also to evaluate practice effects between test occasions. Moreover, a large number of memory tasks are included in the cognitive test battery. These include tasks assumed to assess episodic memory, semantic memory, perceptual representation system, procedural memory, and primary memory. Various biological measures are taken, including sensory function, body measures, blood pressure, and blood samples. In addition there are subjective reports on perceived health status, medication, use of health care, diseases, family history, critical life events, working conditions etc. Interview data about social variables are also included in the database. A series of observations from the first and the second waves of data collection are reported. Interesting dissociations between performances in episodic and semantic memory tests are reported for various health variables. A discussion of the relationship between memory function and some genetic markers is also provided. Memory presents several challenges for molecular genetic analysis. One suitable feature is that memory is a quantitative "trait" with essentially a normal distribution. Another aspect of memory that makes it suitable for a molecular genetic analysis is that it is multifactorial, involving environmental as well as genetic sources of variance. Moreover, it seems reasonable to assume that its heritability is due to multiple genes of varying effect size rather than a few genes of major effect. These three challenges have been proposed for the general factor, g, of human intelligence (Plomin, 1997), and it seems likely to assume that the same would hold true for memory too.

In Chapter 8, Gianfranco Dalla Barba provides an insightful discussion of the illusion of the homunculus and the memory trace paradox in the context of confabulation and temporality. Two cases are used as illustrations of the points Dalla Barba wants to make. The first case, PL, is a 57-year-old right handed woman who has developed an amnesic-confabulatory syndrome following a cardiac arrest. This case is reported to test the hypothesis of confabulation as a deficit of strategic retrieval, and to verify the idea that memories are randomly stored without a temporal order. The second case, GA, is a 52-year old right handed woman with five years of education, who had a subarachnoid hemorrhage clipped. Clipping near the aneurysm was followed by widespread bilateral frontal ischemia and infarction. CAT, MRI and PET scans showed bilateral frontal degenerative areas extending from the orbito-frontal regions to the dorsal areas, involving the anterior cyngulum and the anterior two thirds of the Corpus Callosum. GA's confabulations are reported as being restricted to episodic memory and orientation in time and place. It is also reported that GA's confabulations are independent of the availability of the correct answer. With these two cases as a base Dalla Barba proposes a hypothesis about the relation between memory, consciousness and temporality. Among other things this hypothesis states that an episodic memory deficit is always accompanied by an impairment of planning the personal future since both are functions of temporal consciousness.

In Chapter 9, Hans Markowitsch discusses possible environmental influences on memory performance. His central theme is the possible similarity between amnesia originating from a known organic cause (brain injury) and those referred to as psychogenic, that is without an overt or measurable organic basis. Referring to psychoanalytic terms like repressed memories, he provides a selection of astonishing examples of selective autobiographic amnesia of the total life period which may be triggered by psychic or physical (somatic) stress situations. He postulates that there are enormous inter-individual differences in coping with stress situations, depending on the individual's previous exposure to stress, both quantitatively and qualitatively. With certain constellations, the brain's biochemistry – the transmitter, neuromodulator, and neurohormonal levels – may change their set points and their availability, with the consequence of improper information processing.

Both the case examples given in support of this thesis and the evidence available from animal experimentation clearly underline the possibility of lasting environmental influences on brain activity and mnestic performance. They also reinforce the view that mood states (e. g., depression) can have a tremendous impact on memory. The amnesia induced by such stressful phenomena is termed "mnestic block syndrome."

In Chapter 10, Giovanni A. Carlesimo presents a summary of his own research and that of others reported in the literature with respect to impaired and spared memory functions in both pure amnesics and demented patients. The discussion is focused on perceptual and conceptual components of repetition priming in anterograde amnesia, but other tasks than priming are covered too, and other patient groups. The controversy between a memory systems approach and a processing approach is discussed in relation to how neuropsychological data can contribute in understanding the dichotomy between episodic memory and repetition priming. The overall purpose of this review is to be able to characterize the impaired and spared memory functions better than has been done previously. The pattern of data that seems to be emerging is that the deficit in pure amnesics is specific for the explicit retrieval of the product of conceptually driven information. In demented patients, the repetition priming effect is still able to sustain improved identification of previously experienced information, but it is not strong enough to sustain generation of previously studied information.

In Chapter 11, Jean Delacour provides a synthetic view of the neurobiology of learning and memory on the basis of both animal studies and human studies. The model described is based on three interacting systems: C for coding, A for action, and S for supervision. The first system, C, comprises the neurons which code sensory information or motor programs with the greatest precision. According to Delacour, this system is distributed among modules such as the visual and motor structures, and its organization is, at least partly, topographic. System A comprises the neurons that control arousal, attention and motivation. Unlike the organization of C, the organization of A is neither modular nor topographic, but integrative. Information is not analyzed by separate, encapsulated, and specialized modules. Rather, A neurons receive convergent afferents from heterogeneous sources and project onto multiple targets through highly divergent efferents. In trying to define and delimit system S Delacour runs into some difficulties. This system is assumed to account for the goal-directed nature of behavior. The voluntary act in humans is perhaps the best illustration of the function of system S. Delacour refers to data from brain imaging studies in normal humans and to data from studies on behavioral neurophysiology in monkeys when suggesting that the frontal cortex is at least one crucial part of S. According to Delacour, interactions between C, A, and S constitute the memory system. That is, according to Delacour, the memory system is not a separate anatomical structure. In these interactions, the three systems have different and complementary roles. The role of C is specific for the to-be-remembered information. The A structures implicated in the global amnestic syndromes (the medial diencephalon and the temporal lobe) are involved in memory requiring a conscious recollection of a study episode, independently of what the to-be-remembered information is. The role of system S for memory is said to be characterized by cognitive processes involved in working memory and metacognition. All three systems are assumed to be involved in encoding, storage, and retrieval, since they have comparable plastic capacities at the cellular and molecular levels.

Finally, in Chapter 12, Hans Markowitsch and Lars-Göran Nilsson discuss some unresolved issues in neurobehavioral memory research. In particular, they center on the representation of memory in the brain, on the brain's action in consolidating memories, structures involved in this process and its possible length. In spite of the still missing evidence these topics show that it will be quite rewarding for this and for future generations to study the cognitive neuroscience of memory.

## References

Baltes, P.B., & Lindenberger, U. (1997). Emergence of a powerful connection between sensory and cognitive functions across the adult lifespan: A new window to the study of cognitive aging? *Psychology and Aging, 12*, 12–21.

Cohen, N.J., & Eichenbaum, H. (1993). *Memory, amnesia, and the hippocampal system.* Cambridge, MA: MIT Press.

Henke, K., Buck, A., Weber, B., & Wieser, H.G. (1997). Human hippocampus establishes associations in memory. *Hippocampus, 7*, 249–256.

Knight, R.T. (1996). Contribution of human hippocampal region to novelty detection. *Nature, 383*, 256–259.

O'Keefe, J., & Nadel, L. (1978). *The hippocampus as a cognitive map.* Oxford: Oxford University Press.

Plomin, R. (1997). Identifying genes for cognitive abilities and disabilities. In R.J. Sternberg & E.L. Grigorenko (Eds.), *Intelligence: Heredity and environment* (pp. 89–104). New York: Cambridge University Press.

Schacter, D.L., & Tulving, E. (1994). What are the memory systems of 1994? In D.L. Schacter & E. Tulving (Eds.), *Memory systems 1994* (pp. 1–38). Cambridge: MIT Press.

Semon, R. (1909). *Die mnemischen Empfindungen.* Leipzig.

Squire, L.R. (1992). Memory and the hippocampus: A synthesis from findings with rats, monkeys, and humans. *Psychological Review, 99*, 195–231.

Squire, L.R., & Alvarez, P. (1995). Retrograde amnesia and memory consolidation: A neurobiological perspective. *Current Opinion in Neurobiology, 5,* 169–177.

Tulving, E. (1972).Episodic and semantic memory. In E. Tulving & W. Donaldson (Eds.), *Organization of memory* (pp. 381–403). New York: Academic Press.

Tulving, E. (1976). Ecphoric processes in recall and recognition. In J. Brown (Ed.), *Recall and recognition* (pp. 37–73). New York: Wiley.

Tulving, E. (1983*). Elements of episodic memory.* Oxford: Clarendon.

Tulving, E., Kapur, S., Craik, F.I.M., Moscovitch, M., & Houle, S.(1994). Hemispheric encoding/retrieval asymmetry in episodic memory: Positron emission tomography findings. *Proceedings of the National Academy of Sciences USA, 91,* 2016–2020.

Tulving, E., Markowitsch, H.J., Craik, F.I.M., Habib, R., & Houle, S. (1996). Novelty and familiarity activations in PET studies of memory encoding and retrieval. *Cerebral Cortex, 6,* 71–79.

Tulving, E., Markowitsch, H.J., Kapur, S., Habib, R., & Houle, S. (1994). Novelty encoding networks in the human brain: Positron emission tomography data. *NeuroReport, 5,* 2525–2528.

# On the Uniqueness of Episodic Memory

*Endel Tulving*

In his monumental *Principles of Psychology*, William James wrote a chapter on memory that even today makes for interesting and refreshing reading. In it James defined memory in the way in which it had become known in Western thought over the millennia, and in the way in which many people even now understand it. Memory for James then was equated with remembering what one has learned and experienced in the past. Formally, James wrote that memory is the knowledge of a former state of mind, or *"the knowledge of an event, or fact,* of which meantime we have not been thinking, *with the additional consciousness that we have thought or experienced it before"* (James, 1983, p. 610, emphasis in the original). A number of elements, James wrote, had to be present for a bit of knowledge to be acceptable as a memory: (i) revival in the mind of a "copy" of an original event, (ii) the requirement that the present image be held as standing for a "past original," and (iii) the requirement that the "pastness" refer not just to the past in general but rather to the personal past of the rememberer. Memory thus defined, James further elaborated, possesses the kind of subjectively experienced "warmth and intimacy" that mere conception, that is, mere thought about some previously learned fact, did not evoke.

Today, over a hundred years later, the concept of memory has changed in many ways even though its heart has not. Human memory, which James was writing about, has become much better understood, and infinitely more complex; the concept of memory has spread over vast domains of living organisms and their abilities to learn and benefit from their environments, from conditioning in nematodes to awareness of the past in humans; and the scientific study of memory now involves many different disciplines from molecular biology to cognitive science. But the progress in understanding memory has been more rapid in some respects than in others, and more rapid for some forms than others. The heart of Jamesian memory – one's awareness of the experienced past – was ignored for a long time by all students of memory. Only recently has it been declared to possess not only scientific interest but also being scientifically tractable. We now refer to is as episodic memory.

This chapter is about episodic memory, with especial emphasis on two key ideas that James had about memory and that characterize the thinking about episodic memory today. One idea is that memory has to do with the remember's own *personal* past. The other central idea is that the knowledge provided by episodic memory comes wrapped in the shell of a unique kind of conscious awareness that James tried to convey in terms of the notion of affective "warmth and intimacy" and that we today refer to as "*autonoetic*" awareness.

The central proposition of the chapter is that episodic memory is the only form of evolved memory that deals with the past and makes the personally experienced past accessible through autonoetic awareness. These two features – pastness of experiences and autonoetic awareness – differentiate episodic memory from all other forms of memory, and thereby make it unique. The central issue of the chapter has to do with the *neural correlates* of these two features of episodic memory: What, if anything, is known about the structures and circuits of the brain that subserve the awareness of the past? For a long time this question was completely beyond the pale of scientific methods. Today, thanks to the advances in theoretical thought about memory and to the recently developed techniques of functional brain imaging, we have available bits and pieces of fragmentary evidence that speak to the question. The chapter is a report of the initial progress that has been made.

## What is Episodic Memory?

The concept of episodic memory has changed considerably since its introduction almost 30 years ago (Tulving, 1972). At that time it was thought of as an information processing system that (a) receives and stores information about temporally dated episodes or events, and about temporal-spatial relations among these events, (b) retains various aspects of this information, and (c) upon instructions transmits specific retained information to other systems, including those responsible for translating it into behavior and conscious awareness. It was contrasted with "semantic" memory to which it was assumed to be closely related and by which it was assumed to be influenced in its workings.

This conceptualization was largely shaped by the then dominant verbal learning orientation to memory (Tulving & Madigan, 1970), the nearly exclusive use of list-learning tasks and paradigms (Crowder, 1976), and the virtual absence of any directly relevant empirical evidence. The term "episodic memory" is widely used today, and many writers still think of it in terms similar to those proposed in 1972.

The meaning of "episodic memory" in this paper derives from the orienting attitude that is known as "multiple memory systems" (Foster & Jelicic, 1999; Perani et al., 1993; Schacter & Tulving, 1994a. Episodic memory is one of several specific memory systems. The criteria used for postulating and defining memory systems, the distinction between systems and other classificatory concepts of memory – such as forms or kinds of memory, and memory tasks – and descriptions of currently known or assumed systems have been aired at some length elsewhere (Schacter & Tulving, 1994a, 1994b). The term "episodic memory" has also been used, and still is being used, in its earlier senses, but in this paper it always refers to its system-oriented concept.

Thus in this paper episodic memory refers to a memory system that makes possible mental "time travel" through subjective time, from the present to the past and to the future, a feat that other memory systems cannot perform. It does so by allowing the individual to re-experience, through autonoetic awareness, previous experiences as such, and to project similar experiences into the future. Episodic memory evolved more recently than other systems, it is probably unique to humans, and it develops late in childhood. Its operations depend on semantic and other forms of memory. Therefore, it shares neural mechanisms and cognitive processes with other systems, but in addition it is subserved by specific mechanisms and processes that are not components of any other system.

There are many other terms that are closely related even if not equivalent to episodic memory. Autobiographical memory, event memory, personal memory, source memory, memory for temporal-spatial context are the most frequently used ones. The choice of the terms reflects the user's knowledge, history, intention, and preference. Many of these other terms refer to the kind of remembered information rather than to any hypothetical memory system with specified properties, either of the kind specified by Schacter and Tulving (1994b) or any other kind. Thus, as mentioned, autobiographical memory, has to do with the recollection of significant events from a person's life. Source memory, and memory for "context," refer to the subject's expressed knowledge concerning temporal, spatial, and other environmental conditions prevailing at the time of the acquisition of some particular information. Neither term implies the postulated existence of a special neurocognitive system, as does episodic memory, and neither refers to any unique recollective experience, as does episodic memory.

## Episodic and Declarative (Semantic) Memory

The meaning of episodic memory can be clarified by contrasting it with semantic memory, because they are similar in many ways. Semantic memory – it has also been referred to as generic memory, or knowledge memory – is a memory system that makes possible acquisition, retention, and use of factual information in the broadest sense. Despite its name it is not concerned with language or with verbal information, although much of human knowledge can be expressed linguistically. The knowledge acquired by, held in, and retrieved from semantic memory is about, or represents, the world as it is, or as it could be. This kind of knowledge provides the individual with the necessary material for thought, that is, for cognitive operations on the aspects of the world beyond the reach of immediate perception. Semantic-memory operations – encoding and retrieval – are accompanied by a state of conscious awareness that the individual can differentiate from other possible states of awareness familiar from experience, such as awareness that accompanies imaging visual scenes or auditory stimuli, daydreaming, dreaming, and remembering past happenings, as well as a considerable variety of affective states of awareness. We refer to the kind of awareness that accompanies semantic-memory operations as "noetic" awareness (Tulving, 1985c, 1993).

Episodic and semantic memory are in many ways very similar, and therefore many people, in the past and even today, have tended to think of them as basically the same kind of memory. Both are large and complex, capable of storing vast amounts of information of many different kinds. Both are cognitive (declarative, or representational) systems whose "contents" can be described in terms of propositions about objects and their relations. Information in both can, in a sense, be compared with the external world, and assertions made about the world on the basis of the stored information can be judged for their truth value. Encoding of new information into one of the two systems is difficult to distinguish from encoding of information into the other. There is no simple method that could be used, even in experimental settings, for adding new information to semantic knowledge of a normal adult, without corresponding information being encoded into episodic memory, or vice versa. Both episodic and semantic memory enable individuals to acquire factual information through different sensory modalities, and in both such acquisition can occur very rapidly, sometimes as a consequence of a single glimpse or sound of a relevant input. Both episodic and semantic memory can register, and hold information about, various states of the world, including the internal states of the individual, and both can form representations of the occurrence of events that have a beginning and an end in time. Stored information in both forms of memory is flexibly accessible, a given chunk or bundle of available information being ecphorizable (activatable, actualizable) by a variety of instructions, prompts, and cues. The operations of both memory systems obey the principles of encoding specificity and transfer appropriate processing: the effectiveness of given retrieval cues is determined not only by the nominal identity of target information in the memory store, but also by its episodically and semantically encoded context. Finally, both systems can be thought of as being concerned with "remembering that" rather than "remembering how": the results of acts of retrieval from either memory system can be expressed symbolically, in language or through graphic representations, unlike the skills mediated by procedural memory that can only be expressed through nonsymbolic behavior.

Episodic and semantic memory have been generally thought of as two "subsystems" of declarative memory. In some theories (Squire, 1987) they are assumed to be organized as two parallel branches of a hierarchy, in others (Tulving, 1984, 1993) their relation is one of "embeddedness": the episodic system including the semantic but not vice versa . Recently, however, in order to better accommodate some new and intriguing findings from patients with early onset amnesia (Vargha-Khadem et al., 1997), a realignment in the organization of memory was proposed (Tulving & Markowitsch, 1998). The proposal was that "declarative memory" be equated with "semantic memory," and defined in terms of properties and features that have been assumed to be *common* to semantic and episodic memory in previous formulations. Semantic memory would be retained as a term referring to declarative memory expressed through language. Episodic memory, in this new formulation, would then represent a system that has many features in common with declarative memory but also possess features, such as autonoetic awareness of the personal past, that declarative (semantic) memory does not possess.

## Uniqueness of Episodic Memory

Despite the numerous similarities between episodic and declarative (semantic) memory – similarities that have made it difficult to separate the two – episodic memory does possess critical features not shared by the other systems. Some of these have already been mentioned or alluded to. A more detailed description is available elsewhere (Wheeler et al., 1997; Tulving & Markowitsch, 1998). I summarize episodic memory's unique features here.

First and foremost, episodic memory is the only form of memory that, at the time of retrieval, is oriented towards the past: Retrieval in episodic memory means "mental time travel" through and to one's past. All other forms of memory, including semantic, declarative, and procedural memory, are, at retrieval, oriented to the present. When an animal knows, whether "innately" or by virtue of the consequences of something learned in the past, what an appropriate response is in a given situation, it need not "think back to" earlier *experiences*. Even human beings who are capable of consciously recollecting past experiences seldom engage in such recollection when they make use of previously acquired "declarative" information and knowledge.

Second, and in many ways equally important, is the fact that episodic re-membering (mental time travel) is accompanied by a special kind of "autono-etic" conscious awareness that is clearly different from the kind of conscious awareness ("noetic" awareness) that accompanies retrieval of declarative in-formation (Tulving, 1993). The earlier experience remembered now may be hazy or fragmentary or even false by objective standards, but its phenomenal quality is not mistaken for any other kind of conscious awareness. A normal individual can distinguish between recollecting a personal experience and re-calling an impersonal fact as readily as she can distinguish between, say, per-ceiving and imaging. This ability of humans makes possible an operational definition of autonoetic and noetic awareness in terms of the "remem-ber"/"know" (R/K) paradigm (Dalla Barba et al. 1997; Gardiner & Java, 1993; Gardiner et al., 1998; Knowlton & Squire, 1995; Tulving, 1885), and the segre-gation of the two kinds of awareness at the level of electrophysiological activity of the brain (Düzel et al 1997).

Thus, combining the first two unique features, we can say that the function of episodic memory is conscious recollection of one's personal past. This is the crux of episodic memory: it has to do with conscious recollection of previous *experiences* of events, happenings, and situations. The emphasis is on "experi-ence," rather than "event" or "happening." Declarative memory, on the other hand, is concerned with facts and events of the physical world, that is, with the acquisition and use of the knowledge of what is, or what could be, in the world, and what is appropriate behavior in a given situation.

Other features that characterize episodic memory are less striking, and some of them are more questionable, their verity still being evaluated and their reality debated. Thus, episodic memory lags behind declarative memory in human development (Perner & Ruffman, 1995; Pillemer & White, 1989). In general, it is more vulnerable than declarative memory to a number of patho-logical conditions of the brain (Bäckman & Small, 1998; Evans et al., 1993; Duffy & O'Carroll, 1994; Greene et al., 1996; Desgranges et al., 1998), as well as to the normal process of aging (Herlitz & Forsell, 1996; Nilsson et al., 1997). There are also clear gender differences: women consistently do better on epi-sodic memory tasks than do men, although on tests of general knowledge, word knowledge, primary memory and perceptual priming both populations per-form equally well (Herlitz, Nilsson, & Bäckman, 1997). Episodic memory prob-ably evolved more recently than any other form of memory and there is no evidence that any other species possesses a similar kind of memory (Sudden-dorf & Corballis, 1997). Finally, although it is well established that episodic memory is like declarative memory in that both depend on MTL and dien-cephalic structures, it has also been suspected that episodic memory depends on the frontal lobes in a way that declarative and other forms of memory do not (Schacter, 1987; Squire, 1987). Equally instructive have been the findings from functional neuroimaging studies of the kind that are discussed at some length in the second half of the present paper (Fletcher et al., 1995; Fletcher, Frith, & Rugg, 1997; Haxby et al., 1996; Kapur et al., 1994a; Nyberg, 1998; Nyberg et al., 1996).

In summary, episodic memory is unique in that it is the only form of memory that has the capability of registering and storing personally experienced happenings in subjective time, and making information about such experiences available in the form of a special form of conscious awareness, named autonoetic awareness. All other forms of evolved memory function to provide the individual with information as to how to respond to environmental contingencies and how to behave effectively in various situations.

## Memory and Time

Because the uniqueness of episodic memory as described is not always appreciated, or not sufficiently appreciated, it may be worth while to discuss the issue a bit more fully. I do so next, dealing first with learning and memory that does not have much to do with remembering past experiences, and then with episodic memory, which has everything to do with it.

The behavior of organisms is always and inevitably shaped by heredity and environment. Many organisms, including human beings, begin life with biologically useful behavior patterns, or with the potential of postnatal maturation of such patterns that are "released" in appropriate situations. These innate capabilities can be very complex, as is the case in what is probably the most thoroughly studied human "instinct," namely language (Pinker, 1995). All these "instincts" are effective ways of coping with problems set by one's environment. They are built into the nervous systems of organisms independently of experience. For example, very young children, like the very young of many other species, do not crawl off a "visual cliff" when given an opportunity to do so, but cling to the safe side of the divide, even during the very first test (Gibson & Walk, 1960). Numerous other examples could be given how the genetically determined workings of an organism's brain guide the organism's behavior in a myriad life situations.

Environmentally shaped changes in behavior and cognition, that is learning and memory, represent another effective means of coping with the demands for survival. Learning something now that is useful for achieving desirable goals in the future complements genetically determined behavior patterns, and in higher organisms, such as many mammals, constitutes the source of the better part of the organism's knowledge about its world. Because young children lack innate knowledge about hot stoves, they must learn, through actual experience or vicariously, about what are good and what are bad things to do around hot stoves. Because the world in which the children grow up is exceedingly complex, they must learn a myriad things to cope with it.

All forms of learning and memory, from the lowliest to the highest, serve very much the same function as do the "instincts": they provide the organisms with means of behaving more effectively than would have been possible in the absence of the relevant acquired knowledge or skill. An organism learns something today to behave more effectively in the future. In this sense, when learning occurs, it is oriented to the future; when its fruits are subsequently used, the memory is oriented to the present. The important criterion in judging the worth of any act of learning or memory has to do with their usefulness in guiding ongoing activity here and now.

Thus, all forms of learning and memory that are known throughout the whole animal kingdom could be said to be "proscopic," a term derived from Greek that means "forward-looking." From sensitization and habituation, through simple and complex classical and instrumental conditioning, through the learning of perceptual-motor and cognitive skills, through various forms of "implicit" memory, such as priming, through the imitative learning that occurs in higher animals, all the way to the immense quantities of concrete and abstract knowledge of the world that an adult human beings have accumulated throughout their lives, memory is proscopic: it is important solely because it shapes and effectively enhances the organism's interaction with its future environment. This basic truth holds as much for the Aplysia learning to withdraw its gill to a conditioned stimulus, the mouse learning the location of the sunken platform in a Morris water maze, for the monkey remembering the location of the peanut in a delayed non-matching-to-sample task, the child avoiding touching the hot stove, the pinch hitter hitting the ball out of the ball-park, the Scrabble player coming up with a clever word that astounds the opponents, the scientist thinking of a new kind of a distinction that is important in the study of the brain/mind, and so on, and on, and on, essentially *ad infinitum*.

In none of these future-oriented learning situations and the present-oriented memory situations does it matter how the knowledge was acquired. There is no necessity for any conscious access to the past, and no necessity to be consciously aware of past experiences. The only thing that matters is the efficacy of the current behavior. The child does not remember where and how she touched the hot stove in the past, but she knows how to treat the stove now; the amnesic patient does not remember that the examining physician hid a pin in his hand while shaking the patient's hand an hour ago, but she knows that it is not good to shake the doctor's hand now; the contestant in a TV show does not remember when or where or how she acquired the knowledge that Hannibal is associated with elephants, but she answers the question correctly and profitably now. Because all these people can efficiently rely on their proscopic memory, remembering the past is irrelevant.

Thus, despite the traditional association between memory and the past, the remembering of the past, in the sense of conscious recollection of what happened on an earlier occasion, does not play any critical role in making use of what has been learned and how the fruits of the learning are used. Sometimes, of course, the expression of acquired skills and knowledge is accompanied by conscious recollections of past experiences, but these occurrences are epiphenomenal only. The circumstances surrounding the origin and creation of knowledge that guides effective behavior may be of interest to the scientist studying such behavior, but to the behaving organism it makes no difference.

The singular exception to all the ubiquity and evolutionary significance of the proscopic forms of learning and memory that serve the future without bothering about the past is episodic memory. Episodic memory does exactly what the other forms of memory do not and cannot do – it makes it possible for the individual to recollect previously experienced events as such. It enables the individual to mentally "travel back into her personal past." It shares with proscopic memory the basic function – it provides the individual with useful information as to the effective courses of actions in various situations – but it goes beyond the proscopic function in that it does allow us to remember (to consciously recollect) what happened in the past. A child remembers what happened at a friend's birthday party the day before, a young lover remembers the expression on the beloved's face in the moonlight, the scientist remembers the first time when a speaker at a conference mentioned her name and work, and so on, and on. Because episodic memory is oriented towards the past, we can think of episodic memory as "palinscopic" (backward-looking) memory. An individual who "possesses" palinscopic memory can at Time 2 "mentally travel back" to Time 1.

In summary, then, he main points I make here are these. Despite common sense, most forms of memory have no special connection with the past. Events happen in time, of course, and this means that the learned behavior being made use of now (memory information being retrieved now) had its origin in the past, but the pastness of the origin is no more relevant to these "proscopic" forms of memory than, say, eating a meal "in the past" is relevant to the current feeling of satiation, in the short run, or physical growth and development, in the long run. The singular exception is episodic memory, which is "palinscopic" and unique in two senses: it makes it possible for the individual to remember personally experienced past happenings, and it makes it possible for the individual to experience such "mental time travel" in the form of autonoetic awareness.

The theory of episodic memory as summarized here naturally leads to the question of what is known about the brain side of the story. Are there any specific brain regions that are involved in mediating autonoetic episodic re-membering? Because we now have available techniques for identifying regional differences in brain activity, we can test this expectation empirically. We now turn to examine some available evidence provided by PET studies of memory.

## PET Studies of Memory

### Episodic Memory in the Laboratory

In the laboratory, episodic memory is studied by means of experimentally created "miniature events." One such event consists in the presentation by the experimenter, and perception by the subject, of a discrete stimulus object, such as a word, a simple sentence, a drawing of an object, a picture, a photographed face, and the like. When the subject perceives the appearance of a stimulus object on the display device (e. g., computer screen) for a short interval, usually measured in a few seconds, information about certain aspects of the event is encoded into different memory systems (Tulving, 1999). Some of this information is potentially retrievable under appropriate conditions. These conditions include experimental task instructions and the presentation of more or less specific retrieval cues (Tulving, 1983, Ch. 9). The subject needs to make no special effort to encode information about stimulus items into memory systems: encoding occurs automatically by virtue of the (situational) novelty of the occurrence of the miniature events. Less-than-perfect subsequent retrieval of the event information is usually attributable to the interference caused by the presence of other events in the presentation series, as well as inadequate retrieval cues. Various kinds of "encoding operations," usually consisting of subjects making specific judgments about presented items (Craik & Tulving, 1975), may "immunize" individual events against intralist interference and thus facilitate subsequent retrieval.

Retrieval means "utilization of stored information for the purpose of carrying out a task requiring the information." In a typical "explicit" memory task the subject has to demonstrate his or her knowledge of the previously encoded events by either recalling the name of the presented item, recognizing a copy of the item, or in some other fashion. The level of behavioral retrieval performance depends on a multitude of factors, including individual differences among subjects, the nature of to-be-remembered events, conditions under which encoding occurred, conditions prevailing at retrieval, and especially the relation between encoding and retrieval conditions (Roediger & Guynn, 1996).

Modern neuroimaging studies of memory have been directed at various aspects of memory. One of the most popular approaches has turned out to be studies of two kinds: (i) those comparing semantic and episodic retrieval, and (ii) those comparing episodic-memory encoding and retrieval. Because an act of retrieval of information from semantic memory in a typical memory experiment is a novel experience for the subject (Tulving, 1983), and because novel experiences are assumed to be automatically encoded into long-term memory (Tulving et al., 1996; Tulving & Kroll, 1995), semantic retrieval and episodic encoding are difficult to separate experimentally (Tulving et al., 1994a). Therefore, the two kinds of studies just mentioned are usually indistinguishable experimentally although they may differ in the interpretation of the obtained results. We now consider these studies.

## The Logic of PET

The logic of PET "activation studies" of memory is straightforward. Different mental activities are supported by the activities in different brain regions. When the subject engages in a given cognitive task, PET provides information about the level of cerebral blood flow in different regions that are associated with the processes involved in the task. Because changes in blood flow are known to be correlated with changes in neuronal activity, their patterns (maps) provide information about neuronal activity in different brain sites that reflect these processes (Frackowiak & Friston, 1994; Posner & Raichle, 1995; Raichle, 1994).

Traditionally, PET data are presented in the form of "brain maps." A brain map reflects differences in the patterns of regional blood flow associated with two different tasks, A and B. The tasks are usually selected to differ from one another with respect to readily specifiable cognitive processes. A brain map shows regions in which blood flow, and hence neuronal activity, was higher in Task A than B, regions in which the level of blood flow could not be distinguished between the two tasks, as well as regions in which the level of blood flow was lower in task A than task B. The logic of PET studies holds that these "activation" maps reflect the differences between the two comparison tasks. The experimental challenge in such a situation is to describe the correlation between the functional neuroanatomy and the cognitive processes in a disciplined, systematic, and theoretically meaningful fashion. Although the "subtraction method" (Fox, 1991; Friston et al., 1995) of positron emission tomography (PET) that underlies these analyses has severe limitations (Friston et al., 1996; Jennings et al., 1997), it is widely used and, more important, it has yielded some surprisingly systematic data.

## Encoding and Retrieval

The subtraction method used in PET studies can be illustrated with an example from a study done at Toronto involving a *direct comparison* between episodic encoding and retrieval in healthy young adults (Cabeza et al., 1997b; Kapur et al., 1996). Subjects' brains were scanned under two conditions. One condition involved encoding of novel verbal information into memory. Subjects were shown pairs of words, such as PENGUIN – TUXEDO, and they were instructed to think of some meaningful relation between the words of each pair. They were also told that their memory for these pairs would be tested. We know that at least two things occur in this situation. The first is semantic-memory retrieval: subjects have to make use of their semantic knowledge (general "knowledge of the world") in relating the paired words to each other. Second, each miniature event of seeing a pair of words and thinking of a meaningful relation between then is encoded and stored in episodic memory: subjects can later on remember that such and such word pairs occurred in the study list. The other experimental condition involved retrieval of information thus encoded and stored. Subjects again saw pairs of words, such as PENGUIN – TUXEDO, but now they had to decide whether the pair had or had not appeared in the study list. This is an episodic-memory retrieval (recognition) condition. Responding correctly in this task requires that the subject be able to "think back" to a particular "period" in his life, the encoding trial, and make a decision about the relation between the present stimulus, the test pair, and the "contents" of the episode experienced earlier.

The two conditions are very similar in many ways: the subjects always saw a pair of words on the display screen, the pairs were presented at the same rate, they had to make a binary decision about each pair in both conditions, and the overt responses they made were also similar. The main difference had to do with the presentation history of the material (seen for the first time in encoding, and second time in retrieval) and the task instructions – encode versus retrieve.

The PET results of interest have to with the differences in the patterns of regional cerebral blood flow, and hence neuronal activity, associated with the two tasks. There are two such difference patterns in this study. One results when the regional activation during retrieval is subtracted from the regional activation during encoding. This pattern shows brain regions more active during encoding than during retrieval. The other pattern results when the activation during encoding is subtracted from the activation during retrieval. This pattern shows brain regions more active during retrieval than during encoding. Note that areas that are activated to the same (high or low) extent during both encoding and retrieval will not show up in the comparison, because they are "subtracted out."

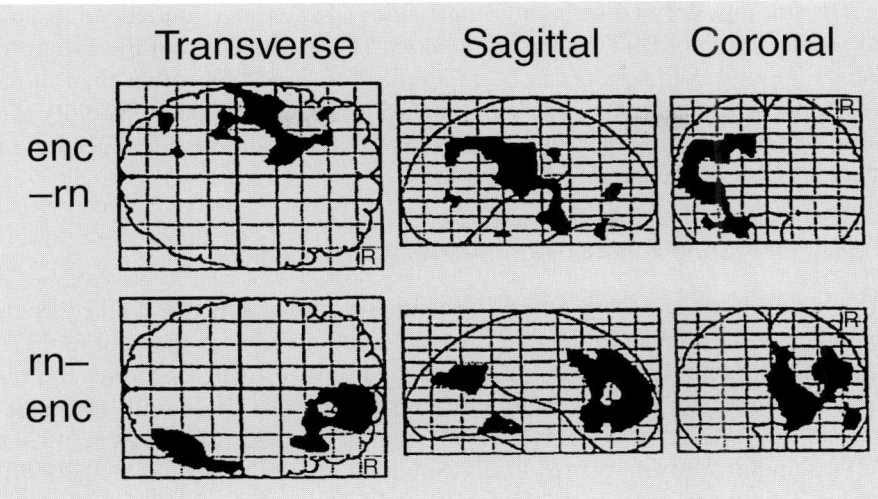

*Figure 1.* Brain maps illustrating differences in regional cerebral blood flow, and hence neuronal activity, in a PET study in which semantic retrieval (episodic encoding) of word pairs was directly compared with episodic retrieval of the same material. The blood flow data were averaged over all subjects and projected to three views – transverse, sagittal, and coronal – of a "see-through brain." The maps in the upper bank show "encoding activations," that is brain regions more active during encoding than during retrieval. The maps in the lower bank show "retrieval activations," that is brain regions more active during retrieval than during encoding. (Figure reprinted from Nyberg, Cabeza, & Tulving, *Psychonomic Bulletin & Review*, 1996, *3*, 135–148).

Figure 1 shows the results of the study. The blood flow data were averaged over all 12 subjects. The brain maps in the upper bank show "encoding activations," that is brain regions more active during encoding than during retrieval. The brain maps in the lower bank show "retrieval activations," that is brain regions more active during retrieval than during encoding.

Two observations are of interest regarding the data in Figure 1. First, there are considerable differences between the brain maps of encoding and those of retrieval. We can assume that there are common regions as well, activated during both encoding and retrieval, although they do not show in Figure 1, for reasons stated. Nevertheless, in light of the commonly held assumption that encoding and retrieval differ but little in psychological processes, and hence presumably in neuronal circuits, the extensive differences seen in Figure 1 are surprising. Second, the two sets of activation are heavily lateralized in the two hemispheres: encoding activations are all in the left hemisphere, and retrieval activations are all in the right hemisphere. Why such a striking hemispheric asymmetry? This second result becomes critical as we proceed.

The findings derived from any single study always have limited value, and the same is true of PET studies of memory. The problem is that the extent to which the observed results can be generalized to conditions other than those of the particular study is unknown. Conclusions regarding generalizability can only be drawn from larger collections of studies. We will consider such larger samples later in the paper.

## HERA: Hemispheric Encoding/Retrieval Asymmetry

The hemispheric encoding/retrieval asymmetry shown in Figure 1 nicely complements similar data obtained in the frontal lobe regions in many other PET studies, including the very first ones designed to investigate encoding and retrieval processes in episodic memory. These studies were done at the Hammersmith Hospital in London, England (Fletcher et al., 1995; Shallice et al., 1994), at Washington University in St Louis (Squire et al., 1992; Buckner et al., 1995), and at Toronto (Kapur et al., 1994a, 1994b; Moscovitch et al., 1995; Tulving et al., 1994a, 1994b). Taken together, the data from these studies suggested a surprising empirical regularity: Left prefrontal cortex seemed to be differentially more involved than right in encoding information into episodic memory, whereas right prefrontal cortex seemed to be differentially more involved than left in episodic memory retrieval.

This pattern is referred to as HERA: hemispheric encoding/retrieval asymmetry in the frontal lobes (Tulving et al., 1994a). Although initially unexpected, and therefore greeted sceptically (Roskies, 1994), the HERA pattern is now well established and indeed represents one of the most robust facts of the PET-memory literature. Figure 2 presents a schematic summary of the results from 25 different PET studies, available in May 1996, that had reported relevant data (Nyberg et al., 1996). The pattern of the data depicts the asymmetry: Episodic-memory encoding (intentional or incidental study) is associated with the activation of the left prefrontal cortex, and not with the right. Episodic-memory retrieval (recognition or recall) is associated predominantly with the activation of the right prefrontal cortex. Because in many cases episodic encoding involves semantically based judgments about the to-be-remembered information, the left-frontal activation associated with such encoding also reflects semantic memory retrieval. This is why the HERA model associates semantic-memory encoding also with the left frontal lobe.

The overall HERA pattern can be economically described in terms of the interaction among three pairs of concepts: (i) encoding versus retrieval, (ii) episodic versus semantic memory, and (iii) left and right frontal lobes. This overall regularity is largely unaffected by specific conditions of the relevant experiments. Available evidence suggests that it holds both for verbal and

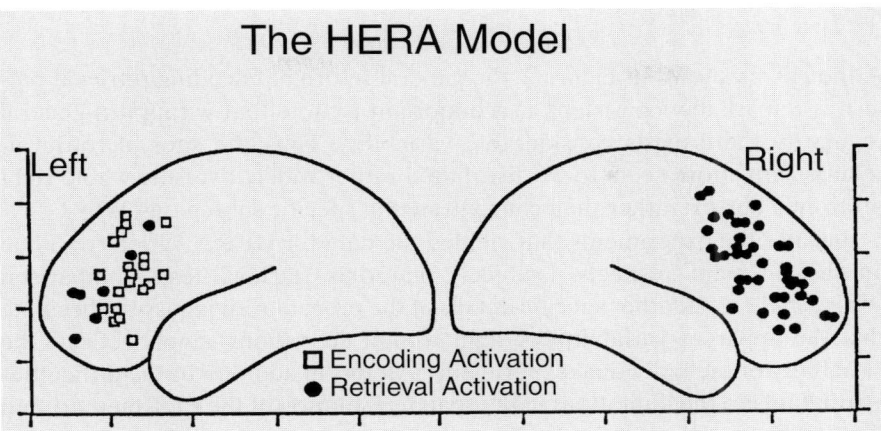

*Figure 2.* A schematic representation of the HERA model based on a meta-analysis of published data. Each data point, projected to the lateral surface of the cerebrum, represents the peak of an activation, obtained in one of the 25 studies in the data base, of encoding (on the left) or retrieval (on the right) against an appropriate reference conditio. (Figure reprinted from Nyberg, Cabeza, & Tulving, *Psychonomic Bulletin & Review*, 1996, *3*, 135–148).

nonverbal materials. For instance, encoding of human faces has been shown to activate the left prefrontal cortex, in the absence of comparable activation on the right, while recognition of previously studied faces has been shown to activate the right prefrontal cortex, in the absence of comparable activation on the left (Grady et al., 1995; Haxby et al., 1996; see also Andreasen et al., 1995). Relevant observations have also been reported for other nonverbal materials and line drawings of objects (Buckner et al., 1996; Köhler et al., 1998; Moscovitch et al., 1995; Owen et al., 1996). The encoding activations on the left have been observed under conditions of both intentional and incidental learning; the retrieval activations on the right have been observed in both recall and recognition tasks.

Before we ask the obvious question now, what does HERA mean theoretically, we raise two other issues that have been directly suggested by HERA. Once concerns refinement and elaboration of HERA: Is there regional specificity in prefrontal cortex that goes beyond the broad hemispheric asymmetry? The second has to do with extension of HERA: Are there other regions in the brain that are differentially involved in semantic-memory retrieval (episodic encoding) and episodic-memory retrieval?

## Refinement of HERA

Although, as shown in Figure 2, the general left/right encoding/retrieval pattern is remarkably consistent, it is important to note that within this general regularity there exists considerable variability. Thus, the sites of retrieval-related activations seem to be distributed rather widely over the whole right prefrontal cortex, rather than concentrated in specific subregions. Why?

Because the experiments that yielded the data for HERA varied from one another in many respects – subjects, materials, retrieval tests, comparison ("baseline") tasks, other specific details of the procedure, it is easy to speculate that the apparent variability of right frontal activations simply reflects the variability of the individual experiments. All this in addition to the difficulties attributable to the limitations in the spatial resolution of the PET method, and the limitations inherent in the typically used subtraction method (Friston et al., 1996; Jennings et al., 1997). As a result, there is nothing very much that can be done at this time by way of a more enlightened analysis and conclusions as to exactly why a given activation site is where it is rather than somewhere else. Future studies no doubt will clarify the issues.

Buckner (1996; see also Buckner & Petersen, 1996) did undertake a more detailed analysis of the HERA data, and suggested that there was indeed evidence for the involvement of different frontal regions in different kinds of encoding and retrieval tasks. He did his analysis at a time when the relevant data were still sparse. We now have a more extensive data base to work with, and can therefore address the issue with more adequate tools.

Recently, with the help of Martin Lepage at Rotman Research Institute, I conducted an "exercise" aimed at refinement of the neuroanatomical picture of HERA. Its purpose was to examine the extent to which the HERA-type pattern of activation is found in different subregions of prefrontal cortex, specified in terms of the classical Brodmann system in which brain areas are distinguished by their cytoarchitectonic differences and labelled numerically (Markowitsch, 1993).

We began with a data base consisting of a listing of 1131 cerebral activation sites that have been identified by PET as involved in memory-related processes in 56 published reports. It is a very slightly modified version of one that was described and used in a recent report of an empirical regularity, the so-called HIPER model, of PET activations in the hippocampal region (Lepage, Habib, & Tulving, 1998). For convenience, and in anticipation of its extension in the future, I refer to this modified version as the "June 98" memory data base. Each activation in the data base is specified in terms of the study it came from, the subtracted conditions, and Talairach and Tournoux (1988) stereotaxic coordinates, the "address" of a given site in the three-dimensional brain. A fuller description of how PET studies of memory and other kinds of cognitive studies are conducted and their results described are available elsewhere (Buckner & Tulving, 1995; Posner & Raichle, 1994).

From the "June 98" data base we extracted an "encoding/retrieval" subset, consisting of all the activations that had been produced by "encoding conditions" and "retrieval conditions" in the original PET studies. Encoding conditions were defined as "subtractive" task comparisons in which the target task requires more elaborative processing of the materials than the (subtracted) reference task. Retrieval conditions were defined as subtractive task comparisons in which the target task produces a greater degree of recovery of previously experimentally encoded material than would the corresponding reference task. To qualify for the inclusion in the encoding/retrieval subset, the same stimulus materials had to be used in within any given comparison.

The "encoding/retrieval" subset of the data base thus constructed consisted of 280 activated sites produced by encoding conditions, and 516 activated sites produced by retrieval conditions. Of the 280 encoding activations, 195 were in the left hemisphere, and 85 in the right. Of the 516 retrieval activations, 230 were in the left hemisphere, and 286 in the right. (There is always some uncertainty in dealing with activations at or near the midline of the cerebrum, and therefore some corresponding error.)

The next step was the essential one. From the encoding/retrieval set of 796 activations we extracted all those that were located in or near prefrontal cortex, bilaterally. We included Brodmann area 6 in the analysis, although it is usually classified as "pre-motor" area. We did so because it has been frequently "sighted" in functional imaging studies of cognition.

This whole exercise is fraught with a number of difficulties and uncertainties, attributed to the random errors in the initial identification of an activated site in the original study, the identification of the Talairach and Tournoux coordinates of the activated site, the uncertainty, and inconsistency, of designations of Brodmann areas in the Talairach and Tournoux (1988) atlas, and the subjectivity of decisions involved in the assignment of an activation to a single Brodmann area (BA). The last source of uncertainty is especially vexing, because in many cases an activated cluster of voxels lies in a border region between two Brodmann areas, and sometimes even three areas. In carrying out the exercise, I assigned activations near two or more Brodmann areas to both, or to all. This means that there is some duplication of activations in the results.

The outcome of the exercise is summarized in Table 1. It shows the numbers of encoding and retrieval activations that were in or near various Brodmann areas. The bottom "total" line of the table shows the extent to which the overall HERA pattern held for this sample of data. The 117 encoding activations were distributed asymmetrically in the two hemispheres: 90 left, 27 right. The 198

*Table 1.* Distribution of frontal encoding and retrieval activations among Brodmann areas in the left and right hemispheres. Data pooled from 56 PET studies. Table entries are absolute frequencies of activations. See text for details. BA = Brodmann Area.

| BA | Encoding | | Retrieval | |
|---|---|---|---|---|
| | Left | Right | Left | Right |
| 6 | 15 | 6 | 19 | 22 |
| 8 | 9 | 4 | 6 | 10 |
| 9 | 18 | 5 | 10 | 30 |
| 46 | 10 | 0 | 3 | 6 |
| 10 | 6 | 4 | 11 | 39 |
| 45 | 9 | 1 | 1 | 6 |
| 44 | 3 | 1 | 4 | 3 |
| 47 | 18 | 2 | 2 | 13 |
| 11 | 2 | 4 | 4 | 9 |
| Total | 90 | 27 | 60 | 138 |

retrieval activations were also distributed asymmetrically, although in the opposite pattern: 59 left, 139 right. These frequencies are in keeping with the HERA pattern. Because there was only partial overlap between the studies used by Nyberg et al. (1996) on which the data depicted in Figure 2 were based, and the studies that contributed data to the sample used here, the replication of the pattern speaks to its reliability.

Table 1 shows that different Brodmann areas contributed differently to the overall HERA pattern. When examining these data, and especially when comparing encoding and retrieval entries directly, one should keep in mind the fact that there are recorded in the table almost twice as many retrieval activations as encoding activations. Contrasts between the two hemispheres, left and right, within each of these two categories, encoding and retrieval, however, are not affected by differences in the base rates.

Distinctive HERA-type "symmetrical asymmetry" is seen in these data in the dorsolateral Brodmann area 9, and especially starkly in Brodmann area 47 on the prefrontal inferior convexity. Symmetrical asymmetry refers to the fact that in both these areas encoding is strongly left-lateralized whereas retrieval is strongly right-lateralized. In other regions data conform to HERA less symmetrically. Thus, Brodmann area 10 (anterior prefrontal cortex) shows clear HERA-type asymmetry for retrieval (11 left, 39 right), but not for encoding. And Brodmann areas 46 and 45 (lateral prefrontal cortex) show similarly clear HERA-type asymmetry for encoding (19 left, 1 right), but less convincingly so for retrieval. A surprising feature of the data in Table 1 is the relatively high overall involvement of Brodmann area 6 in encoding and especially retrieval, although in the latter case there is little evidence of HERA-type asymmetry.

These data thus do refine and clarify the HERA pattern of encoding and retrieval activations in prefrontal cortex. Some of the subregions in the frontal lobes reflect the overall pattern, whereas others differ from it in specific ways. Thus, some regions (BA 47 and 9) are clearly "symmetrically asymmetric," while others show clearer asymmetry for only one of the two sets of processes (BA 46 and 45 for encoding, and BA 10 for retrieval).

Some of these findings confirm expectations based on the existing literature. Thus, the involvement of anterior prefrontal cortex (BA 10) and dorsolateral (BA 46 and 9) regions in encoding and retrieval has been frequently noted (Cabeza & Nyberg, 1996; Grady, 1998; MacLeod et al., 1998; Rugg et al., 1996; Nyberg et al., 1996). The data in Table 1 nicely corroborate these earlier impressions.

Another HERA-type regularity suggested by Table 1 is a bit more surprising, namely the strong "symmetric" encoding/retrieval laterality seen in area 47. The involvement of the *left* inferior prefrontal cortex in encoding-related processes is well known (Buckner, 1996), although activations are typically found at sites superior to area 47. Furthermore, the involvement of the homologous *right* region in episodic-memory retrieval has so far largely escaped systematic attention. Brodmann area 47 was discussed by Grady (1998) in a review of frontal activations observed in PET studies of cognition. She noted that the left area 47 "has more activations from semantic processing and language tasks than any other region" (Grady, 1998). It is of some interest that Talairach and Tournoux characterized it as one concerned with "vegetative functions" (Talairach & Tournoux, 1988, p 11).

In summary, then, there is some evidence that the well known functional heterogeneity of prefrontal cortex also shows up in the analysis of encoding and retrieval. Some regions, such as Brodmann areas 10, 9, 46, and 47 especially seem to contribute to the overall HERA pattern.

## Extension of HERA

We now ask whether a HERA-type activation pattern extends to other, posterior parts of the brain? That is, is there any evidence of hemispheric encoding/retrieval asymmetry in regions other than prefrontal cortex?

Earlier in the paper we already saw a sample presented by the Cabeza-Kapur study. More important, reviews of the relevant studies show that in many cases intentional as well as incidental encoding in episodic memory activated left but not right temporal regions (Cabeza & Nyberg, 1996; Fletcher et al., 1995). As to retrieval, several studies have found increased activation in the parietal lobes. In some cases, the activation has been bilateral (e. g., Schacter et al., 1995; Tulving et al., 1994). In other cases, unilateral activation has been observed, and in these cases it has predominantly been located on the

right side (Grady et al., 1995; N. Kapur et al., 1995; Kapur et al., 1995; Moscovitch et al., 1995).

Again, however, individual studies are not sufficiently informative. One cannot draw strong conclusions from the results of isolated experiments or meta-
analyses based on relatively small samples of data. The HERA pattern, after
all, is nothing more than a statistical tendency. It survives by virtue of the fact
that, and as long as, findings that conform to the pattern are observed more
frequently than findings that seem to be exceptions to it. This means that if we
wish to contemplate the extension of HERA seriously, we must examine a
larger sample of data.

Using the "June 98" data base described above, I performed another exercise, this time aimed at the issue of hemispheric encoding/retrieval asymmetry
in posterior regions. I chose, somewhat arbitrarily, two voxels in the temporal
lobe bilaterally (Talairach xyz = 30  0 –10, and xyz = 32  –32 6), and drew a
rectangular "volume of interest" (VOI) around each voxel. The VOIs had an
overall extension of 64 mm in the left-right (x), 32 mm in the anterior-posterior
(y), and 48 mm in the inferior-superior (z) dimension. These VOIs encompass
not only cortical regions, but also subcortical ones. (Their separation would
constitute one improvement of the method.) I then identified all the encoding
and retrieval activations in the data base that were localized within the two
VOIs thus specified. I repeated the same procedure for a voxel (bilaterally) in
the parietal lobes. The stereotaxic coordinates of the two voxels, one left, one
right, were –30 –66 36 and 30 –66 36, and the rectangular VOIs had extensions
of 60, 36, and 48 mm in the x, y, and z dimensions, respectively. Finally, for
purposes of comparison with HERA, I repeated the procedure for two frontal
voxels (–18 30 16 and 18 30 16), with VOI extensions of 36 mm, 48 mm, and
72 mm in the x, y, and z dimensions, respectively. Given the extensions of the
frontal, "temporal," and "parietal" VOIs, there was some overlap between
them, with the consequence that some activations in the data base were
assigned to more than one of these regions.

The procedure I used is admittedly quite gross; it is easy to think of ways in
which it could be improved, and improved considerably. But refining the procedure would involve additional effort and time, and this is why it has to await for
the future. What is lacking in refinement of the method, however, can be expected
to be compensated for by the relatively large sample size, as there were a total
of 280 encoding and 516 retrieval activations in the June 98 data base. The whole
point of the exercise has to do with the question about hemispheric asymmetry,
if any, in grossly defined brain areas other than the frontal lobes.

The results of this "HERA extension" exercise are summarized in Table 2
that shows the relative frequency of occurrence of encoding and retrieval activations in the three large areas mentioned – frontal, temporal, and parietal

*Table 2*. Relative density of encoding and retrieval activations in large and approximately designated cerebral regions in the left and right hemisphere. Pooled data from 56 different PET studies. Table entries are percentages of all encoding activations, and all retrieval activations, localized within the regions. See text for details.

| | Frontal | Temporal | | Parietal/ | Total |
| | | Anterior | Posterior | Occipital | |
|---|---|---|---|---|---|
| Encoding | | | | | |
| Left | 14.3 | 9.6 | 11.1 | 7.1 | 42.1 |
| Right | 5.0 | 3.6 | 3.2 | 3.6 | 15.4 |
| | | | | | |
| Retrieval | | | | | |
| Left | 10.3 | 2.3 | 8.5 | 7.6 | 28.7 |
| Right | 19.9 | 1.7 | 7.8 | 9.3 | 38.7 |

– and in the two hemispheres. The percentages given in the table are expressed relative to the overall frequency of encoding and retrieval activations, separately for each. For example, the entry of 15.0 for left frontal encoding means that 42 (15.1 per cent) of the total of 280 encoding activations in the data base were found in the VOI for that region, as specified above. The entry of 19.8 for right frontal retrieval means that 102 activations (19.8 per cent) of the total of 516 retrieval activations in the data base were found in the VOI.

The major lesson to be learned from the data in Table 2 is that the HERA-like pattern of hemispheric encoding/retrieval asymmetry does extend towards posterior regions, although not as clearly as it holds in frontal regions. In the right temporal areas, encoding and retrieval activations occur more or less evenly. In the left temporal region, however, encoding activations predominate. A temporal encoding activation is about two and a half times more likely to occur in the left than the right hemisphere, whereas a temporal retrieval activation seems equally likely in the temporal regions in both hemispheres. The picture in the parietal area shows that the hemispheric asymmetry holds for the right hemisphere where retrieval activations are more likely to occur than encoding activations, but not for the left hemisphere where both are equally likely.

In summary, the overall picture that emerges from this exercise is that the two hemispheres show an overall disposition for specialization in episodic memory processes: the left more actively involved in encoding than the right, and the right more actively involved in retrieval than the left. The HERA-like pattern is not as striking in posterior regions as it is in prefrontal cortex, but it is discernible in the meta-analysis, and does describe a definite tendency. The future will tell how this tendency is related, if at all, to the specific conditions under which the data were generated, a problem that is too early to tackle now.

## The Meaning of HERA

We now return to the original HERA model, in the frontal lobes, and pose the question: What does the right frontal retrieval activation mean? We are especially interested, of course, in the possible relevance of this activation for the theoretical concept of "mental time travel," the ability of individuals to hold in mind a temporally defined segment of their past life and to become autonoetically aware of the happenings in it.

We know that retrieval is not a single process, as its label implies, but rather consists of a complex concatenation and combination of a number of component subprocesses. One way of tackling the question about the theoretical meaning of right-frontal activation therefore lies in the analysis of the overall retrieval process into subprocesses, and trying to find out to what extent these subprocesses are associated with right prefrontal cortex.

A major distinction within retrieval process can be made between retrieval "mode" and recovery of stored information. Retrieval mode is a necessary condition for any episodic retrieval to occur, it is a "set for treating stimulus events as cues to stored episodes" (Tulving, 1983, p. 170). It can be assumed to consist of several component processes.

One component process of *retrieval mode* allows the individual to actively hold, in the background of focal attention, a particular past segment of one's life that defines the temporal boundaries of the past events of interest. I refer to this component of retrieval mode as the "epoch set." When the individual answers a question about what she did "last night," or what she remembers from her first day in school, she is very clear in her mind about the period in question. Similarly, when a subject in an experiment tries to remember whether a certain word occurred in the first or the second half of the presented list, she is not confused about the temporal demands of the task – even if carrying out the task may be difficult and performance accuracy poor. In one of the "simplest" explicit memory tasks, yes/no recognition, the subject also must be able to somehow hold in mind the previously studied list if she is to perform the task. To a normal healthy person, to assume a particular epoch set comes easily and naturally. How this marvellous mental feat is accomplished at the neural level, however, is a deep mystery.

A second component process of retrieval mode involves assuming an orientation towards retrieval cues as pointers to past happenings rather than just current, here-and-now, occurrences. A cue represents a specific query about the "contents" of the epoch in question. Did an item like this one appear in the list? What item appeared in the list together with this item? This component of retrieval mode operates within the epoch set and reaches beyond it, in that it involves specific stimuli whereas epoch orienting can occur independently of the contents of the sub-attended epochs. The two component processes further differ in that epoch set is a task-dependent variable, manipulated by instructions, whereas treating stimulus objects as retrieval cues an item-dependent variable (Düzel et al., 1999).

The second major constituent of the *retrieval process* is "ecphory," or actual recovery of stored information. According to theory, ecphory occurs when the retrieval cue "contacts" relevant stored information (Tulving, 1983, Ch. 9). Also according to theory, no recovery of episodic information can occur unless the system is in the appropriate state or mode. Whether or not such recovery occurs, as well as the specification of exactly what is recovered, depend critically on the nature of the relation between the information as encoded in the past and the retrieval cues as interpreted by the system in the present, the so-called encoding specificity principle (Tulving, 1983, Ch. 11). Ecphory too presumably embraces a number of as yet unanalyzed and unspecified component processes.

Given the known involvement of the frontal lobes, especially the right one, in episodic retrieval, and given the several hypothesized component processes of such retrieval, the obvious question to ask concerns the relations involved. Does the right-frontal activations signify retrieval mode, ecphory, both of these, or something else? A beginning has been made in answering this question using the PET and fMRI methods. The basic logic here can be put in the form of a question: Are there brain regions, especially in the frontal areas, that show activation during intentional retrieval independently of the degree of the extent to which studied items are recognized? If yes, the brain regions thus identified become candidate components of the neural circuits that are involved in the maintenance of the episodic retrieval mode.

Based on this logic and variations on the theme, a number of studies have been conducted that have addressed the issue (Buckner et al., 1998; Kapur et al., 1995, Nyberg et al., 1995, Schacter et al., 1996; Rugg et al., 1996, 1997; Wagner et al., 1998). The results of the initial experiments (Kapur et al., 1995, Nyberg et al., 1995) showed that when subjects have been set into the episodic retrieval mode through appropriate task instructions, a number of cerebral regions, especially prominently in the right prefrontal cortex, become activated regardless of the extent of ecphory, that is, actual recovery of the specific stored information. Other studies have largely confirmed these findings (Buckner et al., 1998; Rugg et al., 1997; Schacter et al., 1996; Wagner et al., 1998).

A particularly thorough examination of the whole issue of retrieval mode and right prefrontal cortex was recently conducted by Wagner and colleagues (Wagner et al., 1998). They identified five sites in the frontal lobes that showed activation associated with episodic retrieval mode. (They referred to the conditions as "retrieval attempt," a phrase descriptive of the subject's *task*). Three

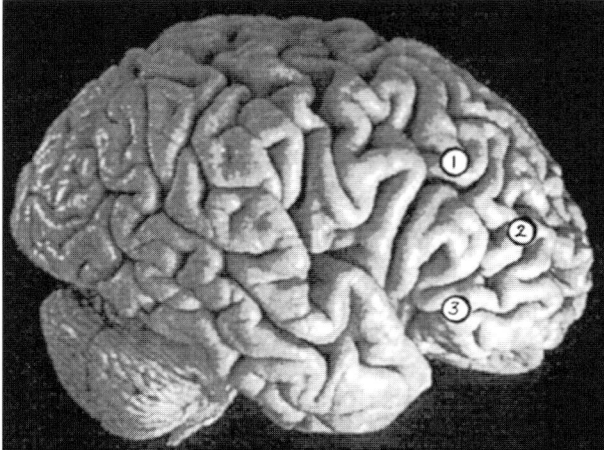

*Figure 3.* Approximate locations of three hypothetical right-frontal "epicenters" of episodic retrieval that are associated with "retrieval mode" projected onto the lateral surface of the brain.

of these were in the right prefrontal cortex. Their approximate location is schematically presented in Figure 3, projected onto the lateral surface of the right hemisphere. We can specify their locations in terms of Brodmann areas (BAs) and the Talairach and Tournoux stereotaxic coordinates) as follows. Site 1 is near the middle frontal gyrus (BA 46, xyz = 44 35 18), Site 2 is near the border of the middle frontal gyrus and precentral gyrus (BA 9, xyz = 40 14 34), and Site 3 is near the inferior frontal gyrus and the frontal operculum (BA 47, xyz = 35 21 –2).

These three right lateral sites turn out to be veritable "epicenters of retrieval" when they are compared with the data in our "June 98" data base. In that data base, there are 34 retrieval activations and only 2 encoding activations that are near (within 16 mm) of Site 1 as specified above, 31 retrieval and 2 encoding activations near (within 16 mm) Site 2, and 22 retrieval activations and a single encoding activation near Site 3.

Future research, no doubt, will illuminate the situation more fully. In the mean time, other evidence is converging on the relation between right prefrontal cortex and episodic retrieval. In a PET study specifically designed to distinguish between recovery of information about remembered items as such versus information about the time of their appearance in the learning list, retrieval of item information activated anterior medial temporal lobe regions bilaterally, whereas retrieval of item information activated frontal regions (Cabeza et al., 1997). The center of one of these "past time" regions was within a few millimeters of Site 2 in Figure 3 (BA 9, Wagner: xyz = 40 14 34; Cabeza: xyz = 48 18 32). The finding suggests that this area may be associated with "epoch set."

Also relevant is a finding reported by McIntosh et al (1997), using data from a previous study (Nyberg et al, 1995), that was produced by an analysis of functional connectivity of brain regions that are activated in retrieval. The analysis showed that Site 3 of Figure 3 (McIntosh's xyz = 32 22 0) participated in the prefrontal medial-temporal "retrieval circuit" only when the to-be-remembered words had originally been encoded at a "deep" semantic level, whereas more anterior regions (BA 10, xyz = 28 44 4) were a part of the circuit regardless of the type of prior encoding. This finding suggests that this area may be associated with retrieval mode for verbal semantic information.

Wagner and his colleagues (1998) concluded that the consistent prefrontal activation seen in tasks involving episodic retrieval signifies a general orientation of the subject towards the past. They further suggested, on the basis of their findings, that the specific brain regions associated with such an orientation depend on the "context," that is specific features of the retrieval task and subjects' "strategies" in carrying out the task. The other data we have briefly reviewed here support this idea of specificity of retrieval sets.

There are other findings that fit into the emerging picture. In a recent PET study it was found that subjects' thinking thoughts about themselves as compared to thinking similar thoughts about others is associated with right frontal activation (Craik et al., 1998). Also, clinical evidence suggests that patients who have suffered right anterior brain damage have difficulty in autonoetically reminiscing about their premorbid personal experiences (Calabrese et al., 1996; Markowitsch et al., 1993; Markowitsch, 1995). In a particularly revealing PET activation study, in which recognition of recently heard sentences about others was compared with recognition of similar sentences taken out of the subjects' own autobiographical notes, Fink et al. (1996) found a largely right hemispheric activation that included temporal lobes, posterior cingulate insula, and prefrontal regions. They interpreted their results as suggesting that a right hemispheric network of brain areas, including prefrontal cortex, is engaged in the remembering of autobiographical information. And, in a remarkable convergence, Levine et al. (1997, in press) have provided a thorough analysis of the case of a young man who, subsequent to traumatic brain injury that resulted in a white-matter lesion in the same right frontotemporal region identified by Fink et al. (1996), lost his ability to autonoetically recollect past events, although his learning and memory abilities otherwise were not adversely affected.

Frontal lobes are known or assumed to have many functions, summarized under concepts such as supervision, organization, integration, executive functions, working-with-memory, self-awareness, and the like (Moscovitch, 1994; Shallice, 1988; Stuss & Benson, 1986; Stuss, Eskes, & Foster, 1994). The data we have considered here, in search of the "meaning" of HERA, suggest several additions to the list: episodic retrieval mode, epoch set, and autonoetic awareness of the past. The functions named are still fuzzy, and the relations among them not entirely clear. Nevertheless, we can think of retrieval mode as a specific form of the general "supervisory" function of the frontal lobes, and autonoetic awareness as a specific form (extension of) self awareness. A more complete account of these relations can be found elsewhere (Wheeler et al. 1997). For the present purposes, we can conclude that the right-frontal activations in PET studies of memory can be interpreted as reflecting some of the major components of mental time travel that make episodic memory unique.

## Conclusions

Contrary to traditional thinking, most forms of learning and memory have little to do with has been in the past. Instead they are oriented towards what is to come: Present experiences allow more effective ways of behaving in the future. In these forms of memory and learning, the kind of conscious awareness of specific past happenings that we usually associate with the term "remembering" is irrelevant. The singular, and in many ways a most remarkable, exception to the future-oriented learning mechanisms and systems is episodic memory. Episodic memory makes possible a form of purely mental activity that is known as remembering of past experiences. This mental activity, highly familiar to all normal healthy humans, differs from other forms of mental activity, and is referred to a "autonoetic awareness." Time-orientation towards the past and autonoetic awareness of what happened in the past differentiate episodic memory from all other forms of memory, and thereby make it unique.

In this chapter I have explored the issue of uniqueness of episodic memory at the level of brain activity. PET and other functional neuroimaging studies have begun to yield data that speak to the issue, by pointing to specific neuro-anatomical regions involved in episodic memory retrieval. An especially interesting finding, because completely unheralded by previous research, is the so called HERA (hemispheric encoding/retrieval asymmetry) pattern of neural activation in the frontal lobes: The *left* frontal lobe is more active in *semantic-memory retrieval* (and episodic-memory encoding), whereas the *right* frontal lobe is more active in *episodic-memory retrieval*. Results of meta-analyses of available data suggest that the frontal hemispheric asymmetry tends to be specific to particular subregions of prefrontal cortex – Brodmann areas 9, 46, 10, and 47 – and also that the HERA-type pattern extends posteriorly to temporal and parietal cortical areas.

Available evidence also suggests that the right-frontal activation, commonly seen in PET and fMRI studies, signifies the involvement of these regions in episodic "retrieval mode," and that specific regions in prefrontal cortex may contribute to separate components of retrieval mode. These components include the "epoch set," the neurocognitive operation that allows an individual to "tune into" a specific temporally extended period of past life. It is also reasonable to assume that right frontal regions play a critical role in enabling autonoetic awareness, although the evidence on this issue is still fragmentary. In comparison with where we were only a few years ago in our understanding of episodic memory and its neural basis, however, we have come a long way.

## Acknowledgments

My research is supported by the Natural Sciences and Engineering research Council of Canada (Grant A8632), and by an endowment in support of research in cognitive neuroscience by Anne and Max Tanenbaum. I thank Martin Lepage for help with data manipulation.

## References

Andreasen, N.C., O'Leary, D.S., Arndt, S., Cizadlo, T., Hurtig, R., Rezai, K., Watkins, G.L., Boles Ponto, L.L., & Hichwa, R.D. (1995). Short-term and long-term verbal memory: A positron emission tomography study. *Proceedings of the National Academy of Sciences USA, 92*, 5111–5115.

Bäckman, L., & Small, B.J. (1998). Influences of cognitive support on episodic remembering: Tracing the process of loss from normal aging to Alzheimer's disease. *Psychology and Aging, 13*, 267–276.

Buckner, R.L. (1996). Beyond HERA: Contributions of specific prefrontal brain areas to long- term memory. *Psychonomic Bulletin & Review, 3*, 149–158.

Buckner, R.L., & Petersen, S.E. (1996). What does neuroimaging tell us about the role of prefrontal cortex in memory retrieval? *Seminars in Neurosciences, 98*, 47–55.

Buckner, R.L., & Tulving, E. (1995). Neuroimaging studies of memory: Theory and recent PET results. In F. Boller & J. Grafman (Eds.), *Handbook of neuropsychology* (10, pp. 439–466). Amsterdam: Elsevier.

Buckner, R.L., Petersen, S.E., Ojemann, J.G., Miezin, F.M., Squire, L.R., & Raichle, M.E. (1995). Functional anatomical studies of explicit and implicit memory retrieval tasks. *Journal of Neuroscience, 15*, 12–29.

Buckner, R.L., Raichle, M.E., Miezin, F.M., & Petersen, S.E. (1996). Functional anatomical studies of memory retrieval for auditory words and visual pictures. *Journal of Neuroscience, 16*, 6219–6235.

Buckner, R.L., Koutstaal, W., Schacter, D.L., Dale, A.M., Rotte, M., & Rosen, B.R. (1998). Functional-anatomic study of episodic memory retrieval II: Selective averaging of event-related fMRI trials to test the retrieval success hypothesis. *NeuroImage, 7*, 163–175.

Cabeza, R., & Nyberg, L. (1996). Imaging cognition: An empirical review of PET studies with normal subjects. *Journal of Cognitive Neuroscience, 9*, 1–26.

Cabeza, R., Kapur, S., Craik, F.I.M., McIntosh, A.R., Houle, S., & Tulving, E. (1997a). Functional neuroanatomy of recall and recognition: A PET study of episodic memory. *Journal of Cognitive Neuroscience, 9*, 254–265.

Cabeza, R., Mangels, J., Nyberg, L., Habib, R., Houle, S., McIntosh, A.R., & Tulving E. (1997b). Functional imaging of neural systems differentially involved in remembering what and when. *Neuron, 19*, 863–870.

Calabrese, P., Markowitsch, H.J., Durwen, H.F., Widlitzek, H., Haupts, M., Holinka, B., & Gehlen, W. (1996). Right temporofrontal cortex as critical locus for ecphory of old episodic memories. *Journal of Neurology, Neurosurgery, and Psychiatry, 61*, 304–310.

Craik, F.I.M., & Tulving, E. (1975). Depth of processing and the retention of words in episodic memory. *Journal of Experimental Psychology: General, 104*, 268–294.

Craik, F.I.M., Moroz, T.M., Moscovitch, M., Stuss, D.T., Winocur, G., & Tulving E. (in press). In search of the self: A PET investigation of self-referential information. *Psychological Science.*

Crowder, R.G. (1976). *Principles of learning and memory.* Hillsdale, NJ: Erlbaum.

Dalla Barba, G., Mantovan, M.C., Ferruzza, E., & Denes, G. (1997). Remembering and knowing the past: A case study of isolated retrograde amnesia. *Cortex, 33*, 143–154.

Desgranges, B., Baron, J.C., de la Sayette, V., Petit-Taboué, M.C., Benali, K., Landeau, B., Lechevalier, B., & Eustache, F. (1998). The neural substrates of memory system impairment in Alzheimer's disease: A PET study of resting brain glucose utilization. *Brain, 121*, 611–631.

Duffy, L., & O'Carroll, R. (1994). Memory impairment in schizophrenia: A comparison with that observed in the Alcoholic Korsakoff Syndrome. *Psychological Medicine, 24*, 155–165.

Düzel, E., Cabeza, R., Picton, T.W., Yonelinas, A.P., Scheich, H., Heinze, H.-J., & Tulving, E. (1999). Task-related and item-related brain processes of memory retrieval. *Proceedings of the National Academy of Science USA, 96*, 1794–1799.

Düzel, E., Yonelinas, A.P., Mangun, G.R., Heinze, H.-J., & Tulving, E. (1997). Event-related brain potential correlates of two states of conscious awareness in memory. *Proceedings of the National Academy of Science USA, 94*, 5973–5978.

Evans, J., Wilson, B., Wraight, E.P., & Hodges, J.R. (1993) Neuropsychological and SPECT scan findings during and after transient global amnesia: evidence for the differential impairment of remote episodic memory. *Journal of Neurology Neurosurgery and Psychiatry, 56*, 1227–1230.

Fink, G.R., Markowitsch, H.J., Reinkemeier, M., Bruckbauer, T., Kessler, J., & Heiss, W.-D. (1996). Cerebral representation of one's own past: Neural networks involved in autobiographical memory. *Journal of Neuroscience, 16*, 4275–4282.

Fletcher, P.C., Frith, C.D., Grasby, P.M., Shallice, T., Frackowiak, R.S.J., & Dolan, R.J. (1995a). Brain systems for encoding and retrieval of auditory-verbal memory: An in vivo study in humans. *Brain, 118*, 401–416.

Fletcher, P.C., Dolan, R.J., & Frith, C.D. (1995b). The functional anatomy of memory. *Experientia (Basel), 51*, 1197–1207.

Fletcher, P.C., Frith, C.D., & Rugg, M.D. (1997). The functional neuroanatomy of episodic memory. *Trends in Neurosciences, 20*, 213–218.

Foster, J.K., & Jelicic, M. (Eds.). (in press). *Unitary versus multiple systems account of memory.* London: Oxford University Press.

Fox, P.T. (1991). Physiological ROI definition by image subtraction. *Journal of Cerebral Blood Flow & Metabolism, 11*, A79–A82.

Frackowiak, R.S.J. & Friston, K.J. (1994). Functional neuroanatomy of the human brain: positron emission tomography: A new neuroanatomical technique. *Journal of Anatomy, 184*, 211–225.

Friston, K.J., Holmes, A.P., Worsley, K.J., Poline, J.-P., Frith, C.D., & Frackowiak, R.S.J.

(1995). Statistical parametric maps in functional imaging: A general linear approach. *Human Brain Mapping, 2*, 189–210.

Friston, K.J., Price, C.J., Fletcher, P., Moore, C., Frackowiak, R.S.J., & Dolan, R.J. (1996). The trouble with cognitive subtraction. *Neuroimage, 4*, 97–104.

Gardiner, J.M., & Java, R.I. (1993). Recognizing and remembering. In A.F. Collins, M.A. Gathercole, M. Conway, & P.E. Morris (Eds.), *Theories of memory*. Hillsdale, NJ: Erlbaum.

Gardiner, J.M., Ramponi, C., & Richardson-Klavehn, A. (1998). Experience of remembering, knowing, and guessing. *Consciousness and Cognition, 7*, 1–26.

Gibson, E.J., & Walk, R.D. (1960). The "visual cliff." *Scientific American, 202*, 64–71.

Grady, C.L. (1998). Neuroimaging and activation of the frontal lobe. In B.L. Miller & J.L. Cummings (Eds.), *The human frontal lobes* (pp. 196–230). New York: Guilford.

Grady, C.L., McIntosh, A.R., Horwitz, B., Maisog, J.M., Ungerleider, L.G., Mentis, M.J., Pietrini, P., Schapiro, M.B., & Haxby, J.V. (1995). Age-related reductions in human recognition memory due to impaired encoding. *Science, 269*, 218–221.

Greene, J.D., Baddeley, A.D., & Hodges, J.R. (1996). Analysis of the episodic memory deficit in early Alzheimer's disease: evidence from the doors and people test. *Neuropsychologia, 34*, 537–551.

Haxby, J.V., Ungerleider, L.G., Horwitz, B., Maisog, J.M., Rapoport, S.I., & Grady, C.L. (1996). Face encoding and recognition in the human brain. *Proceedings of the National Academy of Science USA, 93*, 922–927.

Herlitz, A., & Forsell, Y. (1996). Episodic memory deficit in elderly adults with suspected delusional disorder. *Acta Psychiatrica Scandinavi_ca, 93*, 355–361.

Herlitz, A., Nilsson, L.-G., & Bäckman, L. (1997). Gender differences in episodic memory. *Memory & Cognition, 25*, 801–811.

Ingvar, D.H. (1985). "Memory of the future": An essay on the temporal organization of conscious awareness. *Human Neurobiology, 4*, 127–136.

James, W. (1890). *Principles of psychology*. New York: Holt.

Jennings, J.M., McIntosh, A.R., Kapur, S., Tulving, E., & Houle, S. (1997). Cognitive subtractions may not add up: The interaction between semantic processing and response mode. *Neuroimage, 5*, 229–239.

Kapur, N., Friston, K.J., Young, A., Frith, C.D., & Frackowiak, R.S.J. (1995). Activation of human hippocampal formation during memory for faces: A PET study. *Cortex, 31*, 99–108.

Kapur, S., Craik, F.I.M., Tulving, E., Wilson, A.A., Houle, S., & Brown, G.M. (1994a). Neuroanatomical correlates of encoding in episodic memory: levels of processing effect. *Proceedings of the National Academy of Science USA, 91*, 2008–2011.

Kapur, S., Rose, R., Liddle, P.F., Zipursky, R.B., Brown, G.M., Stuss, D.T., Houle, S., & Tulving, E. (1994b). The role of the left prefrontal cortex in verbal processing: Semantic processing or willed action? *NeuroReport, 5*, 2193–2196.

Kapur, S., Craik, F.I.M., Jones, C., Brown, G.M., Houle, S., & Tulving, E. (1995). Functional role of the prefrontal cortex in retrieval of memories: A PET study. *NeuroReport, 6*, 1880–1884.

Kapur, S., Tulving E., Cabeza, R., McIntosh, A.R., Houle, S., & Craik, F.I.M. (1996). Neural correlates of intentional learning of verbal materials: A PET study in humans. *Cognitive Brain Research, 4*, 243–249.

Knowlton, B.J., & Squire, L.R. (1995). Remembering and knowing: Two different expressions of declarative memory. *Journal of Experimental Psychology: Learning, Memory, and Cognition, 21*, 699–710.

Köhler, S., Moscovitch, M., Winocur, G., Houle, S., & McIntosh, A.R. (1998). Networks of domain-specific and general regions involved in episodic memory for spatial location and object identity. *Neuropsychologia, 36*, 129–142.

Lepage, M., Habib, R., & Tulving, E. (1998). Hippocampal PET activations of memory encoding and retrieval: The HIPER model. *Hippocampus, 8*, 313–322.

Levine, B., Black, S.E., Cabeza, R., Sinden, M., McIntosh, A.R., Toth, J.P., Tulving, E., & Stuss, D.T. (1998). Episodic memory and the self in a case of isolated retrograde amnesia. *Brain, 121*, 1951–1973.

Levine, B., Cabeza, R., Black, S., Sinden, M., Toth, J.P., Tulving, E., & Stuss, D.T. (1997). Functional and structural neuroimaging correlates of selective retrograde amnesia: A case study with MRI and PET. *Brain and Cognition, 35*, 372–376.

MacLeod, A.K., Buckner, R.L., Miezin, F.M., Petersen, S.E., & Raichle, M.E. (1998). Right anterior prefrontal cortex activation during semantic monitoring and working memory. *NeuroImage, 7*, 41–48.

Markowitsch, H.J. (1993). Brodmann's numbers. *Neurology, 43*, 1863–1864.

Markowitsch, H.J. (1995). Which brain regions are critically involved in the retrieval of old episodic memory? *Brain Research Reviews, 21*, 117–127.

Markowitsch, H.J., Calabrese, P., Liess, J., Haupts, M., Durwen, H.F., & Gehlen, W. (1993). Retrograde amnesia after traumatic injury of the fronto-temporal cortex. *Journal of Neurology, Neurosurgery, and Psychiatry, 56*, 988–992.

McIntosh, A.R., Nyberg, L., Bookstein, F.L., & Tulving, E. Differential functional connectivity of prefrontal and medial temporal cortices during episodic memory retrieval. *Human Brain Mapping, 5*, 323–327.

Moscovitch, M. (1994). Memory and working with memory: Evaluation of a component process model and comparisons with other models. In D.L. Schacter & E. Tulving (Eds.), *Memory systems 1994* (pp. 269–310). Cambridge, MA: MIT Press.

Moscovitch, M., Kapur, S., Köhler, S., & Houle, S. (1995). Distinct neural correlates of visual long-term memory for spatial location and object identity: A positron emission tomography (PET) study in humans. *Proceedings of the National Academy of Science USA, 92*, 3721–3725.

Nilsson, L.-G., Bäckman, L., Erngrund, K., Nyberg, L., Adolfsson, R., Bucht, G., Karlsson, S., Widing, M., & Winblad, B. (1997). The Betula prospective cohort study: Memory, health, and aging. *Aging, Neuropsychology, and Cognition, 4*, 1–36.

Nyberg, L. (1998). Mapping episodic memory. *Behavioral Brain Research, 90*, 107–114.

Nyberg, L., Tulving, E., Habib, R., Nilsson, L.-G., Kapur, S., Houle, S., Cabeza, R.E.L., & McIntosh, A.R. (1995). Functional brain maps of retrieval mode and recovery of episodic information. *NeuroReport, 7*, 249–252.

Nyberg, L., Cabeza, R., & Tulving, E. (1996a). PET studies of encoding and retrieval: The HERA model. *Psychonomic Bulletin and Review, 3*, 135–148.

Nyberg, L., McIntosh, A.R., Cabeza, R., Habib, R, & Tulving, E. (1996b). General and specific brain regions involved in encoding and retrieval of events: What, where, and when. *Proceedings of the National Academy of Sciences USA, 93*, 11280–11285.

Nyberg, L., McIntosh, A.R., Houle, S., Nilsson, L.-G., & Tulving, E. (1996c). Activation of medial temporal structures during episodic memory retrieval in individual subjects. *Nature, 380*, 715–717.

Owen, A.M., Milner, B., Petrides, M., & Evans, A.C. (1996). Memory for object features versus memory for object location: A positron-emission tomography study of encoding and retrieval processes. *Proceedings of the National Academy of Science USA, 93,* 9212–9217.

Perani, D., Bressi, S., Cappa, S.F., Vallar, G., Alberoni, M., Grassi, F., Caltagirone, C., Cipolotti, L., Franceschi, M., Lenzi, G.L., & Fazio, F. (1993). Evidence of multiple memory systems in the human brain A [¹⁸F]FDG PET metabolic study. *Brain, 116,* 903–919.

Perner, J., & Ruffman, T. (1995). Episodic memory and autonoetic consciousness: Developmental evidence and a theory of childhood amnesia. *Journal of Experimental Child Psychology, 59,* 516–548.

Pillemer, D.B., & White, S.H. (1989). Childhood events recalled by children and adults. *Advances in Child Development and Behavior, 21,* 297–340.

Pinker, S. (1994). *The language instinct.* New York: Morrow.

Posner, M.I., & Raichle, M.E. (1994). *Images of mind.* New York: Scientific American Library.

Raichle, M.E. (1994b). Images of the mind: Studies with modern imaging techniques. *Annual Review of Psychology, 45,* 333–356.

Roediger, H.L. III, & Guynn, M.J. (1996). Retrieval processes. In R.A. Bjork & E.L. Bjork (Eds.), *Memory: Handbook of perception and cognition, 2* (pp. 197–236). San Diego: Academic Press.

Roskies, A. (1994). Commentary: Mapping memory with positron emission tomography. *Proceedings of the National Academy of Science USA, 91,* 1989–1991.

Rugg, M.D., Fletcher, P.C., Frith, C.D., Frackowiak, R.S.J., & Dolan, R.J. (1996). Differential activation of the prefrontal cortex in successful and unsuccessful memory retrieval. *Brain, 119,* 2073–2083.

Rugg, M.D., Fletcher, P.C, Frith, C.D., Frackowiak, R.S., & Dolan, R.J. (1997). Brain regions supporting intentional and incidental memory: A PET study. *NeuroReport, 8,* 1283–1287.

Schacter, D.L. (1987). Memory, amnesia, and frontal lobe dysfunction. *Psychobiology, 15,* 21–36.

Schacter, D.L., & Tulving, E. (1994). What are the memory systems of 1994? In D.L. Schacter & E. Tulving (Eds.), *Memory systems 1994* (pp. 1–38). Cambridge, MA: MIT Press.

Schacter, D.L., Reiman, E., Uecker, A., Polster, M.R., Yun, L.S., & Cooper, L.A. (1995). Brain regions associated with retrieval of structurally coherent visual information. *Nature, 376,* 587–590.

Schacter, D.L., Savage, C.R., Alpert, N.M., Rauch, S.L., & Albert, M.S. (1996). The role of the hippocampus and frontal cortex in age-related memory changes: A PET study. *NeuroReport, 7,* 1165–1169.

Shallice, T. (1986). *From neuropsychology to mental structure.* Cambridge, UK: Cambridge University Press.

Shallice, T., Fletcher, P., Frith, C.D., Grasby, P., Frackowiak, R.S.J., & Dolan, R.J. (1994). Brain regions associated with acquisition and retrieval of verbal episodic memory. *Nature, 368,* 633–635.

Squire, L.R. (1987). *Memory and brain.* New York: Oxford University Press.

Squire, L.R., Ojemann, J.G., Miezin, F.M., Petersen, S.E., Videen, T.O., & Raichle, M.E. (1992). Activation of the hippocampus in normal humans: A functional anatomical study of memory. *Proceedings of the National Academy of Science USA, 89,* 1837–1841.

Stuss, D.T., & Benson, D.F. (1986). *The frontal lobes.* New York: Raven Press.

Stuss, D.T., Eskes, G.A., & Foster, J.K. (1994). Experimental neuropsychological studies of frontal lobe functions. In F. Boller & J. Grafman (Eds.), *Handbook of neuropsychology* (Vol. 9, pp. 149–185). Amsterdam: Elsevier.

Suddendorf, T., & Corballis, M.C. (1997). Mental time travel and the evolution of the human mind. *Genetic and Social General Psychological Monographs, 123*, 133–167.

Talairach, J., & Tournoux, P. (1988). *A co-planar sterotactic atlas of the human brain*. Stuttgart: Thieme.

Tulving, E. (1972). Episodic and semantic memory. In E. Tulving & W. Donaldson (Eds.), *Organization of memory* (pp. 381–403). New York: Academic Press.

Tulving, E. (1983). *Elements of episodic memory*. Oxford: Clarendon.

Tulving, E. (1984). Relations among components and processes of memory. *Behavioral and Brain Sciences, 7*, 257–268.

Tulving, E. (1985). Memory and consciousness. *Canadian Psychology, 26*, 1–12.

Tulving, E. (1993). What is episodic memory? *Current Perspectives in Psychological Science, 2*, 67–70.

Tulving, E. (1998). Neurocognitive processes of human memory. In C. von Euler, I. Lundberg, & R.R. Llinas (Eds.), *Basic mechanisms in cognition and language* (pp. 261–281). Amsterdam: Elsevier.

Tulving, E. (1998). Study of memory: Processes and systems. In J.K. Foster & M. Jelicic (Eds.), *Unitary versus multiple systems account of memory* (pp. 11–30). London: Oxford University Press.

Tulving, E., & Kroll, N.E.A. (1995). Novelty assessment in the brain and long-term memory encoding. *Psychonomic Bulletin & Review, 2*, 387–390.

Tulving, E., & Madigan, S.A. (1970). Memory and verbal learning. *Annual Review of Psychology, 21*, 437–484.

Tulving, E., & Markowitsch, H.J. (1998). Episodic and declarative memory: Role of the hippocampus. *Hippocampus, 8*, 198–204.

Tulving, E., Kapur, S., Craik, F.I.M., Moscovitch, M., & Houle, S. (1994a). Hemispheric encoding/retrieval asymmetry in episodic memory: Positron emission tomography findings. *Proceedings of the National Academy of Science USA, 91*, 2016–2020.

Tulving, E., Kapur, S., Markowitsch, H.J., Craik, F.I.M., Habib, R., & Houle, S. (1994b). Neuroanatomical correlates of retrieval in episodic memory: Auditory sentence recognition. *Proceedings of the National Academy of Science USA, 91*, 2012–2015.

Tulving, E., Markowitsch, H.J., Craik, F.I.M., Habib, R., & Houle, S. (1996). Novelty and familiarity activations in PET studies of memory encoding and retrieval. *Cerebral Cortex, 6*, 71–79.

Vargha-Khadem, F., Gadian, D.G., Watkins, K.E., Connelly, A., Van Paesschen, W., & Mishkin, M. (1997). Differential effects of early hippocampal pathology on episodic and semantic memory. *Science, 277*, 376–380.

Wagner, A.D., Desmond, J.E., Glover, G.H., & Gabrieli, J.D.E. (1998). Prefrontal cortex and recognition memory: fMRI evidence for context-dependent retrieval processes. *Brain, 121*, 1985–2002.

Wheeler, M.A., Stuss, D.T., & Tulving, E. (1997). Towards a theory of episodic memory: The frontal lobes and autonoetic consciousness. *Psychological Bulletin, 121*, 331–354.

# Functional Neuroanatomy of Component Processes of Episodic Memory Retrieval

*Lars Nyberg*

Functional brain imaging is used to map regions in the human brain that are involved in lower as well as higher level of information processing. An example of the former is the demonstration of differential involvement of distinct visual areas in motion and color processing (see Zeki, 1993). An example of the latter comes from a study of visual object recognition (Kanwisher, Woods, Iacoboni, & Mazziotta, 1997). One motivation for studying visual object recognition was that there is substantial evidence that visual object recognition is subserved by dedicated brain modules, carrying out domain-specific computations. Theorists have distinguished between three main component processes, and in the Kanwisher et al. study a locus for one of these (visual shape analysis) was identified in extrastriate cortex.

The present chapter is concerned with episodic memory (Tulving, 1983). An act of retrieval from episodic memory takes place when "a rememberer mentally travels back in subjective time to re-experience the personal past" (Wheeler, Stuss, & Tulving, 1997, p. 331). Similar to the above noted modular view of visual object recognition, episodic memory retrieval can be broken down into (at least) three separate component processes (cf. Tulving, 1983, 1984; see also Moscovitch, 1992).

The first component process will be referred to as "retrieval mode" (Tulving, 1983). This process can be thought of as a form of "mental set" which is critical for directing and maintaining the rememberer's attention on a particular previous episode. As noted by Tulving (1984), experiments on episodic memory retrieval have generally taken place under "intentional retrieval" conditions, but as will be exemplified below there are some exceptions. Neuropsychological data suggest that the frontal lobes are critical for maintaining a retrieval mode; "the frontal lobes are necessary for converting remembering from a stupid reflexive act triggered by a cue to an intelligent, reflective goal-directed activity that is under voluntary control" (Moscovitch, 1992, p. 262).

The second component process of episodic retrieval will be referred to as "ecphory." Some sort of retrieval cue, external or internally generated, is necessary for episodic retrieval to take place. The information in the cue is combined with stored information, represented in the form of memory traces or "engrams," to produce ecphoric information. This process is called "ecphory" (Tulving, 1983; cf. Semon, 1921, cited in Schacter, Eich, & Tulving, 1978). What is remembered of an event depends on the quantity and quality of ecphoric information, which in turn depends on the nature of the cue and whether relevant episodic information is stored. It has been suggested that hippocampus and related medial-temporal regions (henceforth hippocampal regions) are critical for ecphory (Moscovitch, 1992).

The third component process of episodic retrieval will be termed "recollective experience." Recollective experience refers to subjective awareness of ecphoric information (Tulving, 1984). Depending on the properties of this information (cf. the above section on ecphory), this awareness will produce a feeling that the recollective experience refers to a past event and is veridical. In a similar vein, Shallice (1988) has argued for the importance of a process that monitors the products of retrieval (the ecphoric information), and verifies that the retrieved information is relevant to current goals. Prefrontal regions have been suggested to be critical for this process (Shallice, 1988). Patients with ventromedial frontal lesions often confabulate, and this is supposed to be due to deficient strategic retrieval processes involved in monitoring and verification (Moscovitch, 1995).

Next, evidence from positron emission tomography (PET) studies of episodic memory retrieval will be reviewed to examine the support for neuroanatomical correlates of each of these component processes of episodic retrieval.

## Retrieval Mode

Three PET studies of episodic memory retrieval have been explicitly designed to isolate brain regions related to retrieval mode. Kapur, Craik, Jones, Brown, Houle, and Tulving (1995) compared two episodic retrieval conditions (yes/no visual word recognition) with a non-episodic reference task. In one of the retrieval conditions, the majority of presented words had been studied (85%), whereas in the other retrieval condition a minority of the presented words were old (15%). The authors hypothesized that in both retrieval conditions, regardless of how many words were recognized as old, subjects should be involved in a retrieval mode (or engaged in retrieval attempt). Therefore, relative to the reference condition, both retrieval conditions were predicted to be associated with increased blood flow in right prefrontal regions. The results supported this hypothesis by showing differential activity in several right prefrontal regions, including a right medial frontopolar region located in

Brodmann area 10. When the two retrieval conditions were directly contrasted, no evidence was found for differential activity in this region.

In a similar study of visual word recognition (Nyberg, Tulving, Habib, Nilsson, Kapur, Houle, Cabeza, & McIntosh, 1995), three retrieval conditions were included. One of these included words that had been deeply processed at study, another condition included words that had been shallowly processed at study, and the third condition included non-studied words. When compared with a non-episodic reference condition, each of the three retrieval conditions was associated with a similar activation pattern. This pattern included a right medial frontopolar region located in Brodmann area 10 (coordinates for this region are given in Nyberg, 1998).

The third relevant study (Schacter, Alpert, Savage, Rauch, & Albert, 1996) included a similar manipulation as the Nyberg et al. (1995) study. In one study condition subjects made semantic judgements for words that were presented four times each. In another study condition subjects made a nonsemantic judgment for words that were presented only once. Subjects were then PET scanned (i) while trying to complete three-letter word stems with words presented in the first study condition (high recall), and (ii) while trying to complete three-letter word stems with words presented in the second study condition (low recall). When comparing the blood-flow pattern associated with each retrieval condition with that associated with a non-episodic reference condition, it was found that the low-recall condition involved increased activity in right anterior prefrontal cortex (area 10) whereas the high-recall condition did not. One hypothesis why right area 10 did not show increased activity in the high-recall condition is that the words were so well-learned that the task did not involve much episodic retrieval effort (cf. Schacter et al., 1996, p. 325).

All of the above discussed studies involved intentional retrieval, which indeed is typical for the majority of studies of episodic retrieval. However, a recent study by Rugg, Fletcher, Frith, Frackowiak, and Dolan (1997) provides a significant exception to this trend. In that study, intentional episodic retrieval (yes/no word recognition) was compared with incidental retrieval. In the latter task, subjects made animate/inanimate judgements. The proportion of old words was the same in both conditions (75%). The outcome of the contrast between intentional and incidental retrieval showed increased activity in a right medial frontopolar region (area 10).

Notably, increased activity in area 10 during intentional retrieval was only observed following shallow encoding of the study words. As the memory performance was very high following deep encoding (96%), this pattern of results is consistent with the hypothesis that episodic tasks that do not involve much retrieval effort may not be associated with differential activity in this specific frontal region (cf. Schacter et al., 1996). By contrast, other areas in right frontal cortex show increased activity during intentional retrieval regardless of type of encoding task (see Rugg et al., 1997).

Taken together, the above reviewed studies converge on the notion that a region in right medial anterior prefrontal cortex (area 10) is differentially activated during episodic memory retrieval (cf. Buckner, Raichle, Miezin, & Petersen, 1996). Activity in this region does not seem to be related to level of memory performance. Rather, activation of this region has been absent during high-retrieval conditions. This suggests that the processing component that activates this region during episodic retrieval is not related to ecphory, but may instead be related to retrieval mode.

Little is known from work in other domains about the functional role of right area 10. Importantly, though, it is known that it has connections to the limbic system (see Tulving, 1995, p. 845). Such connections may provide the link between retrieval mode and ecphory.


## Ecphory

The suggestion that hippocampal regions are critical for ecphory (Moscovitch, 1992) is supported by the results from several PET studies. In an early study, Grasby, Frith, Friston, Frackowiak, and Dolan (1993) showed that blood flow in bilateral hippocampal regions correlated with a measure of long-term memory function ("supraspan" recall of auditorily presented words). Although the design of that study made it difficult to tell whether the correlation reflected neural activity associated with encoding, consolidation, or retrieval processes, subsequent studies have provided additional support for a relation between hippocampal activity and level of recovered episodic information.

In a study by Eustache, Rioux, Desgranges et al. (1995) a positive correlation was found between a measure of verbal episodic memory retrieval (associative learning) and left hippocampal metabolism (oxygen consumption). Similarly, Cahill, Haier, Fallon et al. (1996) demonstrated a significant correlation between delayed recall of film clips and bilateral hippocampal/parahippocampal glucose metabolic rate measured at encoding. Moreover, in a study examining the association between individual level of cerebral blood flow and individual level of episodic memory performance (Nyberg, McIntosh, Houle, Nilsson, & Tulving, 1996), a strong positive correlation was found between blood flow in the left hippocampal region and number of correctly recognized words.

In the latter study, bilateral hippocampal regions were found to be salient components of a pattern of brain regions which discriminated a condition of higher memory retrieval from conditions of lower retrieval. This finding is consistent with the results of the Schacter et al. (1996) study of high- and low-stem-cued recall (see the section on "Retrieval mode"). A direct comparison of the high- and low-recall conditions revealed only one significant increase; in the right hippocampal region (cf. Rugg et al., 1997).

Taken together, several PET studies have shown that activity in the hippocampal region is related to actual recovery of episodic information. This provides converging evidence for the view that the hippocampal region is critical for ecphory (e. g., Moscovitch, 1992; see Blaxton 1996 for a critical review of neuroimaging studies on the functional role of hippocampus). In this context it should be noted, though, that the hippocampal region is believed to interact with neocortical areas during recovery. This is because episodic information is assumed to be represented in the hippocampal region as well as in neocortical areas (e. g., Nadel & Moscovitch, 1997). Thus, other areas than the hippocampal region may be implicated in ecphory.

One prominent candidate for a neocortical region implicated in ecphory is a medial parietal area; the precuneus. In the above mentioned study by Kapur et al. (1995), increased activity was observed in the precuneus region (mainly on the right side) in a direct comparison of the high-recovery condition with the low-recovery condition. One explanation put forward by the authors for their finding of an association between precuneus activity and successful retrieval was that it reflects reactivation of stored engrams. In line with the retrieval model discussed in the present chapter, they noted that this interpretation is consistent with the view that prefrontal regions drive the retrieval attempt, and the attempt is successful when it leads to reactivation of engrams stored in posterior multimodal association cortices. Another possible explanation for their finding is that the activation of the precuneus region reflected visual imagery. There is evidence from other studies in favour of each of these explanations.

Starting with the latter explanation, that precuneus activation reflects visual imagery, Fletcher, Frith, Baker, Shallice, Frackowiak, and Dolan (1995) directly compared cued recall of imageable and nonimageable paired associates. They found that the recall of imageable paired associates was associated with increased activation in the precuneus region, thus confirming a previous hypothesis (Grasby, Frith, Friston, Bench, Frackowiak, & Dolan, 1993; Shallice, Fletcher, Frith, Grasby, Frackowiak, & Dolan, 1994).

Turning to the possibility that precuneus activation reflects reactivation of stored engrams, a study by Roland and Gulyas (1995) provided relevant evidence. These authors studied encoding (storing), recognition, and recall of complex visual geometrical patterns. Relative to a rest condition, each of these conditions involved increased activation in posterior precuneus (a similar pattern was seen for three other regions). Since it was assumed that storage sites would be active in all three conditions, it was suggested that higher-level visual areas, including precuneus, are involved in storing complex visual patterns.

Future studies will no doubt provide further information on the role of precuneus in episodic memory retrieval. As an important component of visual imagery is memory retrieval (Sakai & Miyashita, 1993), it is quite possible that both of these explanations will turn out to be valid. Future studies will also provide information on other neocortical areas that may be implicated in ecphory, such as the middle and superior temporal gyri (Fink, Markowitsch, Reinkemeier, Bruckbauer, Kessler, & Heiss, 1996).

## Recollective Experience

The results from a PET study on episodic word recognition by Rugg, Fletcher, Frith, Frackowiak, and Dolan (1996) yielded results which are important for determining neuroanatomical correlates of the third component process of episodic retrieval. These researchers first compared brain activity associated with episodic recognition memory with that of a control task. They found increased activity in several areas, including bilateral frontal and cuneus/precuneus regions. In a second step, they tested for a positive relationship between activity in any of the identified regions and density of recognition memory targets (0, 20, or 80% targets). Such a relationship was observed for activity in right dorsolateral, right medial and bilateral frontopolar regions.

The finding that activity in prefrontal regions was associated with target density was interpreted in terms of post-retrieval processing; such processing can only proceed if there is retrieved information to process. This interpretation is consistent with the view that prefrontal regions are critical for monitoring and verifying retrieval (Shallice, 1988).

The region in the right frontal pole in which activity was found to covary with target density was more lateral [Talairach & Tournoux (1988) x,y,z coordinates = 38, 48, 8; x = medial/lateral (+ for right hemisphere); y = anterior/posterior; z = superior/inferior] than the typical location of retrieval mode regions (e. g., x,y,z in Kapur et al., 1995 = 20, 52, 8). Thus, there is no apparent inconsistency between the Rugg et al. suggestion of a role of prefrontal regions in post-retrieval operations and previous claims that certain prefrontal regions are related to retrieval mode. Instead, these two sets of findings provide additional evidence on functional heterogeneity of human prefrontal cortex (e. g., Petrides, 1994).

There is, however, an inconsistency between the results of the Rugg et al. study and previous findings of no differential prefrontal activity when conditions of higher recovery have been contrasted with conditions of lower recovery (e. g., Kapur et al., 1995; Nyberg et al., 1995). One possible solution to this conflict is provided by the finding by Rugg et al. of a non-linear relationship between prefrontal activity and target density. Whereas prefrontal activity was significantly higher in both the high and low density conditions than in the zero target condition, there was little difference in prefrontal activity between the high and low conditions. To explain the lack of strong differences between the latter conditions, it was hypothesized that the prefrontal blood flow increases that were elicited by each target persisted for several seconds. For this reason, the accumulated PET counts during the measurement interval may not have differed that much between the high and low conditions.

Possibly, this explanation can be used to explain previous demonstrations of no differences in right prefrontal activity between conditions of higher and lower recovery. Other findings may, however, be more problematic. For example, in the Schacter et al. (1996) study, a direct comparison of a condition of lower recovery with a non-episodic reference condition revealed increased activity in bilateral frontal regions. In a similar contrast involving a condition of high recovery, no prefrontal activation was observed. These results would seem to suggest that no post-retrieval processes were operating in the high-recovery condition, or that post-retrieval operations were operating to the same extent in the reference task as in the memory task. Alternatively, when the retrieval task is very easy (as in the Schacter et al., 1996, high-recovery condition) there may be little need for post-retrieval processing.

Taken together, there is some support from PET studies for a role of prefrontal brain regions in mediating aspects of recollective experience. In this context it should be noted that ecphory and recollective experience are closely related, and if ecphory is used to refer to the "production" of ecphoric information and recollective experience to the subjective experience of the ecphoric information then there is evidence that hippocampus is involved in ecphory (e. g., Moscovitch, 1992; above section on ecphory) as well as in recollective experience (Schacter et al., 1996). However, if one by the term recollective experience more emphasizes the realization that the experienced information actually refers to a specific past event, as in the above discussion of post-retrieval processing and activation of frontal regions, then the conceptual separation between these component processes is clearer (as may be the differentiation in terms of functional neuroanatomy).

## Integrating Component Processes

The results of the above discussed studies suggest (a) that a right anterior, medial prefrontal brain region is related to retrieval mode or retrieval attempt; (b) that hippocampal regions as well as specific neocortical regions are related to ecphory or recovery of information; and (c) that activity in distinct prefron-

tal brain regions may underlie recollective experience or post-retrieval operations. As noted above, connections seem to exist between several of these
regions, and such connections are necessary for the integration of various component processes of retrieval. That is, the different sub-processes need to
"cross-talk" in order for an act of retrieval to be complete.

An important next step for researchers will be to attempt to characterize
this "cross-talk." In some initial analyses, covariance-based techniques have
been applied to blood flow data from studies on episodic retrieval (Nyberg,
McIntosh, Cabeza, Nilsson, Houle, Habib, & Tulving, 1996). Such analyses help
to specify how brain regions interact in a network to produce behavior (see
McIntosh, Grady, Ungerleider, Haxby, Rapoport & Horwitz, 1994 for a network analysis of visual cortical pathways). Other techniques such as event-related brain potentials, with better temporal resolution than PET, will also play
an important role in providing information about the nature and timing of
interactions between brain regions.

## Laterality of Activations

Activations related to retrieval mode/attempt have generally been located in
the right hemisphere, and the prefrontal activations in the Rugg et al. (1996)
study on post-retrieval processes also tended to be right-lateralized. This pattern is consistent with the bulk of data on episodic memory retrieval; activations tend to be right-sided (e. g., Fink et al., 1996). This tendency is especially
pronounced within the prefrontal cortex (Cabeza & Nyberg, 1997; see Figure

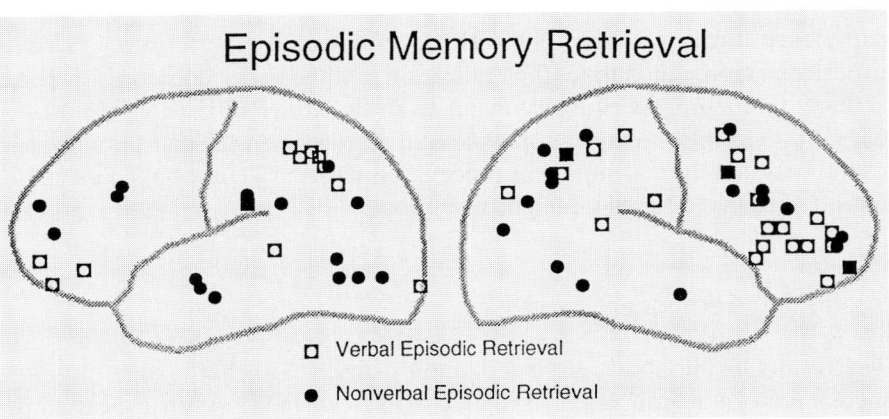

*Figure 1.* Brain regions involved in episodic memory retrieval (from Cabeza & Nyberg, 1997).
Only lateral views of the brain are shown.

1), and forms one basis for the hemispheric encoding/retrieval asymmetry (HERA) model proposed by Tulving and collaborators (Tulving, Kapur, Craik, Moscovitch, & Houle, 1994; see also Nyberg, Cabeza, & Tulving, 1996). According to the HERA model, the right prefrontal cortex is differentially more involved in episodic memory retrieval than the left prefrontal cortex. Instead, left prefrontal cortex is differentially more involved in retrieval from semantic memory, and in encoding novel aspects of the retrieved information into episodic memory, than the right prefrontal cortex.

The reason for the right-sided localization of activations associated with episodic memory retrieval is not clear. One possibility is that it has to do with the autobiographical character of episodic memory (cf. Fink et al., 1996). Another, more general, hypothesis is that the right hemisphere stores and uses representations of specific instances more effectively than the left hemisphere (Brown & Kosslyn, 1993). Future studies will no doubt shed more light on this intriguing issue.

## Component Processes of Episodic Memory Encoding

The present chapter has focused on component processes of episodic retrieval and their neuroanatomical correlates. Briefly, it can be mentioned that there is evidence that another major memory process, encoding or acquisition, can also be broken down into sub-components, and that these sub-components have a distinct neural architecture:

The so-called novelty/encoding hypothesis has been suggested by Tulving and colleagues (Tulving, Markowitsch, Kapur, Habib, & Houle, 1994; Tulving & Kroll. 1995; Tulving, Markowitsch, Craik, Habib, & Houle, 1996). According to this hypothesis, encoding consists of two subprocesses: (i) novelty assessment and (ii) meaning-based encoding operations. If incoming information is identified as novel it is transmitted for further meaning-based processing, and the end product of these processes is the engram.

There is evidence from studies comparing the brain activation pattern associated with processing materials that is familiar or novel within the experimental context that novelty assessment is partly mediated by hippocampal regions and that meaning-based processing is partly mediated by left frontal lobe regions (see Tulving, Markowitsch, Craik, Habib, & Houle, 1996). Recent findings by Dolan and Fletcher (1997) have provided additional evidence that one role of left hippocampal regions in episodic memory encoding is to register the novelty of presented material, and that the role of left prefrontal cortex is related to associative semantic processing.

## Conclusion

A danger with the type of approach taken in the present chapter is that imaging data are forced to fit theoretical models (cf. Gazzaniga, 1996). It should also be stressed that the brain regions discussed here are unlikely to be dedicated to episodic retrieval, but may serve different functional roles depending on which areas they are interacting with (cf. McIntosh, Nyberg, Bookstein, & Tulving, 1997; see also Grady, 1999). Nevertheless, with these caveats in mind, it is concluded that the PET studies discussed above provide strong evidence that different component processes of episodic memory are associated with distinct brain regions.

## *Acknowledgment*

Supported by a grant from HSFR, Sweden.

## References

Blaxton, T.A. (1996). Distinguishing false from true in human memory. *Neuron, 17*, 191–194.

Brown, H.D., & Kosslyn, S.M. (1993). Cerebral lateralization. *Current Opinion in Neurobiology, 3*, 183–186.

Buckner, R.L., Raichle, M.E., Miezin, F.M., & Petersen, S.E. (1996). Functional anatomic studies of memory retrieval for auditory words and visual pictures. *The Journal of Neuroscience, 16*, 6219–6235.

Cabeza, R., & Nyberg, L. (1997). Imaging cognition: An empirical review of PET studies with normal subjects. *Journal of Cognitive Neuroscience, 9*, 1–26.

Cahill, L., Haier, R.J., Fallon, J., Alkire, M.T., Tang, C., Keator, D., Wu, J., & McGaugh, J.L. (1996). Amygdala activity at encoding correlated with long-term, free recall of emotional information. *Proceedings of the National Academy of Sciences, USA, 93*, 8016–8021.

Dolan, R.J., & Fletcher, P.C. (1997). Dissociating prefrontal and hippocampal function in episodic memory encoding. *Nature, 388*, 582–585.

Eustache, F., Rioux, P., Desgranges, B., Marchal, G., Petit-Taboué, M.-C., Dary, M., Lechevalier, B., & Baron, J.-C. (1995). Healthy aging, memory subsystems and regional cerebral oxygen consumption. *Neuropsychologia, 33*, 867–887.

Fink, G.R., Markowitsch, H.J., Reinkemeier, M., Bruckbauer, T., Kessler, J., & Heiss, W.-D. (1996). Cerebral representation of one's own past: Neural networks involved in autobiographical memory. *The Journal of Neuroscience, 16*, 4275–4282.

Fletcher, P.C., Frith, C.D., Baker, S.C., Shallice, T., Frackowiak, R.S.J., & Dolan, R.J. (1995). The mind's eyes – Precuneus activation in memory-related imagery. *Neuroimage, 2*, 195–200.

Gazzaniga, M.S. (1996). Interview with Robert G. Shulman. *Journal of Cognitive Neuroscience, 8*, 474–480.

Grady, C.L. (1999). Neuroimaging and activation of the frontal lobes. In B.L. Miller & J.L.

Cummings (Eds.), *The human frontal lobes: Function and disorders* (pp. 196–230). New York: Guilford Press.

Grasby, P.M., Frith, C.D., Friston, K.J., Bench, C., Frackowiak, R.S.J., & Dolan, R.J. (1993). Functional mapping of brain areas implicated in auditory-verbal memory function. *Brain, 116,* 1–20.

Grasby, P.M., Frith, C.D., Friston, K.J., Frackowiak, R.S.J., & Dolan, R.J. (1993). Activation of the human hippocampal formation during auditory-verbal long-term memory function. *Neuroscience Letters, 163,* 185–188.

Kanwisher, N., Woods, R.P., Iacoboni, M., & Mazziotta, J.C. (1997). A locus in human extrastriate cortex for visual shape analysis. *Journal of Cognitive Neuroscience, 9,* 133–142.

Kapur, S., Craik, F.I.M., Jones, C., Brown, G.M., Houle, S., & Tulving, E. (1995). Functional role of the prefrontal cortex in retrieval of memories: A PET study. *NeuroReport, 6,* 1880–1884.

McIntosh, A.R., Grady, C.L., Ungerleider, L.G., Haxby, J.V., Rapoport, S.I., & Horwitz, B. (1994). Network analysis of cortical visual pathways mapped with PET. *The Journal of Neuroscience, 14,* 655–666.

McIntosh, A.R., Nyberg, L., Bookstein, F.L., & Tulving, E. (1997). Differential functional connectivity of prefrontal and medial temporal cortices during episodic memory retrieval. *Human Brain Mapping, 5,* 323–327.

Moscovitch, M. (1992). Memory and working-with-memory: A component process model based on modules and central systems. *Journal of Cognitive Neuroscience, 4,* 257–267.

Moscovitch, M. (1995). Confabulation. In D.L. Schacter (Ed.), *Memory distortion: How minds, brains, and societies reconstruct the past* (pp. 226–251). Cambridge, MA: Harvard University Press.

Nadel, L., & Moscovitch, M. (1997). Memory consolidation, retrograde amnesia and the hippocampal complex. *Current Opinion in Neurobiology, 7,* 217–227.

Nyberg, L. (1998). Mapping episodic memory. *Behavioral Brain Research, 90,* 107–114.

Nyberg, L., Tulving, E., Habib, R., Nilsson, L.-G., Kapur, S., Houle, S., Cabeza, R., & McIntosh, A.R. (1995). Functional brain maps of retrieval mode and recovery of episodic information. *NeuroReport, 7,* 249–252.

Nyberg, L., Cabeza, R., & Tulving, E. (1996). PET studies of encoding and retrieval: The HERA model. *Psychonomic Bulletin & Review, 3,* 135–148.

Nyberg, L., McIntosh, A.R., Cabeza, R., Nilsson, L.-G., Houle, S., Habib, R., & Tulving, E. (1996). Network analysis of positron emission tomography regional cerebral blood flow data: Ensemble inhibition during episodic memory retrieval. *The Journal of Neuroscience, 16,* 3753–3759.

Nyberg, L., McIntosh, A.R., Houle, S., Nilsson, L.-G., & Tulving, E. (1996). Activation of medial temporal structures during episodic memory retrieval. *Nature, 380,* 715–717.

Petrides, M. (1994). Frontal lobes and behavior. *Current Opinion in Neurobiology, 4,* 207–211.

Roland, P.E., & Gulyas, B. (1995). Visual memory, visual imagery, and visual recognition of large field patterns by the human brain: Functional anatomy by positron emission tomography. *Cerebral Cortex, 5,* 79–93.

Rugg, M.D., Fletcher, P.C., Frith, C.D., Frackowiak, R.S.J., & Dolan, R.J. (1996). Differential activation of the prefrontal cortex in successful and unsuccessful memory retrieval. *Brain, 119,* 2073–2083.

Rugg, M.D., Fletcher, P.C., Frith, C.D., Frackowiak, R.S.J., & Dolan, R.J. (1997). Brain regions supporting intentional and incidental memory: A PET study. *NeuroReport, 8,* 1283–1287.

Sakai, K., & Miyasita, Y. (1993). Memory and imagery in the temporal lobe. *Current Opinion in Neurobiology, 3,* 166–170.

Schacter, D.L., Alpert, N.M., Savage, C.R., Rauch, S.L., & Albert, M.S. (1996). Conscious recollection and the human hippocampal formation: Evidence from positron emission tomography. *Proceedings of the National Academy of Sciences USA, 93,* 321–325.

Schacter, D.L., Eich, J.E., & Tulving, E. (1978). Richard Semon's theory of memory. *Journal of Verbal Learning and Verbal Behavior, 17,* 721–743.

Shallice, T. (1988). *From neuropsychology to mental structure.* Cambridge, UK: Cambridge University Press.

Shallice, T., Fletcher, P.C., Frith, C.D., Grasby, P., Frackowiak, R.S.J., & Dolan, R.J. (1994). Brain regions associated with acquisition and retrieval of verbal episodic memory. *Nature, 368,* 633–635.

Talairach, J., & Tournoux, P. (1988). *Co-planar stereotaxic atlas of the human brain.* New York: Thieme Medical Publishers.

Tulving, E. (1983). *Elements of episodic memory.* New York: Oxford University Press.

Tulving, E. (1984). Précis of Elements of episodic memory. *The Behavioral and Brain Sciences, 7,* 223–268.

Tulving, E. (1995). Organization of memory: Quo vadis? In M.S. Gazzaniga (Ed.), *The cognitive neurosciences* (pp. 839–847). Cambridge, MA: The MIT Press.

Tulving, E., Kapur, S., Craik, F.I.M., Moscovitch, M., & Houle, S. (1994). Hemispheric encoding/retrieval asymmetry in episodic memory: Positron emission tomography findings. *Proceedings of the National Academy of Sciences USA, 91,* 2016–2020.

Tulving, E., & Kroll, N. (1995). Novelty assessment in the brain and long-term memory encoding. *Psychonomic Bulletin & Review, 2,* 387–390.

Tulving, E., Markowitsch, H.J., Craik, F.I.M., Habib, R., & Houle, S. (1996). Novelty and familiarity activations in PET studies of memory encoding and retrieval. *Cerebral Cortex, 6,* 71–79.

Tulving, E., Markowitsch, H.J., Kapur, S., Habib, R., & Houle, S. (1994). Novelty encoding networks in the human brain: positron emission tomography data. *NeuroReport, 5,* 2525–2528.

Wheeler, M.A., Stuss, D.T., & Tulving, E. (1997). Towards a theory of episodic memory: The frontal lobes and autonoetic consciousness. *Psychological Bulletin, 121,* 331–354.

Zeki, S. (1993). The visual image in mind and brain. In *Mind and Brain: Readings from Scientific American* (pp. 27–39). New York: W.H. Freeman.

# The Functional Basis of Memory: PET Mapping of the Memory Systems in Humans

*Daniela Perani*

The investigation of memory disorders in neuropsychology has played a crucial role in the theoretical developments of memory field. The observation of dissociated impairment in the different aspects of memory function in human pathology provided fundamental supports to the "multiple memory system" approach. The idea that memory is not an unitary function, but that multiple memory systems, with different specialization and characteristics are implemented in the brain is nowadays prevalent in the neuroscience field. Different taxonomies of these systems have been proposed: although largely overlapping, the differences in terminology often reflect deep theoretical controversies. This theoretical framework must be however integrated with a process approach, which considers carefully the different stages of the formation of memory traces and the processes related to the retrieval of information. Both approaches have been fruitfully applied to investigation of the neurological basis of memory function in humans using neuroimaging techniques.

The development of neuroimaging methods (such as positron emission tomography, PET, and functional magnetic resonance, fMRI) has provided new impulses to the study of the neural basis of memory functions, and has extended the field of inquiry from the analysis of the consequences of brain lesions to the functional investigations of brain activity, either in patients with selective neuropsychological deficits (steady-state methods in rest condition) or in normal subjects engaged in cognitive tasks (activation procedures). The aim of this chapter is to provide an overview of the contributes of the functional neuroimaging methods in memory research. Technical information has been kept to the minimum required for a correct interpretation of the practical applications of the methodologies.

## The Anatomy of Memory

Computed tomography (CT) and magnetic resonance imaging (MRI) have been used in neuropsychological research as tools to localize the site and extent of focal lesion. Such imaging methods helped to identify morphological damage in amnesics *in vivo* (von Cramon, Hebel, & Schuri, 1985; Press, Amaral, & Squire, 1989). These studies of amnesia-associated lesions in humans have led some uncertainties about crucial lesion(s) sufficient to cause persistent amnesia. It has been repeatedly claimed that the neurological basis of human amnesia is a disconnection between components of Papez's circuit involved in long-term learning and retention (Mair, Warrington, & Weiskrantz, 1979; von Cramon et al., 1985). Memory deficits have been reported in association with damage to the medial temporal lobe (hippocampus, parahippocampal gyrus) (Milner, 1966), the diencephalon (mammillary bodies, mammillo-thalamic tracts, dorso-medial thalamic nucleus) (Mair et al., 1979; von Cramon et al., 1985) and the sectal pre-commissural nuclei of the basal forebrain (Alexander & Freedman, 1984), although less consistently, they have also been reported in association with damage to the cingulate gyrus (Whitty & Lewin, 1960), and to the fornix (Heilman & Sypert, 1977). In the case of vascular thalamic lesions, bilateral damage to the mammillo-thalamic tract and ventro-amygdalofugal pathways is usually found in patients with persistent amnesia (von Cramon et al., 1985; Graff-Radford, Tranel, Van Hoesen, & Brandt, 1990). In post-anoxic amnesia, a selective hippocampal damage in the CA1 field has been reported (Zola-Morgan, Squire, & Amaral, 1986). Amnesia after basal forebrain infarction is considered a consequence of lesions to the septal nuclei, diagonal band of Broca and substantia innominata (Damasio, Graff-Radford, Eslinger, Damasio, & Kassel, 1985). The pathological hallmark of amnesia in Korsakoff's disease is the involvement of several diencephalic structures surrounding the third ventricle, amongst which the dorsomedial nucleus of the thalamus and mammillary bodies are probably playing the most important role (Victor, Adams, & Collins, 1971). Finally, post-encephalitic amnesia usually follows bilateral temporal and hippocampal involvement (Damasio & Van Hoesen, 1985).

The advantage of using MRI for the topographical diagnosis of lesions associated with neuropsychological deficits lies in the excellent spatial and tissue resolution. It allowed a detailed assessment of the morphology of crucial structures for memory, such as the hippocampus and the parahippocampal gyri (Press, Amaral, & Squire, 1989) and the mammillary bodies (Charness & De La Paz, 1987), which can then be submitted to quantitative evaluations. Volumetric measurements have indicated an inverse relationship between age and hippocampal volume (Bhatia, Bookheimer, Gaillard, & Theodore, 1993); a further correlation with performance on memory tests has been found in elderly, non demented subjects (Soininen et al., 1994, Launer et al., 95). Hippocampal, temporal horn (Killiany et al., 1993) and amygdala volume (Cuénod et al., 1993) have all shown some discriminative value between AD and normal aging.

In parallel with methods for the *in vivo* study of brain anatomy, the assessment of the functioning of the human brain (functional brain imaging) has become gradually possible. The original methods for the assessment of cerebral blood flow have been the first steps of a progress which has led to emission tomographic methods (single photon emission computerized tomography – SPECT, and positron emission tomography – PET). Nowadays it is possible to measure in vivo multiple parameters of regional cerebral physiology, such as cerebral blood flow and glucose metabolism. A more recent adjunct to the array of functional imaging methods is functional magnetic resonance (fMRI).

## PET Studies in Steady-State Condition: The Pathological Model

Neuropsychological investigation of patients with memory impairment due to neurological disorders has provided evidence that human memory is a multicomponent system. These components have been separated out in disease states, such as amnesia and different dementing conditions (see Butters & Miliotis, 1985, for a review). Human amnesia is a clinical syndrome characterized by the failure to recall past events and to learn new information. By contrast, amnesic patients have a normal short-term memory, i. e., they can accurately repeat short sequences of stimuli, such as words or numbers, immediately after presentation. This selective disruption of "long-term episodic memory" is the hallmark of human amnesia. While some degree of memory impairment is a frequent consequence of diffuse damage to the central nervous system, such as after severe head trauma or in dementia, amnesia is rarely observed in a "pure" form, that is without any associated disorder of other cognitive functions. Patients with global, "pure" amnesia are characterized by a selective impairment of the episodic component of explicit long-term memory, with preserved short-term, semantic and implicit memory.

As reported above, the investigation of the neurological correlates of memory in man has been primarily based on structural neuroimaging methods. Few anatomo-functional studies have addressed the issue of the relationship between the pattern of brain metabolic impairment and the characteristics of the memory disorders in neurological patients.

Regional cerebral glucose metabolism was assessed with [18F]FDG and PET in a group of patients with pure amnesia and in a group of patients with mild

AD who underwent have an extensive evaluation of memory functions, including short-term memory, episodic memory, semantic memory and implicit memory (Fazio et al., 1992; Perani et al., 1993).

The PET study of brain glucose metabolism in patients with *global amnesia* has identified a bilateral network of interconnected cerebral structures underlying long-term episodic memory, which is selectively impaired in these patients (Fazio et al., 1992). A significant reduction of metabolism in a network of interconnected brain regions (temporal mesial cortex, thalamus, cingulate gyrus and frontal basal cortex) was found in these amnesic patients in comparison with normal controls. The amnesic patients had lesions of different etiologies (anoxia, Korsakoff's syndrome, cerebrovascular lesions), sometimes with restricted or no structural damage on MRI (anoxia cases). This study showed a metabolic impairment, in a series of structures connected in the Papez's circuit, which did not correspond to alterations in structural anatomy as assessed by MRI. The latter was in fact either normal or showed selective and limited damage to structures which have been shown by neuroradiological and pathological studies to be involved in human amnesia. Thus, localized damage to the hippocampus, thalamus or frontal basal cortex can cause a global metabolic depression of the whole of these structures, which behave as a functional circuit. The impairment of brain function is not necessarily associated with tissue death: structurally normal areas with reduced blood flow and metabolism have been observed in several neurological disorders, thus providing an explanation to symptoms apparently unrelated to structural modifications (Feeney & Baron, 1986; Perani, Vallar, Cappa, Messa, & Fazio, 1987). In patients, reductions of cerebral blood flow and metabolism in cerebral regions far removed from the structural damage has been shown by PET (Perani et al., 1988). The mechanism producing such remote effects is likely to be a disconnection between neural structures which causes a reduction of synaptic activity by deprivation of afferent input. The selected impairment of long-term memory of the patients included in this study suggests that episodic learning and memory in man are subserved by a network of interrelated neural structures, including the Papez's circuit and extending to the basal anterior regions, which have important connections with the medial temporal regions (Amaral & Cowan, 1980).

Severe episodic memory impairment is also the hallmark of *Alzheimer's disease* (AD) (Weingartner, Grafman, Boutelle, Kaye, & Martin, 1983). However, the memory disorder in AD is also characterized by defective short-term memory (Morris & Baddeley, 1988), semantic memory (Nebes, 1989) and impairment of some aspects of implicit memory, such as word-stem completion (Salmon, Shimamura, Butters, & Smith, 1988).

Measurements of regional blood flow and metabolism with PET have shown functional brain impairment in AD patients (Herholz et al., 1993). This is typically characterized by bilateral reductions in temporal and parietal regions. A groups of patients with mild AD have been submitted to an extensive evaluation of memory functions and a measurement of regional cerebral glucose metabolism with [$^{18}$F]FDG and PET (Perani et al., 1993). The concept of using disease states associated with different patterns of neuropsychological impairment as a model to map cognitive functions in the human brain was applied in this study. The aim was to investigate the functional correlates of the multiple components of memory. Patients were submitted to an extensive neuropsychological battery for the evaluation of long-term verbal and visual-spatial episodic memory, short-term memory, implicit and procedural memory, language, visual-spatial processing, and non-verbal reasoning. When metabolic values were compared with values from normal controls, significant hypometabolism was found in the frontal, parietal and temporal associative cortex in AD patients. The metabolic values of these AD patients were then correlated with their cognitive performance. The results of a multivariate regression analysis of test scores with metabolic data indicated that different clusters of cerebral areas were associated with each of the main components of memory function. Indeed, specific patterns of metabolic involvement showed correlations between, respectively, short-term and semantic memory and the left perisylvian language areas, and procedural learning and a network of structures including the cerebellum, the basal ganglia and the dorsolateral frontal cortex; the association of episodic memory with the structures of Papez's circuit was also confirmed.

The study of episodic memory disorders in *multiple sclerosis* (MS) has capitalized on the results obtained in the pathological models of memory deficits. Structural neuroimaging has been used to correlate lesional patterns with the cognitive profile of patients with multiple sclerosis (MS), especially for "frontal" dysfunction (Swirsky-Sacchetti et al., 1992; Arnett et al., 1994). However, these methods failed to show a clear-cut anatomical explanation for the long-term memory deficit which is a hallmark of MS cognitive impairment. In addition, MRI cannot assess the actual function of grey matter and the possibility that MS' memory impairment is associated with a reduced functional activity of grey diencephalic and temporal lobe structures. Paulesu and coworkers (1996) using FDG and PET to measure regional cerebral glucose metabolism in a group of MS patients with verbal and/or spatial long-term memory deficits, demonstrated the selective functional involvement of temporal mesial, diencephalic and cingulate structures associated with long-term memory impairment. Thus, the demyelinating process in MS can have an elective, disruptive metabolic effect on deep/cortical and subcortical structures. The regional pattern of these metabolic changes relate to the cognitive profile of these MS patients which was dominated by episodic memory dysfunction.

*Single case study* of amnesia in degenerative disease reported evidence for a "semantic dementia" (Snowden, Neary, Mann, Goulding, & Testa, 1992; Hodges, Patterson, Oxbury, & Funnell, 1992). This is characterized by progressive loss of knowledge of the word meaning, originally described by Warrington (1976). Functional neuroimaging methods in these patients have shown focal reductions of cerebral perfusion and/or metabolism in the left perisylvian temporal regions, including the temporal pole (Hodges & Patterson, 1995). These findings provided converging evidences for an involvement of selected left hemispheric regions in the lexical-semantic processes as already shown by neuropsychological studies of patients with focal lesions (Miozzo, Soardi, & Cappa, 1994; Damasio et al., 1996) and by activation studies in normal subjects (Perani et al., 1995; Martin, Haxby, Lalonde, Wiggs, & Ungerleider, 1996).

These PET experiments provide evidence of the role of distinct functional circuits as the basis of human memory and indicate the usefulness of selected pathological conditions as models for PET studies of cognitive functions.

## In Vivo Mapping of Memory Systems in Normal Subjects: PET Activation Studies

The identification of anatomo-functional networks involved in specific components of memory function in normal subjects is the aim of PET activation methods. The introduction of dynamic methods for the rapid measurement of regional cerebral blood flow while subjects are engaged in specific tasks has played a crucial role for the development of cognitive activation studies. PET is used for the dynamic measurement of the cerebral uptake of a tracer, which, being proportional to blood flow, can reflect the conditions of cerebral activity (Fox, Mintun, Reiman, & Raichle, 1988).

Several data analysis methods have been developed to identify the site and the extent of the modifications in cerebral perfusion associated with specific, localized cerebral activations related to an experimental paradigm. They are based on different approaches to the same set of problems, that is to detect and evaluate the significance of differences or modifications in the spatially extended maps of cerebral radioactivity reflecting genuine changes in function related to the experimental paradigm. These must be separated from the noise due to different confounds, and localized with reference to brain anatomy. Among these, Statistical Parametric Mapping (SPM) is a comprehensive and continuously evolving set of data analysis procedures developed by the Wellcome Department of Cognitive Neurology group (Friston et al., 1989; Friston et al., 1990; Friston, Frith, Liddle, & Frackowiak, 1991a,b; Friston et al., 1995). SPM is the most diffuse data analysis methodology in cognitive neuroscience.

Some basic understanding of the SPM analysis is mandatory for proper experimental design and results interpretation. SPM can detect and evaluate the significance of differences or modifications in the spatially extended maps of cerebral radioactivity reflecting genuine changes in function related to the experimental paradigm. SPM is an open set of operations within the framework of statistical theory, from the general linear model (Friston et al., 1995), to nonparametric (Holmes, Blair, Watson, & Ford, 1996) and multivariate approaches (Friston et al., 1996).

In details, SPMs are spatially extended statistical processes, which are based on the following data analysis steps:

a) *Stereotactic normalization:* PET data acquired for each subject are oriented according to the bicommissural line and transformed to the standard stereotaxic space (Talairach & Tournoux, 1988).

b) *Smoothing,* using a Gaussian filter, in order to suppress the effects of individual anatomical differences and to increase the signal to noise ratio

c) *Analysis of covariance* (ANCOVA): this normalization procedure removes global variations of regional perfusion among individual subjects and among different conditions, which are independent from the local cerebral modifications induced by the experimental manipulations

d) *Hypothesis testing,* which can be performed according to several experimental design. The most widely used, and simplest, design, is the categorical (the so-called subtraction method). It requires a baseline condition which can be compared to an "activated" condition. The resulting differences are submitted to some form of statistical test. Within SPM, the evaluation of significance is based on an estimate of the differences in perfusion and the error variance for each voxel, which are tested against the null hypothesis (lack of differences between baseline and activation) using a known distribution, such as Student's $t$, $F$ or chi-square).

The most recent proposals within SPM is the multivariate method of data analysis, which seems to be ideally suitable for the study of functional connectivity.

In summarizing some selective evidence of functional studies of memory, we will follow the "multiple memory systems" taxonomy.

## Short-Term Memory/Working Memory

A limited-capacity store, which can maintain incoming information for a short period of time, and whose content decays rapidly, in the absence of continuous rehearsal, is a traditional definition of short-term memory (STM) in psychology. All these characteristics are summarized by the textbook example of STM in action: the maintenance of an unfamiliar telephone number for the time required to make a call. We can keep easily in our mind a seven (not a twelve) digit number; if the telephone is busy, we keep rehearsing it overtly or subvocally; if the rehearsal is blocked, for example by a distracting conversation, the number fades from memory.

This simple model of STM was radically revised by Baddeley and coworkers in a series of experiments which led to the working memory model (Baddeley, 1991). Working memory is modelled as a complex system, with multiple subcomponents, which is engaged in all cognitive operations which require the temporary maintenance of information. The "central executive" is the heart of the model, which allocates the resources to the "slave systems": the phonological loop and the visuospatial sketchpad. Keeping the telephone number in mind engages the phonological loop, which comprises a storage compartment and a rehearsal process; trying to save it in the face of a distracting task (such as looking for another telephone if we lose our place in the queue) requires the contribution of the central executive, as any condition of multi-tasking.

Working memory is an active field of PET investigation, and has been particularly focused on the role of the frontal lobe. Two main lines of investigation can be distinguished. Some experiments have tried to map the cerebral correlates of the components of Baddeley's model. Several PET experiments reported comparable and consistent results in the functional investigation of verbal working memory (see Fiez et al., 1996). Auditory-verbal working memory has been studied with a letter-matching task, which was found to be associated with a left perisylvian activation pattern (Paulesu, Frith, & Frackowiak, 1993). Comparing this activation with the one observed during a letter rhyming judgment task, it was possible to separate the areas related to the rehearsal process (mainly Ba 44) from those involved with phonological storage (supramarginal gyrus – Ba 40). Visual working memory has been associated with the activation of a network of frontal, parietal and occipital areas in the right hemisphere (Jonides et al., 1993). These PET results provided evidence for the anatomo-functional dissociation between verbal and visuo-spatial working memory as it was documented by neuropsychology and cognitive psychology. D'Esposito, M. and coworkers (1995) have shown prefrontal cortex activation during dual task performance, but not during single working memory conditions, supporting the role of the frontal lobe in the central executive component of the working memory model.

The other line of investigation has tried to apply to human subjects tasks which in monkeys have been shown to be associated with specific lesion sites within the frontal lobe. Petrides and his coworkers (Petrides et al., 1993a,b) have reported a series of studies emphasizing the different processing components which can be involved in working memory tasks. The visual working memory task, requiring the continuous monitoring of the responses (self-ordered pointing task) was associated with activations in Ba 9 and 46. On the other hand, the learning of arbitrary associations using the same stimuli (conditional task) was associated with bilateral Ba 8 activation, with a left sided prevalence (Petrides, Alivisatos, Meyer, & Evans, 1993a). A verbal tasks similar to the one used in the visual working memory experiment activated the same areas in the left hemisphere, with the addition of a ventral frontal region (Ba 10) when monitoring of externally ordered stimuli was required (Petrides, Alivisatos, Meyer, & Evans, 1993b). The role of the latter area in working memory has been recently confirmed in another investigation with the Tower of London test (Owen, Doyon, Petrides, & Evans, 1996). From these and other investigations (reviewed in Owen, 1997), it has been suggested that different parts of the dorsolateral frontal cortex are involved in different processes: in particular, the ventral part (45 and 47/12) in the maintenance of information, the dorsal part (9, 46), in the manipulation of information (see Rushworth & Owen, 1998 for a review of the neurophysiological evidence in support of this view).

A contrasting hypothesis, also originated from primate studies and tested in humans with imaging experiments, suggests that the fractionation is not related to different processing components, but to stimulus modality (Goldman-Rakic, 1995). The controversy remains open, and will probably be solved by the accumulation of experimental data with a variety of paradigms in monkeys and humans.

## Declarative (Episodic-Semantic) Memory

Declarative memory is the conscious memory of facts and events, associated with the characteristic phenomenal experience of recollection. Event, or episodic memory, is characterized by the presence of a specific spatial and temporal labelling of the memories, while fact, or semantic, memory, refers to our mental lexicon and encyclopedia: memory of the meaning of words, identity of objects, knowledge acquired through study and not through experience (Tulving, 1972). Autobiographical memory is a typical form of declarative memory, which includes both episodic and semantic aspects. Episodic memory can be considered from the point of view of the ability to learn new episodes (anterograde memory), or as retrograde memory, consisting in the recollection of past events. Furthermore, episodic memory, in association with working memory, is responsible for orientation and "prospective memory." The latter term indicates the "memory for the future", whose functioning is usually equated with "memory" in everyday language: remembering appointments, and in general the schedule of a busy day.

Anterograde memory is based on the processed of encoding, storage and retrieval and is the aspect of memory function which is usually assessed by memory tests in which the repeated presentation of a memorandum (words, stories, pictures) is followed, after a distraction interval of several minutes, by the assessment of retrieval or recognition. The differential characteristics with short-term memory is the lack of storage limitation, and the persistence of memories without the need for rehearsal. The format of the material in LTM is also different, and is the result of "deep" encoding: for example, in the case of verbal information, what is stored in episodic memory is not the verbatim, or phonological, form, but the meaning (the gist) of the presented material. The retrograde component of episodic memory is well exemplified by auto-biographical memory, that is the record of the events personally experienced by a subject, which is often identified by non-specialists as memory tout-court.

The study of long-term retention has been an extremely active area of in-vestigation in the neuroimaging field. The neural correlates of *episodic mem-ory* have been investigated with many paradigms, using different stimuli (ver-bal, visual) and different tasks (list learning, paired associates learning, cued recall, free recall, recognition). Individual studies have also focused on differ-ent aspects of memory processing (encoding or retrieval), using a variety of experimental manipulations and designs. While the results have sometimes been unexpected, a coherent picture of the brain correlates of memory pro-cessing is beginning to emerge (for a recent review, see Fletcher, Frith, & Rugg, 1997).

A large number of cortical areas is activated during memory encoding and retrieval. Grasby et al. (1993a) found areas of increased activity bilaterally in the dorsolateral frontal cortex, in the precuneus and in retrosplenial areas. This latter finding supports the hypothesis about the role of the precuneus in mental imagery and provide evidence that it is a key part of the neural substrate of visual imagery occurring in conscious memory recall. The left dorsolateral frontal cortex is consistently activated when encoding meaningful semantic material (Shallice et al., 1994). The activation involves Ba 46 and neighboring cortex (Ba 46, 47) and is related to "deep" processing of information (Kapur et al., 1994), leading to better recall (Kapur et al., 1995). A decreased activation has been observed to be associated with normal aging (Grady et al., 1995), and may reflect defective encoding responsible for age-related memory impair-ments.

The activation does not appear to be related to task difficulty and may reflect the automatic retrieval of semantic information (Thompson-Schill, D'Esposito, Aguirre, & Farah, 1997); in particular, a recent study has suggested that its basic function is to establish meaningful connections between, for example, related word pairs (Dolan & Fletcher, 1997).

Several investigations have assessed the cerebral correlates of retrieval. In this case, it is the the right dorsolateral and medial frontal cortex which has been consistently activated (Shallice et al., 1994; Tulving et al., 1994). Subsequent investigations have attempted to clarify the factors modulating the frontal activation. Kapur and coworkers (1996) found a relationship with retrieval attempt, rather than successful retrieval (ecphory, in Tulving's terminology).

Studies of encoding have indicated a discrepancy between the well-known role of hippocampal lesions in producing human amnesia and the relative difficulty of observing hippocampal activation during PET acquisition processes in normal subjects. Grasby and coworkers (1993), with a parametric design, found a significant correlation between the bilateral hippocampal activation and the number of correctly recalled words from the mid-portion of the serial position curve. Hippocampal activations during encoding have been observed for "novel" stimuli, such as complex colored pictures (Tulving et al., 1994; Stern et al., 1996), unknown faces (Haxby et al., 1996), or new pairings of words (Dolan & Fletcher, 1997); Nyberg and coworkers (1996) found evidence for left hippocampal activation at encoding only when the task required the recollection of the item identity, in contrast with its location or time of presentation. Hippocampal activation seems to be associated with high recall conditions, due to repeated exposure and deep encoding (Schacter, Alpert, Savage, Rauch, & Albert, 1996), and in general to successful recollection (Nyberg et al., 1996). These authors found strong positive correlations between verbal episodic retrieval and blood flow in left medial temporal structures. These regions were dominant components of a series of brain regions that distinguished high retrieval from low retrieval conditions.

There is also evidence that limbic temporal structures are active for language comprehension processing during tasks requiring listening or reading sentences or continuous speech on the basis of specific memory demands (Perani et al., 1996; Perani et al., 1998). In these experiments, verbal memory encoding was clearly engaged in bilinguals subjects who were instructed to listen to stories in order to understand them and report details later during the post-scan interviews. Maternal languages and second languages mastered with high proficiency activated a network of left hemispheric structures including the left hippocampus; low proficiency for the second language was associated with a lack of activation of temporal mesial structures (Figure 1 A and B). These findings support the hypothesis of hippocampal activation in association with successful recollection linked to repeated exposure and deep encoding. In addition, at variance with other verbal memory experiments, with no evidence of hippocampal activation and in which unconnected verbal material was used [word lists (Grasby et al., 1993a; Grasby et al., 1993b) or word pairs (Shallice et al., 1994; Kapur et al., 1996; Cabeza et al., 1997; Dolan & Fletcher,

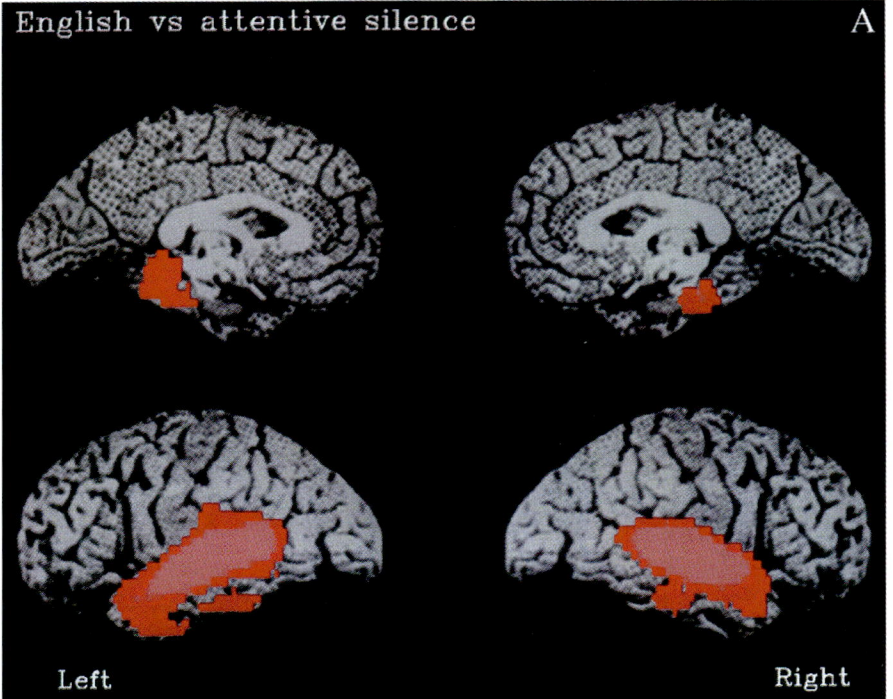

English vs attentive silence · A

Left　　　　　　　　　Right

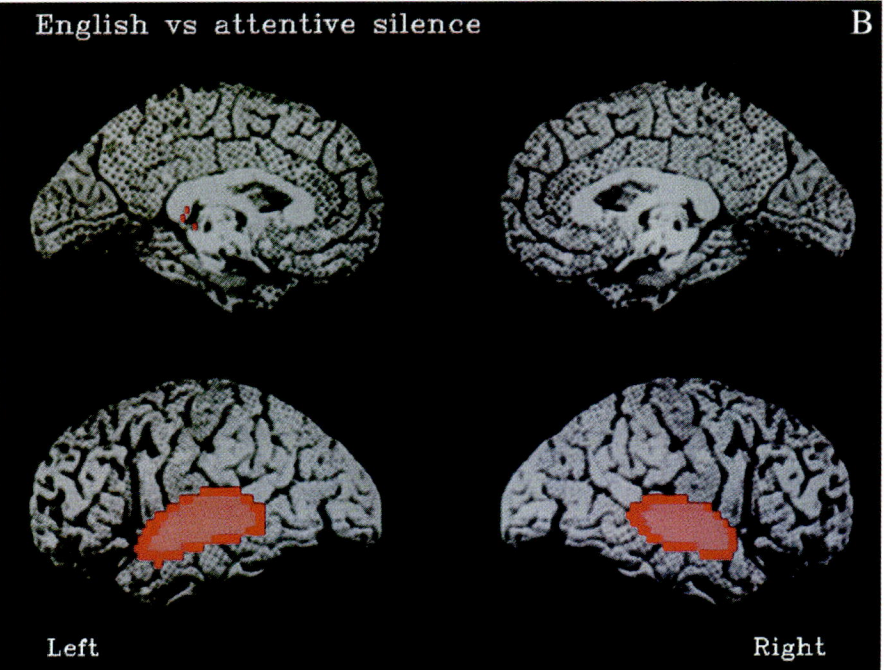

English vs attentive silence · B

Left　　　　　　　　　Right

← *Figure 1.* Activation foci in bilinguals with *high proficiency* (A, top) and *low proficiency* (B, bottom) for the second language (English) (SPM-96, *p* < 0.001, *Z* 3.09). Hippocampal structures are activated only in the former group (see text for details).

1997), in the experiments of Perani and coworkers, subjects were engaged with the more natural task of listening some narrative. The activation seen in the hippocampal structures in these PET experiments offers a further reconciliation between lesional data and functional imaging on memory.

Finally, the same experiments offer an interesting observation: the discrepancy with other recent experiments on verbal memory encoding that indeed revealed a consistent left lateral prefrontal cortex activation (Shallice et al., 1994; Tulving et al., 1994; Fletcher et al., 1995; Kapur et al., 1996; Cabeza et al., 1997). The proposed functional specialization of the left dorso-lateral prefrontal cortex for operations active during encoding may need to be constrained to the particular paradigms in which those activations were observed. One possibility is that left prefrontal cortex may be involved in memory encoding because of its more general role in planning/executive functions, i. e., when arbitrary links between items need to be made. This hypothesis is consistent with the dual-task interference effect demonstrated by Shallice and coworkers (1994) in left prefrontal cortex at encoding, and is supported by recent direct evidence provided by Dolan and Fletcher (1997). The left prefrontal cortex might be not necessary for all forms of verbal memory encoding, and this is also in agreement with the observation that patients with bilateral frontal lobe lesions can act normally in standard tests of recognition and recall (Petrides, 1996).

In a different domain, i. e., the action-motor processes, PET was used to map brain regions that are associated with the observation of meaningful and meaningless hand actions, with the intent to recognize or imitate them later (Decety et al., 1997). Both the strategies involve memory encoding processes, as an observed action can be understood and imitated whenever it becomes the source of a representation of the same action within the observer. Independently by the cognitive strategy, meaningful actions engaged the left hemisphere in frontal and temporal regions (with in addition bilateral hippocampal activation), while meaningless actions involved the right occipito-parieto-frontal pathway. The involvement of dorsolateral prefrontal cortex in this condition is in agreement with previous studies concerning the planning of voluntary actions (Frith, Friston, Liddle, & Frackowiak, 1991) and the mental simulation of actions (Decety et al., 1994; Stephan et al., 1995; Grafton, Arbib, Fadiga, & Rizzolatti, 1996). It is possible that the left prefrontal region would be specialized for generating responses, whereas the right side would be more important for memory and the two sides would equally contribute to the more general function of internal response generation. When the subjects had to memorize meaningful and meaningless actions with the purpose of preparing to identify them among others, the right hippo-campus was the only activated structure. This finding indicate that the hippo-campal activation is crucial when new action-related information had to be acquired for later recognition. In contrast, when the aim of observation was to memorize the same actions with the purpose of imitation, the activation was predominant in brain structures that are usually involved in action planning. Thus, the pattern of brain activation during tasks based on the same visual stimuli (familiar or non familiar actions) changed according to the cognitive task in which the subject was involved. In addition, in the observation of meaningful actions, there was a different involvement either of right or of left hippocampal structures with the imitation or recognition strategy, respectively. These findings indicate the role of hippocampal structures for rapidly acquiring and storing new meaningful action-related information and suggest a different role for the right (imitation/visuospatial encoding) and left-sided (recognition/semantic encoding) hippocampal regions.

*Semantic memory* is considered by some theorists, such as Tulving (1972), as a separate memory system. Other conceive semantic memory as a differentiation of episodic memory, which is characterized by similar acquisition mechanisms (information coming from the external world), but becomes different because of repeated exposure, which leads to the loss of the event-specific characteristics and to a peculiar modality of organization, not according to a spatial or a temporal metrics, but as knowledge structures. The organization of semantic memory is a matter of debate. The traditional models are based on hierarchical organization and more recently others are based on connectionist modelling (see Baddeley, 1991). Additionally, some theories consider the hypothesis of an amodal unique semantic system, whereas others are based on multiple semantic systems. According to the latter, visual information are represented in the visual semantic system, whereas functional-associative information are represented in the verbal component of the semantic system (Warrington & McCarthy, 1991).

Other interesting insights have been provided by the functional study of semantic memory. The neural correlates of semantic memory have been investigated with several different tasks, requiring access to semantic knowledge in order to identify and name pictures and to understand words (see Bly & Kosslyn, 1997 for a review). The research has been largely guided by the effort to understand the neurological correlates of the semantic category and modality effects reported in clinical neuropsychology. Concerning category effects, clear-cut differences according to semantic category have been found by Perani and coworkers (1995) with a picture matching task and by Martin and coworkers (1996) and Damasio and coworkers (1996) with picture naming tasks.

Martin and coworkers (1996), for a picture discrimination task, demonstrated different anatomical activations depending on the category of picture (living or non-living) presented. Damasio and coworkers (1996) reported temporal lobe activations from a PET study where subjects named from pictures, famous people, animals and tools. Naming famous people activated an area in the left ventrolateral temporal pole, while naming animals and tools activated different areas in the left posterior inferotemporal region and left temporal pole, indicating separate cerebral representations involved in the lexical retrieval of words from different categories.

Class of knowledge effects (access to visuo-perceptual and to functional-associative knowledge) have been addressed by Vandenberghe and coworkers (1996): only marginal differences were found (left hippocampal region and cerebellum being more active in the associative task). More extensive differences were found by Cappa, Perani, Schnur, Grassi, and Fazio (1998) in the left dorsolateral frontal cortex, suggesting that the class of knowledge effect might be amplified by tasks requiring self-generated (effortful) lexical access than in externally-driven matching conditions. Complementary evidence for a fractionation of knowledge in the brain is provided by a study (Martin et al., 1995), in which a word generation task was used. Associating to a named object a color name activated the fusiform gyri, with a left sided prevalence, while associating an action name activated the left posterior middle and superior temporal gyri.

The neural correlates of access to semantic knowledge from pictorial or verbal material have been compared by Vandenberghe and coworkers (1996) using a word and picture matching task: the main finding was an extensive area of common activation for words and pictures. Perani and coworkers (in press) also compared the processing of stimuli belonging to different semantic categories (animate and inanimate) in the verbal and visual modality. The results of this study are compatible with the idea that an overlapping, extensive network of brain areas is activated when pictures are identified, and when words are understood. Within this network, some areas appear to be category-specific, suggesting anatomically segregated representations of semantic knowledge pertaining to animate entities and tools. In particular, there is evidence for a crucial role of the left inferior temporal lobe in the processing of animate entities and of the left middle temporal gyrus for tools, both from words and pictures. The activation in dorsolateral frontal cortex appears to be specific for the semantic access of tools only from pictures and may underlie an automatic access to motor imagery which is specific for pictorial material.

Perani and coworkers (1995) found that animal picture recognition (living) activated the inferior temporo-occipital areas, bilaterally, whereas artefact recognition (non-living) engaged a predominantly left hemispheric network,

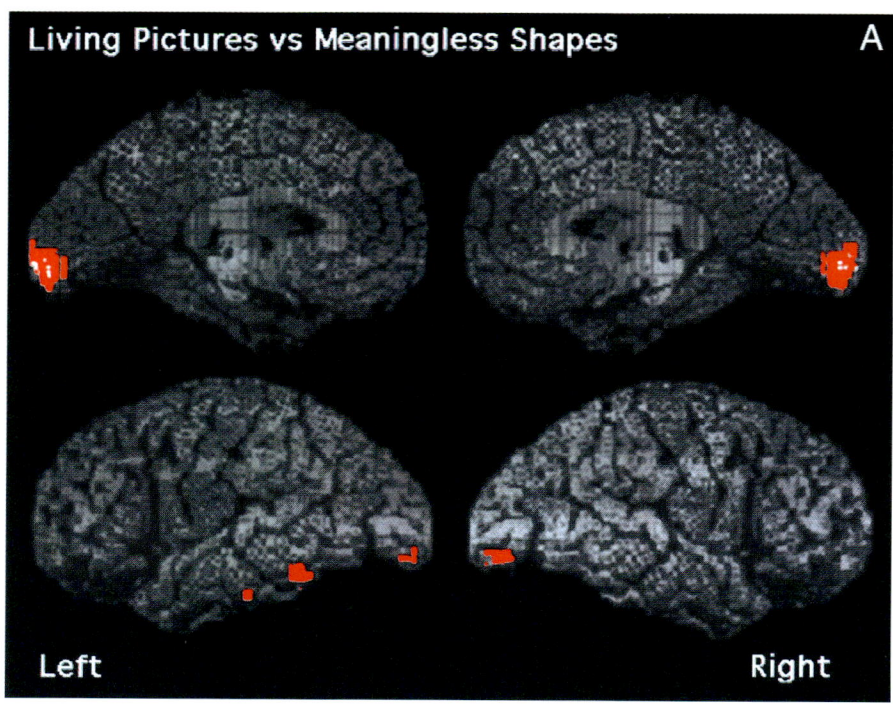

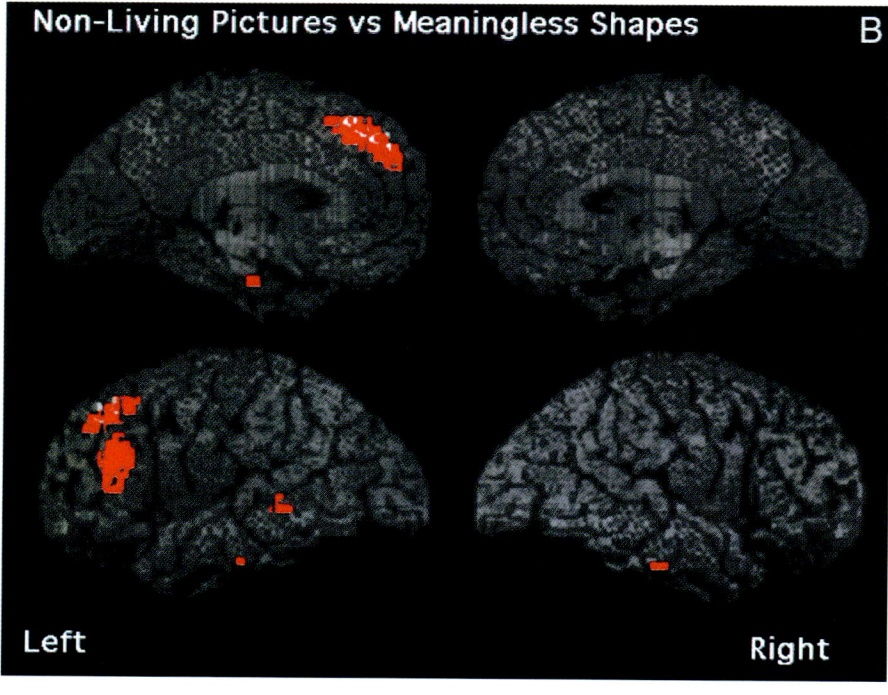

← *Figure 2.* Activation foci for (A, top) animal picture recognition (living) and (B, bottom) for artefact recognition (non-living) (SPM-96, $p < 0.001$, $Z$ 3.09). Living entities activated the inferior temporo-occipital areas, bilaterally, whereas artefact recognition engaged a predominantly left hemispheric network, involving also the left dorsolateral frontal cortex.

---

involving also the left dorsolateral frontal cortex (Figure 2 A and B). These latter findings, which concur with clinical observations in neurological patients, have provided *in vivo* evidence for a fractionation of the neural substrates of semantic knowledge in man. The findings for animal recognition are in agreement with evidences from human pathology and concur with primate, evoked potential and PET studies indicating an important role of the inferior temporal and occipital regions for the recognition of faces and objects. The ventral visual processing pathways may thus be considered to play a central role in the discrimination of living stimuli. The network of neural structures activated by artefact recognition was lateralized to the left hemisphere and involved the prefrontal cortex in particular the inferior frontal gyrus. The possible hypotheses accounting for this pattern of activation might be related to the functional knowledge or to cognitive strategy linked to object manipulation. The fact that man-made tools are manipulable may be associated with different cerebral pathways for naming and recognition: in particular, visuo-motor integration along the perception-to-action route. The left prefrontal activation, namely the inferior frontal, is an interesting issue in the brain functional correlates of semantic memory. In primate, mirror neurons have been described in the left rostral part of the inferior area 6 (the so called F5) which became active when the same action is actively performed by the monkey or when it is made by the experimenter and observed by the monkey (Gallese, Fadiga, Fogassi, & Rizzolatti, 1996). A comparable activation was found in humans while observing motor actions (grasping of meaningful objects with the right hand) (Rizzolatti et al., 1996). The same area was also involved within a network of brain structures which became active during observation of meaningful pantomimes in comparison with meaningless gestures (Decety et al., 1997). These data might be related to the representation of the semantic action and are possibly the basis of recognition of meaningful motor events. There are also PET evidences that support the role of the left inferior frontal gyrus, namely Ba 44 and 45 (Broca's area), in the "representation" of hand motor actions. Bonda and coworkers (1996) found its activation during a self-ordered hand movement sequence and Parsons and coworkers (1995) found comparable functional activation during a task in which normal subjects were required to form a mental imagery of the hand and rotate it. Decety and coworkers (1994) using PET found activation of the inferior frontal gyrus during mental simulation of actions. Again, frontal lesions can cause impairment in pantomime recognition in aphasics (Gainotti & Lemmo, 1976; Bell, 1994). It has been suggested that this deficit could depend on lesions of cortical areas adjacent to Broca's area (Goodglass & Kaplan, 1963).

Taken together, these different lines of evidence appear to indicate that the left inferior frontal cortex might be endowed both with a hand movement representation and action recognition. Many arguments indicate that recognition of actions of conspecifics is a genuine ability, which seems to be highly developed in humans and non-human primates (Premack & Woodruff, 1978). As recently proposed by Vogt (1996) based on psychophysical experiments, the perception-action mediation rely on motor representations which are already activated (or formed) during observation. These neural mechanisms could fit within the influential "motor theory of perception" initially used to account for the perception of speech (see Liberman & Mattingly, 1985). According to this theory, speech perception should not only be related to sounds but also to the phonetic gestures of the speaker, which are represented in the brain.

## Conclusions

This set of results from PET neuroimaging studies is remarkable, because it has suggested important roles in memory processing for several brain structures, which were not predicted on the basis of neuropsychological investigations in amnesic patients. It is noteworthy that a "reverse" approach (i. e., neuropsychological investigations in patients primed by PET results) is appearing in the neuropsychological literature (see, for example, Swick & Knight, 1996). On the other hand, the role of the frontal cortex in "strategic" or "cognitive mediation" (Warrington & Weiskrantz, 1982) aspects of memory seems to be amenable to empirical investigation with PET.

While the results of an integrated approach may be sometimes difficult to reconcile, it is clear that PET has more than a simple confirmatory role of the results of lesion-based neuropsychological investigations.

## References

Alexander, M.P. & Freedman, M. (1984). Amnesia after anterior communicating artery aneurysm rupture. *Neurology, 34*, 752–757.

Amaral, D.G., & Cowan, W.M. (1980) Subcortical afferents to the hippocampal formation in the monkey. *Journal of Comparative Neurology,189*, 573–591.

Arnett, P.A., Rao, S.M., Bernardin, L., Grafman, J., Yetkin, F.Z., & Lobek, L. (1994). Relationship between frontal lobe lesions and Wisconsin Card Sorting Test performance in patients with multiple sclerosis. *Neurology, 44*, 420–425.

Baddeley, A.D. (1991). *Human memory: Theory and practice.* Hove, UK: Erlbaum.

Bell, B.D. (1994). Pantomime recognition impairment in aphasia: An analysis of error type. *Brain and Language, 47,* 269–278.

Bhatia, S., Bookheimer, S.Y., Gaillard, W.D., & Theodore, W.H. (1993). Measurement of whole temporal lobe and hippocampus for MR volumetry: Normative data. *Neurology, 43*, 2006–2010.

Bly, B.M., & Kosslyn, S.M. (1997). Functional anatomy of object recognition in humans: Evidence from positron emission tomography and functional magnetic resonance imaging. *Current Opinion in Neurology, 10,* 5–9.

Bonda, E., Petrides, M., Ostry, D., & Evans, A. (1996). Specific involvement of human parietal systems and the amygdala in the perception of biological motion. *Journal of Neuroscience, 16,* 3737–3744.

Butters, N., & Miliotis, P. (1985). Amnesic disorders. In K.M. Heilman (Ed.), *Valenstein clinical neuropsychology* (2nd ed., pp. 403–451). Oxford: Oxford University Press.

Cabeza, R., Grady, C.L., Nyberg, L. et al. (1997). Age-related differences in neural activity during memory encoding and retrieval: A positron emission tomography study. *Journal of Neuroscience, 17,* 391–400.

Cappa, S.F., Perani, D., Schnur, T., Grassi, F., & Fazio, F. (1998). The effect of semantic category and knowledge-type on lexical-semantic access: A PET study. *Neuroimage, 8,* 350–359.

Charness, M.E., & De La Paz, R.L. (1987). Mammillary body atrophy in Wernicke's encephalopathy: Antemortem identification using magnetic resonance imaging. *Annals of Neurology, 22,* 595–600.

Cramon, D.Y. von, Hebel, N., & Schuri, U. (1985). A contribution to the anatomical basis of thalamic amnesia. *Brain, 108,* 993–1008.

Cuénod, C.A., Denys, A., Michot, J.L., Jehenson, P., Forette, F., Kaplan, D., Sirota, A., & Boller, F. (1993). Amygdala atrophy in Alzheimer's disease. An in vivo magnetic resonance imaging study. *Archives of Neurology, 50,* 941–945.

D'Esposito, M., Detre, J.A., Alsop, D.C., Shin, R.K., Atlas, S., & Grossmann, M. (1995). The neural basis of the central executive component of working memory. *Nature, 378,* 279–281.

Damasio, A.R., Graff-Radford, N.R., Eslinger, P.J., Damasio, H., & Kassel, N. (1985). Amnesia following basal forebrain lesions. *Archives of Neurology 42,* 263–271.

Damasio, A.R., & Van Hoesen, G.W. (1985). The limbic system and the localization of herpes simplex encephalitis. *Journal of Neurology Neurosurgery and Psychiatry 48,* 297–301.

Damasio, H., Grabowski, T.J., Tranel, D., Hichwa R.D., & Damasio, A.R. (1996). A neural basis for lexical retrieval. *Nature, 380,* 499–505.

Decety, J., Grèzes, J., Costes, N., Perani, D., Jeannerod, M., Procyk, E., Grassi F., & Fazio, F. (1997). Brain activity during observation of actions. Influence of action content and subject's strategy. *Brain, 120,* 1763–1777.

Decety, J., Perani, D., Jeannerod, M., Bettinardi, V., Tadary, B., Woods, R., Mazziotta, J.C., & Fazio, F. (1994). Mapping motor representation with PET. *Nature, 371,* 600–602.

Dolan, R., & Fletcher, P. (1997). Dissociating prefrontal and hippocampal function in episodic memory encoding. *Nature, 388,* 582–585.

Fazio, F., Perani, D., Gilardi, M.C., Colombo, F., Cappa, S.F., Vallar, G., Bettinardi, V., Paulesu, E., Alberoni, M., Bressi, S., Franceschi, M., & Lenzi, G.L. (1992). Metabolic impairment in human amnesia: A PET study of memory networks. *Journal of Cerebral Blood Flow and Metabolism, 12,* 353–358.

Feeney, D.M., & Baron, J.C. (1986). Diaschisis. *Stroke 17,* 817–830.

Fiez, J.A., Raife, E.A., Balota, D.A., Schwarz, J.P., Raichle, M.E., & Petersen, S.E. (1996). A positron emission tomography study of the short-term maintenance of verbal information. *Journal of Neuroscience, 16,* 808–822.

Fletcher, P.C., Frith, C.D., & Rugg, M.D. (1997). The functional neuroanatomy of episodic memory. *Trends in Neuroscience, 20,* 213–218.

Fletcher, P.C., Frith, C.D., Grasby, P.M., Shallice, T., Frackowiak, R.S., & Dolan, R.J. (1995). Brain systems for encoding and retrieval of auditory-verbal memory. An in vivo study in humans. *Brain, 118,* 401–416.

Fox, P.T., Mintun, M.A., Reiman, E.M., & Raichle, M.E. (1988). Enhanced detection of focal brain responses using intersubject averaging and change-distribution analysis of subtracted PET images. *Journal of Cerebral Blood Flow and Metabolism, 85,* 642–653.

Friston, K., Passingham, R.E., Nutt, J.G., Heather, J.D., Sawle, G.V., & Frackowiak, R.S.J. (1989). Localisation in PET images: Direct fitting of the intercommissural (AC-PC) line. *Journal of Cerebral Blood Flow and Metabolism, 9,* 690–695.

Friston, K.J., Frith, C.D., Liddle, P.F., Dolan, R.J., Lammerstsma, A.A., & Frackowiak, R.S.J. (1990). The relationship between global and local changes in PET scans. *Journal of Cerebral Blood Flow and Metabolism, 10,* 458–466.

Friston, K., Frith, C.D., Liddle, P.F., & Frackowiak, R.S.J. (1991a). Plastic transformation of PET images. *Journal of Computer Assisted Tomography, 15,* 634–639.

Friston, K., Frith, C.D., Liddle, P.F., & Frackowiak, R.S.J. (1991b). Comparing functional (PET) images: The assessment of significant change. *Journal of Cerebral Blood Flow and Metabolism, 11,* 690–699.

Friston, K.J., Holmes, A.P., Worsley, K.J., Poline, J.-B., Frith, C.D., & Frackowiak, R.S.J. (1995). Statistical parametric maps in functional imaging: A general linear approach. *Human Brain Mapping, 2,* 189–210.

Friston, K.J., Poline, J.-B., Holmes, A.P., Frith, C.D., & Frackowiak, R.S.J. (1996). A multivariate analysis of PET activation studies. *Human Brain Mapping, 4,* 140–151.

Frith, C.D., Friston, K., Liddle, P.F., & Frackowiak, R.S.J. (1991). Willed action and the prefrontal cortex in man: A study with PET. *Proceeding of the Royal Society London, 244,* 241–246.

Gainotti, G., & Lemmo, M.S. (1976). Comprehension of symbolic gestures in aphasia. *Brain and Language, 3,* 451–460.

Gallese, V., Fadiga, L., Fogassi, L., & Rizzolatti, G. (1996). Action recognition in the premotor cortex. *Brain, 119,* 593–609.

Goldman-Rakic, P. (1995). Architecture of the prefrontal cortex and the central executive. *Annals of the New York Academy of Sciences, 769,* 71–83.

Goodglass, H., & Kaplan, E. (1963). Disturbances of gesture and pantomime in aphasia. *Brain, 86,* 703–720.

Grady, C.L., McIntosh, A.R., Horwitz, B., Maisog, J.M., Ungerleider, L.G., Mentis, M.J., Pietrini, P., Schapiro, M.B., & Haxby, J.V. (1995). Age-related reductions in human recognition memory due to impaired encoding. *Science, 269,* 218–221.

Graff-Radford, N.R., Tranel, D., Van Hoesen, G.W., & Brandt, J.P. (1990). Diencephalic amnesia. *Brain, 113,* 1–25.

Grafton, S.T., Arbib, M.A., Fadiga, L., & Rizzolatti, G. (1996). Localisation of grasp representations in humans by positron emission tomography. *Experimental Brain Research, 112,* 103–111.

Grasby, P.M., Frith,C.D., Friston, K.J., Bench, C., Frackowiak, R.S.J., & Dolan, R.J. (1993a). Functional mapping of brain areas implicated in auditory-verbal memory function. *Brain, 116,* 1–20.

Grasby, P.M., Frith, C.D., Friston, K.J., Frackowiak, R.S.J., & Dolan, R.J. (1993b). Activation of the human hippocampal formation during auditory-verbal long-term memory function. *Neuroscience Letters, 163,* 185–188.

Haxby, J.V., Ungerleider, L.G., Horwitz, B., Maisog, J.M., Rapoport, S.I., & Grady, C.L. (1996). Face encoding and recognition in the human brain. *Proceedings of the National Academy of Science USA, 93,* 922–927.

Heilman, K.M., & Sypert, G.W. (1977). Korsakoff's syndrome resulting from bilateral fornix lesions. *Neurology, 27,* 490–493.

Herholz, K., Perani, D., Salmon, E., Franck, G., Fazio, F., Heiss, W.D., & Comar, D. (1993). Comparability of FDG PET studies in probable Alzheimer's disease. *Journal of Nuclear Medicine, 34,* 1460–1466.

Hodges, J.R., Patterson, K., Oxbury, S., & Funnell, E. (1992). Semantic dementia: Progressive fluent aphasia with temporal lobe atrophy. *Brain, 115,* 1783–1806.

Hodges, J.R., & Patterson, K. (1995). Is the semantic memory consistently impaired early in the course of Alzheimer's disease? Neuroanatomical and diagnostic implications. *Neuropsychologia, 33,* 441–459.

Holmes, A.P., Blair, R.C., Watson, J.D.G., & Ford, I. (1996). Non-parametric analysis of statistic images from functional mapping experiments. *Journal of Cerebral Blood Flow and Metabolism, 16,* 7–22.

Jonides, J., Smith, E.E., Koeppe, R.A., Awh, E., Minoshima, S., & Mintun, M.A. (1993). Spatial working memory in humans as revealed by PET. *Science, 363,* 623–625.

Kapur, S., Craik, F.I.M., Tulving, E., Wilson, A.A., Houle, S., & Brown, G.M. (1994). Neuroanatomical correlates of encoding in episodic memory: Levels of processing effect. *Proceedings of the National Academy of Science USA, 91,* 2008–2011.

Kapur, S., Craik, F.I.M., Jones, C., Brown, G.M., Houle, S., & Tulving, E. (1995). Functional role of the prefrontal cortex in retrieval of memories: A PET study. *NeuroReport, 6,* 1880–1884.

Kapur, S., Tulving, E., Cabeza, R., McIntosh, A.R., Houle, S., & Craik, F.I. (1996). The neural correlates of intentional learning of verbal materials: A PET study in humans. *Cognitive Brain Research, 4,* 243–9.

Killiany, R.J., Moss, M.B., Albert, M.S., Sandor, T., Tieman, J., & Jolesz, F. (1993). Temporal lobe regions on magnetic resonance imaging identify patients with early Alzheimer's disease. *Archives of Neurology, 50,* 949–954.

Launer, L.J., Scheltens, P., Lindeboom, J., Barkhof, F., Weinstein, H.C., & Jonker, C. (1995). Medial temporal lobe atrophy in an open population of very old persons: Cognitive, brain atrophy, and sociomedical correlates. *Neurology, 45,* 747–752.

Liberman, A.M., & Mattingly, I.G. (1985). The motor theory of speech perception revised. *Cognition, 21,* 1–36.

Mair, W.G.P., Warrington, E.K., & Weiskrantz, L. (1979). Memory disorder in Korsakoff's psychosis: A neuropathological and neuropsychological investigation of two cases. *Brain, 102,* 749–783.

Martin, A., Haxby, J.V., Lalonde, F.M., Wiggs, C.L., & Ungerleider, L.G. (1995). Discrete cortical regions associated with knowledge of color and knowledge of action. *Science, 270,* 102–105.

Martin, A., Wiggs, C.L., Ungerleider, L.G., & Haxby, J.V. (1996). Neural correlates of category-specific knowledge. *Nature 379,* 649–652.

Milner, B. (1966). Amnesia following operation on the temporal lobes. In C.W.M. Whitty & O.L. Zangwill (Eds.), *Amnesia* (pp. 109–133). London: Butterworths.

Miozzo, A., Soardi, M., & Cappa, S.F. (1994). Pure anomia with spared action naming due to a left temporal lesion. *Neuropsychologia, 32,* 1101–1109.

Morris, R.G., & Baddeley, A.D. (1988). Primary and working memory functioning in Alzheimer-type dementia. *Journal of Clinical and Experimental Neuropsychology, 10,* 279–296.

Nebes, R.D. (1989). Semantic memory in Alzheimer's disease. *Psychological Bulletin, 106,* 377–394.

Nyberg, L., McIntosh, A.R., Houle, S., Nilsson, L.-G., & Tulving, E. (1996). Activation of medial temporal structures during episodic memory retrieval. *Nature, 380,* 715–717.

Owen, A.M., Doyon, J., Petrides, M., & Evans, A.C. (1996). Planning and spatial working memory: A positron emission tomography study in humans. *European Journal of Neuroscience, 8,* 353–364.

Owen, A. (1997). The functional organisation of working memory processes within human lateral frontal cortex: The contribution of functional neuroimaging. *European Journal of Neuroscience, 9,* 1329–1339.

Parsons, L.M., Fox, P.T., Downs, J.H., Glass, T., Hirsch, T.B., Martin, C.C., Jerabek, P.A., & Lancaster, J.L. (1995). Use of implicit motor imagery for visual shape discrimination as revealed by PET. *Nature, 375,* 54–58.

Paulesu, E., Frith, C.D., & Frackowiak, R.S.J. (1993). The neural correlates of the verbal component of working memory. *Nature, 362,* 342–345.

Paulesu, E., Perani, D., Fazio, F., Comi, G., Pozzilli, C., Martinelli, V., Filippi, M., Bettinardi, V., Sirabian, G., Passafiume, D., Anzini, A., Lenzi, G.L., Canal, N., & Fieschi, C. (1996). Functional basis of memory impairment in multiple sclerosis: A [$^{18}$F]FDG PET study. *Neuroimage, 4,* 87–96.

Perani, D., Vallar, G., Cappa, S.F., Messa, C. & Fazio, F. (1987). Aphasia and neglect after subcortical stroke. A clinical/cerebral perfusion correlation study. *Brain, 110,* 1211–1229.

Perani, D., Di Piero, V., Gilardi, M.C., Lucignani, G., Pantano, P., Rossetti, C., Pozzilli, C., Gerundini, P., Lenzi, G.L., & Fazio, F. (1988). Remote effects of subcortical cerebrovascular lesions: A SPECT cerebral perfusion study. *Journal of Cerebral Blood Flow and Metabolism, 8,* 560–567.

Perani, D., Bressi, S., Cappa, S.F., Vallar, G., Alberoni, M., Grassi, F., Caltagirone, C., Cipollotti, L., Franceschi, M., Lenzi, G.L., & Fazio, F. (1993). Evidence of multiple memory systems in the human brain: A ($^{18}$F)FDG PET metabolic study. *Brain, 116,* 903–919.

Perani, D., Cappa, S.F., Bettinardi, V., Bressi, S., Gorno Tempini, M.L., Matarrese, M., & Fazio, F. (1995). Different neural networks for the recognition of biological and man-made entities. *NeuroReport 6,* 1637–1641.

Perani, D., Dehaene, S., Grassi, F., Cohen, L., Cappa, S.F., Paulesu, E., Dupoux, E., Fazio, F., & Mehler, J. (1996). A PET study of native and foreign language processing. *Neuroreport 7,* 2439–2444.

Perani, D., Paulesu, E., Sebastian Galles, N., Dupoux, E., Dehaene, S., Bettinardi, V., Cappa, S.F., Fazio, F., & Mehler, J. (1998). The bilingual brain: Proficiency and age of acquisition of the second language. *Brain, 121,* 1841–1852.

Perani, D., Schnur, T., Tettamanti, M., Gorno-Tempini, M., Cappa, S.F., & Fazio, F. (in press). Word and picture matching: A PET study of semantic category effects. *Neuropsychologia.*

Petrides, M., Alivisatos, B., Meyer, E., & Evans, A.C. (1993a). Dissociation of the human mid-dorsolateral from posterior dorsolateral frontal cortex in memory processing. *Proceedings of the National Academy of Science USA, 90,* 873–877.

Petrides, M., Alivisatos, B., Meyer E., & Evans A.C. (1993b). Functional activation of the human frontal cortex during the performance of verbal working memory tasks. *Proceedings of the National Academy of Science USA, 90,* 878–882.

Petrides, M. (1996). Specialized systems for processing of mnemonic information within the primate frontal cortex. Review. *Philosophical Transactions of the Royal Society of London, Series B: Biological Sciences, 351,* 1455–1461.

Premack, D., & Woodruff, G. (1978). Does the chimpanzee have a theory of mind? *Behavioral Brain Sciences,4,* 515–526.

Press, G.A., Amaral, D.G., & Squire, L.R. (1989). Hippocampal abnormalities in amnesics patients revealed by high resolution magnetic resonance imaging. *Nature, 341,* 54–57.

Rizzolatti, G., Fadiga, L., Matelli, M., Bettinardi, V., Perani, D., & Fazio, F. (1996). Localization of cortical areas responsive to the observation of hand grasping movements in humans: A PET study. *Experimental Brain Research, 111,* 246–252.

Rushworth, M.F.S., & Owen, A.M. (1998). The functional organisation of the lateral frontal cortex: Conjecture or conjuncture in the electrophysiology literature. *Trends in Cognitive Science, 2,* 46–53.

Salmon, D.P., Shimamura, A.P., Butters, N., & Smith, S. (1988). Lexical and semantic priming deficits in patients with Alzheimer's disease. *Journal of Clinical and Experimental Neuropsychology, 10,* 477–494.

Schacter, D.L., Alpert, N.M., Savage, C.R., Rauch, S.L., & Albert, M.S. (1996). Conscious recollection and the human hippocampal formation: Evidence from positron emission tomography. *Proceedings of the National Academy of Sciences USA, 93,* 321–325.

Shallice, T., Fletcher, P., Frith C.D., Grasby, P., Frackowiak, R.S.J., & Dolan, R.J. (1994). Brain regions associated with acquisition and retrieval of verbal episodic memory. *Nature, 368,* 633–635.

Snowden, J.S., Neary, D., Mann, D.M.A., Goulding, P.J., & Testa, H.J. (1992). Progressive language disorder due to lobar atrophy. *Annals of Neurology, 31,* 174–183.

Soininen, H.S., Partanen, K., Pitkaenen, A., Vainio, P., Haenninen, T., Hallikaininen, M., Koivisto, K., & Riekkinen, P.J. (1994). Volumetric MRI analysis of the amygdala and hippocampus in subjects with age-associated memory impairment: Correlation to visual and verbal memory. *Neurology, 44,* 1660–1668.

Stephan, K.M., Fink, G.R., Passingham, R.E., Silbersweig, D., Ceballos-Baumann, A.O., Frith, C.D., & Frackowiak, R.S.J. (1995). Functional anatomy of the mental representation of upper extremity movements in healthy subjects. *Journal of Neurophysiology, 73,* 373–386.

Stern, C.E., Corkin, S., Gonzalez, R.G., Guimaraes, A.R., Baker, J.R., Jennings, P.J., Carr, C.A., Sugiura, R.M., Vedantham, V., & Rosen, B.R. (1996). The hippocampal formation participates in novel picture encoding: Evidence from functional magnetic resonance imaging. *Proceedings of the National Academy of Sciences USA, 93,* 8660–8665.

Swick, D., & Knight, R.T. (1996). Is prefrontal cortex involved in cued recall? A neuropsychological test of PET findings. *Neuropsychologia, 10,* 1019–1028.

Swirsky-Sacchetti, T., Mitchell, D.R., Seward, J., Gonzales, C., Lublin, F., Knobler, R., &

Field, H.L. (1992). Neuropsychological and structural brain lesions in multiple sclerosis: A regional analysis. *Neurology, 42,* 1291–1295.

Talairach, J., & Tournoux, P. (1988). *Co-planar stereotaxic atlas of the human brain.* Stuttgart: Thieme.

Thompson-Schill, S., D'Esposito, M., Aguirre, G.K., & Farah, M.J. (1997). Role of left inferior prefrontal cortex in retrieval of semantic knowledge: A revaluation. *Proceedings of the National Academy of Sciences USA, 94,* 14792–14797.

Tulving, E. (1972). Episodic and semantic memory. In E. Tulving & W. Donaldson (Eds.), *Organization of memory* (pp. 381–403). New York: Academic Press.

Tulving, E., Kapur, S., Markowitsch, H.J., Craik, F.I.M., Habib, R., & Houle, S. (1994). Neuroanatomical correlates of retrieval in episodic memory: Auditory sentence recognition. *Proceedings of the National Academy of Science USA, 91,* 2012–2015.

Vandenberghe, R., Price, C., Wise, R., Josephs, O., & Frackowiak, R.S.J. (1996). Functional anatomy of a common semantic system for words and pictures. *Nature, 383,* 254–256.

Victor, M., Adams, R.D., & Collins, G.H. (1971). *The Wernicke-Korsakoff Syndrome.* Philadelphia: FA Davis.

Vogt, S. (1996). Imagery and perception-action mediation in imitative actions. *Cognitive Brain Research, 3,* 79–86.

Warrington, E.K. (1976). The selective impairment of semantic memory. *Quarterly Journal of Experimental Psychology, 27,* 635–657.

Warrington, E.K., & Weiskrantz, L. (1982). Amnesia: A disconnection syndrome? *Neuropsychologia 20,* 233–249.

Warrington, E.K., & McCarthy, R.A. (1991). Categories of knowledge: Further fractionation and an attempted integration. *Brain, 110,* 1273–1296.

Weingartner, H., Grafman, J., Boutelle, W., Kaye, W., & Martin, P. (1983). Forms of memory failure. *Science, 21,* 380–382.

Whitty, C.W.M., & Lewin, W. (1960). Korsakoff syndrome in the postcingulectomy confusional state. *Brain, 83,* 648–653.

Zola-Morgan, S., Squire, L.R., & Amaral, D.G. (1986). Human amnesia and the medial temporal region: Enduring memory impairment following a bilateral lesion limited to the CA1 field of the hippocampus. *Journal of Neuroscience, 6,* 2950–2967.

# The Roles of the Hippocampus in Memory

*Katharina Henke*

In the first part of this chapter I will introduce the hippocampal memory hypothesis and discuss it on grounds of evidence from four different fields of neuroscience: Studies of brain-damaged patients, animal ablation studies, epilepsy surgery, and functional neuroimaging. In the second part, I will proceed to a summary of specific hypotheses about the function of the hippocampus in declarative memory. This leads to the third part, our positron emission tomography (PET) experiment (Henke, Buck, Weber, & Wieser, 1997), which was designed to test some of these hypotheses about the role of the hippocampus in memory.

## Evidence from Four Fields of Neuroscience

### The Hippocampal Memory Hypothesis

The hippocampus formation (HF) is a bilateral, archicortical structure in the medial part of the temporal lobe (TL). The HF consists of the hippocampus proper (CA1, CA2, CA3, and CA4), the dentate gyrus and the subiculum (see Figure 1). The parahippocampal gyrus, the entorhinal and perirhinal cortices are located inferiorly and laterally to the HF.

The HF was once related to olfaction, later to emotion, and for the past 40 years to learning and memory. There are early German reports (Bechterew, 1900; Kohnstamm, 1917; Uchimura, 1928; Grünthal & Störring, 1930, 1933) describing patients who became amnesic following damage to both medial TL regions. Glees and Griffith (1952) described an amnesic patient with a presumably vascular lesion destroying left TL structures including the HF, the parahippocampal gyrus, part of the fusiform and lingual gyrus, the fornix and the tip of the TL. They concluded that the HF was essential for the maintenance of recent memory and for carrying on normal mental activity. Yet, it was not until the influential reports by Scoville and Milner (1957) and Penfield and Milner (1958) that the mediotemporal region was more widely acknowledged

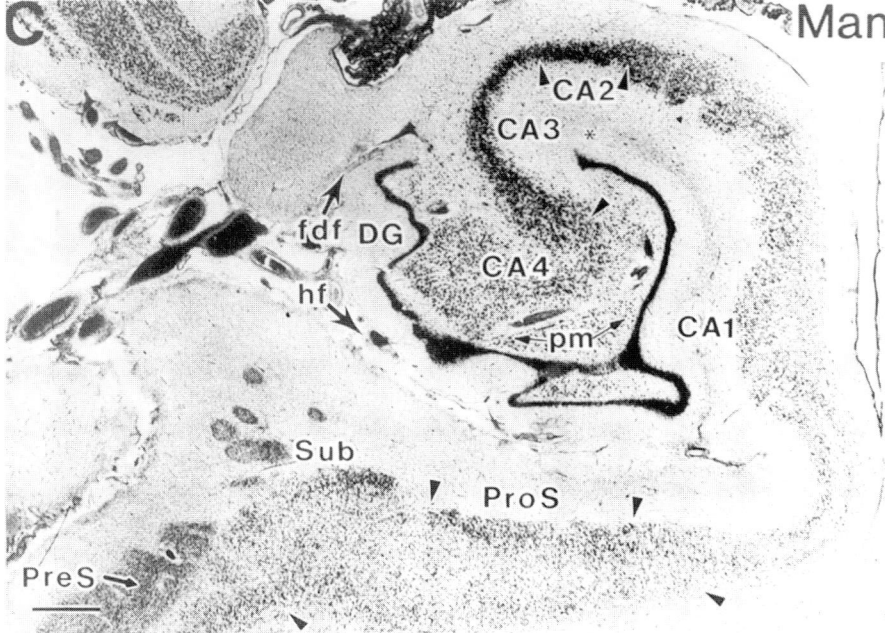

*Figure 1.* Hippocampal cytoarchitecture. Nissl-stained coronal section through the HF of man with the approximate boundaries of the corresponding subdivisions marked by arrowheads. DG, dentate gyrus; Sub, subiculum; PreS, presubiculum; ProS, prosubiculum; CA1, CA2, CA3, CA4, fields of Ammon's horn or hippocampus proper; hf, hippocampal fissure; pm, polymorph layer of the dentate gyrus; fdf, fimbrio-dentate fissure. Figure from Rosene and Van Hoesen (1987), by permission of Plenum Press.

to be crucial for memory functions. This is illustrated by Penfield and Milner's (1958) first paragraph:

> It has often been assumed that memory depends upon the total action of the brain rather than upon some specialized intracerebral neuron mechanism. There is recent evidence, however, in support of the view that the recording of experience is localizable in the same sense that sensory functions and speech functions are localizable (p. 475).

Penfield and Milner (1958) reported 90 patients with medial TL epilepsy who underwent unilateral partial temporal lobectomy, including the HF and parahippocampal gyrus, the uncus and the amygdala. These patients suffered only minor memory deficits after surgery. The resulting deficits were more pronounced after resection of the left than the right mediotemporal structures. Yet, in two cases of left partial temporal lobectomy, the operation resulted in an unexpected general loss of recent memory. Postmortem autopsy revealed

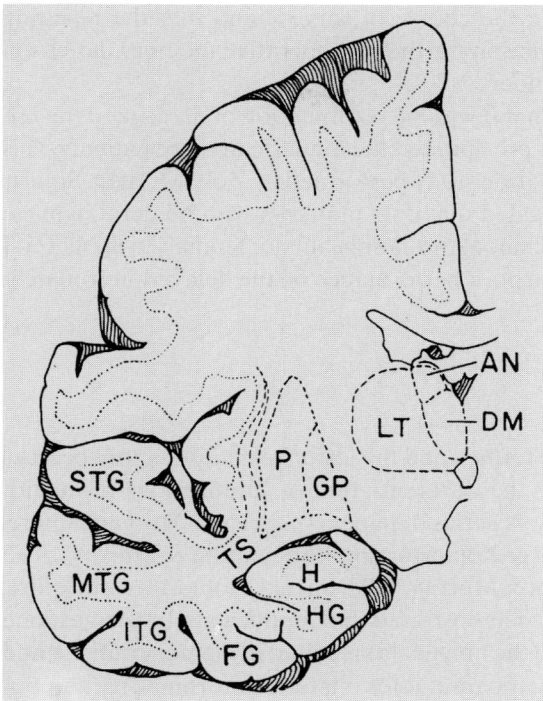

*Figure 2.* Anatomy of the TL: Hippocampus and temporal stem. AN, anterior nuclear group of thalamus; DM, dorsomedial nucleus of thalamus; FG, fusiform gyrus; GP, globus pallidus; H, hippocampus; HG, parahippocampal gyrus; STG/MTG/ITG, superior/middle/inferior temporal gyrus; LT, lateral thalamus; P, putamen; TS, temporal stem. Figure from Horel (1978), by permission of Oxford University Press.

that both of these patients had preexisting damage to the contralateral right hippocampal zone, leaving them with bilateral mediotemporal damage. Somewhat later, Scoville and Milner (1957; the sequence of publications does not reflect the sequence of events) made a similar discovery: They reported 9 patients with bilateral medial TL resections. In one of these patients (H. M.), surgery was a treatment for medically refractory epilepsy, in the other patients it was a treatment for psychotic disorders. Scoville extended the orbital undercutting to include the resection of medial temporal structures such as the amygdala, the uncus, and the pes of the hippocampus. He experimented by trying progressively larger bilateral resections extending up to 8 cm back from the tips of the TL. Two of these patients (H. M. and M. B.) who had received the largest bilateral resections (without orbital undercutting) developed a severe amnesic syndrome. Scoville and Milner reported a positive relationship between the extent of destruction of the medial temporal area and the degree of memory impairment. Specifically, they attributed the memory loss in these patients to the resection of the hippocampal formation. This interpretation was questioned subsequently by Horel (1978) and Mishkin (1978). Horel advanced the alternative hypothesis that the temporal stem overlying the HF (see Figure

2) might have been severed in the course of surgery and that the resulting damage might have been the reason for the postoperative memory deficits in the patients of Scoville and Milner.

Mishkin, instead, proposed that it was the combination of damage to the HF and to the amygdala which has precipitated the amnesia in these patients. This argument was settled by an ablation study performed by Zola-Morgan, Squire, and Mishkin (1982) which revealed that only monkeys with bilateral damage to the amygdala and the hippocampal formation, but not animals with bilateral temporal stem lesions, showed a poor performance on the delayed-non-match-to-sample task.

## Animal Ablation Studies

Ablation studies became more refined and the lesion techniques more precise. This development allowed for the differentiation of subfunctions of medio-temporal structures in memory. A series of papers (e. g., Zola-Morgan, Squire, Amaral, & Suzuki, 1989; Squire & Zola-Morgan, 1991; Gaffan & Murray, 1992; Meunier, Bachevalier, Mishkin, & Murray, 1993; Suzuki, Zola-Morgan, Squire, & Amaral, 1993; Murray, 1996) demonstrated that hippocampal damage alone (without concurrent damage to the amygdala) resulted in memory deficits, and that memory deficits were also apparent after bilateral entorhinal, parahippo-campal and perirhinal damage. Indeed, the severest impairments in visual rec-ognition memory were obtained after bilateral perirhinal damage. Murray (1996) concluded that the medial TL structures do not comprise a single func-tional system supporting declarative memory. She advanced the hypothesis that the rhinal cortex might be part of a memory system that corresponds to semantic memory in the human.

## Human Lesion Studies

In the field of human lesion studies, several patients with damage limited to the hippocampus were reported (Zola-Morgan, Squire, & Amaral, 1986; Kart-sounis, Rudge, & Stevens, 1995; Rempel-Clower, Zola, Squire, & Amaral, 1996). These patients were neuropsychologically well documented. Zola-Mor-gan et al. (1986) reported patient R. B. with ischemic damage of the CA1 region of both hippocampi and a moderately severe amnesia. Kartsounis, Rudge, and Stevens (1995) presented a patient who became moderately am-nesic following bilateral ischemic lesions to both the CA1 and CA2 region of the hippocampus. These studies provided evidence that bilateral damage lim-ited to the hippocampus proper is sufficient to cause amnesia in the human.

Rempel-Clower et al. (1996) described three further patients with bilateral ischemic damage to hippocampal regions. Postmortem neuropathological analyses demonstrated that one of these patients had damage limited to the field CA1 (like R. B.), another patient had damage to the fields CA1, CA2, CA3, the dentate gyrus and the entorhinal cortex, and the third patient presented with damage to the fields CA1, CA2, CA3, the dentate gyrus, subiculum, and entorhinal cortex. The authors concluded that the severity of anterograde and retrograde amnesia is dependent on the locus and extent of damage in the hippocampal region. This view is not completely congruent with Murray (1996) who infers from monkey ablation studies that the mediotemporal structures do not comprise a homogeneously functioning system.

Vargha-Khadem et al. (1997) analyzed the memory deficits in three patients who had sustained selective bilateral hippocampal damage early in life. Their results support the notion that the HF is critical for everyday episodic memory (memory for autobiographical events and their spatio-temporal reference), but not for semantic memory (general factual knowledge; Tulving, 1972).

## Epilepsy Surgery

New discoveries have also been made in the field of neurosurgery since Scoville and Milner (1957). A few subsequent reports took some weight off the hippocampal memory hypothesis. Gol and Fabisch (1967) presented 7 patients who underwent unilateral or bilateral hippocampectomy for the relief of pain. These authors found that their patients' memory deficits varied with the size of their lesions and appeared to be more influenced by neocortical than archicortical damage. Loring et al. (1991) found no significant difference in memory when contrasting dominant temporal lobectomy patients in whom the anterior HF was spared to those in whom the anterior HF was resected. Jones-Gotman et al. (1997) published a postoperative comparison of three groups of patients who underwent different partial unilateral TL resections as a treatment for TL epilepsy. The patients from Dublin underwent a neocorticectomy, the patients from Zurich a selective amygdalohippocampectomy, and the patients from Montreal an anterior lobe resection including the amygdala and the anterior hippocampal formation. The largest hippocampal and amygdala resections were found in the Zurich patients. If the HF were the crucial structure in the TL for learning material, one would therefore expect the Zurich patients to perform worst on tests of learning. All patients received the same verbal and nonverbal learning and recall tasks. Matched control groups to each of the three patient samples were also examined. The results revealed a similar memory outcome in all patients suggesting that the HF does not have the prominent role in learning that has been ascribed to it on grounds of results from other epileptic patients (Scoville & Milner, 1957; Penfield & Milner, 1958). Results from patients with TL epilepsy have to be interpreted with caution, since most of these individuals have seizures since their early childhood which might have changed the functional organization of their brains. If, e. g., the seizures originate from the left medial temporal region, the dysfunction of the left HF might become compensated by other brain structures in the same or opposite hemisphere.

As mentioned in the foregoing paragraph, patients with medically intractable mesial TL epilepsy may receive a selective mesial TL resection which was pioneered by Wieser and Yasargil (1982) in Zurich, namely the unilateral selective amygdalohippocampectomy (AHE). The eligible patients usually have unilateral seizure origin. Postoperatively, these patients may show some mild decline of memory, more so after left than right AHE. Hajek, Khan, Leenders, and Wieser (1995) published 4 patients with bilateral seizure origins. The seizures in these patients originated independently in the right or left mesiobasal TL structures. The 4 patients received an AHE on either the left or right side, depending on which TL contained the epileptogenic zone producing the greater number of seizures. The laterality indices (defined as greater number of seizures originating in one TL divided by the total number of seizures × 100) were between 66% and 76% in these patients. Two of the patients were operated on the right and two on the left side. Three patients were seizure free postoperatively. One of the patients with a right AHE was initially seizure-free, but later developed rare complex partial seizures. Postoperatively, the patients who were operated on the right side showed improved nonverbal learning and memory and equal (to the preoperative status) verbal learning and memory. One of these patients exhibited bilateral language comprehension, the other left hemisphere language comprehension. The patients who underwent surgery on the left side showed left hemisphere language comprehension, and exhibited a postoperative decrease of learning and memory. This decrease was apparent for verbal material in one patient and for both verbal and nonverbal memory in the other patient. These four cases are somewhat similar to the two patients reported by Penfield and Milner (1958) who received a left partial temporal lobectomy with preexisting damage to the contralateral hippocampal zone, and who suffered a severe postoperative amnesia. The four patients from Zurich did not have structural damage as examined with magnetic resonance imaging (MRI) in the contralateral hippocampal formation, but had an electroencephalographically confirmed dysfunction in the contralateral hippocampal formation. Nevertheless, two of the four patients did not experience any change in memory and one suffered some decline in verbal memory only. The fourth patient, however, had exhibited a continuous decrease in memory performance preoperatively and continued to deteriorate

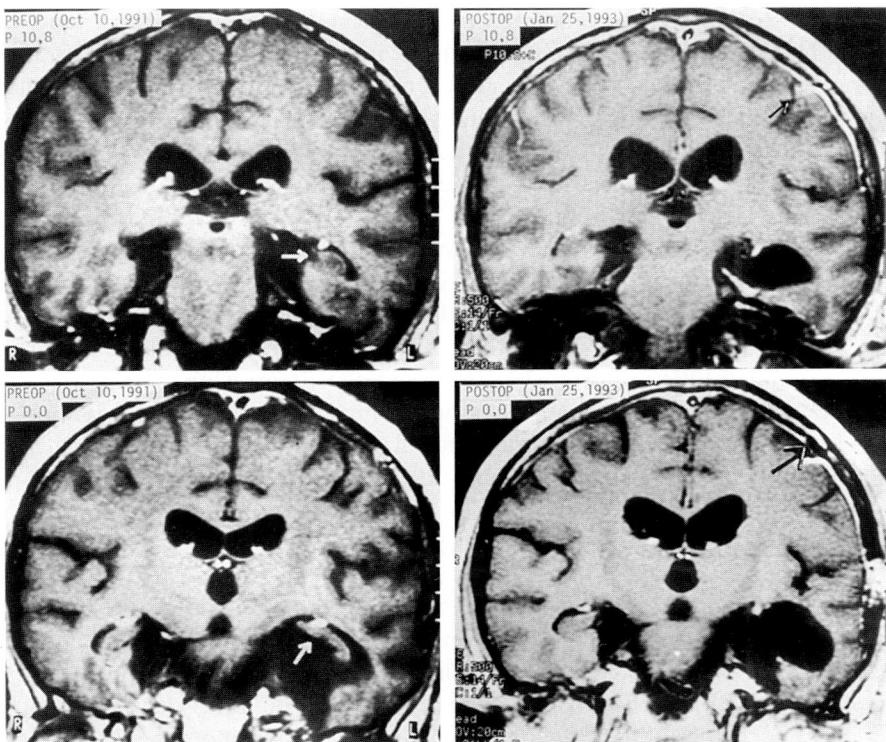

*Figure 3.* Preoperative and postoperative MRIs of patient KHJ. Comparable coronal sections with a distance of 10.8 mm allowing a comparison of preoperative (left) and postoperative (right) MRI (T1-weighted, with Gadolinium) of patient KHJ. The compressed, laterally displaced and flattened left HF (left, with white arrows) has been completely resected far back to the level of the aqueductus Silvii. Black arrows in the postoperative MRI denote artifacts (metal abrasion) from the craniotomy. Figure from Henke and Wieser (1996), by permission of Elsevier Science.

postoperatively. It should be mentioned that multiple factors apart from epilepsy and surgery accounted for this unfortunate trend.

A more similar condition to that in the two patients of Penfield and Milner (1958) was present in another Zurich patient reported by Henke and Wieser (1996). Penfield and Milner (1958) and Scoville and Milner (1957) had published their cases with postoperative amnesia as a warning not to perform hippocampal resections if damage is present in the contralateral hippocampal area. Our patient K. H. J. (Henke & Wieser, 1996) was such a case. He exhibited a left medial temporal seizure origin with bilateral structural pathology in the medial temporal areas. K. H. J. had bilateral excentric medial TL arachnoidal cysts compressing both HF (Figure 3) and suffered from severe, drug-resistant complex partial seizures generated in the left medial TL area with frequent secondary generalization. A surgical intervention on the left medial TL for the removal of the displaced left amygdala and the left HF was considered adequate for seizure control. After extensive presurgical evaluation, including selective TL amobarbital testing (Wieser, Valavanis, Roos, Isler, & Renella, 1989; Wieser, Landis, Regard, & Schiess, 1989) for learning and memory a left-sided AHE was performed (Figure 3). K. H. J. was postoperatively seizure-free. His nonverbal learning and memory was deficient preoperatively and recovered to normal postoperatively. Yet, his verbal learning and memory had suffered from the operation. Nevertheless, K. H. J. did not show a postoperative global amnesia. He was able to manage his life and to fulfill the requirements of a half-time position. This case is in line with growing evidence that a too rigid "hippocampal memory hypothesis" must be revised. K. H. J. is another example showing that bilateral medical TL pathology by itself must not necessarily lead to a classic amnesic syndrome.

## Functional Imaging

A fourth area of interest concerning the hippocampal memory hypothesis is functional neuroimaging (e. g., positron emission tomography, PET; functional magnetic resonance imaging, fMRI). The initial $H_2{}^{15}O$ and $[^{18}F]$2-fluoro-2-de-oxy-D-glucose PET studies of learning and memory did rarely reveal a significant hippocampal blood flow or metabolic increase during the execution of memory tasks (e. g., Grasby et al., 1994; Kapur et al., 1994; Shallice et al., 1994; Tulving, Kapur, Markowitsch et al., 1994; Andreasen et al., 1995; Fletcher et al., 1995). Subsequent functional neuroimaging studies on learning and memory using nonverbal stimulus material, such as faces, photographs of houses and landscapes, line drawings, and films of urban environments, did lead to significant hippocampal blood flow increases, more so on the right than the left side (e. g., Kapur, Friston, Young, Frith, & Frackowiak, 1995; Haxby et al., 1996; Maguire, Frackowiak, & Frith, 1996; Stern et al., 1996; Gabrieli, Brewer, Desmond, & Glover, 1997; Henke et al., 1997). There are also some recent reports of hippocampal activation during single word learning (Nyberg et al., 1996), during paired-associate word learning (Dolan & Fletcher, 1997), and during the retrieval of single words (Schacter, Alpert, Savage, Rauch, & Albert, 1996; Rugg, Fletcher, Frith, Frackowiak, & Dolan, 1997). As will be discussed at the end of this chapter, the variable determining whether significant hippocampal activation can be obtained, seems not to be the verbal versus nonverbal nature of the stimuli, but the kind of learning involved. Instructions which emphasize associative learning, in the sense of establishing new semantic linkages between stimuli, lead to information processing with elevated hippocampal blood flow both during encoding and during the retrieval of material which has been encoded that way.

In conclusion, the evidence from four different fields of research, namely functional imaging, human lesion studies, neurosurgery, and animal ablation studies, draws a heterogeneous picture of the function of the hippocampal formation in memory. It remains unclear how important the HF is for declarative memory and what its specific role or roles in memory might be.

## Theories of Hippocampal Function in Memory

In the following I will concentrate on the most prominent theories of hippocampal function in memory, focusing on the consolidation hypothesis advanced by Squire and collaborators (e. g., Squire, 1992; Squire & Alvarez, 1995) and on Cohen and Eichenbaum's (1993) hypothesis about the flexibility of the hippocampus-dependent declarative memory.

### Spatial Learning

In 1978 O'Keefe and Nadel published their "cognitive map" theory of the hippocampus. Based on O'Keefe and Dostrovsky's (1971) findings that there are cells in the CA1 and CA3 fields of the rat hippocampus which fire specifically when the animal is located in a certain place in space, O'Keefe and Nadel developed their theory about memory for spatial layouts. The authors emphasize the importance of the hippocampus for a high-level internal representation of allocentric spatial relationships and for learning to solve problems that require memory for these relationships. The cognitive map is computed from the animal's movements and on grounds of visual landmark information. The notion that the hippocampus might have a particular function in memory for spatial information, such as memory for spatial locations, did not receive much support by evidence in the human. Spatial information appeared to be one of several information categories for which learning was poor after bilateral hippocampal damage (e. g., Backer Cave & Squire, 1991). Nonetheless, recent imaging studies did find parahippocampal and hippocampal activation while subjects were recalling the location of objects in space (Owen, Milner, Petrides, & Evans, 1996) or a way through an urban environment (Maguire, Frackowiak, & Frith, 1996). Furthermore, Henke et al. (in press) found a selective spatial learning deficit in a patient with bilateral hippocampal damage.

*Novelty Detection*

The claim that the HF is engaged in the novelty assessment of stimuli is founded on broad experimental evidence from studies in humans and animals. Electrophysiological recordings from scalp and from intracranial electrodes have shown that novel stimuli activate a large distributed network involving prefrontal, temporal and parietal areas (Halgren & Marinkovic, 1995; Knight, 1996). Event-related potential studies (e. g., Knight, 1996), single neuron recording studies (e. g., Fahy, Riches, & Brown, 1993; Rolls, Cahusac, Feigenbaum, & Miyashita, 1993), and functional neuroimaging studies (Tulving, Markowitsch et al., 1994; Tulving et al., 1996; Martin, Wiggs, Ungerleider, & Haxby, 1996) suggested that the HF is part of this novelty detection network. Novelty assessment is considered an early stage of long-term memory encoding (Tulving et al., 1996). Before elaborate, meaning-based encoding processes become operational, perceived stimuli must be judged old or new. Obviously, there is no use in learning "old" items, since these are stored in memory already. Therefore, the probability of long-term storage of items varies with their novelty value. Items are stored to the extent that they are new. Tulving et al. (1996) suggested that

> "... novelty assessment involves the limbic system and temporal/opercular regions, that elaborative encoding is associated with neuronal activity in the left prefrontal cortex, and that explicit retrieval is based on the activity of the right frontal, anterior cingulate, parietal, and cerebellar regions." (pp. 77).

Thus, in their opinion, the HF is rather taking part in the selection of the to-be-stored material than actively being involved with encoding, storage or retrieval.

*Consolidation*

Another interesting view about the function of the HF in memory was advanced by Squire and collaborators (Zola-Morgan & Squire, 1990; Squire & Zola-Morgan, 1991; Squire, 1992; Alvarez & Squire, 1994; Squire & Alvarez, 1995). These authors claim that the consolidation of information from short-term to long-term memory is a typical function of the HF. The fact that retrograde amnesia is temporally graded in patients and experimental animals with amnesia due to bilateral hippocampal damage, is interpreted as evidence for a time-limited role of the HF in memory storage. According to this view, the HF is initially indispensable for the retrieval of information, but after a certain time period during which consolidation takes place, information becomes independent of hippocampal function and can be retrieved in the absence of both hippocampal formations. Thus, the HF is not considered a repository of permanent memory, but temporarily stores "aspects" of information held in short-term memory. The HF has several characteristics which make it a prime candidate for consolidation: It is reciprocally connected with virtually all association cortices and exhibits long-term potentiation (LTP) which is thought to induce fast changes in the synaptic connectivity. Converging inputs arriving simultaneously lead to an increase in synaptic efficacy lasting for hours to weeks. LTP induces cellular changes which allow for a well formed representation of the pattern of co-activations on a single trial. Unlike the neocortex, the HF is not believed to possess a large storage capacity. This makes it a bad candidate structure for the permanent storage of information. By virtue of its connections with the neocortex, however, the HF can instantly store patterns of neocortical coactivations at the time of encoding of a perceived scene. The cortico-cortical connections between the simultaneously activated neocortical regions are less plastic and therefore need repeated simultaneous activations in order to become strengthened. According to Squire's hypothesis, the HF forms a temporary memory trace holding the information about what neocortical regions were simultaneously activated when event A has been registered. Subsequently, the HF repeatedly reactivates the cortical (and subcortical) sites in the same way that they were activated during encoding. It thereby helps strengthening the connections between these participating regions over time. This process is considered the neuronal correlate of consolidation. By the time the cortico-cortical connections between the storage sites of event A are established, event A can be retrieved without the participation of the hippocampi.

## Representational Flexibility

Eichenbaum and Cohen (Cohen & Eichenbaum, 1993; Eichenbaum, Otto, & Cohen, 1994; Eichenbaum, 1997) took this theory a step further by stressing two characteristics which are unique to declarative memory and which may depend on the ability of the HF to store and reactivate patterns of coactivations. These characteristics are *representational flexibility* and *compositionality*. In the following, I will try to explain what these terms mean:

   Stored patterns of coactivations are believed to overlap with other stored patterns of coactivations in the HF. When a new event B shares features with a previously stored event A, the representations of the old event A will become reactivated in concert with the new event B. This allows for the retrieval of an old event A on grounds of only one cue which is also part of a new event B. Due to this partial overlap with the new event B the whole hippocampal memory trace of the first event A can become reactivated as event B is experienced. The complete cortical-subcortical network which was involved in processing the experience of event A may simultaneously become activated. This mechanism might underlie the phenomenon of "cued recall." It works even in cases, where the cue in event B has been manipulated such that it only vaguely resembles the corresponding component of event A. The interaction of current representations with the representations of earlier events in the hippocampal network creates what Cohen and Eichenbaum (1993, p. 289) call a "memory space." A memory space contains new events composed of items which have relations to other items constituting previously encountered events. These earlier events are still being in the process of consolidation and are still dependent on hippocampal function. Such reinstantiations occur repetitively over time and may modify the later long-term neocortical representation of an event. This might also be one possible source for the introduction of memory errors.

Another feature of compositionality and flexibility is the ability to retrieve either event A as a whole or to retrieve only a certain part of event A, like zooming in the recollection of only one aspect of event A. The hippocampal representations consist of both, the complete learned episode and its constituents. Therefore, the HF can reactivate all neocortical storage sites simultaneously and recover the memory of the whole event A or it can reactivate only a certain neocortical storage site which represents part of the memory of event A and thereby recover the recollection of only one aspect of event A. Hence, the HF provides the means for gaining access to the various neocortical representations that together constitute the learned episode. It permits access to both the representations of the *parts* of a learned event and their *conjunctions*.

## The Human Hippocampus Establishes Associations in Memory: A PET Experiment

As laid out in the previous section, there are different views about what the function or functions of the HF in memory might be. According to the latter view, the hippocampal system binds together the different components of a learning event by linking neuronal activation in distributed brain regions (Squire & Zola-Morgan, 1991; Squire, 1992; Cohen & Eichenbaum, 1993; Eichenbaum et al., 1994). Temporary storage of such patterns of coactivations allows the hippocampal system to maintain the coherence and relational properties of the learning event (Cohen & Eichenbaum, 1993; Eichenbaum et al., 1994). According to this perspective, the HF is expected to be active during both the establishment of inter-item associations and during the retrieval of recently formed associations. The HF is also expected to be more involved in the encoding of associations between items of a scene than during the encoding of these items in isolation.

As mentioned, another view implicates the HF in the detection of novelty of stimuli, which might be a prerequisite to learning (Tulving, Markowitsch et al., 1994; Tulving et al., 1996; Knight, 1996).

We designed a $H_2^{15}O$ PET experiment (Henke et al., 1997) with encoding and retrieval tasks that allowed us to isolate the following memory functions: Learning single novel items, establishing inter-item associations between novel items, retrieving recently formed associations between items, and detecting novel constellations of studied items.

Our experiment consisted of two learning conditions, two retrieval conditions, and a perceptual task (Figure 4). During the learning and retrieval tasks, our 12 subjects were presented with photographs that contained houses next to individuals (Figure 4). Subjects responded in all tasks by either pressing the right or the left key of a computer mouse. The first learning task required subjects to decide whether the presented individual might either be an inhabitant or a visitor of the house (Associative Learning). The left key was pressed for inhabitant, the right for visitor. This judgment is based on subjective criteria such as style or age, individual knowledge and stereotypes. There was no correct or wrong answer. The purpose of the task was to engage subjects in an evaluation of the person and the house with regard to the relation the person might have to the house. This evaluation process necessarily leads to the establishment of associations between houses and people in memory, irrespective of the decision about their fit. The second learning task required subjects to determine the gender of the presented person and to decide whether an outside or an inside view of the house was presented (Single Item Learning). The left key was pressed when a man and an exterior was presented or when a woman and an interior was presented. In all other combinations, subjects pressed the right key. This task engaged subjects in an evaluation of the person and the house independently of each other. It therefore leads to the storage of the house and the person as separate entities rather than associates. Thus, the first learning task should lead to a better retention of the house-person pairs than the second learning task. Associative Learning was carried out twice and was followed after 10 minutes by either of two retrieval tasks. In both retrieval tasks the studied houses and people were presented again, either in the previously viewed combination (Retrieval Old) or in a new combination (Retrieval New). No new material was presented. The task in both retrieval conditions was to decide whether an old or a new combination was presented. The left key was pressed for "old combination," the right for "new combination." Retrieval Old thus required the recovery of stored associations, while Retrieval New required a search for formed associations and led to the detec-

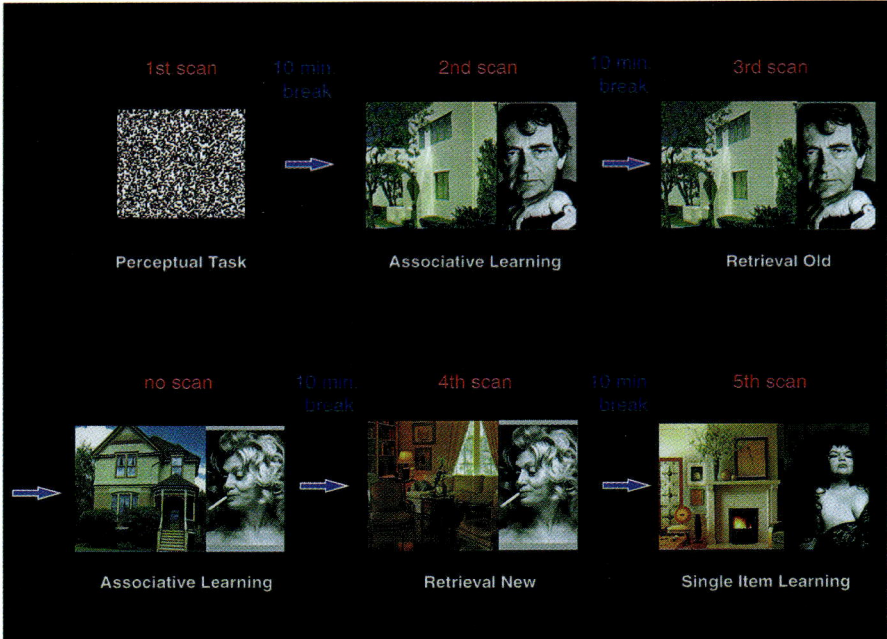

*Figure 4.* Examples of stimuli and an example sequence of tasks. The sequence of tasks was varied across subjects to avoid order effects. Yet, the Associative Learning tasks always immediately preceded the retrieval tasks to keep the delay time between encoding and retrieval at 10 minutes. Only one Associative Learning procedure was accompanied by scanning. Figure from Henke, Buck, Weber, and Wieser (1997), by permission of Wiley & Sons,

tion of novel combinations. Old and new combinations were mixed during the prescanning period (= 30 s) and postscanning period (also 30 s). During scanning (60 s) either only old (Retrieval Old) or new combinations (Retrieval New) were presented.

The Perceptual Task served as a comparison task and required subjects to judge whether a square or a rectangle (filled with black-and-white random dot patterns) was presented (Figure 4).

We first conducted a behavioral study (without PET) with different subjects to test the suitability of our learning tasks. The Associative Learning task led to a substantially better retention of house-person combinations than the Single Item Learning task.

Time spent on task per trial (stimuli were exposed for 3 s) in the PET experiment was comparable between Associative Learning and the two retrieval tasks ($1847 \pm 168$ ms for Associative Learning, $1890 \pm 173$ ms for Retrieval Old, $1900 \pm 152$ ms for Retrieval New), but was shorter in the Single Item Learning task ($1510 \pm 189$ ms) and the Perceptual Task ($650 \pm 107$ ms).

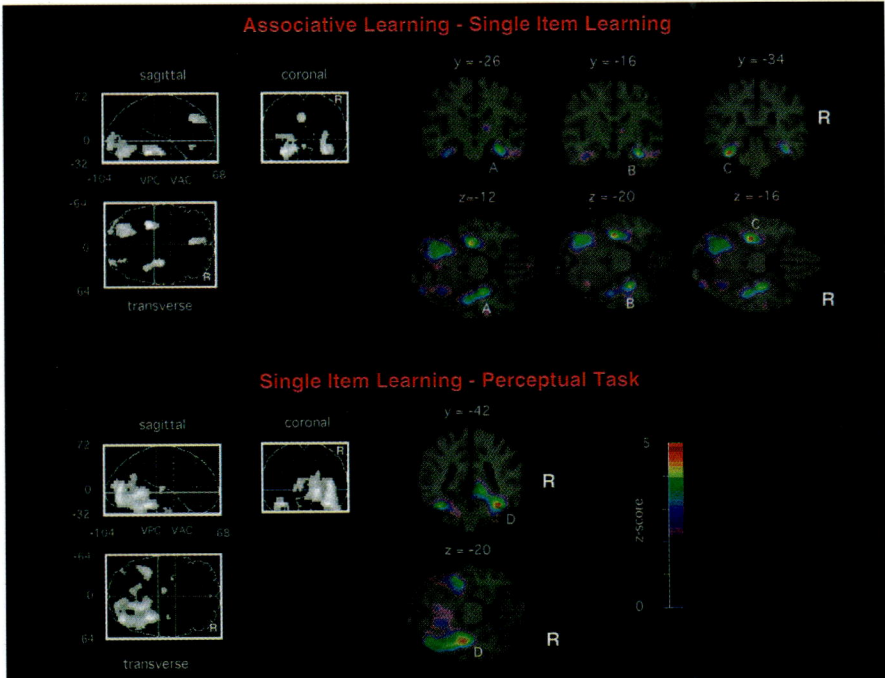

*Figure 5.* Relative rCBF changes during Associative Learning and Single Item Learning. Left side: Areas of relative rCBF increase are demonstrated as through projections onto representations of standard stereotaxic space (Frackowiak & Friston, 1994). R, right; VAC, vertical plane through the anterior commissure; VPC, vertical plane through the posterior commissure. Numbers at axes refer to coordinates of stereotaxic space.
Right side: Coronal (top) and transverse (bottom) SPM{z} maps at the indicated coordinate position superimposed on a magnetic resonance image that had been spatially normalized into the same stereotaxic space. A, right hippocampus; B, right parahippocampal gyrus; C, left fusiform gyrus; D, right fusiform gyrus. Figure from Henke, Buck, Weber and Wieser (1997), by permission of Wiley & Sons, Inc.).

Pairwise subtraction analysis of the inter-subject averaged PET images was performed. The comparison of Associative Learning to Single Item Learning isolates regional cerebral blood flow (rCBF) changes due to the establishment of associations between items. This comparison yielded significant blood flow increases in the left anterior fusiform gyrus, the right parahippocampal gyrus, the right HF and a medial frontal area (Figure 5, Table 1).

No brain area was significantly more activated during Single Item Learning than Associative Learning. Single Item Learning weighed against the Perceptual Task revealed relative blood flow increases in visual areas: right occipital cortex, right lingual gyrus and both fusiform gyri. The fusiform gyri and the occipital cortex have been activated in many studies during visual perception

*Table 1.* Peaks of blood flow increases and decreases. The coordinates (x, y, z) locate the maxima within an area of rCBF increase (positive z-values) or decrease (negative z-value) associated with a given contrast; +indicates p < 0.05 (corrected for multiple comparisons), all other z-values correspond to p < 0.001 (uncorrected for multiple comparisons). R, right; L, left; PT, Perceptual Task. (Table from Henke, Buck, Weber, and Wieser, 1997, by permission of Wiley & Sons, Inc.)

| Task | Brain area | Coordinates | Contrast | z-value |
|---|---|---|---|---|
| Associative Learning | L. anterior fusiform | −30,−34,−16 | AL-SIL | 4.97+ |
| | R. parahippocampal gyrus | 32,−16,−20 | AL-SIL | 4.62+ |
| | R. hippocampus | 30,−26,−12 | AL-SIL | 4.11 |
| | Anterior cingulate | −2,34,32 | AL-SIL | 4.14 |
| Single Item Learning | R. fusiform gyrus | 34,−42,−20 | SIL-PT | 5.20+ |
| | R. middle occipital | 38,−80,8 | SIL-PT | 4.90+ |
| | R. lingual gyrus | 20,−52,0 | SIL-PT | 4.85+ |
| | L. fusiform gyrus | −34,−42,−20 | SIL-PT | 4.41+ |
| | L. fusiform gyrus | −38,−48,−24 | SIL-PT | 4.35+ |
| | R. inferior parietal | 52,−32,28 | SIL-PT | −5.45+ |
| | R. superior temporal | 58,−32,20 | SIL-PT | −5.01+ |
| Retrieval Old | R. frontal cortex | 36,16,36 | RO-AL | 3.91 |
| | R. visual striatum | 30,−26,0 | RO-RN | 3.41 |
| | R. inferotemporal | 38,−42,0 | RO-RN | 3.40 |
| Retrieval New | R. thalamus | 4,−8,0 | RN-RO | 3.48 |
| | R. thalamus | 16,−22,4 | RN-RO | 3.29 |

of object identity and spatial location (Haxby et al., 1993, 1994; McIntosh et al., 1994; Moscovitch, Kapur, Köhler, & Houle, 1995; Martin et al., 1996; Stern et al., 1996). Thus, the Associative Learning and Single Item Learning tasks share some activations in the higher visual areas. Associative Learning, however, in addition activated the HF and parahippocampal gyrus. We attribute this hippocampal activation to the difference in associative learning between the two encoding tasks rather than to the mentioned difference in time spent on task (subjects took 300 ms longer per trial during Associative than Single Item Learning). If time spent on task were critical for hippocampal blood flow, we would also expect significantly increased hippocampal blood flow during Single Item Learning compared to the Perceptual Task, since time spent on task differed by 860 ms. This was, however, not the case. According to a third interpretation, the observed hippocampal activation reflects depth of processing rather than associative learning, since the Associative Learning task involves deeper encoding than the Single Item Learning task. We consider semantic encoding a necessary component of most single-trial associative learning tasks in humans, since associations between unrelated items are necessarily formed through stored knowledge (semantic memory), unless the associations are purely perceptual (nonsemantic), in which case the task is rather a hippocampus-independent perceptual priming task than a declarative task. Depth of processing and associative learning are thus confounded. Yet, Kapur et al. (1994) varied depth of encoding in a single item learning task and did not find hippocampal activation during deep as compared to shallow encoding. The associative task component seems necessary for a strong hippocampal activation. Therefore, we believe that the observed activations in the hippocampal region during Associative Learning as compared to Single Item Learning reflect associative processing. We conclude that the hippocampal system supports the establishment of meaningful associations between items (Cohen and Eichenbaum, 1993; Eichenbaum et al., 1994), while the higher visual areas subserve the formation of rather isolated visual memories.

Retrieval Old compared to Associative Learning indicates blood flow changes due to executive retrieval processes rather than changes due to the recovery of memory traces, since these are likely to be cancelled out in this comparison. This comparison did not leave significant blood flow residuals; the largest rCBF residual was located in the right frontal cortex. Activation of the right frontal cortex has been consistently observed during the retrieval of information from episodic memory (Tulving, Kapur, Markowitsch et al., 1994; Tulving, Kapur, Craik, Moscovitch, & Houle, 1994) and has been related to the retrieval attempt (Kapur, Craik et al., 1995) rather than the recovery of stored information. Activations due to the recovery of formed associations become apparent in the comparison of Retrieval Old with Retrieval New. This comparison did not result in any significant rCBF residuals either; the largest net blood flow increases were located in two areas: in the right visual striatum, i. e., between the tail of the caudate nucleus and the caudal/ventral portions of the putamen, and in the right inferotemporal cortex, on the border between the right fusiform and lingual gyrus. The inferotemporal cortex (IT) is known to mediate visual recognition. IT lesions in monkeys produce deficits in pattern discrimination or recognition (e. g., Mishkin, Ungerleider, & Macko, 1983) and recordings from single neurons in IT show activity related to the visual presentation of complex patterns, objects and faces (e. g., Schwartz, Desimone, Albright, & Gross, 1983). That the reactivation of associations 10 minutes after their formation did not lead to a recurrent activation in the HF and parahippocampal gyrus is rather unexpected, since bilateral damage to the HF usually abolishes recently formed memories. Yet, concordant evidence comes from another PET study (Haxby et al., 1996), where a region in the right HF and adjacent cortex was activated during encoding of faces, but not 16 minutes later during recognition of these same faces.

The comparison of Retrieval New to Retrieval Old reveals blood flow changes related to the detection of novel combinations of previously learned items. This comparison yielded no significant activations. There were two peaks of relatively increased blood flow in the right thalamus. The thalamus has been activated in previous PET studies of novelty detection (Tulving, Markowitsch et al., 1994; Tulving et al., 1996). However, unlike the findings of other studies of the detection of novel single items (Tulving, Markowitsch et al., 1994; Tulving et al., 1996; Martin et al., 1996; Knight, 1996), the right hippocampal region was (significantly) activated neither during the Single Item Learning task, which included the presentation of novel single pictures, nor during the detection of novel combinations of studied items. Instead, the HF was exclusively activated during the establishment of associations between items. The additional comparison of the memory tasks to the Perceptual Task and to a baseline scan confirmed these results. Therefore, the lack of hippocampal activation during the retrieval of old combinations and during the detection of novel combinations is not likely to be a consequence of medial temporal activations in the comparison tasks.

These results support Cohen and Eichenbaum's (1993) theory which is based on animal learning experiments and indicate its validity for encoding in the human brain. Our data predict that human amnesics with bilateral hippocampal damage would be more impaired on tests of associative memory than tests of single item memory. Indeed, it was recently reported that patients with damage to the HF (, N.E.A.VKroll, Knight, Metcalfe, Wolf, & Tulving, 1996) suffered from a selective impairment in binding the constituent parts of individual stimuli in memory. The patients retained some ability to remember studied stimulus parts, but not the combinations of parts.

In light of our results we conducted a review of functional imaging studies of episodic memory. We found that hippocampal and/or parahippocampal activations were typically reported when stimuli were unfamiliar (never seen before the experiment) rather than familiar (e. g., words), when they were complex, multi-facetted and nonverbal (e. g., Kapur, Friston et al., 1995; Haxby et al., 1996; Maguire, Frackowiak, & Frith, 1996; Stern et al., 1996; Gabrieli et al., 1997). The reason for this selectivity might be that the memorization of such stimuli requires the establishment of many associations among the subcomponents of the stimuli. Most experiments using verbal stimuli failed to demonstrate hippocampal activations (Grasby et al., 1994; Kapur et al., 1994; Shallice et al., 1994; Tulving, Kapur, Markowitsch et al., 1994; Andreasen et al., 1995; Fletcher et al., 1995). Although learning a list of words for later retrieval also requires some associative learning, e. g., linking the presentation of a word to the place and time of the learning event, the demand for associative learning is not as high as for more complex material. Schacter et al. (1996), however, reported right hippocampal activation during the recall of words. Since these words were encoded by counting the number of meanings associated with each word – a task that binds the presented word to various stored concepts – the hippocampal activation during retrieval might reflect the recovery of previously formed associations. Similarly, Rugg et al. (1997) found left hippocampal activation during the retrieval of words which had been encoded by producing a sentence which includes that word. Like Schacter et al.'s encoding task, this encoding task also binds the presented word into the self-created context of the sentence. At the time of retrieval, the presented old word might reactivate the formed associations, i. e., the sentence. Interestingly, these two studies report hippocampal activations during the *retrieval* of previously formed associations, while we could not identify significant hippocampal activation with retrieval of studied house-person combinations in our study. Dolan and Fletcher (1997) reported left hippocampal and parahippocampal activation during an associative learning task with "contextually new" word pairs. These are word pairs that have not been studied during two preceding runs of paired-associates learning. They found less left hippocampal activation if one word of each pair had been studied during the two preceding study runs, and even less hippocampal activation if the presented word pairs had been studied twice already. The authors interpret the left hippocampal activation during the study of new (= not yet learned) word pairs as a correlate of novelty detection: The newer the learning material (with reference to the two previously given study lists), the more hippocampal activation was present. An alternative interpretation which the authors do not mention, is that hippocampal activation increased as a function of associative learning: Previously learned word pairs need less associative learning than new word pairs. Their experiment demonstrates that the left hippocampal region can be activated using a verbal associative learning task. Thus, the hippocampal and parahippocampal activations found in other functional imaging studies of memory can also be interpreted as correlates of establishing (or retrieving) associations.


## Conclusions

The HF does not have the prominent role in learning and memory that was ascribed to it following the reports of Scoville and Milner (1957) and Penfield and Milner (1958). The HF is merely one amongst several medial temporal lobe structures which support memory, and it does not subserve all kinds of declarative memory functions equally.

The other medial temporal lobe structures such as the entorhinal, perirhinal, and parahippocampal cortices are also important for learning and memory. Their function in memory cannot only be explained by their position as input or output channels of the hippocampal formation, but they seem to have their independent contributions to declarative memory storage and retrieval. Each of these structures might have its individual functional specialization within declarative memory.

The episodic and semantic components of declarative memory seem to be dissociable, with the episodic component being more dependent on the hippocampal formation than the semantic component. There is evidence that the HF is part of a network supporting the screening of incoming information for its novelty value – a process which precedes encoding. At encoding, the HF might be particularly engaged in forming associations between previously unrelated items and in encoding spatial relations. At retrieval, the HF helps recover the formed associations between recently stored items.

## Acknowledgment

This research was supported by a scholarship (8210–040202) from the Swiss National Science Foundation (SNF) to the author and by SNF grant 31–47'203.96.

## References

Alvarez, P., & Squire, L.R. (1994). Memory consolidation and the medial temporal lobe: A simple network model. *Proceedings of the National Academy of Sciences USA, 91*, 7041–7045.

Andreasen, N.C., O'Leary, D.S., Arndt, S., Cizadlo, T., Hurtig, R., Rezai, K., Watkins, G.L., Boles Ponto, L.L., & Hichwa, R.D. (1995). Short-term and long-term verbal memory: A positron emission tomography study. *Proceedings of the National Academy of Sciences USA, 92*, 5111–5115.

Backer Cave, C., & Squire, L.R. (1991). Equivalent impairment of spatial and nonspatial memory following damage to the human hippocampus. *Hippocampus, 1*, 329–340.

Bechterew, W. von (1900). Demonstration eines Gehirns mit Zerstörung der vorderen und inneren Theile der Hirnrinde beider Schläfenlappen. *Neurologisches Zentralblatt, 19*, 990–991.

Cohen, N.J., & Eichenbaum, H. (1993). *Memory, amnesia, and the hippocampal system.* Cambridge, MA: MIT Press.

Dolan, R.J., & Fletcher, P.C. (1997). Dissociating prefrontal and hippocampal function in episodic memory encoding. *Nature, 388*, 582–585.

Eichenbaum, H. (1997). How does the brain organize memories? *Science, 277*, 330–332.

Eichenbaum, H., Otto, T., & Cohen, N.J. (1994). Two functional components of the hippocampal memory system. *Behavioral and Brain Sciences, 17*, 449–518.

Fahy, F.L., Riches, I.P., & Brown, M.W. (1993). Neuronal activity related to visual recognition memory: Long-term memory and encoding of recency and familiarity information in the primate anterior and medial inferior temporal and rhinal cortex. *Experimental Brain Research, 96*, 457–472.

Fletcher, P.C., Frith, C.D., Grasby, P.M., Shallice, T., Frackowiak, R.S.J., & Dolan, R.J.

(1995). Brain systems for encoding and retrieval of auditory-verbal memory. An in vivo study in humans. *Brain, 118,* 401–416.

Frackowiak, R.S.J., & Friston, K.J. (1994). Functional neuroanatomy of the human brain: Positron emission tomography – a new neuroanatomical technique. *Journal of Anatomy, 184,* 211–225.

Gabrieli, J.D.E., Brewer, J.B., Desmond, J.E., & Glover, G.H. (1997). Separate neural bases of two fundamental memory processes in the human medial temporal lobe. *Science, 276,* 264–266.

Gaffan, D., & Murray, E.A. (1992). Monkeys *(Macaca fascicularis)* with rhinal cortex ablations succeed in object discrimination learning despite 24-hr intertrial intervals and fail at matching to sample despite double sample presentations. *Behavioral Neuroscience, 106,* 30–38.

Glees, P., & Griffith, H.B. (1952). Bilateral destruction of the hippocampus *(cornu ammonis)* in a case of dementia. *Monatsschrift für Psychiatrie und Neurologie, 123,* 193–204.

Gol, A., & Fabisch, G.M. (1967). Effects of human hippocampal ablation. *Journal of Neurosurgery, 26,* 390–398.

Grasby, P.M., Frith, C.D., Friston, K.J., Simpson, J., Fletcher, P.C., Frackowiak, R.S.J., & Dolan, R.J. (1994). A graded task approach to the functional mapping of brain areas implicated in auditory-verbal memory. *Brain, 117,* 1271–1282.

Grünthal, E., & Störring, G.E. (1930). Über das Verhalten bei umschriebener, völliger Merkunfähigkeit. *Monatszeitschrift für Psychiatrie und Neurologie, 74,* 354–369.

Grünthal, E., & Störring, G.E. (1933). Ergänzende Beobachtungen und Bemerkungen zu dem in Band 74 (1930) dieser Zeitschrift beschriebenen Fall mit reiner Merkunfähigkeit. *Monatszeitschrift für Psychiatrie und Neurologie, 77,* 374–382.

Hajek, M., Khan, N., Leenders, K.L., & Wieser, H.G. (1995). Temporal lobe epilepsy with bilateral seizure origin studied by [18F]FDG-positron emission tomography. *European Journal of Neurology, 2,* 211–217.

Halgren, E., & Marinkovic, K. (1995). Neurophysiological networks integrating human emotions. In M.S. Gazzaniga (Ed.), *The cognitive neurosciences* (pp. 1137–1151). Cambridge, MA: MIT Press.

Haxby, J.V., Horwitz, B., Maisog, J.M., Ungerleider, L.G., Mishkin, M., Schapiro, M.B., Rapoport, S.I., & Grady, C.L. (1993). Frontal and temporal participation in long-term recognition memory for faces: A PET-rCBF activation study. *Journal of Cerebral Blood Flow and Metabolism, 13* (Suppl. 1), 499.

Haxby, J.V., Horwitz, B., Ungerleider, L.G., Maisog, J.M., Pietrini, P., & Grady, C.L. (1994). The functional organization of human extrastriate cortex: A PET-rCBF study of selective attention to faces and locations. *Journal of Neuroscience, 14,* 6336–6353.

Haxby, J.V., Ungerleider, L.G., Horwitz, B., Maisog, J.M., Rapoport, S.I., & Grady, C.L. (1996). Face encoding and recognition in the human brain. *Proceedings of the National Academy of Sciences USA, 93,* 922–927.

Henke, K., & Wieser, H.G. (1996). Bilateral medial temporal lobe damage without amnesic syndrome: A case report. *Epilepsy Research, 24,* 147–161.

Henke, K., Buck, A., Weber, B., & Wieser, H.G. (1997). Human hippocampus establishes associations in memory. *Hippocampus, 7,* 249–256.

Henke, K., Kroll, N.E.A., Behniea, H., Amaral, D.G., Miller, M.B., Rafal, R., & Gazzaniga, M.S. (1999). Memory lost and regained following bilateral hippocampal damage. *Journal of Cognitive Neuroscience.* In press.

Horel, J.A. (1978). The neuroanatomy of amnesia. A critique of the hippocampal memory hypothesis. *Brain, 101,* 403–445.

Jones-Gotman, M., Zatorre, R.J., Olivier, A., Andermann, F., Cendes, F., Staunton, H., McMackin, D., Siegel, A.M., & Wieser, H.G. (1997). Learning and retention of words and designs following excision from medial or lateral temporal-lobe structures. *Neuropsychologia, 35,* 963–973.

Kapur, N., Friston, K.J., Young, A., Frith, C.D., & Frackowiak, R.S.J. (1995). Activation of human hippocampal formation during memory for faces: A PET study. *Cortex, 31,* 99–108.

Kapur, S., Craik, F.I.M., Tulving, E., Wilson, A.A., Houle, S., & Brown, G.W. (1994). Neuroanatomical correlates of encoding in episodic memory: Levels of processing effect. *Proceedings of the National Academy of Sciences USA, 91,* 2008–2011.

Kapur, S., Craik, F.I.M., Jones, C., Brown, G.M., Houle, S., & Tulving, E. (1995). Functional role of the prefrontal cortex in retrieval of memories: A PET study. *NeuroReport, 6,* 1880–1884.

Kartsounis, L.D., Rudge, P., & Stevens, J.M. (1995). Bilateral lesions of CA1 and CA2 fields of the hippocampus are sufficient to cause a severe amnesic syndrome in humans. *Journal of Neurology, Neurosurgery, and Psychiatry, 59,* 95–98.

Knight, R.T. (1996). Contribution of human hippocampal region to novelty detection. *Nature, 383,* 256–259.

Kohnstamm, O. (1917). Über das Krankheitsbild der retro-graden Amnesie und die Unterscheidung des spontanen und des lernenden Merkens. *Monatszeitschrift für Psychiatrie und Neurologie, 41,* 373–382.

Kroll, N.E.A., Knight, R.T., Metcalfe, J., Wolf, E.S., & Tulving, E. (1996). Cohesion failure as a source of memory illusions. *Journal of Memory and Language, 35,* 176–196.

Loring, D.W., Lee, G.P., Meador, K.J., Smith, J.R., Martin, R.C., Ackell, A.B., & Flanigin, H.F. (1991). Hippocampal contribution to verbal recent memory following dominant-hemisphere temporal lobectomy. *Journal of Clinical and Experimental Neuropsychology, 13,* 575–586.

Maguire, E.A., Frackowiak, R.S.J., & Frith, C.D. (1996). Learning to find your way: A role for the human hippocampal formation. *Proceedings of the Royal Society of London B, 263,* 1745–1750.

Martin, A., Wiggs, C.L., Ungerleider, L.G., & Haxby, J.V. (1996). Neuronal correlates of category-specific knowledge. *Nature, 379,* 649–652.

McIntosh, A.R., Grady, C.L., Ungerleider, L.G., Haxby J.V., Rapoport, S.I., & Horwitz, B. (1994). Network analysis of cortical visual pathways mapped with PET. *Journal of Neuroscience, 14,* 655–666.

Meunier, M., Bachevalier, J., Mishkin, M., & Murray, E.A. (1993). Effects on visual recognition of combined and separate ablations of the entorhinal and perirhinal cortex in rhesus monkeys. *Journal of Neuroscience, 13,* 5418–5432.

Mishkin, M. (1978). Memory in monkeys severely impaired by combined but not by separate removal of amygdala and hippocampus. *Nature, 273,* 297–298.

Mishkin, M., Ungerleider, L.G., & Macko, K.A. (1983). Object vision: Two cortical pathways. *Trends in Neuroscience, 6,* 414–417.

Moscovitch, M., Kapur, S., Köhler, S., & Houle, S. (1995). Distinct neural correlates of visual long-term memory for spatial location and object identity: A positron emission tomography study in humans. *Proceedings of the National Academy of Sciences USA, 92,* 3721–3725.

Murray, E.A. (1996). What have ablation studies told us about the neural substrates of stimulus memory? *Seminars in the Neurosciences, 8,* 13–22.

Nyberg, L., McIntosh, A.R., Cabeza, R., Habib, R., Houle, S., & Tulving, E. (1996). General and specific brain regions involved in encoding and retrieval of events: What, where, and when. *Proceedings of the National Academy of Sciences USA, 93,* 11280–11285.

O'Keefe, J., & Dostrovsky, J. (1971). The hippocampus as a spatial map. Preliminary evidence from unit activity in the freely-moving rat. *Brain Research, 34,* 171–175.

O'Keefe, J., & Nadel, L. (1978). *The hippocampus as a cognitive map.* Oxford: Oxford University Press.

Owen, A.M., Milner, B., Petrides, M., & Evans, A.C. (1996). Memory for object features versus memory for object location – a positron-emission tomography study of encoding and retrieval processes. *Proceedings of the National Academy of Sciences USA, 93,* 9212–9217.

Penfield, W., & Milner, B. (1958). Memory deficit produced by bilateral lesions in the hippocampal zone. *Archives of Neurology and Psychiatry, 79,* 475–497.

Rempel-Clower, N.L., Zola, S.M., Squire, L.R., & Amaral, D.G. (1996). Three cases of enduring memory impairment after bilateral damage limited to the hippocampal formation. *Journal of Neuroscience, 16,* 5233–5255.

Rolls, E.T., Cahusac, P.M.B., Feigenbaum, J.D., & Miyashita, Y. (1993). Responses of single neurons in the hippocampus of the macaque related to recognition memory. *Experimental Brain Research, 93,* 299–306.

Rosene, D.L., & Van Hoesen, G.W. (1987). The hippocampal formation of the primate brain: A review of some comparative aspects of cytoarchitecture and connections. In E.G. Jones & A. Peters (Eds.), *Cerebral cortex, Vol. 6: Further aspects of cortical function, including hippocampus* (chapter 9, pp. 345–456). New York: Plenum.

Rugg, M.D., Fletcher, P.C., Frith, C.D., Frackowiak, R.S.J., & Dolan, R.J. (1997). Brain regions supporting intentional and incidental memory: A PET study. *NeuroReport, 8,* 1283–1287.

Schacter, D.L., Alpert, N.M., Savage, C.R., Rauch, S.L., & Albert, M.S. (1996). Conscious recollection and the human hippocampal formation: Evidence from positron emission tomography. *Proceedings of the National Academy of Sciences USA, 93,* 321–325.

Schwartz, E.L., Desimone, R., Albright, T.D., & Gross, C.G. (1983). Shape recognition and inferior temporal neurons. *Proceedings of the National Academy of Sciences USA, 80,* 5776–5778.

Scoville, W., & Milner, B. (1957). Loss of recent memory after bilateral hippocampal lesions. *Journal of Neurology, Neurosurgery, and Psychiatry, 20,* 11–21.

Shallice, T., Fletcher, P.C., Frith, C.D., Grasby, P.M., Frackowiak, R.S.J., & Dolan, R.J. (1994). Brain regions associated with acquisition and retrieval of verbal episodic memory. *Nature, 368,* 633–635.

Squire, L.R. (1992). Memory and the hippocampus: A synthesis from findings with rats, monkeys, and humans. *Psychological Review, 99,* 195–231.

Squire, L.R., & Alvarez, P. (1995). Retrograde amnesia and memory consolidation: A neurobiological perspective. *Current Opinion in Neurobiology, 5,* 169–177.

Squire, L.R., & Zola-Morgan, S.M. (1991). The medial temporal lobe memory system. *Science, 253,* 1380–1386.

Stern, C.E., Corkin, S., Gonzalez, R.G., Guimaraes, A.R., Baker, J.R., Jennings, P.J., Carr, C.A., Sugiura, R.M., Vedantham, V., & Rosen, B.R. (1996). The hippocampal formation participates in novel picture encoding: Evidence from functional magnetic resonance imaging. *Proceedings of the National Academy of Sciences USA, 93,* 8660–8665.

Suzuki, W.A., Zola-Morgan, S., Squire, L.R., & Amaral, D.G. (1993). Lesions of the perirhinal and parahippocampal cortices in the monkey produce long-lasting memory impairment in the visual and tactual modalities. *Journal of Neuroscience, 13,* 2430–2451.

Tulving, E. (1972). Episodic and semantic memory. In E. Tulving & W. Donaldson (Eds.), *Organization of memory* (pp. 381–403). New York: Academic Press.

Tulving, E., Kapur, S., Markowitsch, H.J., Craik, F.I.M., Habib, R., & Houle, S. (1994). Neuroanatomical correlates of retrieval in episodic memory: Auditory sentence recognition. *Proceedings of the National Academy of Sciences USA, 91,* 2012–2015.

Tulving, E., Markowitsch, H.J., Kapur, S., Habib, R., & Houle, S. (1994). Novelty encoding networks in the human brain: Positron emission tomography data. *NeuroReport, 5,* 2525–2528.

Tulving, E., Kapur, S., Craik, F.I.M., Moscovitch, M., & Houle, S. (1994). Hemispheric encoding/retrieval asymmetry in episodic memory: Positron emission tomography findings. *Proceedings of the National Academy of Sciences USA, 91,* 2016–2020.

Tulving, E., Markowitsch, H.J., Craik, F.I.M., Habib, R., & Houle, S. (1996). Novelty and familiarity activations in PET studies of memory encoding and retrieval. *Cerebral Cortex, 6,* 71–79.

Uchimura, J. (1928). Zur Pathogenese der örtlich elektiven Ammonshornerkrankung. *Zeitschrift für Neurologie und Psychiatrie, 114,* 567–601.

Vargha-Khadem, F., Gadian, D.G., Watkins, K.E., Connelly, A., Van Paesschen, W., & Mishkin, M. (1997). Differential effects of early hippocampal pathology on episodic and semantic memory. *Science, 277,* 376–380.

Wieser, H.G., & Yasargil, M.G. (1982). Selective amygdalohippocampectomy as a surgical treatment of mesiobasal limbic epilepsy. *Surgical Neurology, 17,* 445–457.

Wieser, H.G., Valavanis, A., Roos, A., Isler, P., & Renella, R.R. (1989). "Selective" and "superselective" temporal lobe Amytal tests: I. Neuroradiological, neuroanatomical, and electrical data. In J. Manelis, E. Bental, J.N. Loeber, & F.E. Dreifus (Eds.), *Advances in epileptology* (vol. 17, pp. 20–27). New York: Raven Press.

Wieser, H.G., Landis, T., Regard, M., & Schiess, R. (1989). "Selective" and "superselective" temporal lobe Amytal tests: II. Neuropsychological test procedure and results. In J. Manelis, E. Bental, J.N. Loeber, & F.E. Dreifus (Eds.), *Advances in epileptology* (vol. 17, pp. 28–33). New York: Raven Press.

Zola-Morgan, S.M., & Squire, L.R. (1990). The primate hippocampal formation: Evidence for a time-limited role in memory storage. *Science, 250,* 288–290.

Zola-Morgan, S., Squire, L.R., & Amaral, D.G. (1986). Human amnesia and the medial temporal region: Enduring memory impairment following a bilateral lesion limited to field CA1 of the hippocampus. *Journal of Neuroscience, 6,* 2950–2967.

Zola-Morgan, S., Squire, L.R., Amaral, D.G., & Suzuki, W.A. (1989). Lesions of perirhinal and parahippocampal cortex that spare the amygdala and hippocampal formation produce severe memory impairment. *Journal of Neuroscience, 9,* 4355–4370.

Zola-Morgan, S., Squire, L.R., & Mishkin, M. (1982). The neuroanatomy of amnesia: Amygdala-hippocampus versus temporal stem. *Science, 218,* 1337–1339.

# Cross-Level Unification: A Computational Exploration of the Link Between Deterioration of Neurotransmitter Systems and Dedifferentiation of Cognitive Abilities in Old Age

*Shu-Chen Li and Ulman Lindenberger*

## Introduction

In the last few decades, much research progress has been made in neuroscience and in many subfields of psychology such as cognition and development. Alas, while empirical data and theories have been accumulating within each of these disciplines rapidly, overarching theoretical orientations which aim at integrating subsets of these fields are scarce, the importance of cross-domain or cross-level unification as revealed in the history of science notwithstanding. Take psychology as a particular example of disunity either in terms of methodologies, domains of research, or levels of analysis: Not only is there a lack of integration, to the contrary, strong bifurcations exist between the experimental and psychometric traditions (Cronbach, 1957, 1975), between the studies of child development and adult development/aging (Baltes, Staudinger, & Lindenberger, in press), and between the behavioral and biological studies of cognition (Churchland & Sejnowski, 1988). Segregation, either within a given discipline or between disciplines, is not optimal. According to Leibniz (1690/1951, p. 73), who thought that scientific inquiry can be viewed as "an ocean that is continuous everywhere without a break or division" (cf. Gigerenzer, 1991), interdisciplinary exchange and integration are not only desirable but also necessary for science to progress.

### Unification via Interdisciplinary Coevolution: The Example of Cognitive Neuroscience

Although it has not been stressed until recently, a positive change towards a zeitgeist of interdisciplinary integration among subfields of psychology and neuroscience is slowly emerging. Many philosophers of science, neuroscientists and psychologists now assert that unification of theories and findings at different levels and in different domains is a *process* within which the *coevolution* of theories in related fields can take place by ways of cross-level hypothesis generation and testing (e. g., Baltes et al., in press; Bechtel, 1988; Churchland, 1988; Churchland & Sejnowski, 1988; Llinas & Churchland, 1996; Newell, 1990; Plude, Enns, & Brodeur, 1994; Posner, 1992; Royce, 1987; Schacter, 1992; Schneider, 1993; Shepard, 1987; Staats, 1991).

In the last decade of the 20th century, an example of a fruitful convergence of research from formerly isolated fields is the emergence of cognitive neuroscience. With the goal of uniting computational cognitive science, experimental cognitive psychology and neuroscience, researchers endorsing the cognitive neuroscience orientation have been working towards bridging the gap between the descriptions of information processing and the specifications of brain functioning. Indeed, the various studies reported in this volume exemplify some attempts at more integrated views of memory functioning by drawing together data and theories from different levels.

Given that the agenda of cognitive neuroscience is to unify empirical regularities *and* theories of cognition at the behavioral, information processing, and biological levels, the research strategy has been to simultaneously collect, via neural imaging techniques, experimental data concerning both behavioral manifestations and neuronal properties of cognitive systems. In addition to such experimental endeavors, theoretical efforts have also been devoted to the construction of two types of neural models serving different but complementary purposes: (a) specific models which aim at capturing the dynamics and anatomy of particular neural circuitry (e. g., Houk, Davis, & Beiser, 1995; Berns & Sejnowski, 1998), and (b) general models which try to capture global principles of neural information processing, such as signal coding, transmission, and storage, that might overall apply in many different cortical networks (cf. Churchland & Sejnowski, 1988; e. g., McClelland, McNaughton, & O'Reilly, 1995; Servan-Schreiber, Printz, & Cohen, 1990).

## Research Goal and Organization

The computational investigations described in this chapter belong to the class of general models. Specifically, we explore, via connectionist simulations, a potential theoretical path from the deterioration of neural information processing to the dedifferentiation of cognitive abilities that is empirically observed in old people. To investigate this theoretical link, we looked at two sets of mechanisms. The first set concerns the effect of neurotransmitters, in particularly catecholamines, on the signal-to-noise ratio of neural transmission and the subsequent effect on the level of random variability within the central nervous system (CNS). The second set has to do with the relations between these biological processes and age-related increase in intraindividual and interindividual variability and the concomitant dedifferentiation of ability structure in old age.

The organization of this chapter is as follows: We first describe experimental results regarding age-related dedifferentiation in old people's ability profiles and age-related increase in interindividual and intraindividual variability. A few general conceptual accounts for these empirical findings will be presented, along with a short description of an attempt to formally integrate these two sets of findings and explanations at a purely descriptive level. We then present empirical findings on aging-induced deterioration of neurotransmitter systems (Morrison & Hof, 1997) and the increase in CNS variability at the biological level. In trying to bridge the gap between the empirical phenomena observed at these two levels, we propose a computational approach which varies the responsivity of the processing units and the internal variability of connectionist networks by manipulating the gain parameter of the sigmoid activation function. Specifically, the aging-induced depletion of catecholamines (Gabrieli, 1995) is simulated by reducing the value of the gain parameter. After describing the foundations upon which our computational model is based, we then report two sets of simulations, each involving three groups of networks that *differ only* in the means of the uniform distributions from which values of gain parameters were sampled. Then, we examine the effect of this gain parameter manipulation on the intercorrelations between the networks' performances in two task domains (i. e., episodic memory and categorization learning). At the end, we discuss limitations of the present formalization and its implications for the study of lifespan cognitive development.

## Dedifferentiation of Ability Structure, Variability, and Some Conceptual Accounts

In this section, we review two separate sets of empirical findings at the behavioral level that are taken from cognitive aging research and psychometric studies of intelligence. To our knowledge, these two sets of findings have been rarely reviewed together, implying that they are formerly thought to be independent. The first set of findings concerns the tendency towards dedifferentiation of intellectual abilities from early adulthood to old age. The second set of results pertains to age-related increase in both interindividual and intraindividual variability in old age. General explanations previously proposed to account for these findings are also discussed.

## Dedifferentiation of Ability Structure

At the behavioral level, one of the most replicable and important psychometric findings about mental abilities is the positive manifold (i. e., patterns of positive correlations) between tests of different cognitive abilities. As early as the turn of this century, Spearman (1904) identified a factor of general intelligence *(g)* to indicate the degree of the positive manifold. Patterns of positive manifold, as represented in factor analytical models, are usually taken as descriptive indicators for the organizations of the mental abilities measured by intelligence tests. Given that a central issue in developmental and especially lifespan research concerns changes in the organization of behaviors, the notion that development may modulate the degree of differentiation or lack of differentiation (i. e., dedifferentiation) among mental abilities has been of great interest to researchers of intelligence and its development (e. g., Burt, 1954; Garrett, 1946; Reinert, 1970; Spearman, 1927). To date, results from cross-sectional psychometric studies of intelligence show a general trend from a lack of differentiation to differentiation to dedifferentiation across the lifespan, as the ontogeny of cognition proceeds, respectively, from childhood to adulthood and finally into old age. Empirical findings regarding the differentiation of cognitive abilities in child development will be discussed later. Here we first focus on data pertaining to cognitive aging. Empirical evidence for age-related dedifferentiation of cognitive abilities has been found both with respect to intercorrelations among tasks that are within the same domain of functioning (i. e., intrasystemic relations) and across different domains of functioning (i. e., intersystemic relations).

### Dedifferentiation of Intrasystemic Relations in Psychometric Studies

As people age, the statistical structural patterns involving different types of mental abilities become less differentiable. For instance, using Wechsler's normative data, Balinsky (1941) found that differentiation increased from early adolescence to adulthood and then reversed in later adulthood. Similarly, Lienert and Crott (1964) tested adolescents (age 10–12 years), young adults (age 18–20 years), and older adults (age 45–60 years) on 14 ability tests, and found that the percentage of variance in the first centroid factor was 45, 41 and 47. Baltes, Cornelius, Spiro, Nesselroade and Willis (1980) found that the factor structure of fluid and crystallized intelligence was less differentiable in old people (60 to 89 years old). Likewise, Hayslip and Sterns (1979) found that intercorrelations among tests of fluid and crystallized intelligence were higher for older than for younger adults. Cunningham (1980) compared the ability structures of several adult age groups, and found that although similar factor loading patterns could be obtained for adults of increasing age, there was an age-related increase in the magnitude of factor covariance. Besides the results from cross-sectional studies, in a longitudinal study, McHugh and Owens (1954) found that the first unrotated principal component accounted for 53% of the variance in the Army Alpha Test when the participants were at the age of 19, and increased to 63.4% when the participants reached the age of 50. In addition to these earlier findings, two very recent studies provide new support for age-related dedifferentiation in intrasystemic relationships. For instance, Baltes and Lindenberger (1997) found that the strengths of intercorrelations between five intellectual abilities were stronger (median $r = 0.71$ vs. median $r = 0.37$) for old people (age 70–103 years) than for young people (age 25–69 years). Babcock, Laguna, and Roesch (1997) examined the factor structure of processing speed (involving a total of nine speed measures) in young (age 18–24 years) and old (age 55–80 years) people. Their results showed that although the number of factors and factor loadings were invariant across the two age groups, the interfactor correlations, the variance-covariance matrices, and the unique variances differed between the groups, all indicating a greater degree of dedifferentiation in the old group.

## Dedifferentiation of Intersystemic Relations in Cognitive Aging Research

Besides the age-related strengthening of intrasystemic relationships that is evident in psychometric studies, recent cognitive aging research has also identified an intersystemic relationship between cognitive and simple sensory and sensorimotor functioning. For instance, Granick, Kleban, and Weiss (1976) reported high correlations between auditory threshold at various frequencies and scores of the verbal ($r = 0.44$) and digit symbol ($r = 0.36$) subtests of the Wechsler's Intelligence Scale. Baltes and Lindenberger (1997) and Lindenberger and Baltes (1994) found that the relationship between the performance measures of sensory (i. e., auditory and visual acuity) and sensorimotor (i. e., balance and gait) functioning and those of cognitive functioning (including tests of processing speed, memory, reasoning, practical knowledge and verbal fluency) was of such magnitude that, for the age range from 70 to 100 years, practically all age differences (91%) in cognitive functioning, which corresponds to about 40% of the total interindividual differences in cognitive functioning, were associated with and therefore can be predicted by relatively simple sensory and sensorimotor measures. Likewise, Salthouse, Hancock, Meinz, and Hambrick (1996) showed that, for the age range from 18 to 92 years, visual acuity shared a very large proportion of age-related interindividual differences in measures of working memory, associative learning, and concept identification.

Indications of Dedifferentiation in Neural Information Processing

In addition to the findings of age-related dedifferentiation of old people's ability structure at the behavioral level, recent results from studies of brain imaging also gave initial indications of a parallel trend at the biological level. For instance, Grady and colleagues (Grady et al., 1992, 1994) examined aging-induced changes in object and spatial visual processing at the level of regional cerebral blood flow (rCBF). Their results demonstrated that during object matching, old people showed more activation than young people in the right prefrontal cortex; and during location matching, old people showed more rCBF activation than young people in several areas of prefrontal cortex (i. e., in bilateral inferior parietal cortex and left medial parietal cortex). Based on these results, Grady et al. (1994) suggested that during visual processing the neural circuitry in the occipital visual area is more efficiently used in young people; whereas in old people there is more reliance on other additional cortical networks (in particularly for spatial vision), indicating a stronger degree of interdependence among different processes at the cortical level. Animal models of aging also provide evidence in support of a tendency of age-related functional dedifferentiation at the cortical level. For instance, it was found that the receptive fields of the hind-paw representations in sensorimotor cortex and the cortical areas excited by tactile point-stimulation to be large and highly overlapping in old rates, but relatively small and focused in young rates (Spengler, Godde, & Dinse, 1995).

In summary, the phenomenon of increasing interdependence among different functions and processes in old age is relatively ubiquitous. At the behavioral level, empirical evidence has been found both with respect to intrasystemic and intersystemic relationships; and with different types of performance measures, ranging from standardized intelligence tests and elementary experimental cognitive tasks of memory and processing speed to sensory acuity. At the biological level, empirical supports came both from neural imaging studies on the dynamics of brain metabolism in humans and from animal models of brain aging.

## *Age-Related Increase in Variability*

We now turn to describe the phenomena of age-related increase in both interindividual and intraindividual variability. Although the idea of relating cognitive aging deficits to aging-induced increase in neural noise was first introduced in about four decades ago (e. g., Crossman & Szafran, 1956; Welford, 1965), most studies of cognitive aging, however, focus only on measures of central tendency. Issues on age-related increase in dispersion (i. e., intraindividual variability) or diversity (i. e., interindividual variability) and the relationship between these two types of variability, on the other hand, have not been emphasized in gerontological research (cf. Nesselroade, 1991a,b). Nevertheless, meta-analyses based on longitudinal and cross-sectional studies which reported measures of variability indicated an age-related increase in variability.

Interindividual Variability

For instance, with respect to cognitive variables, (i. e., memory and other measures of intelligence) 79% of the studies (6 longitudinal and 48 cross-sectional) reviewed by Nelson and Dannefer (1992) reported an increase of variability with age. Similarly, results from Morse's (1993) meta-analysis (only cross-sectional studies were included) showed that interindividual variability in measures of response time (RT), memory, and fluid intelligence increased with age. Hale, Myerson, Smith, and Poon (1988) examined the question exclusively with respect to RT, and found age-related increase in interindividual variability. In addition to these meta-analytical studies, other experimental studies also showed that interindividual variability in episodic memory, measures of fluid intelligence (Christensen, Mackinnon, Jorm, Henderson, Scott, & Korten, 1994), and digit memory span (Rabbitt, 1993) increased with age.

Intraindividual Variability

Besides age-related increase in interindividual variability, there is also evidence for age-related increase in *intra*individual variability. For instance, intertrial variability in RT was also found to increase with age (e. g., Fozard, Thomas, & Waugh, 1976; Salthouse, 1993). In addition to results regarding intraindividual variability of response latency, Li, Aggen, Nesselroade, and Baltes (1998) measured memory and sensorimotor performances in a small sample of community-dwelling elderly (age 64–86 years) in 13 biweekly measurement occasions that spanned across six months. Their results showed a trend in the direction of a positive correlations between age and the magnitude of intraindividual variability in memory ($r = 0.46, p < 0.05$, n = 19) and sensorimotor ($r = 0.20, p = 0.4$, n = 19) performance.

Indications of Increased CNS Variability

In addition to the aforementioned empirical evidence of age-related increase in intraindividual and interindividual variability in RT and other performance measures at the behavioral level, neurobiological studies have also shown indications of a trend of increased CNS variability. For instance, Kraiuhin, Gordon, Stanfield, and Meares (1986) examined the relationship between age and auditory P300 latency (a component of event related potentials) via a tone discrimination task in normal adults (age 15 to 89 years). In addition to a significant relationship between age and P300 latency, their results also showed significantly more latency variability in the subsample of older adults (i. e., adults over 45 years). Kugler, Taghavy, and Platt's (1993) review of studies involving the P300 potential analysis of cognitive human brain aging also indicated a trend of age-related increase in P300 variability.

In brief, although the issue of age changes in interindividual and intraindividual variability has been somewhat ignored in gerontological research, the available empirical evidence seems to suggest a trend of age-related increase in both types of variability. Data supporting this tendency have been found both at the behavioral and biological levels.

## Conceptual Explanations of Dedifferentiation and Increased Variability

A few explanations for the two sets of empirical phenomena reviewed above have been suggested at the conceptual level. In this section, we present some of these general accounts. Controversies associated with some of these explanations are also discussed.

### Common-Cause Hypothesis and Dedifferentiation

Regarding the phenomenon of age-related dedifferentiation of ability structure, one explanation, known as the common-cause hypothesis (Baltes & Lindenberger, 1997; Lindenberger & Baltes, 1994; Lindenberger, Marsiske, & Baltes, 1998), proposes that normal aging is associated with a general loss of cognitive capacity and plasticity that is in turn caused by aging-induced deterioration of general neurobiological mechanisms which compromise the integrity of the brain across a wide range of areas and functional circuitry. Mechanisms and processes of brain aging are then postulated to constrict the functional cerebral space (Kinsbourne & Hicks, 1978), which could manifest at the behavioral level as the dedifferentiation of ability structure.

### Some Controversies Regarding the Explanations of Increased Behavioral-Level Variability

With respect to the phenomenon of increased variability in old age, some researches have proposed that age-related increase in *inter*individual differences might be associated with individual differences in the rates of neurobioogical deterioration that are associated with aging (Birren, Woods & Williams, 1980; Rabbitt, 1981; Welford, 1980). However, within the cognitive aging literature, this view has been specifically questioned with respect to age-related increase in RT variability. It has been demonstrated that the correlation between age and the standard deviation of RT is greatly attenuated or, in some cases, eliminated when the effect of mean RT is statistically controlled* (e. g., Hale et al., 1988; Salthouse, 1993). Therefore, it was argued that a general mechanism of age-related slowing, in and of itself, is sufficient to cause the increase in *inter*individual variability, and that increased variability in RT should be viewed as a consequence, rather than a cause, of age-related slowing. Nonetheless, age-related slowing itself as a phenomenon at the behavioral level still needs to be explained. In addition, interpretations of causality that are based on statistical control rather than direct experimental manipulation should be taken with constraints. Specifically, with respect to the statistical explanatory advantage of mean RT over the variability of RT in predicting age, one should at least note that in addition to the causal relationship interpreted by Hale et al. (1988) and Salthouse (1993), a difference in measurement reliability of these two types of measures, favoring the measure of central tendency, can be one other important factor contributing to the explanatory advantage of mean RT. Besides, central-tendency measures of RT also do not exhibit explanatory advantage when predicting other variables. For instance, some psychometric studies of intelligence have shown that trial-by-trial intraindividual variability in RT consistently correlates more highly with the factor of general intelligence than mean RT, despite the fact that the test-retest reliability of the measures of variability is usually lower than that of mean RT or median RT (e. g., Jensen, 1992; Smith & Stanley, 1987). People who show greater intraindividual variability in their response latencies tend to score lower on IQ tests. In addition, it was demonstrated that although the standard deviation of RT and median RT are highly correlated, they still reflect independent sources of variance that are specific to each of the two variables. Using Spearman's (1904, 1927) formula to compute the true-score correlation between the standard deviation and the median of the RT distribution, Jensen (1992) found that the overall specificity (i. e., variance specific to each of the two variables) is still about 34.4% of the total true-score variance.

---

* The generalizability of this finding to performance measures other than response times is not clear. For instance, Li et al. (1998) found that the positive relationship between age and the magnitude of intraindividual variability in memory performance was not affected after controlling for mean-level performance ($r = 0.460$ before controlling for mean performance, and $r = 0.456$ after controlling for mean performance). However, the relationship between age and the magnitude of intraindividual variability in sensorimotor functioning was eliminated after controlling for mean-level performance.

CNS Variability as an Explanation for Intraindividual Response Variability

Psychologists interested in understanding biological correlates of intelligence have proposed that intraindividual variability in RT at the behavioral level could be related to CNS variability, which in turn is one of the biological bases of intelligence. For instance, both Eysenck (1982) and Hendrickson (1982) hypothesized that intraindividual response variability in RT could be caused by random errors, or what might be called "neural noise" in the transmission of neural signal in the CNS. This view parallels the neural-noise hypothesis in the gerontological literature (e. g., Crossman & Szafran, 1956; Welford, 1965, 1981, 1984). Indeed, as Hale et al. (1988) have argued, the finding that RT variability can be predicted, independent of age, from mean RT does lend support to the contention that there is no need to postulate an extra hypothesis of differential rates of brain aging in order to account for age-related increase in *inter*individual variability. However, such a result does not exclude the possibility that *intra*individual response variability could be an indicator of some kinds of base conditions (or more metaphorically put as "hums" of a living system by Nesselroade, 1991a) produced by organic processes taking place within the organism, for example, processes such as metabolic activities within the nervous systems (Fiske & Rice, 1955, pp. 219–220). Specifically, the explanatory advantage of measures of central tendency over measures of variability at the behavioral level does not preclude the possibility that at the level of the CNS, biochemical mechanisms which increase the level of random variability either in neural coding or neural transmission might be one of the causes for age-related slowing and other aspects of cognitive aging, such as the dedifferentiation of ability structure.

## Linking Dedifferentiation to Increased Variability within Computational Frameworks

Up to this point, we have reviewed two sets of empirical findings, namely, age-related dedifferentiation of ability structure and age-related increase in variability at both the behavioral and biological levels. We have also presented some conceptual explanations that have been proposed to account for these results. As revealed in the preceding review, there is an apparent lack of integration both at the level of data and at the level of theory. Just as the empirical phenomena themselves have been investigated independently, explanations of these data have also been advanced separately. In addition, the theoretical notions been offered so far have remained at the conceptual level. Therefore, the main purpose of our study is to explore a joint platform for the explanation of age changes in level, variability, and covariance within formal computational frameworks. The central issues is how aging-induced changes in the fidelity of neural transmission may bring about, at the behavioral level, not only decrements in performance level (as seen in longer reaction times and less accurate performance) and increments in variability, but also increments in the degree of covariation between different dimensions and domains of cognitive performance. In other words, is it possible, or even necessary, that generalized decrements in the efficacy of neural transmission simultaneously affect all three aspects of behavior? To our knowledge, no prior theoretical work has been done to formally address this question. However, a few general ideas hinting at potential relationships among subsets of these phenomena have been suggested in some researchers' earlier writings.

For instance, Cerella (1990) suggested a possible relationship between neural connectivity and mean response latency. Specifically, Cerella proposed that aging disrupts the connectivity between neurons, and that the loss in connectivity extends the length of the pathway through which a signal travels, because a signal must step around broken links in its path. Longer pathways lead then to longer response latencies.

In trying to link Reed and Jensen's (1991) finding of a positive correlation ($r = 0.26, p < 0.002, n = 200$) between IQ and brain nerve conduction velocity (NCV) measured in the visual tract with Eysenck's (1982) and Hendrickson's (1982) views on the biological basis of intraindividual variability in RT, Jensen (1992) speculated that:

> "... it is a reasonable hypothesis that the correlation between nerve conduction velocity (NCV) in the visual tract and IQ is the indirect result of similarity of NCV throughout different regions of the brain, including the higher association centers involved in complex reasoning. However, the fact that there are three synapses in the visual tract, at each of which there could be some probability of a momentary 'error' in transmission, means that the Reed-Jensen finding could also possibly support Eysenck's theory that the average latency of the neural response registered at the visual cortex results, not from NCV per se, but from the accumulation of delays due to random errors in transmission, the errors presumably occurring at the synapses." (p. 871)

The "error" in the above quotation was taken by these researchers to represent the lack of fidelity of neural information processing (i. e., the probability that a given message encoded in a series of pulse trains will arrive at its destination in the identical form in which it was encoded, Eysenck, 1982, p. 9). From the quote, it is clear that Jensen (1992) along with Eysenck (1982) and

Hendrickson (1982) suggested a relationship between the fidelity of neural transmission and response latency. However, the issues of how errors in neural transmission might affect variability observed both at the biological and behavioral level and what might be the relationship between variability level and intercorrelations among different cognitive functioning were not clearly specified. Similarly, although the neural-noise hypothesis of cognitive aging (Crossman & Szafran, 1956; Welford, 1965) suggests that age-related behavioral slowing and other deficits are likely to be associated with the increased noise level in neural transmission, the potential relationships between variabilities at the biological and behavioral levels and the patterns of covariations are not specified or discussed.

Following these lines of reasoning, we further speculate that less accurate information transmissions would lead to a higher level of random variability in the total information content within the system. Furthermore, increased random variability in the CNS might in turn play a role in age-related changes in variability at the behavioral level and in patterns of intercorrelations between different cognitive processes. We have formally instantiated these two sets of conceptual notions at the descriptive and implementation levels. Before presenting these formalisms, we discuss a set of recent empirical findings which, in part, inspired our theorizing about the relationships between CNS variability, behavioral variability, and dedifferentiation.

### Intraindividual Variability and Intersystemic Relationship: Initial Empirical Indications

In terms of initial empirical findings that are at least related, if not directly parallel, to the above theoretical speculations, Li et al. (1998) recently investigated the link between memory and sensorimotor functioning within a sample of old adults via intraindividual response variability at the behavioral level. They found suggestive trends of positive correlations between the strength of a given individual's intersystemic link between memory and sensorimotor functioning and the magnitude of his or her own intraindividual variability in memory ($r = 0.29$; $p = 0.22$, $n = 19$) and sensorimotor ($r = 0.22$, $p = 0.37$, $n = 19$) performance. Li et al. (1998) argued that such a relation between the magnitude of intraindividual variability in different domains of functioning and the strength of the intersystemic link between these functions should not be trivialized as a mere statistical artifact.

Indeed, the topic of range restriction is commonly discussed within the context of interindividual difference research, and it has to do with restricted selectivity in sampling. If the range of a sample is selectively restricted, the intercorrelations among a set of variables that one observes in this given sample might *underestimate* the true correlations in the population (e. g., Lawley, 1943; Pearson, 1903). Hence, within the context of interindividual differences, a finding of a relationship between the magnitude of interindividual variability in different performance measures and the strength of the intercorrelations among these variables might not have *substantive* value and should be interpreted cautiously, because such a relation, if not merely reflects the extent of range selectivity in the sample, is at least confounded by it.

A relationship between the magnitude of *intraindividual* response variability and the strength of intersystemic link is, however, conceptually different. While sampling variability usually bears no direct relevance to many of the theoretical constructs of cognitive functioning at the individual's level, intra-individual variability and its biological basis, on the other hand, have been central to many theories of intelligence (e. g., Eysenck, 1982; Hendrickson, 1982; Jensen, 1982), cognitive development (e. g., Siegler, 1994; Siegler & Ellis, 1996; van der Maas & Molenaar, 1992) and cognitive aging (Hanno & Hoyer, 1994; Li, Lindenberger, & Frensch, 1996; Welford, 1965, 1981, 1984). Hence, it may be of some interest to researchers in these areas, if one could more formally examine the link between age-related increase in intraindividual variability, dedifferentiation of ability structure, and aging-induced degeneration in neurotransmitter systems within computational models.

## *A Formalization at the Descriptive Level*

As an initial attempt, Li and Lindenberger (1998) carried out Monte Carlo simulations to quantitatively examine this issue at a purely descriptive level. In these simulations, it was assumed that the brain state (i. e., total neural information content within the brain at a given moment) could be represented by a random state vector (cf. Anderson, 1983). Elements of the brain state vector were sampled from a normal distribution with a given mean and standard deviation. Two mathematical functions, A and B, represented two different processes; but both functions utilized the information content in the common brain state vector. In other words, the distributional properties of the information in the brain state vector were shared by both processes, but were transformed differently, depending on the specific function types. Furthermore, it was assumed that these two processes were not perfectly reliable, hence each of them was associated with some processing noise. The processing noise of each function was assumed to be independent.

The simulation results showed that across three different pairings of the A and B function types (i. e., logistic and polynomial, linear and linear, and exponential and power) and three different levels of processing noise, the magnitude of the correlation between the outcomes of the two functions increased as the level of variability in the random vector representing brain state increased. Admittedly, this model oversimplifies many issues. However, it does allow one to start exploring mathematical or statistical principles addressing the issue of correlations between dependent random variables (e. g., Zimmerman, 1976) as potential mathematical formalisms that could describe and support the relationship(s) between CNS variability and the intercorrelations among different cognitive functions.

If one adopts the cognitive neuroscience orientation, it is then not satisfying to only address these phenomena descriptively. At the empirical level, one question still needs to be answered is what kinds of aging-induced neurobiological changes are likely to increase random variability in the CNS, presumably, via affecting the fidelity of neural information processing? At the level of formal modeling, one question awaiting answers is what other types of formalism can "implement" an increase in within system variability in ways that capture, at least, some functional properties of the related biological mechanisms, as opposed to a formalism, such as that of Li and Lindenberger (1998), which treats variability as a primitive in the formulation and only describes the phenomena? Therefore, with the simulations reported in this chapter we attempted to extend the descriptive results from Li and Lindenberger's (1998) Monte Carlo simulations to one type of processing model within which variability does not have to be treated as a primitive that is to be manipulated directly; rather it is the derivative of other mechanisms which mimic functional aspects of neural information processing. We now turn to present some empirical findings on aging-induced degeneration in neurotransmitter systems, and describe the computational foundations for the simulations to be presented.

## Aging-Induced Deterioration of Catecholaminergic System

Epinephrine, norepinephrine, and dopamine belong to a family of neurotransmitters called catecholamines. To date, some biochemical evidence has accumulated, suggesting the role of catecholamines as neuromodulators of information processing in the brain. This is to say that catecholamines themselves do not directly change the firing rate of a neuron; however, the release of catecholamines enhances the responsivity of a neuron to other incoming afferent signals. This effect has been interpreted as the modulation of the neuron's signal-to-noise ratio (e. g., Clark, Geffen, & Geffen, 1987; DeFrance, Sikes, & Chronister, 1985; Mamelak & Hobson, 1989; Servan-Schreiber et al., 1990; Spitzer, 1997; Yang & Mogenson, 1990). In the course of normal aging, the concentration of catecholamines in the striatum and basal ganglia decreases by 7% or 8% during each decade of life (e. g., see Gabrieli, 1995; Morgan & May, 1990; Rogers & Bloom, 1985, for reviews). By extension, because of the decline in its catecholamine concentration, the aging brain might be a noisier (or with a higher level of random variability) information processing system, as suggested by the neural-noise hypothesis.

Afew potential links between catecholamines and age-related behavioral variations in rats, non-human primates, and humans, have been documented. For instance, in training young and old rats to perform escape-and-avoidance tasks, Spirduso and colleagues found that the density of dopamine receptors was associated with response speed and its variance: the higher the density, the faster and less variable the RT (MacRae, Spirduso, & Wilcox, 1988; Spirduso, Mayfield, Grant, & Schallert, 1989). Similarly, Schultz, Studer, Romo et al.'s (1989) results showed that depletions of nigrostriatal dopamine neurons in monkeys not only increased motor reaction time and movement time, it also increased RT variability. With respect to memory performance, in a delayed-response task designed to test short-term memory capacity in non-human primates, Arnsten and Goldman-Rakic (1985) showed that memory deficits of aged monkeys, who suffered from 50% dopamine depletion in their prefrontal cortex, can be alleviated by catecholaminergic agonists. Similar associations have also been found between degeneration of the dopaminergic system and working-memory deficits (Sawaguchi & Goldman-Rakic, 1991), as well as attentional impairment (Corwin, Kanter, Watson, Heilman, Valenstein, & Hashimoto, 1986; Rothman, 1996). In humans, Kischka, Kammer, Maier, and Weisbrod et al. (1996) found that the injection of L-dopa, a dopamine agonist, reduced the magnitude of semantic priming marginally and the magnitude of indirect priming significantly. This finding suggests that the increase of semantic priming effects in old age (see Laver & Burke, 1993 for review) could be related to compromised dopaminergic mechanisms.

*Formalization at the Implementation Level:*
*Modeling the Effects of Catecholamines*

A Unit's Responsivity

Within the framework of connectionist modeling, Servan-Schreiber et al. (1990) demonstrated that the modulatory effects of catecholamines (i. e., the sharpening of a neuron's signal-to-noise ratio) can be simulated by the gain parameter of the logistic activation. Equation 1 defines the activation function,

$$Output\ Activation_i = \frac{1}{1+e^{-(gain \times netinput_i + bias)}} \tag{1}$$

Figure 1 shows that reducing the value of the gain parameter (simulating attenuated efficacy of the catecholaminergic system) flattens the activation pro-

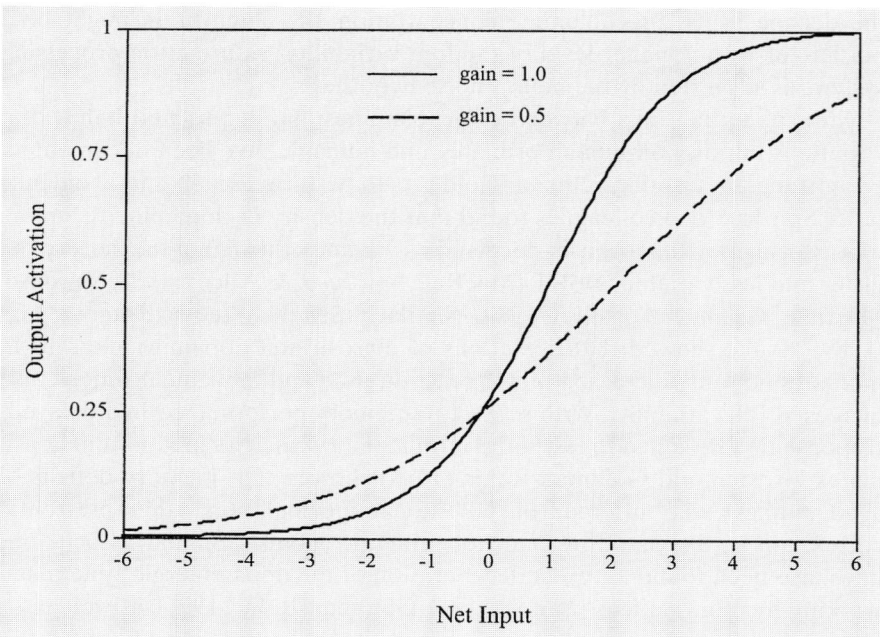

*Figure 1.* Gain parameter's effect on responsivity: sigmoid activation function of units in back-propagation network for two values of gain (the bias parameter of the activation function was set to –1.0).

file, hence the unit become less sensitive to changes in incoming afferent signals. Under conditions of static gain (i. e., gain parameters of all units are fixed at a given value and remain the same across all processing steps), the manipulation proposed by Servan-Schreiber et al. (1990) captures, however, only one aspect of the modulatory effects of the catecholamines, namely, the fine tuning of a neuron's responsivity.

Intra-Network Variability

Li et al. (1996) demonstrated a second property of the gain parameter when it is assumed to be stochastic (i. e., values of the gain parameters of units in a network were sampled from a uniform distribution at each processing step). When stochastic gains are used to simulate fluctuations in the concentration of transmitter substances (e. g., Kempf, Mandel, Oliverio, & Pulisi-Allegra, 1982; Manshardt & Wurtman, 1968; Reis, Weinbren, & Corvelli, 1968), the variability in a given unit's output activation in response to an input signal across different processing steps is systematically related to the mean of the

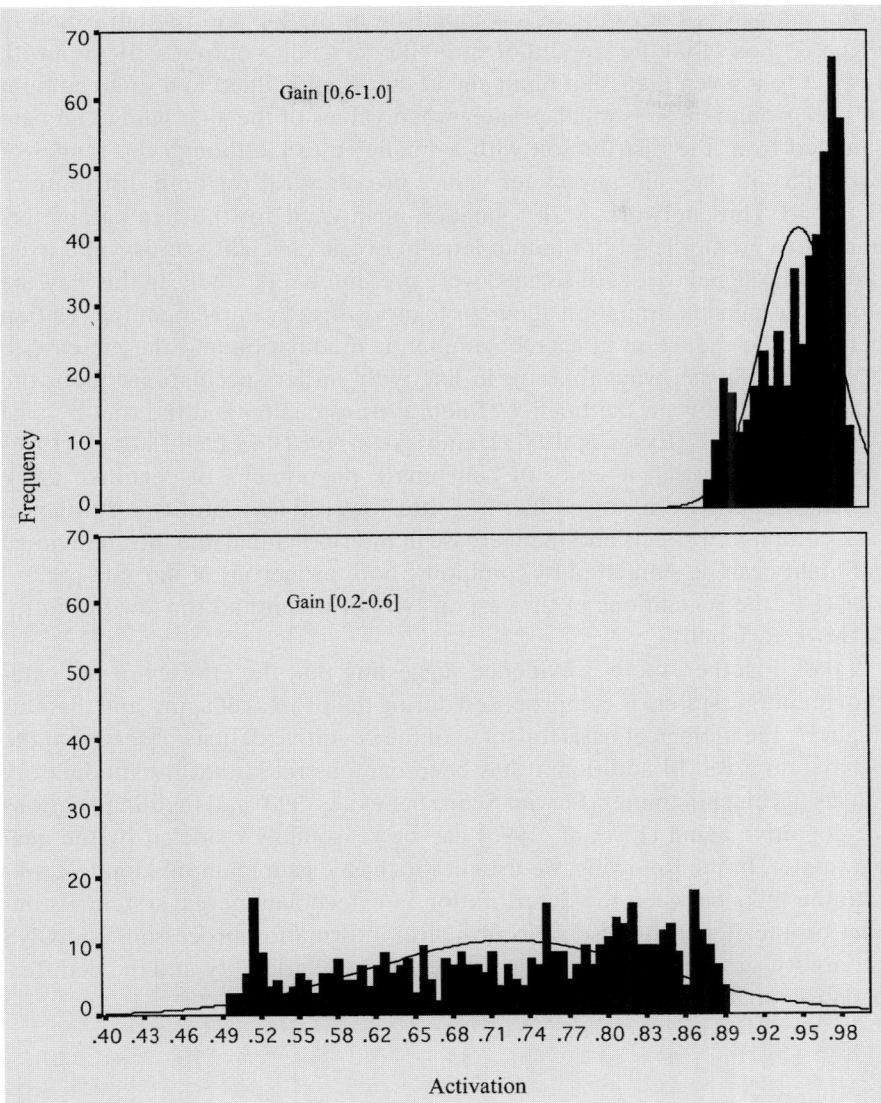

*Figure 2.* Gain parameter's effect on internal variability: distributions of output activations with respect to a fixed Gaussian signal with small noise across 500 trials for two ranges of gain parameter values.

gain parameters. For example, a comparison of the top and bottom panels in Figure 2 shows that the amount of variability in a unit's output activation with respect to a given Gaussian input signal that is embedded in a small amount of background noise is much greater when values of the gain parameters are sampled from the distribution with a smaller mean, although the ranges of variability in the gain parameter values are identical for both distributions (i. e., 0.4). Thus, networks with a smaller mean value for the gain parameters undergo a greater level of random intra-network variability across time, even if the same signal (or set of signals) were presented repeatedly. In this way, the stochastic gain manipulation allows us to more directly implement the relation between the reduction in catecholaminergic modulation and the increase in CNS variability in ways that are in line with earlier speculations about the relationship between the fidelity of neural transmission and the trial-by-trial variability in RT (Eysenck, 1982; Hendrickson, 1982). In fact, Li et al. (1996) already showed that a series of benchmark phenomena of cognitive aging deficits, ranging from slowed learning rate, lowered asymptotic performance, task-complexity effects and the increase in interindividual and intraindividual variability can be simulated by combining both properties of the gain parameter (i. e., the regulations of the responsivity of a unit and the level of intra-network variability).

Taken together, there is evidence suggesting that the efficacy of the catecholaminergic system is compromised during the process of aging, and that this might be the biological basis for some of the cognitive deficits observed at the behavioral level. In addition, it has been demonstrated that the modulatory effects of catecholamines (Servan-Schreiber et al., 1990) and their implications for cognitive aging (Li et al., 1996) can be reasonably modeled by the gain parameter. In the following, we use the stochastic gain manipulation to explicate the links between the deterioration in catecholaminergic system, its impact on the signal-to-noise ratio of neural information processing and CNS variability, age-related increase in interindividual variability, and the dedifferentiation of ability structure observed in old age.

## Simulations

Two sets of simulations are presented. Both sets of simulations involved the standard back-propagation networks with fully interconnected layers of input, hidden and output units. Three groups of otherwise identical networks that differed only in the mean value of their gain parameters were trained and tested in each simulation. Using the stochastic gain manipulation to simulate the effect of aging-induced deterioration of catecholamine effects, the values of the gain parameters of the "young networks" were randomly sampled from a uniform distribution within the range [0.6, 1.0], the gain parameters of the "middle networks" were sampled from the range [0.4,0.8], and lastly, the parameters of the "old networks" were sampled from the range [0.2,0.6]. One hundred networks, each started with a different random initial weight configuration, were included for each of the three network groups. It is well-known that the initial weight configuration of a network affects learning (Baldi & Chauvin, 1991; Kolen & Goel, 1991). At the beginning of learning, the initial weight configuration defines a specific starting position in the hyperspace that is jointly defined by values of all the weights and the minimum error point as defined in downhill gradient descent learning. During learning, the network must try to gradually minimize the difference (also called error) between its output activation and the target output activation. Therefore, depending on the starting location defined by the initial weight configuration, a network can have a fast or slow rate in reaching the criterion performance. Hence, interindividual differences in initial learning ability can be simulated by networks that start with different initial weight configurations. An identical set of 100 random seeds was used to define the initial weight configurations for networks in each of the three groups. This controls for the effect of initial weight configuration on learning across groups and ensures that differences observed in the performances across the three groups of networks arise only from the gain parameter manipulation.

## Simulation 1: Intercorrelations among Paired-Associate Recall of Different List Length

In empirical studies using the paired-associate learning paradigm (Barnes & Underwood, 1959), participants first learn a list of word pairs, for instance, *computer* and *typewriter*, *automobile* and *airplane*, and etc. to some performance criterion. At test, the participants are expected to recall the second item (or the B item) of the pair (*typewriter* and *airplane* in the example given here), when probed with the first item (*computer* and *automobile* in the above example) of the pair (the A item). In order to simulate paired-associate learning using back-propagation networks, random asymmetric binary (0 1) input and output vectors were used to represent the A and B items. In this simulation, the architecture of the networks involved 14 input, 5 hidden, and 14 output units. The first four input and output units represented context information of a given list, and were kept the same across all items of a given list. The remaining 10 input and output units represented unique item information. On average, all item patterns consisted of an equal number of 1s and 0s. In this simulation, the gain manipulation was applied only to the output units. Three additional network parameters, learning rate, momentum, and bias were set, respectively, at 0.1, 0.9, and −1.0, for all networks throughout the simulations.

The networks were trained to learn three paired-associate recall tasks that were defined by list length (i. e., 3, 5, and 8 items per list). Five lists were included for each of the three tasks. Lists with different length were constructed such that the shorter lists were nested within the longer lists. More specifically, five-item lists contained five items from the 8-item lists, and the 3-item lists contained 3 items from the five-item lists. This nesting of shorter lists within the longer lists was necessary to ensure that intercorrelations among the three tasks could arise from the shared information content (i. e., the specific input-output mapping) between the lists. Learning in connectionist networks is adaptive. This implies that the network's performance is jointly determined by the network architecture, parameter settings, initial weight configuration, and task requirements defined by the input-output mapping of a given task. In the simulations reported here, all of these aspects were kept constant, with the exception that task requirements differed across task conditions. However, if the tasks do not share some aspects of the input-output mapping, one cannot expect that the rank order of the effects of a set of initial weight configurations (simulating interindividual differences in initial learning ability in a given sample) on learning in one task should relate systematically to the rank order of the same set of initial weight configurations in a completely different task. Therefore, it was important to ensure that different tasks at least share some related input-output mappings.

Recall performance was determined by the similarity between target and actual output activation patterns. Similarity of the two output vectors were defined by the retrieved cosine. Specifically, given two vectors, **a** and **b**, the retrieved cosine is the ratio of the dot product between **a** and **b** to the product of the lengths of the two vectors (Goebel & Lewandowsky, 1991). Retrieved cosine is a preferred measure of vector similarity because it is invariant of the length of the vector and is scaled within the range of 0 to 1, with 0 representing maximum dissimilarity, and 1 representing maximum similarity. Performances of all networks in all three tasks were evaluated after 100 learning trials, at which point the retrieved cosine measure of the "middle networks" in the most difficult task (i. e., the 8-item condition) reached 0.965.

## Results

### Gain Parameter and Mean-Level Performance

The mean performance of each network group in recalling lists of different list lengths are plotted in Figure 3. Results from analysis of variance (ANOVA)

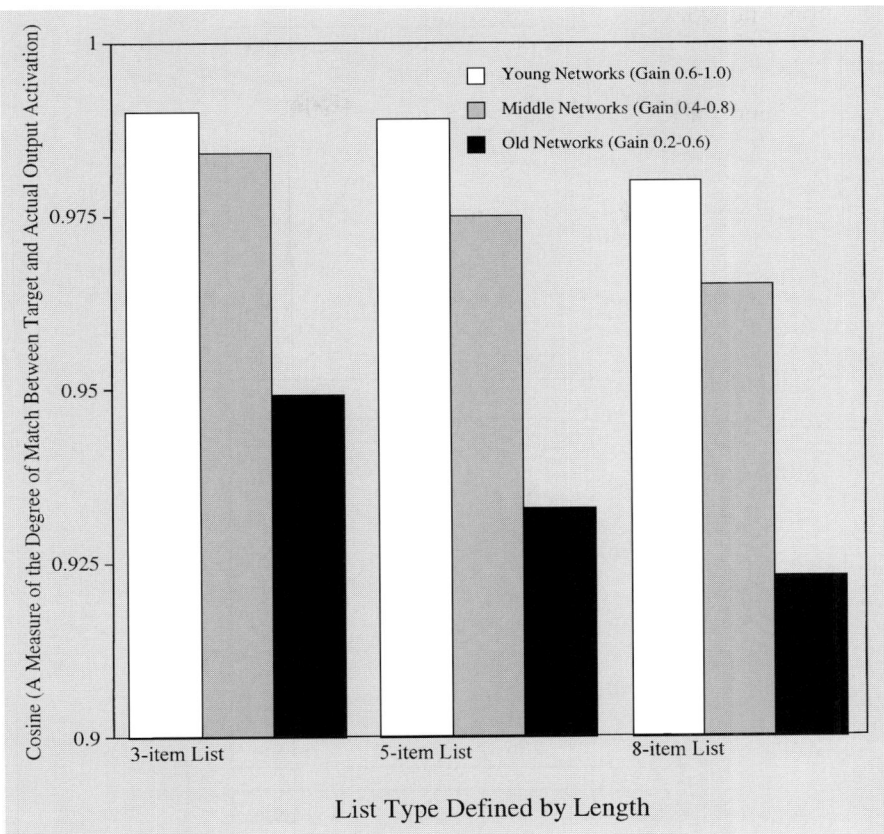

*Figure 3.* Neural networks' performance in the paired-associate recall task as a function of gain parameter and list length.

of a two-way split-plot factorial design involving three treatment levels and three groups showed that the main effects of list length and group, and the length by group interaction were all significant with $p$ values less than 0.001. For all network groups, performance was best for short lists – a result that is in line with the classical list-length effects found in a wide range of memory performance, ranging from recognition, free recall, to cued recall (e. g., Strong, 1912; Gillund & Shiffrin, 1984). In addition, the "cost" of learning longer lists in comparison to the shorter lists was largest for the old networks and smallest for the young networks, as indicated by the significant interaction between group and list length. This finding is in good agreement with the age by complexity effect that is often reported in the cognitive aging literature (e. g., McDowd & Craik, 1988).

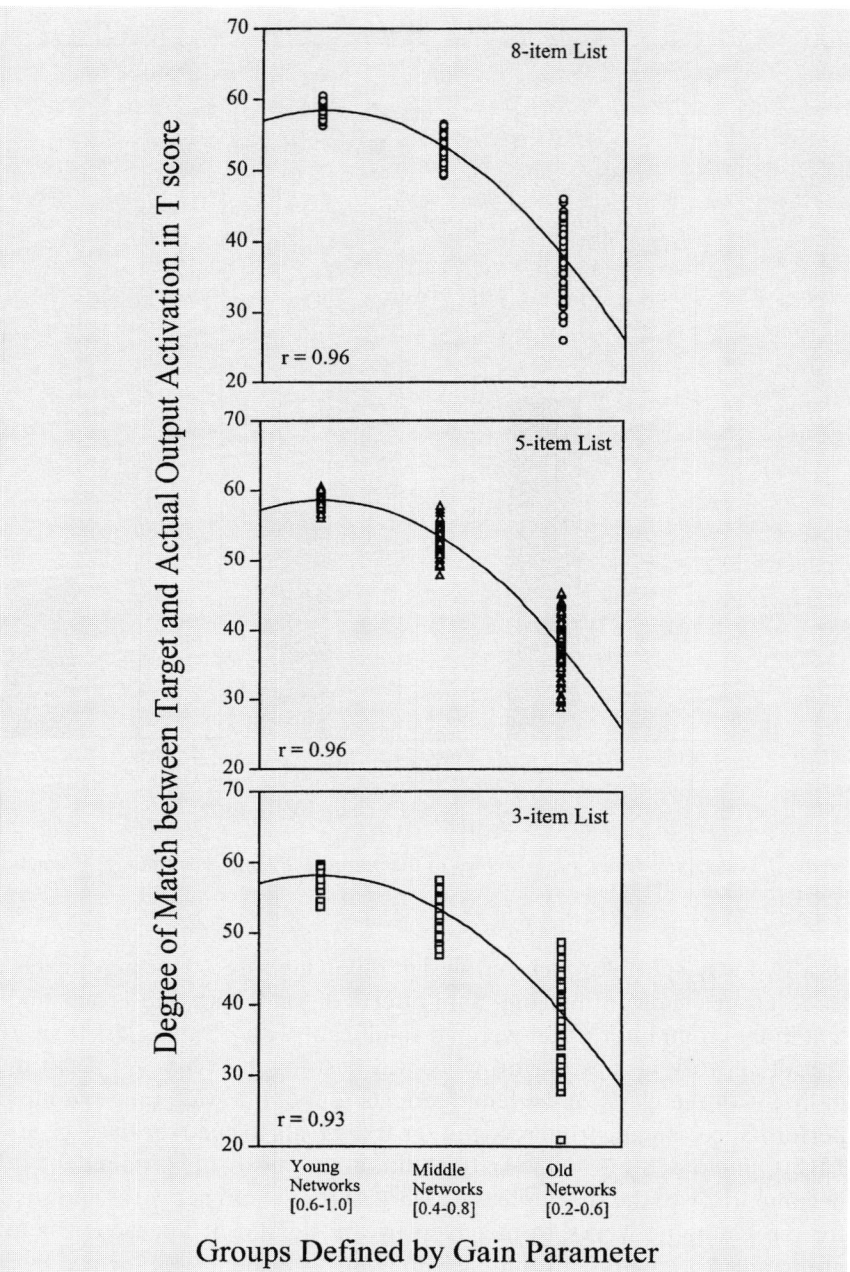

*Figure 4.* Inter-network variability as a function of the gain parameter in paired-associate recall of three different list lengths.

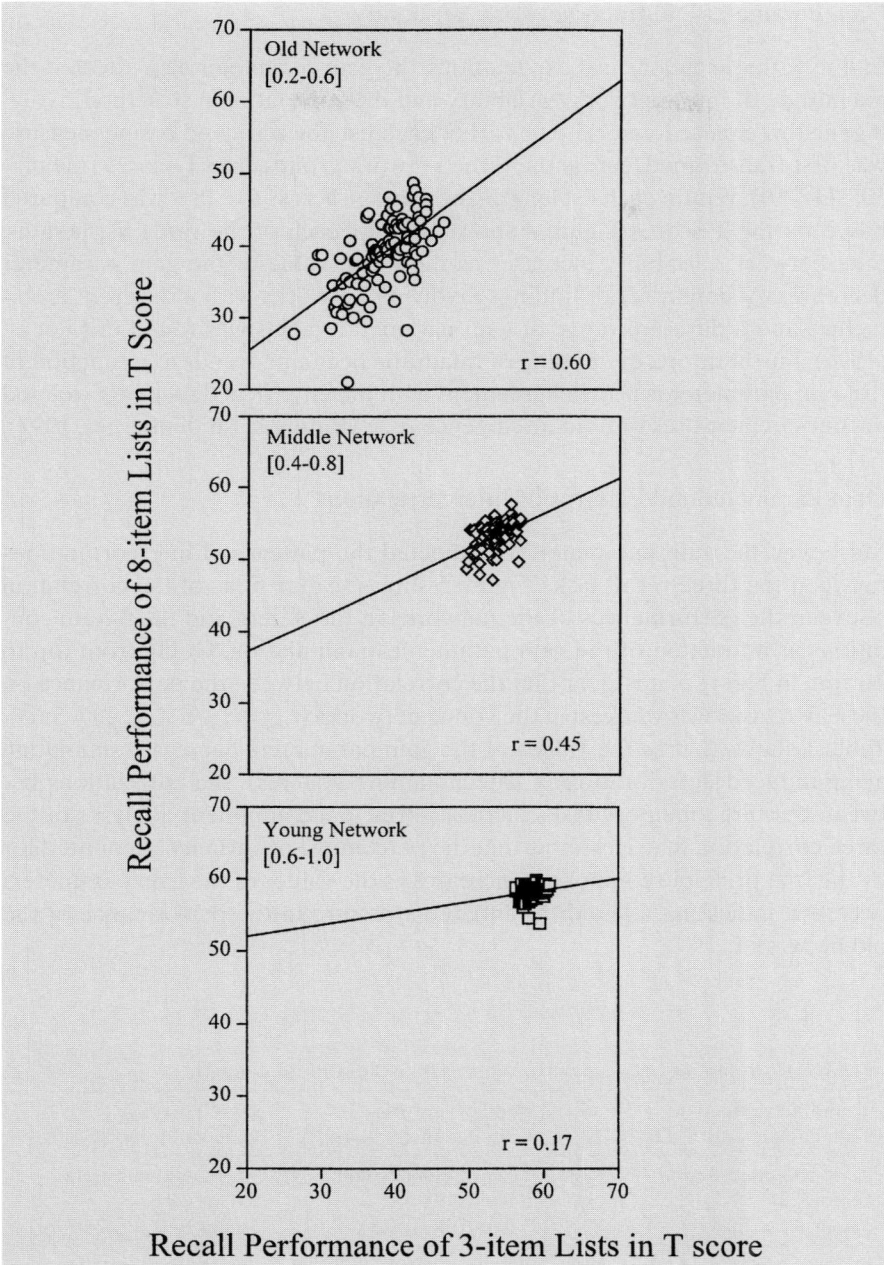

*Figure 5.* Correlations between performances in long and short lists as a function of the gain parameter.

Gain Parameter and Inter-Network Variability

In line with our theoretical expectations, the gain parameter also affected the magnitude of inter-network variability and the correlational structure involving the three paired-associate tasks. For each list, the retrieved cosine measure was first transformed, across the three network groups, into T scores (mean = 50, SD = 10). Within each list length, the average across five lists was computed based on the T scores. Figure 4 shows that for each of the three list lengths, inter-network variability increases as the mean value of the gain parameter decreases. A similar set of findings involving networks with a different architecture and a different range of gain parameter values was found in Li et al. (1996). Furthermore, the finding of quadratic declining trends as a function of the gain parameter is also in agreement with the empirical data of age-related declines in measures of fluid intelligence (e. g., Baltes & Lindenberger, 1997).

Gain Parameter and Patterns of Intercorrelations

Moreover, the gain parameter also affected the patterns of intercorrelations between the three recall tasks. Figure 5 shows scatter plots of the correlation between the performances of the networks in the 8-item and the 3-item conditions as a function of the gain parameter manipulation. Going from top to bottom in Figure 5, it is clear that the correlation between the performance on these two tasks was weakest in the young networks ($r_{old} = r_{mid} > r_{young}$, $z = 3.63$). Table 1 shows that as the values of the gain parameters decrease (simulating aging-induced deterioration in catecholamine systems), the correlations between the three memory tasks increase. Principal component analyses of the three correlation matrices show that the percentage of variance accounted for by the first principle component increases as the values of the gain parameters decrease, indicating a less differentiated structure in the performance of the old networks.

*Table 1.* Correlations between performances of lists of different length

| Young Networks Gain Parameter [0.6–1.0] | | Middle Networks Gain Parameter [0.4–0.8] | | Old Networks Gain Parameter [0.2–0.6] | |
|---|---|---|---|---|---|
| 8-item | 5-item | 8-item | 5-item | 8-item | 5-item |
| 5-item 0.31 | – | 5-item 0.59 | – | 5-item 0.74 | – |
| 3-item 0.17 | 0.24 | 3-item 0.45 | 0.54 | 3-item 0.60 | 0.74 |
| Variance accounted for by 1st PC: | 49.3% | Variance accounted for by 1st PC: | 68.3% | Variance accounted for by 1st PC: | 79.6% |

## Simulation 2: Intercorrelations among Categorization Tasks of Different Discriminability

In this simulation we examined the effect of the gain parameter on the correlational structure of the networks' performances in three categorization tasks with different levels of between-category discriminability. Again, three groups of networks, with 100 networks in each group, were trained to learn 2-choice categorization tasks involving bivariate normal stimuli. A bivariate normal category is defined by normally distributed values (with known mean and variance) on two stimulus dimensions (e. g., Ashby & Gott, 1988; Ashby & Maddox, 1992). In this simulation, each network had two input, hidden, and output units. The gain manipulation was applied to all units in the network. Each of the two input units represented one of the two stimulus dimensions, and each of the two output units represented one of the two response categories. The networks were trained to categorize the stimuli into two categories, A and B, depending on whether Dimension 1 was greater or smaller than Dimension 2. Training exemplars for each of the two categories were sampled from bivariate normal distributions with means of 0.3 and 0.7 for the first and second dimensions of category A, and a reverse set of means, 0.7 and 0.3, for the two dimensions of category B. The networks were trained to learn categorization tasks with three levels of between-category discriminability. Within each condition, the networks were trained on a total of 2000 stimulus exemplars during learning. During testing, 400 testing patterns were constructed by crossing 20 values (ranging from –0.5 to 1.4 with a stepsize of 0.1) for the first input dimension and 20 identical values for the second dimension. The degree of discriminability between categories was manipulated by varying the extent of overlap between categories. This was defined by the standard deviations of the two stimulus dimensions. Figure 6 shows the extent of overlap between the probability density functions of two sets of binomial categories that are defined by less (top panel, $SD = 0.2$) or more spread (bottom panel, $SD = 0.6$) stimulus dimensions. As shown here, when the standard deviation is large (bottom panel), the overlap between categories increases and the between-category discriminability decreases. Three additional parameters, learning rate, momentum, and bias were set, respectively, at 0.1, 0.7, and –1.0, for all networks throughout the simulations

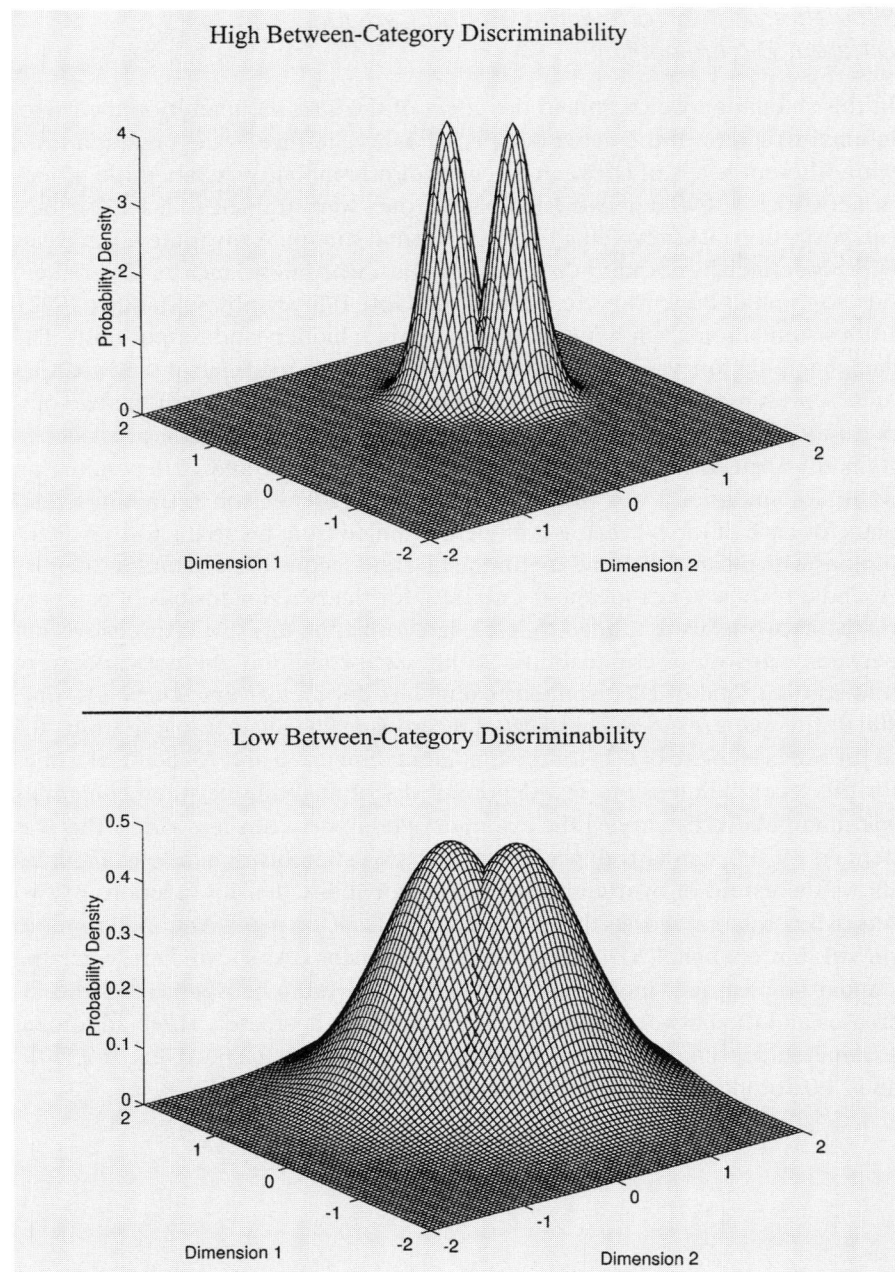

*Figure 6.* Bivariate distributions of categories with high (top panel) and low (bottom panel) between-category discriminability.

## Results

### Gain Parameter and Mean-Level Performance

Performance of the three groups of networks as a function of between-category discriminability are plotted in Figure 7. Results from ANOVA using a two-way split-plot factorial design involving three treatment levels and three groups showed that the main effects of discriminability, group, and the interaction between discriminability and group, were all significant, with $p$ values less than 0.001. For all network groups, performance decreased as between-category discriminability decreased. With respect to the main effect of group, young and middle networks performed comparably; however the old networks performed much more poorly in all conditions and was disproportionately worse in the low discriminability condition.

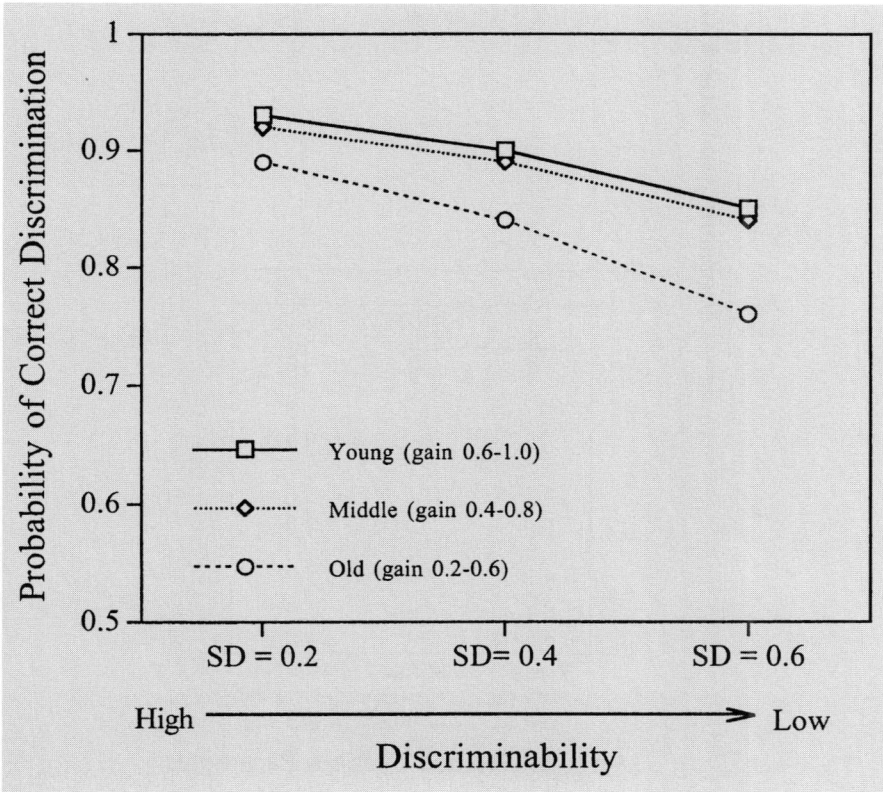

*Figure 7.* Neural networks' performance in the two-choice categorization task as a function of gain parameter and discriminability (chance performance is 50%).

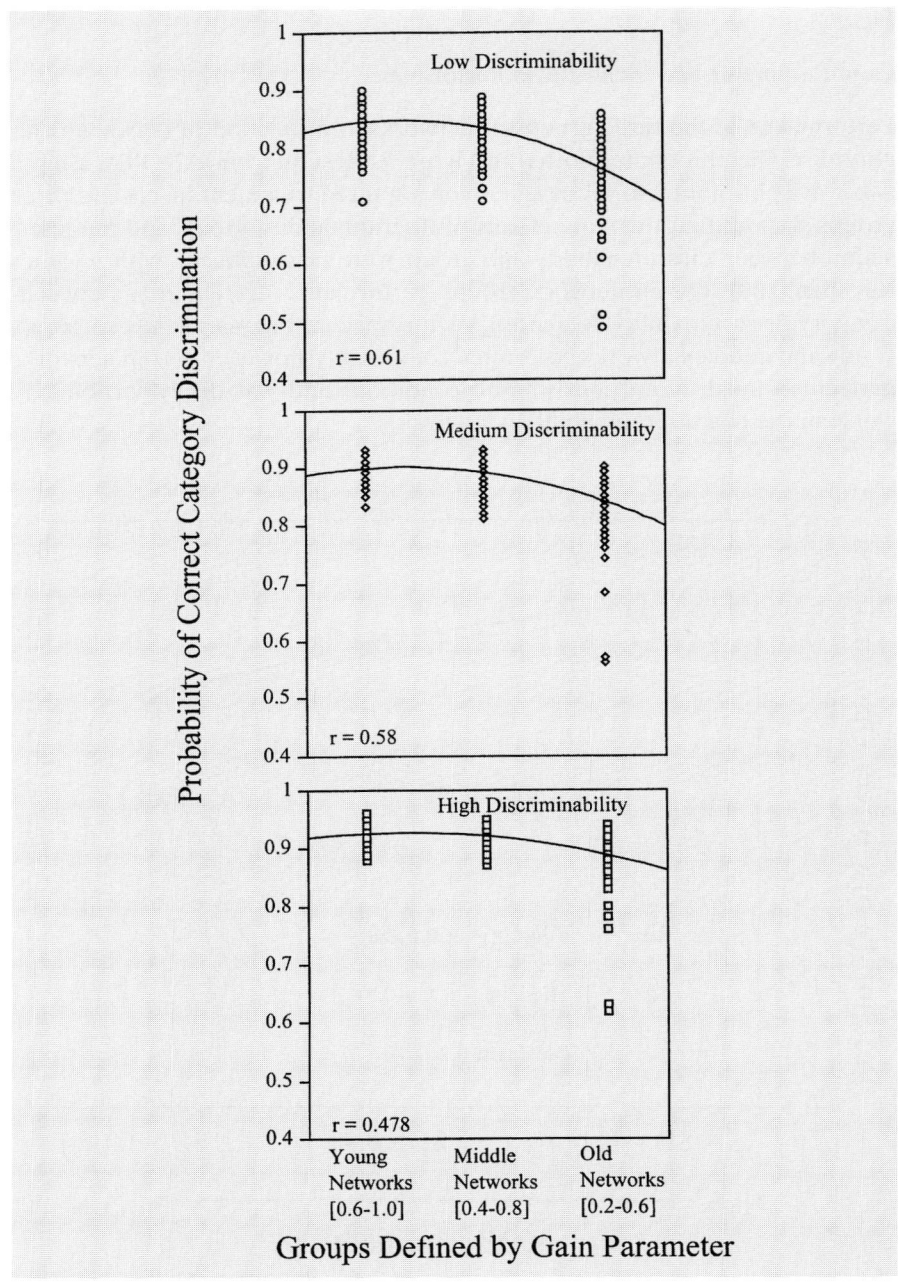

*Figure 8.* Inter-network variability as a function of the gain parameter in two-choice categorization with three levels of between-category discriminability.

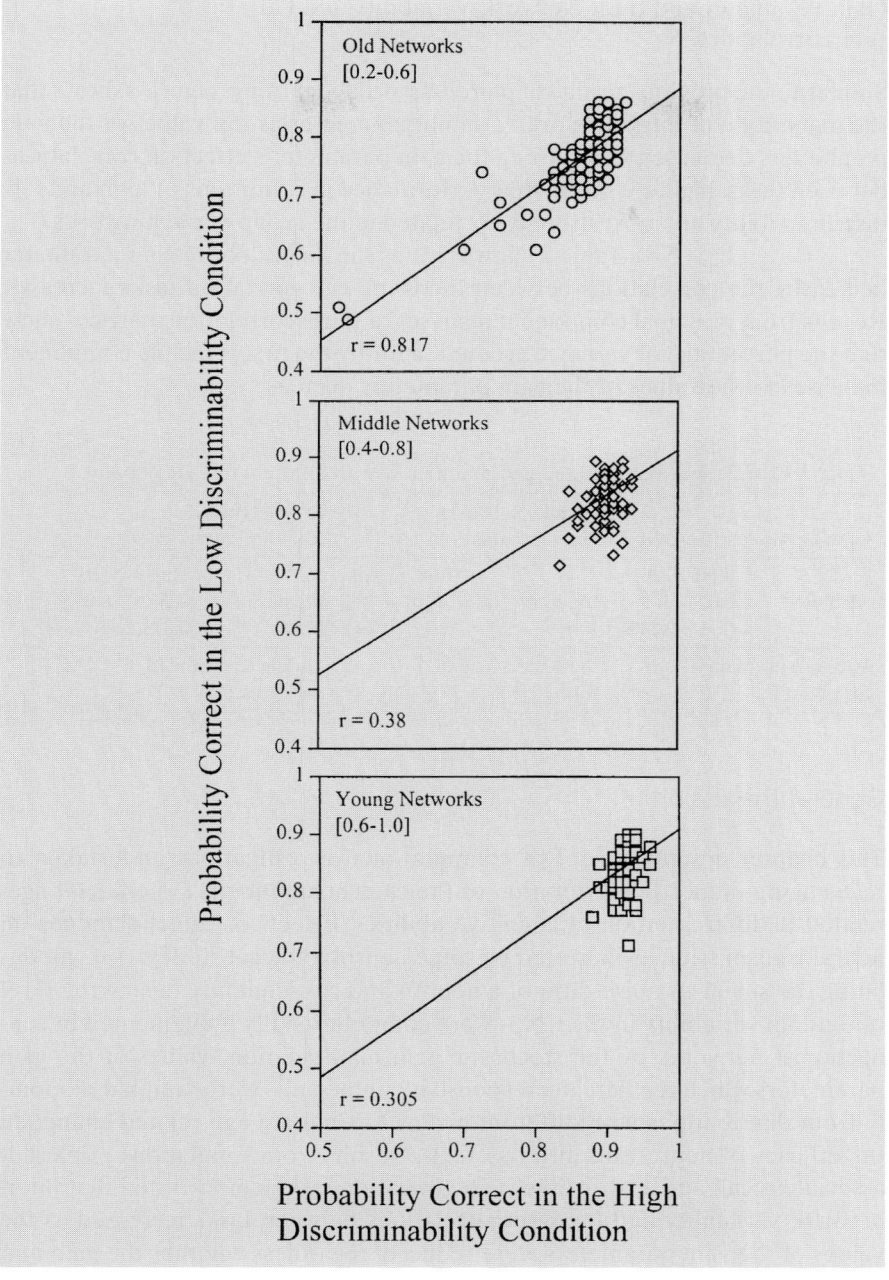

*Figure 9.* Correlations between performances in conditions of high and low discriminability as a function of the gain parameter.

## Gain Parameter and Inter-Network Variability and Patterns of Intercorrelations

Similar to the previous results of paired-associate learning, Figure 8 shows that the magnitude of inter-network variability increases as the values of the gain parameters decreases. Concerning the gain parameter's effect on correlations between tasks, Figure 9 shows that performance in conditions of high and low discriminability are most strongly correlated in the group of old networks ($r_{old}$ > $r_{mid}$ = $r_{young}$, $z$ = 5.8). Table 2 shows that as the values of the gain parameter decreases, the correlations between the three categorization tasks increases. Results from principal component analyses of these correlation matrices show that the percentage of variance accounted for by the first principle component increases as the values of the gain parameters decrease.

*Table 2.* Correlations between categorization tasks with different discriminability.

| Young Networks Gain Parameter [0.6–1.0] | | | Middle Networks Gain Parameter [0.4–0.8] | | | Old Networks Gain Parameter [0.2–0.6] | | |
|---|---|---|---|---|---|---|---|---|
| | High | Med. | | High | Med. | | High | Med. |
| Medium | 0.62 | – | Medium | 0.70 | – | Medium | 0.94 | – |
| Low | 0.31 | 0.80 | Low | 0.38 | 0.79 | Low | 0.81 | 0.9 |
| Variance accounted for by 1st PC: 72.2% | | | Variance accounted for by 1st PC: 75.0% | | | Variance accounted for by 1st PC: 92.8% | | |

## General Discussion

This chapter describes a set of computational investigations undertaken to *relate* aging-induced deterioration of the catecholaminergic system *with* age-related dedifferentiation in cognitive abilities. Effects of catecholamines on neural transmission as indicated by some neurobiological studies (i. e., modulating the signal-to-noise ratio of a neuron and consequently raising the level of random variability in the CNS) were computationally implemented in connectionist networks by the stochastic gain manipulation. Values of the gain parameters which regulate the responsivity of the units were sampled randomly from distributions with different means to simulate age-related change in the efficacy of neurotransmitter systems. Results from simulations of paired-associate recall and a two-choice categorization task demonstrated that inter-network variability and the intercorrelations between tasks increased as the values of the gain parameters were reduced, regardless whether the gain manipulation was applied to a subset of the units (Simulation 1) or to all units (Simulation 2).

## Disclaimers and Limitations

Before we further discuss the implications of our simulation results, some disclaimers and limitations about the present implementation should be pointed out. It should be made clear that we do not claim that the simulations presented here are, by themselves, sufficient enough to constitute a "theory" that relates the efficacy of neural transmission and the dedifferentiation of ability structure in old age. Rather, we view the connectionist approach taken here as a computational tool to aid the development of such a theory (cf. McCloskey, 1991). We have demonstrated that connectionist networks provided a computational framework for implementing the neuromodulatory effects of catecholamines as the gain parameter's effects on tuning a unit's responsivity and the level of intra-network variability. With this implementation, the simulations allow us to observe two sets of relationships. First, the relation between reducing the responsivity at the level of a single unit and the overall level of intra-network variability during information processing (referring back to Figures 1 and 2). And second, the relation between responsivity and intra-network variability at the system's level and the extent of inter-network variability and the magnitude of intercorrelations among different tasks at the performance level (refer back to Figures 4, 5, 8, and 9). Whether these relationships between the gain parameter, a unit's responsivity, intra-network variability and intercorrelations between tasks mimic closely the mechanisms underlying neural information processing and their behavioral manifestations is an open empirical question awaiting rigorous experimental validation. However, the simulation results do demonstrate a set of computational formalisms that would support these relationships if they indeed exist.

One additional limitation which applies to all quantitative models with even a moderate degree of complexity is the difficulty in discerning the analytical boundary of the specific manipulations implemented. Given that connectionist networks are adaptive learning systems, other network parameters, such as learning rate, momentum, bias, number of units, initial weights and even the task requirement specified by the actual input-output mappings are likely to interact with the gain parameter. We have kept all these other parameters constant within each of the two simulations reported here. However, we have not tested the generalizability of our simulation results in other parameter settings, nor is the investigation entailing a sufficient portion of the entire parameter space possible. Rather than searching through the parameter space, we think a more principled research strategy is to work out analytical solutions that could describe the simulated effects. Note, however, that such analytical solutions are not always attainable.

One observation from the process of implementing the simulations suggests that the gain parameter's effects on the level of inter-network variability and the magnitude of cross-task intercorrelations could dependent on whether the gain manipulation is effective enough to produce a difference in mean-level performance. In other words, given specific task requirements and number of training trials, is the difference in the means of the gain parameters large enough to produce a difference in mean-level performance. On the one hand, this suggests that the gain manipulation demonstrated in our simulations are necessarily constrained by other parameters of the network and the task requirements. On the other hand, this additional condition on the gain parameter's effects is actually not at odds with the experimental data. Results from psychometric studies have shown that the phenomenon of differentiation and dedifferentiation of ability structure can also be found along the dimension of ability, besides the age dimension. Specifically, the ability structure is less differentiated among groups of low performers than among groups of high performers (e. g., Deary et al., 1996; Detterman & Daniel, 1989). In addition, age-related decrements in the cognitive mechanics (e. g., processing speed and memory) are pervasive phenomena. In cases where age-related increase in variability or dedifferentiation are found, there are almost always age-related decrease in performance level as well.

One other limitation concerns the general issue about the level of abstraction that a given task should be represented. Arbitrary random vectors have been commonly used as the stimulus and response patterns in most connectionist simulations. During learning, connection weights are adjusted to reduce error between the network's actual output and the target output that's specified by the stimulus-response mapping defined by a given task. At the end of learning, the network stores the learned internal representation of the stimulus-response mapping in its weight patterns. The network's final weight patterns which determines its performance are jointly defined by a large number of network parameters *and* the to-be-learned task. Even in conditions when all other network parameters are held constant, a network can still "develop" quite different weight patterns, depending on the differences in the input-output mappings that are specified by different tasks. Relations between a network's internal representations of different tasks depend on the similarity between the stimulus-response mappings specified by the tasks. When random vectors are used to represent the stimulus and response patterns, there is no guarantee that a network's internal representations of different tasks would be related to each other; nor would the performances, being the outward expressions of the internal representations, of a group of networks in one task be systematically related to their performances in other tasks. In our simulation of paired-associate recall, similarities between the input-output mappings of different tasks were created by nesting the shorter lists within the longer lists. Hence, we first generated a certain degree of intercorrelations between the tasks, before observing the effect of the gain manipulation on patterns of covariation. It is foreseeable that in conditions when more realistic representations of the stimuli and responses can be used (such as in simulations of facial recognition, pixel densities from the image of a face can be transcribed into a matrix of values; e. g., Valentin & Abdi, 1996), overlaps between different stimulus-response mappings can arise more naturally from the similarities between the stimuli. However, in many cases it is not clear as to what would be the realistic ways to represent the stimuli. Relatively few work has been done with respect to this issue, and it is not within the purview of this chapter to provide the solutions. Given that our goal is to demonstrate general principles between the gain parameter's effect on regulating intra-network variability, inter-network variability and patterns of covariations, as opposed to answer specific questions about performances in what types of tasks would be related, we feel justified to stay at the more abstract level of representing task requirements. Keeping these limitations in mind, we now turn to discuss implications of our simulation results with respect to the possible sources of interindividual variability and cognitive development.

## Sources of Interindividual Variability

In this section, we highlight the implications of our results for the relationship between intraindividual and interindividual variability. One early proposal for the age-related increase in interindividual variability in cognitive performance (Birren et al., 1980; Rabbitt, 1981; Welford, 1980) is interindividual differences in the rate of brain aging (e. g., Birren, Woods, & Williams, 1980; Rabbitt, 1981; Welford, 1980). Results from our simulations together with some empirical results suggest, however, this need not be the case. At least, there exist other plausible explanations. Age-related increase in intraindividual variability or age-related behavioral slowing are two possible alternatives.

In the simulations, we demonstrated that as the stochastic gain manipulation increased the level of intra-network variability within each of the old networks, the inter-network variability measured across all networks in the group at the performance level also increased. This indicates that a greater degree of intra-individual variability in old people's cognitive functioning either at behavioral or biological level is at least one alternative explanation for the greater inter-individual variability observed at the group level. Aging-induced increase in CNS variability alone could also lead to an increase in interindividual variability at the group level. It is, therefore, not necessary to invoke a hypothesis about interindividual differences in the "rate" of neurobiological deterioration, in order to account for age-related increase in interindividual variability observed at the behavioral level. One should also note a principle difference between these two hypotheses. This intraindividual-variability hypothesis accounts for a group-level phenomenon by an individual-level mechanism, whereas the hypothesis of individual differences in the rates of brain aging still uses a group-level mechanism to account for the group-level phenomenon. Hence, it is reasonable to argue that the hypothesis of increased intraindividual variability, supported by the simulation results, is more parsimonious and fundamental than the hypothesis of individual difference in the rates of neurobiological deterioration.

However, one should note that this mapping from intra-network to inter-network variability is not "unique" in the sense that the increase in inter-network variability can also be produced by reducing the network's learning rate (e. g., Li et al., 1996). Indeed, analyses at the behavioral level have also shown that the relationship between age and variability in RT is, to a great extent, channeled through age-related difference in RT itself. In other words, age-related slowing measured at the performance level is sufficient to account for age-related increase in interindividual variability (e. g., Hale, Myerson, Smith, & Poon, 1988; Salthouse, 1993). Both the simulation results and the empirical findings suggest then that age-related slowing can be yet another alternative account for age-related increase of interindividual variability.

Based on these simulation results alone one cannot choose between the two alternatives, favoring a age-related behavioral slowing or a neural-noise explanation, if the only issue of interest is whether these two alternatives can account for the phenomenon of age-related increase in interindividual variability. Likewise, one also cannot decide which of the two parameters, gain or learning rate, can better capture age-related increase in interindividual variability. However, these two hypotheses can be better contrasted if additional criteria, such as the feasibility of cross-level hypothesis generation and the scope of the explanation, are considered. These two explanations are not entirely compatible in the sense that they were proposed for phenomena at two different levels. Consequently, they also are not in direct conflict with each other. Cognitive aging researchers who subscribe to the behavioral-slowing view in general agree that what they take as a primitive in their explanations (i. e., behavioral slowing) needs to be somehow instantiated at the biological level (e. g., Salthouse, 1996). The stochastic gain manipulation has been shown to be able to account for both age-related slowing and additional cognitive aging phenomena that were formerly shown to be within the purview of the age-related slowing hypothesis (Li et al., 1996). Given that the gain parameter computationally implements the efficiency of neural information transmission, the gain parameter account of cognitive aging deficits provides at least one version of computational formalism which demonstrates how behavioral slowing might be instantiated biochemically. From a modeling perspective, the learning rate parameter has a more restricted simulation scope than the gain manipulation. Specifically, although reducing the learning rate can also simulate a greater degree of inter-network variability, learning rate alone was not able (or less able in some cases) to account for some benchmark cognitive aging deficits, such as the age difference in asymptotic performance, the age by task complexity effect, and susceptibility to interference, all of which can be better accounted for by the stochastic gain manipulation (Li et al., 1996).

## Implications for Cognitive Child Development

The question concerning variations in the structure of mental ability has also been investigated from a cognitive child development perspective. For instance, Garrett, Bryan, and Perl (1935) found that the first unrotated factor accounted for, respectively, 31%, 32% and 12% of the variance in a 10-tests battery for boys aged 9, 12, and 15 years (and 31.5%, 24% and 19.5% for girls of the same ages). These findings led Garrett (1946), who coined the term *differentiation hypothesis*, to state that "with increasing age there appears to be a gradual breakdown of an amorphous general ability into a group of fairly distinct aptitudes" (p. 375). In addition, initial biological evidence suggests that as infants mature from 2 to 17 weeks of age, the variability in both the latency and amplitude of the evoke potential in response to tones decreased (e. g., Thomas, Whitaker, Crow, Little et al., 1997). Behavioral level results with respect to word and phrase duration in speech also indicate a decline in variability from early childhood (age 7 year) to teenage (age 13 year) to adulthood (Chermak & Schneiderman, 1985), and this effect could not be explained by mean speaking rate.

Taken together, results both from developmental and cognitive aging studies seem to suggest two continua as the ontogeny of cognition goes from early childhood to adulthood and then into late adulthood. With respect to the structure issue, cognitive abilities are less differentiated in early childhood, become increasingly differentiated from childhood to adulthood, and start to dedifferentiate again going from adulthood to old age. (e. g., Baltes & Lindenberger, 1997; Burt, 1954; Reinert, 1970). With respect to the variability issue, the trend seems to be that variability is high in early childhood, decreases in adulthood, then increases again in late adulthood. However, empirical data supporting age-related decrease in interindividual and intraindividual variability from infancy to adulthood is not as available as the findings supporting age-related increase in variability during the aging process.

Given the similarities between the developmental and aging patterns, one can expect that the gain manipulation can also account for related cognitive developmental phenomena at the formal level. However, one should ask whether there are reasons for assuming that the general neurobiological mechanisms associated with aging are also operative in child development but in a reversed direction? Empirical data at both the behavioral and biological level indicated that this might possibly be the case. Behavioral studies of lifespan cognitive development have shown that cognitive abilities, such as processing speed, selective attention, and memory span, show an inverted-U shaped lifespan function. For instance, using two tests of perceptual speed from the Woodcock-Johnson Tests, Kail and Salthouse (1994) showed that perceptual speed increases from age six to early adulthood, then becomes stable until mid-adulthood, and eventually starts to decline. In their review of lifespan development of selective attention, Plude et al. (1994) reported that the abilities to filter visual distractors and to search for attribute conjunctions improve throughout childhood, remain stable in adulthood, and decline in late adulthood. Similarly, others have shown that the ability to resist interference in paradigms involving Wisconsin Card Sorting Test (WCST) and the Stroop Test increases from age seven to early adulthood, remains stable until mid adulthood, then declines again as people age (e. g., Chelune & Baer, 1986; Comalli, Wapner, & Werner, 1962; Haaland, Vranes, Goodwin, & Garry, 1987). With respect to memory performance, a few studies have also shown a similar inverted-U lifespan developmental function for memory span (e. g., Case, 1985; Hasselhorn, 1988; Salthouse, 1990; Siegel, 1994). In light of these data, some developmental psychologists have proposed conceptual accounts to explain the phenomena of cognitive development and aging within a unified framework. For instance, lifespan variations in the efficacy of inhibitory mechanism (e. g., Bjorklund & Harnishfeger, 1995; Dempster, 1992), the amount of neural noise (cf. Plude, Enns, & Brodeur, 1994), and the speed of processing (Kail & Salthouse, 1994; Park, Smith, Lautenschlager, Earles et al., 1996) have all been *independently* proposed as the connecting thread for lifespan cognitive development. Interestingly, at the biochemical level, lifespan data concerning the efficacy of the dopaminergic system also indicated a continuum of age-related increase in dopamine metabolites extracted from human urine samples in the age range from 1 day old to 18 years old and a decrease from 18 to 55 years old (Dalmaz, Peyrin, Sann, & Dutruge, 1979). Given the roles of catecholamines in regulating the spontaneous firing rate of neurons in the prefrontal cortex, the related attentional and inhibitory mechanisms (e. g., Jay, Glowinski, & Thierry, 1995; Mora, Sweeney, Rolls, & Sannguinetti, 1976; Shelley, Catts, Ward, & Andrews, 1997), and processing speed (e. g., MacRae et al., 1988; Schultz et al., 1989; Spirduso et al., 1989), one might speculate that the rise and fall in the efficacy of neural transmission as modulated by the catecholamines (or other transmitter substances showing similar functional properties) could be an important thread at the biological level for cognitive development across the lifespan.

## Conclusion

In this chapter, we have reviewed empirical evidence for age-related dedifferentiation in cognitive abilities and age-related increase in variability at both the biological and behavioral levels, along with age-related differences in the integrity of neurotransmitter systems. A computational approach capturing the effects of the catecholaminergic system on regulating the sensitivity and variability of neural information processing was proposed to theoretically link findings at these different levels. Based on the simulation results, we suggest that a causal path from the responsivity of a neuron to the level of random variability within the CNS, and the behavioral manifestations of intraindividual variability, interindividual variability, and the ontogeny of the structure of cognitive abilities can at least be supported by the computational formalism specified here. We acknowledge that such cross-level theorizing runs the risk of losing the specifics for the general, and that the cross-level links we proposed here stay quite speculative, despite initial support from the simulations. However, we have demonstrated in this chapter that theorizing from a cognitive neuroscience orientation offers more possibilities for cross-level data integration, hypothesis generation and testing. Hopefully this will in the future provide us with a more integrated picture of lifespan cognitive development.

## Acknowledgments

We thank Patricia Hawley and Karen Li for their helpful comments on earlier versions of this chapter. Thanks are also due to John R. Nesselroade who throughout the years had written many articles and chapters on the conceptual and measurement issues of intraindividual variability, and to Paul B. Baltes who has always been recommending firmly an integrative lifespan approach to the study of development.

## References

Anderson, J.A. (1983). Cognitive and psychological computation with neural models. *IEEE Transactions on Systems, Man, and Cybernetics, 13*, 799–814.

Arnsten, A.F.T., & Goldman-Rakic, P.S. (1985). Alpha 2-adrenergic mechanisms in prefrontal cortex associated with cognitive declines in aged non human primates. *Science, 230*, 1273–1276.

Ashby, F.G., & Gott, R.E. (1988). Decision rules in the perception and categorization of multidimensional stimuli. *Journal of Experimental Psychology: Learning, Memory and Cognition, 14,* 33–53.

Ashby, F.G., & Maddox, W.T. (1992). Complex decision rules in categorization: Contrasting novice and experienced performance. *Journal of Experimental Psychology: Human Perception and Performance, 18,* 50–71.

Babcock, R.L., Laguna, K.D., & Roesch, S.C. (1997). A comparison of the factor structure of processing speed for younger and older adults: Testing the assumption of measurement equivalence across age groups. *Psychology and Aging, 12,* 268–276.

Baldi, P., & Chauvin, Y. (1991). Temporal evolution of generalization during learning in linear network. *Neural Computation, 3,* 589–603.

Balinsky, B. (1941). An analysis of the mental factors of various groups from nine to sixty. *Genetic Psychology Monographs, 23,* 191–234.

Baltes, P.B., Cornelius, S.W., Spiro, A., Nesselroade, J.R., & Willis, S.L. (1980). Integration versus differentiation of fluid/crystallized intelligence in old age. *Developmental Psychology, 6,* 625–635.

Baltes, P.B., & Lindenberger, U. (1997). Emergence of a powerful connection between sensory and cognitive functions across the adult lifespan: A new window to the study of cognitive aging? *Psychology and Aging, 12,* 12–21.

Baltes, P.B., Staudinger, U.M., & Lindenberger, U. (in press). Life-span developmental psychology. *Annual Review of Psychology.*

Barnes, J.M., & Underwood, B.J. (1959). "Fate" of first-learned associations in transfer theory. *Journal of Experimental Psychology, 58,* 97–105.

Berns, G.S., & Sejnowski, T.J. (1998). A computational model of how the basal ganglia produce sequences. *Journal of Cognitive Neuroscience, 10,* 108–121.

Bechtel, W. (1988). *Philosophy of science.* Hillsdale, NJ: Erlbaum.

Birren, J.E., Woods, A.M., & Williams, M.V. (1980). Behavioral slowing with age: Causes, organization and consequences. In L.W. Poon (Ed.), *Aging in the 1980's: Psychological issues* (pp. 293–308). Washington, DC: American Psychological Association.

Bjorklund, D.F., & Harnishfeger, K.K. (1995). The evolution of inhibition mechanisms and their role in human cognition and behavior. In F.N. Dempster & C.J. Brainerd (Eds.), *Interference and inhibition in cognition* (pp. 141–173). New York: Academic Press.

Burt, C. (1954). The differentiation of intellectual ability. *British Journal of Educational Psychology, 24,* 76–90.

Case, R. (1985). *Intellectual development.* New York: Academic Press.

Cerella, J. (1990). Aging and information-processing rate. In J.E. Birren & R.W. Schaie (Eds.), *Handbook of psychology and aging* (pp. 201–221). San Diego, CA: Academic Press.

Chelune, G.J., & Baer, R.A. (1986). Developmental norms for the Wisconsin Card Sorting Test. *Journal of Clinical and Experimental Neuropsychology, 8,* 219–228.

Chermak, G.D., & Schneiderman, C.R. (1985). Speech timing variability of children and adults. *Journal of Phonetics, 13,* 477–480.

Christensen, H., Mackinnon, A., Jorm, A.F., Henderson, A.S., Scott, L.R., & Korten, A.E. (1994). Age differences and interindividual variation in cognition in community-dwelling elderly. *Psychology and Aging, 9,* 381–390.

Churchland, P.S. (1988). The significance of neuroscience for philosophy. *Trends in Neurosciences, 11,* 304–307.

Churchland, P.S., & Sejnowski, T.J. (1988). Perspectives on cognitive neuroscience. *Science*, *242*, 741–745.

Clark, C.R., Geffen, G.M., & Geffen, I.B. (1987). Catecholamines and attention: II. Pharmacological studies in normal humans. *Neuroscience and Biobehavioral Reviews*, *11*, 353–364.

Comalli, P.E., Wapner, S., & Werner, H. (1962). Interference effects of Stroop color-word test in children, adulthood and aging. *Journal of Genetic Psychology*, *100*, 47–53.

Corwin, J.V., Kanter, S., Watson, R.T., Heilman, K.M., Valenstein, E., & Hashimoto, A. (1986). Apomorphine has a therapeutic effect on neglect proposed by unilateral dorsal medial prefrontal cortex lesion in rate. *Experimental Neurology*, *94*, 683–698.

Cronbach, L.J. (1957). The two disciplines of scientific psychology. *American Psychologist*, *12*, 671–684.

Cronbach, L.J. (1975). Beyond the two disciplines of scientific psychology. *American Psychologist*, *30*, 116–127.

Crossman, E.R.F.W., & Szafran, J. (1956). Changes with age in the speed of information intake and discrimination. *Experimental supplementum IV: Symposium on Experimental Gerontology*, *4*, 128–135.

Cunningham, W.R. (1980). Age comparative factor analysis of ability variables in adulthood and old age. *Intelligence*, *4*, 133–149.

Dalmaz, Y., Peyrin, L., Sann, L., & Dutruge, J. (1979). Age-related changes in catecholamines metabolites of human urine from birth to adulthood. *Journal Neural Transmission*, *46*, 153–174.

Deary, I.J., Egan, V., Gibson, G.J., Austin, E.J., Brand, C.R., & Kellaghan, T. (1996). Intelligence and the differentiation hypothesis. *Intelligence, 23*, 105–132.

DeFrance, J.F., Sikes, R.W., & Chronister, R.B. (1985). Dopamine action in the nucleus accumbens. *Journal of Neurophysiology*, *54*, 1568–1577.

Dempster, F.N. (1992). The rise and fall of the inhibitory mechanism: Toward a unified theory of cognitive development and aging. *Developmental Review*, *12*, 45–75.

Detterman, D.K., & Daniel, M.H. (1989). Correlations of mental tests with each other and with cognitive variables are highest for low IQ groups. *Intelligence, 13*, 349–359.

Eysenck, H.J. (1982). Introduction. In H.J. Eysenck (Ed.), *A model for intelligence* (pp. 1–10). Berlin: Springer-Verlag.

Eysenck, H.J. (1987). Intelligence and reaction time: The contribution of Arthur Jensen. In S. Modgil & C. Modgil (Eds.), *Arthur Jensen: Consensus and controversy*. New York: Falmer Press.

Fiske, D.W., & Rice, L. (1955). Intra-individual response variability. *Psychological Bulletin*, *52*, 217–250.

Fozard, J.L., Thomas, J.C., & Waugh, N.C. (1976). Effects of age and frequency of stimulus repetitions on two-choice reaction time. *Journal of Gerontology*, *38*, 556–563.

Gabrieli, J. (1995). Contribution of the basal ganglia to skill learning and working memory in humans. In J.C. Houk, J.L. Davis, & D.G. Beiser (Eds.), *Models of information processing in the basal ganglia* (pp. 277–294). Cambridge MA: Bradford.

Garrett, H.E. (1946). A developmental theory of intelligence. *American Psychologist, 1*, 372–378.

Garrett, H.E., Bryan, A.I., & Perl, R. (1935). The age factor in mental organization. *Archives of Psychology*, Columbia University, No. 176: 29.

Gigerenzer, G. (1991). From tool to theories: A heuristic of discovery in cognitive psychology. *Psychological Review*, *98*, 254–267.

Gillund, G., & Shiffrin, R.M. (1984). A retrieval model for both recognition and recall. *Psychological Review*, *91*, 1–67.

Goebel, R.P., & Lewandowsky, S. (1991). Retrieval measures in distributed memory models. In W.E. Hockley & S. Lewandowsky (Eds.), *Relating theory and data: Essays on human memory in honor of Bennet B. Murdock* (pp. 509–527). Hillsdale, NJ: Erlbaum.

Grady, C.L., Haxby, J.V., Horwitz, B., Schapiro, M.B., Rapoport, S.I., Ungerleider, L.G., Mishkin, M., Carson, R.E., & Herscovitch, P. (1992). Dissociation of object and spatial vision in human extrastriate cortex: Age-related changes in activation of regional cerebral blood flow measured with [¹⁵O]water and positron emission tomography. *Journal of Cognitive Neuroscience*, *4*, 23–34.

Grady, C.L., Maisog, J.M., Horwitz, B., Ungerleider, L.G., Mentis, M.J., Salerno, J.A., Pietrini, P., Wagner, E., & Haxby, J.V. (1994). Age-related changes in cortical blood flow activation during visual processing of faces and location. *Journal of Neuroscience*, *14*, 1450–1462.

Granick, S., Kleban, M.H., & Weiss, A.D. (1976). Relationships between hearing loss and cognition in normally hearing aged person. *Journal of Gerontology*, *31*, 434–440.

Haaland, K.Y., Vranes, L.F., Goodwin, J.S., & Garry, P.J. (1987). Wisconsin Card Sort Test performance in a healthy elderly population. *Journal of Gerontology*, *42*, 345–346.

Hale, S., Myerson, J., Smith, G.A., & Poon, L.W. (1988). Age, variability, and speed: Between-subject diversity. *Psychology and Aging*, *3*, 407–410.

Hanno, D.J., & Hoyer, W.J. (1994). Mechanisms of visual-cognitive aging: A neural network account. *Aging and Cognition*, *1*, 105–119.

Hasselhorn, M. (1988). Wie und warum verändert sich die Gedächtnisspanne über die Lebensspanne? [How and why does memory span change over the life span?]. *Zeitschrift für Entwicklungspsychologie und Pädagogische Psychologie*, *20*, 322–337

Hayslip, B., Jr., & Sterns, H.L. (1979). Age differences in relationships between crystallized and fluid intelligence and problem solving. *Journal of Gerontology*, *34*, 404–414.

Hendrickson, A.E. (1982). The biological basis of intelligence: Part I Theory. In H.J. Eysenck (Ed.), *A model for intelligence* (pp. 134–151). Berlin: Springer-Verlag.

Hendrickson, D.E. (1982). The biological basis of intelligence: Part II Measurement. In H.J. Eysenck (Ed.), *A model for intelligence* (pp. 152–197). Berlin: Springer-Verlag.

Houk, J.C., Davis, J.L., & Beiser, D.G. (Eds.) (1995). *Models of information processing in the basal ganglia*. Cambridge, MA: MIT Press.

Jay, T.M., Glowinski, J., & Thierry, A.M. (1995). Inhibition of hippocampo-prefrontal cortex excitatory responses by the mesocortical DA system. *Neuroreport: An International Journal for the Rapid Communication of Research in Neuroscience*, *6*, 1845–1848.

Jensen, A.R. (1982). Reaction time and psychometric g. In H.J. Eysenck (Ed.), *A model for intelligence* (pp.9 3–132). Berlin: Springer-Verlag.

Jensen, A.R. (1992). The importance of intraindividual variation in reaction time. *Personality and Individual Differences*, *13*, 869–881.

Kail, R., & Salthouse, T.A. (1994). Processing speed as a mental capacity. Special Issue: Life span changes in human performance. *Acta Psychologica*, *86*, 199–225.

Kempf, E., Mandel, P., Oliverio, A., & Pulisi-Allegra, S. (1982). Circadian variations of noradrenaline, 5-hydroxytryptamine and dopamine in specific brain areas of C56B1/6 and BALB/c mice. *Brain Research*, *232*, 472–478.

Kinsbourne, M., & Hicks, R.E. (1978). Functional cerebral space: A model for overflow, transfer, and interference effects in human performance. In J. Requin (Ed.), *Attention and performance VII* (pp. 345–362). Hillsdale, NJ: Erlbaum.

Kischka, U., Kammer, Th., Maier, S., Weisbrod, M. et al. (1996). Dopaminergic modulation of semantic network activation. *Neuropsychologia, 34,* 1107–1113.

Kolen, J.F., & Goel, A.K. (1991). Learning in parallel distributed processing network: Computational complexity and information content. *IEEE Transactions on Systems, Man, and Cybernetics, 21,* 359–367.

Kraiuhin, C., Gordon, E., Stanfield, P., Meares, R. et al. (1986). P300 and the effects of aging: Relevance to the diagnosis of dementia. *Experimental Aging Research, 12,* 187–192.

Kugler, C.F.A., Taghavy, A., & Platt, D. (1993). The event-related P300 potential analysis of cognitive human aging: A review, *Gerontology, 39,* 280–303.

Laver, G.D., & Burke, D.M. (1993). Why do semantic priming effects increase in old age? A meta-analysis. *Psychology and Aging, 8,* 34–43.

Lawley, D.N. (1943). A note on Karl Pearson's selection formulae. *Royal Society of Edinburgh Proceedings, Section A, 62,* 28–30.

Leibniz, G.W. von (1951). The horizon of human doctrine. In P.P. Wiener (Ed.), *Selections* (pp. 73–77). New York: Scribner. (Original work published after 1690).

Li, S.-C., & Lindenberger, U. (1998). *Towards a theoretical demonstration of a unified principle relating intraindividual variability and the differentiation and dedifferentiation of cognitive functioning across the lifespan.* Manuscript in preparation.

Li, S.-C., Lindenberger, U., & Frensch, P. (1996). *In search of an integrative framework of cognitive aging: A computational exploration of the link between processing efficiency and brain catecholamines.* Unpublished manuscript. Berlin, Max Planck Institute for Human Development.

Li, S.-C., Aggen, S.H., Nesselroade, J.R., & Baltes, P.B. (1998). *Revisiting the link between memory and sensorimotor functioning in old age via intraindividual variability: The MacArthur successful aging studies.* Unpublished manuscript. Berlin, Max Planck Institute for Human Development.

Lienert, G.A., & Crott, H.W. (1964). Studies on the factor structure of intelligence in children, adolescents, and adults. *Vita Humana, 7,* 147–163.

Lindenberger, U., & Baltes, P.B. (1994). Sensory functioning and intelligence in old age: A strong connection. *Psychology and Aging, 9,* 339–355.

Lindenberger, U., Marsiske, M., & Baltes, P.B. (1998). *Dual-task costs in sensorimotor and intellectual functioning: Increase from early to old age.* Unpublished manuscript. Berlin, Max Planck Institute for Human Development.

Llinas, R.R., & Churchland, P.S. (1996). *The mind-brain continuum.* Cambridge, MA: MIT Press.

Maas, H.L. van der, & Molenaar, P.C.M. (1992). Stagewise cognitive development: An application of catastrophe theory. *Psychological Review, 99,* 395–417.

MacRae, P.G., Spirduso, W.W., & Wilcox, R.E. (1988). Reaction time and nigrostriatal dopamine function: The effects of age and practice. *Brain Research, 451,* 139–146.

Mamelak, A.N., & Hobson, J. (1989). Dream bizarreness as the cognitive correlate of altered neuronal behavior in REM sleep. *Journal of Cognitive Neuroscience, 1,* 201–222.

Manshardt, J., & Wurtman, R.J. (1968). Daily rhythm in the noradrenaline context of rat hypothalamus. *Nature, 217,* 574–575,

McClelland, J.L., McNaughton, B.L., & O'Reilly, R.C. (1995). Why there are complementary learning systems in the hippocampus and neocortex: Insights from the successes and failures of connectionist models of learning and memory. *Psychological Review, 102,* 419–437.

McCloskey, M. (1991). Networks and theories: The place of connectionism in cognitive science. *Psychological Science, 2,* 387–395.

McDowd, J.M., & Craik, F.I. (1988). Effects of aging and task difficulty on divided attention performance. *Journal of Experimental Psychology: Human Perception and Performance, 14,* 267–280.

McHugh, R.B., & Owens, W.A. (1954). Age changes in mental organization – a longitudinal study. *Journal of Gerontology, 9,* 296–302.

Mora, F., Sweeney, K.F., Rolls, E.T., & Sannguinetti, A.M. (1976). Spontaneous firing rate of neurons in the prefrontal cortex of the rat: Evidence for a dopaminergic inhibition. *Brain Research, 116,* 516–522.

Morgan, D.G., & May, P.C. (1990). Age-related changes in synaptic neurochemistry. In E.L. Schneider & J.W. Rowe (Eds.), *Handbook of the biology of aging* (pp. 219–254). New York: Academic Press.

Morrison, J.H., & Hof, P.R. (1997). Life and death of neurons in the aging brain. *Science, 278,* 412 – 419.

Morse, C.K. (1993). Does variability increase with age? An archival study of cognitive measures. *Psychology and Aging, 8,* 156–164.

Nelson, E.A., & Dannefer, D. (1992). Aged heterogeneity: Facts or fiction? The fate of diversity in gerontological research. *Gerontologist, 32,* 17–23.

Nesselroade, J.R. (1991a). The warp and the woof of the developmental fabric. In R.M. Downs, L.S. Liben, & D.S. Palermo (Eds.), *Visions of aesthetics, the environment and development: The legacy of Joachim F. Wohlwill* (pp. 213–240). Hillsdale, NJ: Erlbaum.

Nesselroade, J.R. (1991b). Interindividual differences in intraindividual change. In J.L. Horn & L.M. Collins (Eds.), *Best methods for the analysis of change: Recent advances, unanswered questions, future directions* (pp. 92–107). Washington, D.C.: American Psychological Association.

Newell, A. (1990). *Unified theory of cognition.* Cambridge, MA: Harvard University Press.

Park, D.C., Smith, A.D., Lautenschlager, G., Earles, J.L. et al. (1996). Mediators of long-term memory performance across the life span. *Psychology and Aging, 11,* 621–637.

Pearson, K. (1903). Mathematical contributions to the theory of evolution: XI. On the influence of natural selection on the variability and correlation of organs. *Transactions of the Royal Society, Series A, 200,* 1–66.

Plude, D.J., Enns, J.T., & Brodeur, D. (1994). The development of selective attention: A life-span overview. *Acta Psychologica, 86,* 227–272.

Posner, M.I. (1992). Attention as a cognitive and neural system. *Current Directions in Psychological Science, 1,* 11–14.

Rabbitt, P.M. (1981). Cognitive psychology needs models for changes in performance with old age. In A. Baddeley, & J. Long (Eds.), *Attention and performance IX* (pp. 555–573). Hillsdale, NJ: Erlbaum.

Rabbitt, P.M. (1993). Does it all go together when it goes? The nineteenth Bartlett Memorial Lecture. *The Quarterly Journal of Experimental Psychology, 46A,* 385–434.

Reed, T.E., & Jensen, A.R. (1991). Arm nerve conduction velocity (NCV), brain NCV, reaction time, and intelligence. *Intelligence, 16, 15,* 33–47.

Reinert, G. (1970). Comparative factor analytic studies of intelligence through the life span. In L.R. Goulet & P.B. Baltes (Eds.), *Life-span developmental psychology: Research and theory* (pp. 115–145). New York: Academic Press.

Reis, D.J., Weinbren, M., & Corvelli, A. (1968). A circadian rhythm of norepinephrine regionally in cat brain: Its relationship to environmental lighting and to regional diurnal variations in brain serotonin. *Journal of Pharmacology and Experimental Therapeutics, 164*, 135–145.

Rogers, J., & Bloom, F.E. (1985). Neurotransmitter metabolism and function in the aging central nervous system. In C.E. Finch & E.L. Schneider (Eds.), *Handbook of the biology of aging* (pp. 645–691). New York: van Nostrand Reinhold.

Rothman, R.B. (1996). Treatment of a 4-year-old boy with ADHA with the dopamine releaser phentermine. *Journal of Clinical Psychiatry, 57*, 308–309.

Royce, J.R. (1987). A strategy for developing unifying theory in psychology. In A.W. Staats & L.P. Mos (Eds.), *Annals of theoretical psychology* (Vol. 5, pp. 275–284). New York: Plenum.

Salthouse, T.A. (1990). Working memory as a processing resource in cognitive aging. *Developmental Review, 10*, 101–124.

Salthouse, T.A. (1993). Attentional blocks are not responsible for age-related slowing. *Journal of Gerontology: Psychological Sciences, 48*, P263–P270.

Salthouse, T.A. (1996). The processing-speed theory of adult age differences in cognition. *Psychological Review, 103*, 403–428.

Salthouse, T.A., Hancock, H.E., Meinz, E.J., & Hambrick, D.Z. (1996). Interrelations of age, visual acuity, and cognitive functioning. *Journal of Gerontology: Psychological Sciences, 51B*, P317–P330.

Sawaguchi, T., & Goldman-Rakic, P.S. (1991). D1 dopamine receptors in prefrontal cortex: Involvement in working memory. *Science, 251*, 947–950.

Schacter, D.L. (1992). Understanding implicit memory. *American Psychologist, 47*, 559–569.

Schneider, W. (1993). Varieties of working memory as seen in biological and connectionist/control architectures. *Memory & Cognition, 21*, 184–192.

Schultz, W., Studer, A., Romo, R., Sundstrom, E. et al. (1989). Deficits in reaction times and movement times as correlates of hypokinesia in monkeys with MPTP-induced striatal dopamine depletion. *Journal of Neurophysiology, 61*, 651–668.

Servan-Schreiber, D., Printz, H.W., & Cohen, J.D. (1990). A network model of catecholamines effects: Gain, signal-to-noise ratio, and behavior. *Science, 249*, 892–895.

Shelley, A.M., Catts, S.V., Ward, P.B., Andrews, S. et al. (1997). The effect of decreased catecholamines transmission on ERP indices of selective attention. *Neuropsychopharmacology, 16*, 202–210.

Shepard, R.N. (1987). Towards a universal law of generalization for psychological science. *Science, 237*, 1317–1323.

Siegel, L.S. (1994). Working memory and reading: A life-span perspective. *International Journal of Behavioral Development, 17*, 109–124

Siegler, R.S. (1994). Cognitive variability: A key to understanding cognitive development. *Current Directions, 3*, 1–5.

Siegler, R.S., & Ellis, S. (1996). Piaget on childhood. *Psychological Science, 7*, 211–215.

Smith, G.A., & Stanley, G. (1987). Comparing subtest profiles of g loadings and correlations with RT measures. *Intelligence, 11*, 291–298.

Spearman, C.E. (1904). "General intelligence" objectively determined and measured. *American Journal of Psychology, 15*, 201–293.

Spearman, C.E. (1927). *The abilities of man*. London: Macmillan.

Spengler, F., Godde, B., & Dinse, H.R. (1995). Effects of aging on topographic organization of somatosensory cortex. *NeuroReport, 6*, 469–473.

Spirduso, W.W., Mayfield, D., Grant, M., & Schallert, T. (1989). Effects of route of administration of ethanol on high-speed reaction time in young and old rats. *Psychopharmacology, 97,* 413–417.

Spitzer, M. (1997). A cognitive neuroscience view of schizophrenic thought disorder. *Schizophrenia Bulletin, 23,* 29–50.

Staats, A.W. (1991). Unified positivism and unification psychology. *American Psychologist, 46,* 899–912.

Strong, E.K. (1912). The effect of length of series upon recognition memory. *Psychological Review, 19,* 447–462.

Thomas, D.G., Whitaker, E., Crow, C.D., Little, V. et al. (1997). Event-related potential variability as a measure of information storage in infant development. *Developmental Neuropsychology, 13,* 205–232.

Valentin, D., & Abdi, H. (1996). Can a linear autoassociator recognize faces from new orientations? *Journal of the Optical Society of America A, 13,* 717–724

Welford, A.T. (1965). Performance, biological mechanisms and age: A theoretical sketch. In A.T. Welford & J.E. Birren (Eds.), *Behavior, aging, and the nervous system* (pp. 3–20). Springfield, IL: Thomas.

Welford, A.T. (1980). Relationships between reaction time and fatigue, stress, age and sex. In A.T. Welford (Ed.), *Reaction times* (pp. 321–354). New York: Academic Press.

Welford, A.T. (1981). Signal, noise, performance and age. *Human Factor, 23,* 97–109.

Welford, A.T. (1984). Between bodily changes and performance: Some possible reasons for slowing with age. *Experimental Aging Research, 10,* 73–88.

Yang, C.R., & Mogenson, G.J. (1990). Dopaminergic modulation of cholinergic response in rat medial prefrontal cortex: An electrophysiological study. *Brain Research, 524,* 271–281.

Zimmerman, D.W. (1976). Test theory with minimal assumptions. *Educational and Psychological Measurement, 36,* 85–96.

# Aging, Dementia, and Memory

*Lars-Göran Nilsson*

As was discussed in the introductory chapter of this volume, there are several reasons for the growing interest in studying memory functions in recent years. In addition to being interested in memory because of its basic importance for a meaningful intelligent life of people, a great deal of interest is due to the emerging role of various memory disorders in everyday life of people. The understanding of memory decline in old age is an example of this. Memory and other cognitive problems, including those accompanying Alzheimer's disease and other progressive brain diseases, are going to increase with the increasing populations of the elderly. As the number of elderly people increases in most countries in the world, there is a growing concern to understand what the reasons for this memory decline are, and whether there is any cure or remedy. About two thirds of the population in Sweden reach the age of 65 and this proportion shows a steady increase. The proportion of people reaching this age varies across countries, but the trend of a general increase is present everywhere. Statistical information in Sweden has revealed that the increase will be most pronounced in the population over 80 years of age, especially among women (Statistiska Centralbyrån, 1976).

This development means a great demand on nursing and medical care and on the system for social care in general, especially so since the prevalence of dementia increases as a function of age. It has been estimated that the demented population will increase almost three times faster than the rest of the population before year 2000. Several studies have reported a prevalence of dementia in the order of 5% for those 65 years and older and 20% for those 80 years and older. On the basis of 12 prevalence studies conducted in Europe during the period 1980–1990, Hofman et al. (1991) showed the average to be 1.4% for persons 65–69 years of age, 4.1% for persons 70–74 years of age, 5.7% for 75–79 years of age, 13.0% for 80–84 years of age, 21.6% for 85–89 years of age, and 32.3% for persons 90–94 years of age.

Several studies have reported an increase in the incidence of dementia as a function of age in the order of 1–2% for 70-year olds and about 10% for 90-year olds (e. g., Marcusson, Blennow, Skoog, & Wallin, 1995). Hagnell,

Lanke, Rorsman, and Öjesjö (1981) reported a higher level of incidence in an urban population (2%) than in a rural population (1%). Hagnell (1966) showed a considerable variation in incidence for severe mental illness as a function of age and gender. Women in the age of 80 years and older show an incidence of 25%, whereas men in the ages between 65 and 69 show an incidence of 6%. Overrepresentation of women with the diagnosis of Alzheimer's disease and a similar overrepresentation of men with the diagnosis of vascular dementia has been detected (Skoog, 1998).

With respect to dementia in general and to risk factors for dementia of the Alzheimer type in particular, Mortimer and Hutton (1985) showed a positive correlation between several factors (e. g., age, genetical factors, Down's syndrome, high age of mother and father at birth, head trauma, thyroid gland disease, low levels of vitamin B12, aluminum) and the disease. Other risk factors like alcohol consumption, smoking habits, and several disorders in the medical history of the patient (e. g., vascular disease and depression) have recently been reported (Van Duijn, 1998). For socioeconomic status the results have been found to be rather mixed; some studies showed a positive correlation whereas others showed no such relationship. It has also been noted that there is some evidence for synergistic effects between environmental and genetic factors (e. g., Van Duijn, 1998). Genes may modify the risk of Alzheimer's disease associated with head trauma and several vascular factors. It can be concluded from these reviews that systematic research on risk factors has merely started and that there is still much research to be done.

Alzheimer's disease is a neurodegenerative disease of the central nervous system with a progressive decline of cognitive function as a cardinal symptom. Disorders in memory function constitutes an early sign of the disease. Neuropathological characteristics of Alzheimer's disease are senile plaques, neurofibrillary tangles, amyloid angiopathy, and neuronal loss. Relatively little is still known about the pathogenesis of Alzheimer's disease, but it has been known for some time now that genetic factors are involved (Davies, 1986). Four genes have been identified in relation to Alzheimer's disease (Van Broeckhoven, 1995): amyloid precursor protein (APP), presenilin-1 (PS-1), presenilin-2 (PS-2), and apolipoprotein (ApoE) genes. Whereas APP, PS-1, and PS-2 are fully penetrant and cause familial presenile dementia of Alzheimer type, ApoE is not a causative gene, but rather a genetic risk factor or a predisposing gene. The frequency of one form of this gene, allele ε4, is about 40% for people with late-onset Alzheimer's disease and 15% in control samples from the normal population (Chorney et al., 1998). Altogether, the four genes mentioned account for about 50% of all known cases of Alzheimer's disease (Van Broeckhoven, 1995).

In this chapter I will discuss some current issues in research on aging, dementia and memory relating to genetic aspects of memory. To illustrate the points to be made, I will use data from an ongoing longitudinal study on memory, health and aging (Nilsson et al., 1997). This project is a multi-cohort longitudinal study of cognition, health and personality in middle- to late-adulthood. It is located in the Swedish city of Umeå, a city of about 100,000 inhabitants in the north of Sweden. Because Umeå is called the city of birch trees and because Betula is Latin for birch tree, we colloquially refer to this project as the Betula study.

## The Betula Study

The project was originally motivated by the wish to explore various aspects of the development of memory functioning and health in adulthood and late life in light of the fact that an increasingly larger portion of the population consists of elderly people. In addition to studying the development of memory and health in general, a more specific purpose was to explore early, preclinical signs and potential risk factors of dementia, and to obtain premorbid measures of memory and health in people who are in accidents or acquire various other diseases during the course of the study. It was argued that the measures to be taken to accomplish these goals require an interdisciplinary approach involving scientists from several medical, social and psychological fields. Specifically, the aims of the study require the planning, conducting and analyzing of data from medical examinations, blood sample testing, health status enquiries, explorations of daily living and leisure activities, critical life events, examination of social and economic factors, and an extensive examination of a wide variety of memory functions.

### Design

The design employed for this study was modelled after Schaie (1965, 1977) to separate the effects of the three major sources of variation in developmental research: age, cohort, and time of measurement. Several studies have shown that different intellectual abilities (e. g., verbal, arithmetic) may show different cohort effects. The role of cohort effects in research on aging and memory is largely unknown; for this reason we consider the study of such effects in the present context to be exploratory. However, with this design it is possible to carry out a series of analyses, which have not been previously permitted in most other studies. These include cross-sectional, cross-sequential, cohort-sequential, time-sequential, and longitudinal analyses with proper controls for practice effects.

The general design of the study includes four samples of subjects with 10 different age cohorts in each sample. Subjects in the first sample (S1) were tested the first time in 1988–1990 (T1), in 1993–1995 (T2), and in 1998–2000 (T3). Subjects in the next two samples (S2 and S3) were tested the first time at T2 and then at T3, whereas subjects in the fourth sample (S4) were tested at T3 only.

Subjects in S1 were 35, 40, 45, 50, 55, 60, 65, 70, 75, and 80 years of age when first tested at T1. Subjects in S2 were also 35, 40, 45, 50, 55, 60, 65, 70, 75, and 80 years of age when they were tested the first time, five years later, at T2. Subjects in S3 were 40, 45, 50, 55, 60, 65, 70, 75, 80, and 85 years of age when they were tested the first time at T2, that is at the same time as the five years younger subjects of S2 were tested for the first time. Subjects in S4 were 40, 45, 50, 55, 60, 65, 70, 75, 80, and 85 years of age when they were tested for the first time at T3. There was a total of 100 subjects in each cohort of S1, S2, and S3, and 50 subjects in each cohort of S4 when each sample was first tested.

## Measures

At each wave of data collection in the Betula study, the subjects took part in extensive memory testing, a health examination and they completed questionnaires about social variables. The measures of cognition were selected to cover various aspects: episodic memory, semantic memory, primary memory, implicit memory, procedural memory, cognitive speed, and spatial cognition. The cognitive tests in the Betula study are listed in Table 1. As can be seen in this table,

*Table 1.* Cognitive tests in the Betula study

| | |
|---|---|
| *Episodic memory tasks* | Source recall of recently acquired facts |
| Free recall of sentences | Prospective memory |
| Cued recall of sentences, category cue | |
| Cued recall of sentences, verb cue | *Semantic memory* |
| Recognition of sentences, free choice | Word fluency |
| Source recall of sentences | Word comprehension |
| Free recall of enacted sentences | General knowledge |
| Cued recall of enacted sentences, category cue | |
| | *Priming* |
| Cued recall of enacted sentences, verb cue | Word stem completion |
| | *Word fragment completion* |
| Recognition of enacted sentences, free choice | *Procedural memory* |
| | Tower of Hanoi |
| Source recall of enacted sentences | |
| Free recall of words, distractor task at study | *Cognitive speed* |
| Free recall of words, distractor task at test | Letter-digit substitution |
| Free recall of words, distractor task at study and test | *Spatial cognition* |
| | Block design |
| Free recall of words, no distractor task | |
| Recall of recently acquired facts | *Cognitive screening* |
| | Mini-Mental State Examination |

there is an emphasis on episodic memory tasks, which is due to the fact that age deficits are most pronounced in such tasks, and signs of dementia are typically seen in such tasks prior to other cognitive tasks (e. g., Becker & Lopez, 1992; Tierney et al., 1996). In addition to the tests used, memory functioning was also assessed by means of subjective ratings.

The health variables included self ratings of health, blood parameters including red and white cells of the blood, hormones, vitamins, blood fat, blood sugar, immune response reactants, liver function, electrolytes and minerals. Urine measures on leukocytes, glucose, protein, electrolytes, and hemoglobin were also included. Measures used for systolic blood pressure, diastolic blood pressure and pulse rate were taken after 10 min of rest in supine position, immediately after standing up, and after standing up for three min. Sensory functions were assessed by means of three relatively crude measures. Hearing status was determined on the basis of whether the subjects accurately could hear a conversation at a distance of 1 m, spoken in a normal tone of voice. Vision was assessed on the basis of whether the subject accurately could see to do finger counting at a distance of 1 m, and read normal newspaper text with or without glasses or lenses. Height, weight, body mass index, biceps, and triceps skinfold were also measured.

Other health related factors include: dental status, health care consumption, previous diseases, diseases of relatives, surgery and anesthesia, medication, substance use, subjective ratings of stress, activities of daily living (hygiene etc.), personality, mood and seasonal variation. The basic rationale used for investigating the development of health in adulthood and old age was to cover a wide range of potentially important physical and psychic factors and to relate these indexes of health status to memory performance. The methods used to collect these data were questionnaires, interviews, and a regular health examination including blood sample testing. The literature on the role of health status for the size of the age effect in memory performance is quite mixed. On the one hand, it has been reported that self-rated health status declines as a function of age (Perlmutter, & Nyquist, 1990), and that decline in self-rated health status is related to a decrease in memory performance (Field, Schaie, & Leino, 1988; Hultsch, Hammer, & Small, 1993; Perlmutter & Nyquist, 1990). On the other hand, it has also been demonstrated that statistical control for self-rated health status does not attenuate the age-related variance in cognitive performance (Salthouse, Kausler, & Saults, 1990). In a recent study Earles and Salthouse (1995) demonstrated that self-rated health only partially mediated the relationship between age and cognitive performance related to speed.

It should also be noted that sample blood has been saved for the investigation of genetic variations as determined by association studies and neurotransmitter-receptor studies, and sample whole blood for "banking" for future genome investigation in different diseases. For a subset of the Sample 1 subjects, data regarding the following serum protein polymorphisms have been registered: complement C3, haptoglobin, properdin factor B, orosomucoid, group-specific components, and transferrin C.

Social variables included marital status, profession, type of dwelling, living conditions, education, leisure activities, current daily activities, profession, profession and activities of spouse, children, parents, friends, as well as activities of childhood and adolescence.

## Attrition

Nilsson et al. (1997) described the study in general, reported data on attrition and selective drop-out, and overall data on health and memory as a function of age. By means of public information from Statistiska Centralbyrån (1985), several demographic variables were used to assess potential differences between participants and nonparticipants. In these analyses we included: gender, marital status, employment, education, income, and number of persons living in the household as variables for comparisons. Comparisons between participants ($n = 1\,000$) and nonparticipants ($n = 481$) revealed that participants were employed to a somewhat greater extent and had a higher income than nonparticipants. Breaking down the data for these two variables separately for each of the ten cohorts, it was found that there are more employed persons for participants than nonparticipants among 40-, 55-, 65-, and 70-year-olds. For the income variable, participants showed a higher income in the three oldest cohorts. Thus, although some differences were observed, participants were indistinguishable from nonparticipants in most variables of interest. Further support for the representativeness of the participants in this study was obtained when comparing participants with the whole of Sweden in the same cohorts. This comparison revealed a somewhat higher level of education and a bit higher income for participants. The difference between participants and Sweden in general for education and income was expected given the fact that Umeå is a city where a university is located.

## Memory Performance

The memory data in Nilsson et al. (1997) revealed a continuous age-related deterioration in tasks assessing episodic memory, no age-related deficit in semantic memory tasks when educational level is partialled out, and no age effects in priming. The relationships between subjective (i. e., self-rating) and objective (blood and urine parameters, blood pressure and pulse, medication, recent contacts with a physician, and sensory function) indexes of health, on the one hand, and memory performance, on the other, were in general relatively weak in all age groups. The health-memory relationship was completely mediated by age, whereas the age-memory relationship was only partially mediated by health.

Bäckman and Nilsson (1996) showed that verbal fluency and vocabulary tests indicated no variation between 35 and 50 years of age, followed by a gradual decline with increasing age. In a test of general knowledge, only the two oldest cohorts showed deficits. When educational level was controlled statistically, a different pattern of results was seen: the middle-aged adults performed at the highest level and, with the exception of one fluency test, no age-related deficits were observed before 75 years of age. These data suggest that, although there may be age-related deficits in semantic memory in the general population, education appears to be a more important factor than adult age per se for semantic memory functioning.

Erngrund, Mäntylä, and Nilsson (1996) investigated potential age differences in source recall. An age-related deterioration of both item and source recall was observed, with source recall being more impaired than item recall. Source error analyses revealed an increase of source amnesia in the ages of 75–80 years. Individual differences in background variables, age, gender, and word comprehension were related to source of well-known items, whereas age and years of formal education were related to source recall of unknown items. Source amnesia was accentuated in the two oldest cohorts and related to word comprehension. The age-related tendency to forget the source even when the fact is retained was suggested to be a specific feature of cognitive aging.

Erngrund, Mäntylä and Rönnlund (1996) extended the study of source recall of facts related to well-known and unknown people (Erngrund, Mäntylä, & Nilsson, 1996) to a study of source recall of how short sentences were encoded, by means of enactment or no enactment. Age-related decrements were observed both in item and source memory, although age differences in source memory were more accentuated than in item memory. Furthermore, the results suggested an overall impairment of source memory across age when individual differences in the demographic, psychometric, and biological variables were taken into consideration.

Herlitz, Nilsson, and Bäckman (1997) examined potential gender differences in episodic memory, semantic memory, primary memory and priming. There were no differences between men and women with regard to age, education, or on a global intellectual functioning. Men outperformed women on a visuospatial task and women outperformed men on tests of verbal fluency. Most importantly, the results demonstrated that women consistently performed at a higher level than men on episodic memory tasks, although there were no differences between men and women on the tasks assessing semantic memory, primary memory, or priming. Women's higher performance on the episodic memory tasks could not be fully explained by their higher verbal ability.

Mäntylä and Nilsson (1997) examined age related effects in a prospective memory task. The prospective memory task was incidental and relatively realistic in the sense that the participants were asked to remind the experimenter to sign a paper after a two-hour memory test session. Results showed an overall deterioration in performance as a function of age. Age-related differences in prospective memory were also observed when differences in background variables were taken into account.

Nyberg, Bäckman, Erngrund, Olofsson, and Nilsson (1996) explored whether an age effect existed in episodic memory, semantic memory and priming after differences on various demographic, intellectual, and biological factors had been controlled for. The simple correlations of age with episodic memory and semantic memory performance were found to be significant, whereas no relationship was found between age and levels of priming. After controlling for differences on the background factors, age predicted episodic but not semantic memory performance. It was proposed that the failure to account for the age effect on episodic memory is because it is caused by age-related neuronal changes.

Nyberg, Nilsson, Olofsson, and Bäckman (1997) explored the effects of division of attention during encoding and retrieval on age differences in episodic memory. It was demonstrated that age differences in memory performance were substantial under single-task conditions, but after correcting memory performance under dual-task conditions for differences in single-task performance age did not predict performance. These results did not support the hypothesis that reduced attentional capacity in old age is underlying age differences in episodic memory.

## Memory Performance and Genetic Markers

During the last 10 years or so there has been an increasing interest in the role of genetic markers on cognitive function (e. g., Cardon, Faulkner, DeFries, & Plomin, 1992). In most of the behavior genetics studies carried out so far, the main emphasis has been on examining the contribution of genetic factors for intelligence. DNA has been extracted in the Betula study too and we are now in the process of examining the associations between various genetic markers and various forms of memory.

In a first study from Betula on this topic, Nilsson et al. (1996) studied associations between six serum protein polymorphisms [complement C3, properdin factor B (BF), haptoglobin (HP), orosomucoid (ORM1), transferrin C

(TF), and group-specific components (GC)] and high versus low scoring on episodic memory tasks in an attempt to identify QTL (quantitative trait loci) contributing to the heritability of this quantitative trait. Of those six serum protein polymorphisms available to relate to memory function, it was generally conceived that complement C3 and the acute-phase reactant HP should be of primary interest as immune response factors.

Since a highly significant sex difference had been found with respect to memory performance (cf. Herlitz, Nilsson, & Bäckman, 1997), with men showing a poorer performance, associations were studied separately for males and females. In females significant differences between the high and low groups were found in four out of six marker systems (C3, HP, TF, and CG), whereas in males a significant difference was found only in the HP system. Significant differences from population frequencies were also found more frequently in females than in males. The strongest marker associations were found with complement C3 and the acute-phase reactant HP, which thus suggests that immune response factors may be of importance in preserving episodic memory function. In the HP system there was evidence of a primary phenotypic association involving heterozygotes (Nilsson et al., 1996). This means that the HP groups may somehow be functionally involved in the preservation of episodic memory. An association involving heterozygotes indicates that linkage disequilibrium with alleles at other loci influencing memory function is unlikely. The association with C3 alleles may be due to either linkage disequilibrium or functional involvement on the protein level. The overall results indicate that episodic memory is a multifactorial and heritable quantitative trait where sex is an important determinant.

In another line of research on the role of genetic markers for memory functions in the Betula project, we explored the gene for Apolipoprotein E (ApoE). ApoE, the gene of which is located on chromosome 19, is a protein on the surface of lipoproteins, thereby influencing the metabolism of lipids, primarily cholesterol. There are genetic forms of ApoE (alleles) coding for three forms of the protein (isoforms), ApoE2, ApoE3, and ApoE4. These isoforms differ in one amino acid. ApoE3 is the most common isoform, occurring in about three fourths of the population. ApoE2 and ApoE4 occur in about 10% and 15% of the population, respectively. ApoE4 is considered to be a strong risk factor for the development of Alzheimer's disease with late onset. ApoE4 is also a risk factor for cardiovascular disease in middle age persons. It has not yet been determined whether ApoE4 is associated with vascular dementia. However, recent data (Skoog, 1998; Skoog, Lernfelt, Landahl et al., 1996) suggest that vascular disorders are common in Alzheimer's disease and ApoE may play a crucial role in this interaction. The pathophysiological mechanism behind ApoE4 and Alzheimer's disease is still not yet fully determined, at least there is still no consensus among several alternative hypotheses. One general claim is that ApoE4 does not protect key neuronal structures from excessive phosphorylation, thus leading to neuronal degeneration. Persons with ApoE2 and ApoE3, on the other hand, receive necessary neuronal protection and are much less likely to develop Alzheimer's disease. Evidence in favor of this hypothesis has been presented in recent years, but there are still many researchers in the field who remain skeptical about its merits. Thus, more research is still needed.

In the Betula study, there is presently much research in progress trying to understand the role of the various forms ApoE for memory function. Nilsson et al. (1998) explored the role of ApoE in memory function in nondemented subjects and in subjects who developed dementia between the first wave of data collection in 1988–1990 and the second wave of data collection in 1993–1995.

Memory performance was determined for subjects with the ApoE4 allele and those subjects without this allele. Analyses of memory performance were based on longitudinal data and those seven factors that had been determined by means of a principal component analysis in Nilsson et al. (1997). Among these seven factors there were four factors classified as being related to episodic memory, two factors related to semantic memory, and one factor to priming. In overall analyses, differences between ApoE4 and nonApoE4 subjects were obtained for episodic memory rather than for semantic memory and priming. Of those four episodic memory factors, the results of further analyses revealed that differences between the ApoE4 subjects and the nonApoE4 subjects hold primarily for one factor, namely action memory.

The basic procedure in the tasks relating to this factor is that subjects are presented with verbal commands (e. g., roll the ball, fold the paper, touch the shirt) and are instructed to perform the actions with objects given to them by the experimenter. Subjects are then given a series of tests based on this enacted encoding. Immediately after study, subjects are given a free recall test of the verbal commands presented, followed by a cued recall test, in which four category cues are presented to aid subjects recall the four instances of each category. After a number of other tasks in the Betula test battery, subjects are then given a yes/no recognition test followed by still another cued recall test with the verb of each command as a cue. The target items in both these tests are the nouns of the verbal commands. For each cued recall response the subjects are also instructed to say whether they studied each command by means of enactment or nonenactment. Just before or just after the study and free recall test of the enacted commands, subjects also studied a similar list of commands without any instructions of enactment. Thus, at the source recall test, subjects are asked to remember how the commands were studied initially, with or without enactment.

Thus, the action memory component, free recall, cued recall, and recognition revealed interactions between ApoE4 or not, dementia or not, and test occasion. One source of these interactions is that type of ApoE allele (ε4 or no ε4) does not matter for nondemented subjects either at the first test occasion in 1988–1990 or at the second test occasion in 1993–1995. However, for those subjects who developed dementia between the two test occasions, type of ε4 allele seems to be of importance. When subjects had been diagnosed as demented, those with the ε4 allele suffered in memory performance more than those without the ε4 allele. Moreover, and perhaps more interestingly is that the demented subjects with the ε4 allele performed very poorly in some tasks already at the first test occasion, that is before they had been diagnosed as demented. These tasks were not only the action memory tasks. Rather, both episodic and semantic memory tasks were found to be involved. More specifically, those tasks that showed this "marker property" were on the one hand episodic memory tasks using a recognition memory procedure and some semantic memory tasks. The recognition memory tasks included recognition of nouns that had been encoded as enacted verbal commands and as nonenacted verbal commands, and face recognition. The semantic memory tasks showing a similar marker property were two word fluency tests and one vocabulary test. In one of these two word fluency tests, subjects were required to generate as many words as possible beginning with the letter "A" during one minute. The other fluency task for which demented subjects with the ε4 allele showed poor performance already when they were nondemented was the task in which they were required to generate as many 5-letter words beginning with "M" as possible during one minute.

It was just mentioned that the performance of nondemented participants at the first and the second test occasion, taken separately, was not affected by the ε4 allele. However, when relating the performance levels at these two occasions, five years apart, there is an interesting pattern emerging. The data were first arranged according to the amount of change in performance that occurred between the first and the second test occasion. Some subjects showed a decrease in performance in some tasks, whereas others showed an increase, and still others performed at the same level when they were tested five years later. Those 20% of the subjects who had increased their performance most and those 20% of the subjects who had decreased their performance most were included in this analysis. For these two categories of subjects, in the four oldest age cohorts, it was found that the presence of the ε4 allele was correlated to memory performance in some of the episodic memory tasks, but not to any of the semantic memory tasks and not to priming. In particular, it was found that the action memory tasks were sensitive enough to detect a difference between those who increased their performance and those who decreased their performance. The ε4 allele was significantly less common among those in the former group than in the latter group. These data suggest that the presence or absence of the ε4 allele is associated with episodic memory performance in a healthy, nondemented population.

It should be observed that the results on genetic markers and memory referred to here (Nilsson et al., 1998; Nilsson et al., 1996) provide some further support to the notion of dissociations as a means to obtain converging evidence for the distinction between episodic memory and semantic memory (Schacter & Tulving, 1994; Tulving, 1972, 1983). Whereas correlations between genetic markers and memory were obtained for episodic memory tasks, there was no significant correlations to semantic memory tasks. It remains to be seen whether this relationship still holds when taking Tulving's conceptual update (this volume) of episodic and semantic memory into account.

Obviously, these results will have to be confirmed in subsequent research before firm conclusions can be made. One opportunity to do this is after the third wave of data collection has been completed in the Betula study in year 2000. A word of caution should also be mentioned with respect to these first steps taken in the Betula study in trying to relate one single genetic marker to memory performance. Plomin (1997) emphasized when trying to relate genetic markers to intelligence that the heritability of intelligence is more likely to be due to many genes of varying effect size than to few genes of a major effect. It is likely that a multifactorial ability like memory should also be related to multiple genes rather than to a single gene. It is indeed a challenging task to try to determine which the genes are that determine the genetic component of memory functioning.

It should also be mentioned in this context that genetic data from the Betula study is used in a broader context as well, not necessarily related to cognitive function. In total, DNA is available at present for close to 3,000 Betula subjects. In combination with the fact that the Betula study involves a large number of psychological, medical, and social variables, the Betula study makes a perfect case for normative data on genetic markers in relation to other variables. For example, in Cruts et al. (1995), ApoE data from the Betula database were used as control for patients with early-onset Alzheimer's disease from another study. In the study by Nelis et al. (1997) data from 262 Betula subjects were used to evaluate the frequency of a rare polymorphism in PMP-22 in northern Sweden. The results are suggestive for a founder effect in the Betula samples. Further studies are needed, however, to determine whether a founder effect would increase the chances to detect new genes involved in episodic memory and personality by reducing the number of genes in the gene pool and by maintaining disequilibrium over larger chromosomal regions.

## Future Work

The fact that data on a wide variety of memory tasks, medical and social variables are available together with genetic data on a large number of subjects of a wide age range in the Betula study presents a challenging case for future research on cognitive neuroscience of memory. The overall goal of this research is to identify some of the genes that are responsible for the genetic portion of the variation of memory function in the population. In the same way as for other mental functions, e. g., intelligence, hard-wired effects are not expected, rather the effects of several genes, each with a relatively small effect size.

With respect to the question of potential early, preclinical, cognitive signs of dementia, coherent knowledge to present date is relatively sparse. It is believed that genetic markers in relation to memory performance might be valuable tools in the search for such early cognitive signs of Alzheimer's disease and other related disorders. The data from Nilsson et al. (1998) referred to earlier on the role of allele ε4 in the search of early signs of dementia in episodic memory tasks seem rather promising in this regard.

Although the focus here has been on the association between genetic markers and memory, it should also be made clear that further understanding of age-related diseases is another, more general goal, of this research. Most of these diseases of the central nervous system become apparent in adult life and their population frequency increases with increasing age. There is considerable evidence that the complex etiology of these diseases is caused by interactions between many genetic and environmental factors. It is believed that cognitive performance as expressed in memory performance may play a crucial role in the risk quantification of these diseases and in the understanding of the pathogenesis of these diseases.

In most other contemporary studies with similar goals, the strategy is to use pathological samples of subjects. The approach used in the Betula study is complementary to this strategy in that it uses genetic variations in normal phenotypic traits as a point of departure for identifying genetic susceptibility loci for complex multifactorial disorders and complex multifactorial cognitive functions.

It was mentioned initially that four genes have been identified in relation to Alzheimer's disease (Van Broeckhoven, 1995) – the APP, PS-1, PS-2, and ApoE genes – that the first three are fully penetrant and cause familial presenile Alzheimer disease, and that the fourth gene is not a causative gene, but rather a genetic risk factor or a predisposing gene. Van Broeckhoven (1995) has estimated that these four genes, taken together, account for about 50% of all cases of Alzheimer's disease. Other predisposing genes, that may interact independently of or synergistically with ApoE, have been identified. These genes are the alpha-1-antichymotrypsin (AACT) gene (Kamboh, Sanghera, Ferrell, & DeKosky, 1995), the very low density lipoprotein receptor (VLDL-R) gene (Okuizumi, Onodera, Namba et al., 1995), the non-amyloid precursor protein (NACP) gene (Xia, Rohan de Silva, Rosi et al., 1996), and the PS-1 gene (Wragg, Hutton, & Malhot, 1996), which is, thus, already known in relation to the presenile form of Alzheimer's disease. In contrast to what was the case for ApoE, there has been some difficulty in replicating the association of these genes with increased risk for Alzheimer's disease. Given the multifactorial approach and the large number of subjects in Betula, it might be possible to solve this controversy by using memory performance as a way to bridge the effects of these genes on the basis of the fact that we are exploring genetic variations underlying normal phenotypic traits or functions, and it might be possible to disentangle susceptible loci for complex multifactorial diseases.

## References

Bäckman, L., & Nilsson, L.-G. (1996). Semantic memory functioning across the adult life span. *European Psychologist, 1*, 27–33.

Becker, J.T., & Lopez, O.L. (1992). Episodic memory in Alzheimer's disease: Breakdown of multiple memory processes. In L. Bäckman (Ed.), *Memory functioning in dementia* (pp. 27–43). Amsterdam: Elsevier.

Broeckhoven, C. Van (1995). Molecular genetics of Alzheimer's disease: Identification of genes and gene mutations. *European Neurology, 35*, 8–19.

Cardon, L.R., Faulkner, D.W., DeFries, J.C., & Plomin, R. (1992). Multivariate genetic analyses of specific cognitive abilities in the Colorado Adoption Project at age 7. *Intelligence, 16*, 383–400.

Chorney, M.J., Chorney, K., Seese, N., Owen, M.J., Daniels, J., McGuffin, P., Thompson, L.A., Detterman, D.K., Benbow, C., Lubinski, D., Eley, T., Plomin, R. et al. (1998). A quantitative trait locus associated with cognitive ability in children. *Psychological Science, 9*, 159–166.

Cruts, M., Backhovens, H., Van, G., Theuns, J., Wang, S.-Y., Wehnert, A., Duijn, C.M. van , Karlsson, T., Hofman, A., Adolfsson, R., Martin, J.J., & Broeckhoven, C. Van (1995). Mutation analysis of the chromosome 14q24.3 dihydropoyl succinyltransferase (DLST) gene in patients with early-onset Alzheimer's disease. *Neuroscience Letters, 199*, 73–77.

Davies, P. (1986). The genetic of Alzheimer's disease: A review and a discussion of the implications. *Neurobiology and Aging, 7*, 459–466.

Duijn, C. van (1998, July). *Genetic and environmental factors and the incidence of Alzheimer's disease.* Paper presented at the 6th International Conference on Alzheimer's Disease and Related Disorders, Amsterdam, The Netherlands.

Earles, J.L., & Salthouse, T.A. (1995). Interrelations of age, health, and speed. *Journal of Gerontology: Psychological Sciences, 50B*, P33–P41.

Erngrund, K., Mäntylä, T., & Nilsson, L.-G. (1996). Adult age differences in source memory:

A population based study. *Journal of Gerontology: Psychological Science, 51B*, P335–P345.

Erngrund, K., Mäntylä, T., & Rönnlund, M. (1996). Acting or listening: Adult age differences in source recall of enacted and nonenacted statements. *Journal of Adult Development, 3*, 217–232.

Field, D., Schaie, K.W., & Leino, E.V. (1988). Continuity in intellectual functioning: The role of self-reported health. *Psychology and Aging, 4*, 385–392.

Hagnell, O. (1966). *A prospective study of the incidence of mental disorders.* Stockholm: Svenska Bokförlaget.

Hagnell, O., Lanke, J., Rorsman, B., & Öjesjö, L. (1981). Does the incidence of age psychosis decrease? A prospective, longitudinal study of a complete population investigated during the 25-year period 1947–1972: The Lundby study. *Neuropsychobiology, 7*, 201–211.

Herlitz, A., Nilsson, L.-G., Bäckman, L. (1997). Gender differences in episodic memory. *Memory and Cognition, 25*, 801–811.

Hofman, A., Rocca, W.A., Brayne, C., Breteler, M.M., Clarke, M., Cooper, B., Copeland, J.R., Dartigues, J.F., da Silva-Droux, A., Hagnell, O. et al. (1991). The prevalence of dementia in Europe: A colloborative study of 1980–1990 findings. *International Journal of Epidemiology, 20*, 736–748.

Hultsch, D.F., Hammer, M., & Small, B.J. (1993). Age differences in cognitive performance in later life: Relationships to self-reported health and activity life style. *Journal of Gerontology: Psychological Sciences, 48*, P1–P11.

Kamboh, M.I., Sanghera, D.K., Ferrell, R.E., & DeKosky, S.T. (1995). APOE*4-associated Alzheimer's disease risk is modified by alpha 1-antichymotrypsin polymorphism. *Nature Genetics, 11*, 104.

Mäntylä, T., & Nilsson, L.-G. (1997). Remembering to remember in adulthood: A population-based study on aging and prospective memory. *Aging, Neuropsychology, and Cognition, 4*, 81–92.

Marcusson, J., Blennow, K., Skoog, I., & Wallin, A. (1995). *Demenssjukdomar* [Dementia diseases]. Stockholm: Almqvist & Wiksell Medicin.

Mortimer, J.A., & Hutton, J.T. (1985). Epidemiology and etiology of Alzheimer's disease. In J.T. Hutton & A.D. Kenny (Eds.), *Senile dementia of the Alzheimer type* (pp. 177–196). New York: Liss.

Nelis, E., Holmberg, B., Adolfsson, R., Holmgren, G., & Broeckhoven, C. Van (1997). PMP22 Thr(118)met: Recessive CMTI mutation or polymorphism. *Nature Genetics, 15*, 13–14.

Nilsson, L.-G., Adolfsson, R., Cruts, M., Bäckman, L., Edvardsson, H., de Knijff, P., Nyberg, L., & Broekhooven, C. Van (1998). The role of Apolipoprotein E for memory function in non-demented and demented persons: A population-based study. Manuscript in preparation.

Nilsson, L.-G., Bäckman, L., Erngrund, K., Nyberg, L., Adolfsson, R., Bucht, G., Karlsson, S., Widing, M., & Winblad, B. (1997). The Betula prospective cohort study: Memory, health, and aging. *Aging, Neuropsychology and Cognition, 1*, 1–32.

Nilsson, L.-G., Sikström, C., Adolfsson, R., Erngrund, K., Nylander, P.-O., Bäckman, L. (1996). Genetic markers with high versus low scoring on episodic memory tasks. *Behavior Genetics, 26*, 555–562.

Nyberg, L., Bäckman, L., Erngrund, K., Olofsson, U., & Nilsson, L.-G. (1996). Age differences in episodic memory, semantic memory, and priming: Relationships to biological, demographic, and psychometric variables. *Journal of Gerontology: Psychological Science, 51B*, P234–P240.

Nyberg, L., Nilsson, L.-G., Olofsson, U., & Bäckman, L. (1997). Effects of division of attention during encoding and retrieval on age differences in episodic memory. *Experimental Aging Research, 23*, 137–143.

Okuizumi, K., Onodera, O., Namba, Y., Ikeda, K., Yamamoto, T., Seki, K., Ueki, A., Nanko, S., Tanaka, H., Takahashi, H. et al. (1995). Genetic association of the very low density lipoprotein (VLDL) receptor gene with sporadic Alzheimer's disease. *Nature Genetics, 11*, 207–209.

Perlmutter, M., & Nyquist, L. (1990). Relationships between self-reported physical and mental health and intelligence performance across adulthood. *Journal of Gerontology: Psychological Sciences, 45*, P145–P155.

Plomin, R. (1997). Current directions in behavioral genetics: Moving into the mainstream. *Current Directions in Psychological Science, 6*, 85.

Salthouse, T.A., Kausler, D.H., & Saults, J.S. (1990). Age, self-assessed health status, and cognition. *Journal of Gerontology: Psychological Sciences, 45*, P156–P160.

Schacter, D.L., & Tulving, E. (1994). What are the memory systems of 1994? In D.L. Schacter & E. Tulving (Eds.), *Memory systems 1994* (pp. 1–38). Cambridge: MIT Press.

Schaie, K.W. (1965). A general model for the study of developmental problems. *Psychological Bulletin, 64*, 92–107.

Schaie, K.W. (1977). Quasi-experimental research designs in the psychology of aging. In J.E. Birren & K.W. Schaie (Eds.), *Handbook of the psychology of aging* (pp. 39–58). New York: Van Nostrand.

Skoog, I. (1998, July). *The interaction between vascular factors and Alzheimer's disease.* Paper presented at the 6th International Conference on Alzheimer's Disease and Related Disorders, Amsterdam, The Netherlands.

Skoog, I., Lernfelt, B., Landahl, S., Palmertz, B., Andreasson, L.A., Nilsson, L., Persson, G., Oden, A., & Svanborg, A. (1996). 15-year longitudinal study of blood pressure and dementia. *Lancet, 347*, 1163–1166.

Statistiska Centralbyrån (1976). *Information i prognosfrågor* [Information in issues of prognosis], SCB, 3. Stockholm: Author.

Statistiska Centralbyrån (1985). *Befolkningens utbildningsnivå* [Level of education for the inhabitants]. Örebro: Author.

Tierney, M.C. et al. (1996). Prediction of probable AD in memory-impaired patients: A prospective longitudinal study. *Neurology, 46*, 661–665.

Tulving, E. (1972). Episodic and semantic memory. In E. Tulving & W. Donaldson (Eds.), *Organization of memory* (pp. 382–403). New York: Academic Press.

Tulving, E. (1983). *Elements of episodic memory.* Oxford: Clarendon Press.

Wragg, M., Hutton, M., & Malhot, C. (1996). Genetic association between intronic polymorphism in presenilin-1 gene and late-onset Alzheimer's disease. *Lancet, 347*, 509–512.

Xia, Y., Rohan de Silva, H.A., Rosi, B.L., Yamaoka, L.H., Rimmler, J.B., Pericak-Vance, M.A., Roses, A.D., Chen, X., Masliah, E., DeTeresa, R., Iwai, A., Sundsmo, M., Thomas, R.G., Hofstetter, C.R., Gregory, E., Hansen, L.A., Katzman, R., Thal, L.J., & Saitoh, T. (1996). Genetic studies in Alzheimer's disease with an NACP/alpha-synuclein polymorphism. *Annals of Neurology, 40*, 207–215.

# Confabulation and Temporality

*Gianfranco Dalla Barba*

Most of the current theories and models of memory (e. g., Baddeley & Wilson, 1986; Burgess & Shallice, 1996; Johnson, 1991; Moscovitch, 1989; Moscovitch, 1995a) are based on two assumptions that contain theoretical problems which have never been clarified. The problems that these theories seem to have ignored can be summarized by the following questions: "Who is controlling the retrieval?" and "What is retrieved?" In the first section of this chapter we show that, as far as the first question is concerned, current theories of memory are based on an illusion, what we will refer to as the *illusion of the homunculus*. We will show next that, as far as the second question is concerned, the answers provided by current theories of memory contain a paradox, what we will be referring to as the *memory trace paradox*. We will then describe the cases of two patients that show previously not described aspects of confabulation. Finally, we will present a set of ideas concerning the relation between memory, consciousness and temporality; we will try to show how normal and pathological memory can be accounted for according to these ideas.

## Confabulation and the Illusion of the Homunculus

Most of the current ideas about the mechanisms underlying confabulation emphasize the role of retrieval and control processes. According to these ideas damage to the frontal lobe and related structures would prevent both the active process of search in the long-term memory storage and the evaluation and monitoring of the result of this search. Moscovitch (1989, 1995a; Moscovitch & Melo, 1997), for example, distinguishes between two components of retrieval. One, associative retrieval, is relatively automatic and independent from frontal functions. The other, strategic retrieval, is self-initiated, goal-directed, effortful and intelligent. Within strategic retrieval processes, two further components are hypothesized. The first involves organizing a memory search that uses whatever knowledge is available, whether semantic or episodic. Once knowledge is recovered, a second strategic process is involved in monitoring the output of the memory search and checking whether it is consistent with other information in semantic and episodic memory. The first type of strategic retrieval is based on functions attributed to the dorsolateral frontal cortex, whereas the ventromedial frontal cortex would be crucial for monitoring processes, the disruption of which would be responsible for confabulation (Moscovitch, 1995a).

Adopting a similar perspective, Johnson (1991) suggested that confabulation results from the disruption of processes normally involved in "reality monitoring" (Johnson, 1988; Johnson & Raye, 1981). Reality monitoring operates on the basis of qualitative characteristics of information (e. g., amount of perceptual details, supporting memories) in combination with judgment processes that use this information as evidence that, for example, something was real and not imagined. Confabulation consisting in minor distortion of information or in the temporal displacement of true memories would reflect the disruption of more automatic monitoring processes involved in reality monitoring, whereas the disruption of monitoring processes that operate on a more deliberate basis would lead to bizarre confabulation. Similar proposals have been advanced in literature on normal (e. g, Burgess & Shallice, 1996; Mandler, 1980; Tulving, 1983) and pathological memory (Baddeley & Wilson, 1986; Delbecq-Derouesne, Beauvois, & Shallice, 1990).

This type of account of normal and pathological memory, however, does not specify clearly whether the retrieval and control processes operate on a conscious and voluntary basis or, alternatively, whether they are unconscious and inaccessible to consciousness. Let's consider more closely this problem, and assume first that control processes operate on a conscious and voluntary basis. If this were to be the case, subjective phenomenal experience should show that every time I try to retrieve an episode, consciousness is presented with different candidate memories. I would then evaluate them, reject those that I consider inappropriate, and choose the one I consider as the correct answer. However, subjective phenomenal experience shows that things do not work this way. If, for example, I try to recall what I was doing last Wednesday at 5 p. m., I would certainly initiate a sort of *strategic retrieval*. I will, for example, remember that on Friday I gave a lecture in Lyon, that Thursday I took the train to reach that city where I was supposed to give the lecture, and that Wednesday at 5 p. m., I was trying to organize something sensible to say in my lecture. In other words, I make a search in my past, I move within my memories until I select one memory that I consider fits most appropriately with the question "What was I doing last Wednesday at 5 p. m.?" The search in memory I am engaged in, however, will never consider as candidates to be rejected, memories such as those produced by confabulators. Consider the following examples of confabulation produced by a patient I described some years ago (Dalla Barba, 1993b). This patient, when asked, would claim that "the day before he won a running race and that he had been awarded a piece of meat which was put on his right knee." When asked to define the word *synagogue,* his answer was: "Something that has to do with physiotherapy."

Now, according to the hypothesis that memories and knowledge are the result of the control and inhibition of inappropriate responses by special cognitive control processes, in order to attribute the correct meaning to the word *synagogue* one should chose between candidates such as – say – "a church," "a temple for Jewish people," "a kind of fruit" or "something that has to do with physiotherapy." Only if one can inhibit all the inappropriate responses will "the temple for Jewish people," come out, otherwise, as in the case of our patient, the answer could be "something that has to do with physiotherapy" or any other type of answer. This kind of reasoning also implies that if, before his amnesia, one would have asked the patient what he did the day before, he would have considered and rejected the possibility of having won a running race and that he had been awarded a piece of meat which was put on his right knee. However, I don't think that these are good examples of the kind of memories that are consciously considered and rejected in a normal process of retrieval.

It could be argued that confabulations are often much more plausible than the examples of the synagogue and of the running race. Actually most confabulators produce tales that are indistinguishable from "true" memories if the observer does not know the history and present situation of the confabulator. For example, a patient, MG, we have studied (Dalla Barba, Boissé, Bartolomeo, & Bachoud-Lévi, 1997), while he was waiting to undergo the CT scan, told the radiologist that he had accompanied a friend to be admitted to the neurology department that day and that the neurologist who was taking care of the patient's (non-existent) friend, realized that he also had neurological problems and so decided to refer him to the radiology department for a CT scan. On that occasion the radiologist did not even suspect that MG was confabulating. Even in this case, however, the confabulation is plausible and indistinguishable from a true memory, as demonstrated by the reaction of the radiologist, it cannot be considered as the result of lack of conscious control on the retrieval's output. In fact, it is quite difficult to imagine that if you are at the hospital for, let's say, a broken arm and somebody asks you the reason for being there, you consciously consider and reject the possibility of being in that place because you are accompanying a friend. The analysis of the subjective phenomenal experience leads us to exclude this possibility.

However, even assuming that the retrieval of an episode or of a meaning is possible thanks to the voluntary and conscious inhibition of inappropriate candidate memories, which phenomenal experience leads us to exclude, it still remains to be established on the basis of which criteria the correct memory would be chosen. It could be argued that one possible criteria is plausibility. Only plausible candidates are accepted. But is not plausibility itself a meaning that I attribute to a possible answer and, as such, should not also this meaning undergo a process of control and verification just like any other meaning? And the criteria I establish in order to decide what plausibility is, should not itself be verified, and so in an endless Chinese boxes game? It has been suggested (Johnson, 1988; Johnson, 1991; Johnson & Raye, 1981) that the correct choice between different candidate memories is based on the qualitative characteristics of information, for example the amount of perceptive details and the amount and type of supporting associate memories. However, again, *quis custodet custodes*? Who can assure that the bright red of the shirt that Paul was wearing last time I met him, is a perceptive detail that comes from my memory and not from my imagination? Why should I grant to the so-called perceptive details the status of veridicity that I refuse to the object of my memory? In the same way who can assure, for example, that the fact that when I last met Paul, Mary was there, is an associate supporting memory that guaranties the veridicity of the main memory, that is meeting Paul, and not a confabulation. As you can see there is no way to get out from this circularity.

So, there is good evidence to exclude that control and monitoring processes of retrieval operate on a voluntary and conscious basis. Are then control and monitoring processes operating outside consciousness and are they inaccessible to consciousness? The acceptance of such a hypothesis, that control and monitoring processes operate outside consciousness, would be based on what we will call the *illusion of the homunculus,* that is the contradiction of postulating the existence of an *unconscious consciousness* which actively and intentionally rejects false memories and provides *conscious consciousness* only with true memories. It is far from being clear on what kind of theoretical evidence we would attribute intentionality to an unconscious process. Intentionality is a characteristic of consciousness, it is indeed the constraint of consciousness to exist as consciousness *of* something. To attribute intentionality to an unconscious process means to provide it with the property of being *subject*, that is to attribute consciousness to the unconscious. Moreover, it would be an unconscious consciousness inaccessible to conscious consciousness. Like in a Chinese boxes game, the subject would contain another subject, an homunculus provided with a shady and inaccessible consciousness, busy solving problems like rejecting false memories and providing conscious consciousness with the result of his accurate selection.

The homunculus illusion goes even further. In the work of selection and control of memories, the homunculus would deal with memories, true or false, already structured in a propositional form, like, for example, "having won a running race yesterday." So the homunculus illusion not only postulates the existence of an unconscious consciousness, but since this unconscious consciousness must also have an object, it also postulates an unconscious mnesic activity already structured in a propositional form. In other words, memories too, which are property of consciousness, are found in the unconscious already specified in syntactic and semantic terms, and ready to be selected by our homunculus.

Furthermore, memories and information that the homunculus selects are not memories and information that come from *his* memory but from the memory of the subject that contains him. According to which criteria the homunculus can then distinguish between true and false information considering that he is dealing with information coming from the memory of "another person." Of course we could say that the homunculus is an accurate witness and infallible recorder of the whole life of the subject for whom he is working. Indeed, in some way the life of the subject and that of the homunculus coincide since the homunculus is contained in the unconscious of the subject for whom he works. But if the life of the subject and that of the homunculus coincide, their memories will also coincide. And if memories coincide does the homunculus not need, as well, an unconscious homunculus that helps him distinguish between true and false memories? Like this the Chinese boxes game continues endlessly, and what we are left with is just a *redutio ad infinitum*. So, the difficulties we met considering control and monitoring processes as operating on a conscious basis, together with the theoretical problems revealed by the illusion of the homunculus, cast serious doubts on the convenience of hypothesizing a role for these processes in successful or unsuccessful retrieval of memories and information. However, these are not the only unsolved problems in theories of memory. An additional and certainly not less relevant problem concerns the nature of what is retrieved. This will be the subject of the next session.

## The Memory Trace Paradox

A common assumption of most theories of memory is that memories are possible because the past is preserved in some form in the organism doing the remembering. According to this assumption if I now perceive this cup of coffee on this table, tomorrow I will be able to remember it because this event has been stored somewhere in my brain or in my cognitive system in the form of a "memory trace." In other words, the event "cup-of-coffee-on-the-table" has determined a modification in the balance of my brain or of my cognitive system, that I call memory trace of the event or, to use a smarter term, an "engram," in which the event is stored in the form of a representation. According

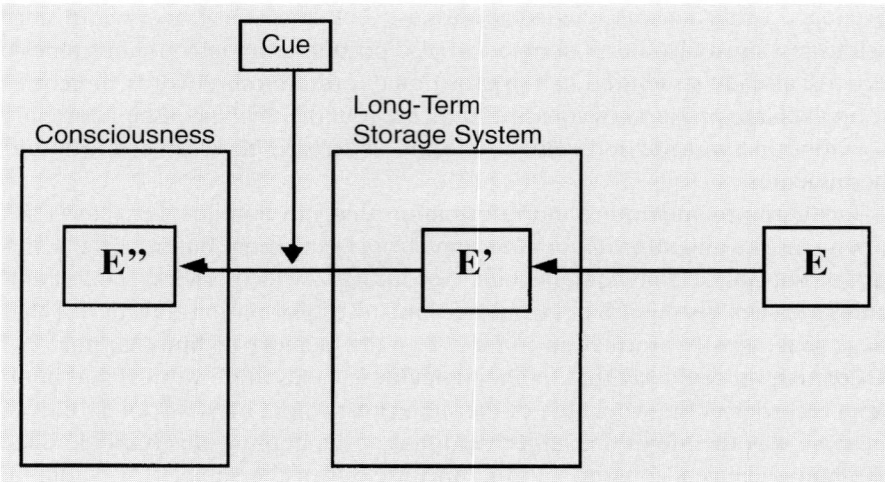

Figure 1.

to this view, the activation of the representation stored in the engram$!Engram, as in copy theories of remembering, or the interaction between a present cue and the stored representation, as in reconstructive models of memory, would give rise to the phenomenal experience of remembering, that is to the conscious awareness of an episode of one's own past. Figure 1 depicts this point of view: the event "E" is stored in the Long-Term Storage System as the memory trace "E'''"; the activation of E', with or without the involvement of a cue, results in "E'','' i. e., the conscious remembering of E.

It is easy to see that any theory, however expressed, that founds the possibility of remembering on the preservation of an event in a memory trace contains a paradox which is the consequence of an illusory assumption. The illusory assumption on which these theories are based consists in believing that time can be contained in the objects. According to these theories the past event that I am now remembering, for example the dinner I had with some friends yesterday, is consciously remembered as a "past" event because as such, i. e., "past," that event was contained in the memory trace, the activation of which produces the remembering. In other words, the past of that event, or its "pastness" in Bergson's terminology (Bergson, 1896), is already there, locked up in that "thing," be it physical or abstract, that I call memory trace of the event. However, things as such are not temporal. *Per se* the objects of the world are neither present, nor past or future, but they acquire a temporal dimension only in presence of a conscious subject who takes the trouble to make them temporal. No matter what kind of status one wants to attribute to the human brain or to what the human brain is thought to do, there can not be any time attribute even in a "thing" like the human brain or the human mind. This wrong assumption on which theories of memory are based reflects itself directly in the paradox of which these theories are victim, i. e., the memory trace paradox. The memory trace paradox consists of deriving the remembering, that is the conscious experience of the past, from elements borrowed from the present. Let's see why. The event I am now perceiving, for example, the cup of coffee on this table, is, without any doubt, a present event. This event, cup-of-coffee-on-the-table, produces a modification in the balance of a system, be it a physical one – the nervous system – or an abstract one – the computational level – that I call memory trace. What is the temporal nature of the modification that the event "cup-of-coffee-on-the-table" produces in the system, that is, what is the temporal nature of the memory trace? Present, without any doubt. The cup of coffee that I now perceive is present and if one wants to maintain that this event produces a modification somewhere in between the brain and the mind, one should also admit that this modification is present and that the event that this modification represents is also present. In one word, whatever it is about, according to the level of explanation one wants to adopt, e. g., the production of new proteins, the growth of new dendritic spines, the activation or reinforcement of synaptic networks, or computational processing of information, it will always be about a *present* modification of something. What happens when the event contained in the memory trace is retrieved? When the event is recalled or recognized, this happens in the present and again as a consequence of a present process, i. e., as the result of the reactivation of the modification that the event determined at whatever level you want to consider, be it molecular, anatomical, physiological or computational. So it is not clear at all how it would be possible that the remembering, who's crucial feature is to be remembering *of* the past, could arise from a set of elements that are present, i. e., perception, memory trace and retrieval. Figure 2 depicts this situation: the event "E" is present and stored as present "E'" in the memory trace; When E' is retrieved this happens as a consequence of a present process, including or not the involvement of a present cue; the result of this processing is "E''," i. e., the conscious remembering of E as "past." The reactivation of an episodic memory trace should, in case, give rise to a new perception of the event stored in the trace, and not to the remembering of that event, because the event stored in the memory trace was present at the time when it was stored and present during all the time it was locked up in the trace. On the contrary, if I recognize that particular event as *past*, this happens because I attribute to that event a specific meaning – being past – a meaning that by definition can not be stored in the memory trace because the memory trace during it's whole existence never stopped to being present.

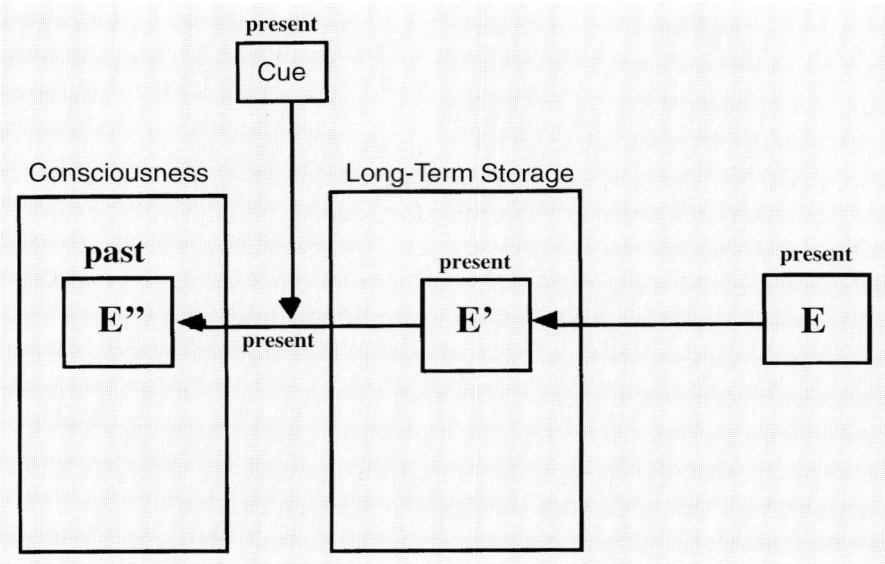

Figure 2.

This does not mean that the events do not produce modifications in the brain or in the cognitive system. However, we can not turn to these modifications in order to explain the remembering. All objects in the universe are subject to modifications caused by the events. Any object carries on itself the signs of the past, yet, if not by metaphor, no one would attribute the ability of remembering to the objects. The signs that the events leave on the objects acquire the meaning of *past*, only for a consciousness that attributes this meaning to them. More than fifty years ago Merleau-Ponty wrote: "This table carries the traces of my past life, I have cut into it my initials, I have made ink spots on it. But, by themselves, these traces do not send back to the past: they are present; and, if I find in them the signs of some 'previous' event, I find them because, by some other way, I have the sense of the past, because I carry in me this meaning" (Merleau-Ponty, 1945). The "warmth and intimacy" of memories, as in James (James, 1890), their "pastness," as in Bergson (Bergson, 1896), or their "meeness" as in Claparède (Claparède, 1911), or recollective experience as in modern psychological and neuropsychological literature, appropriately describe some characteristics of remembering but do not tell us anything about its nature. In fact, they either describe just a present feature of remembering, and so doing they remain in the present, or, if they are already connected to the past, they presuppose what they want to explain.

In support of the memory trace hypothesis one could argue that it is not at all necessary that episodes are contained in the memory trace *as past*. For the remembering to be possible it would be actually sufficient that "something" in the trace indicated that its content concerns some past episode. In other words it would be sufficient, as predicted by some theories of memory (e. g., Anderson & Bower, 1974; Anderson & Bower, 1972; Hintzman, 1978; Morton et al., 1985), that the episodes recorded in the trace were marked with, for example, a sort of tag indicating the date at which they occurred or simply that what is contained in the trace is past. However, this kind of hypothesis does not explain the past but it rather presupposes it. In fact, any tag or label one wants to add to the episode contained in the memory trace will be a cue that by itself it is present, as present as the episode to which it is stuck. The date and the information "past" of the cue don't tell anything by themselves, they are not past but they become past only if the past is already given for the consciousness that seizes that cue. In other terms, the tag or the cue of "past-ness" of an episode does not precede nor "creates" the past but, on the contrary, it is somehow a consequence of the past in the sense that it carries out its function of being a sign of pastness because this notion is already given for the consciousness. When I put my hand in my pocket to take a handkerchief and I realize that it has a knot, I attribute to that knot the meaning of being the cue of a past event that I must remember. If I didn't *already* have the past as meaning, that knot would remain simply what it is and not the cue of something past. In one word, the date, the cue of pastness or whatever, do not tell anything about the past nor do they testify it. Regardless of the number of tags or cues one wants to add to the memory trace, this will never contain the past.

## Confabulation, Amnesia and Temporality

### Case 1

Confabulation is generally considered as reflecting a deficit of the retrieval or post retrieval stage (e. g., Baddeley & Wilson, 1986; Burgess & Shallice, 1996; Johnson, 1991; Moscovitch, 1989; Moscovitch, 1995a; Moscovitch & Melo, 1997). In Moscovitch's (1989, 1995a, Moscovitch & Melo, 1997) view, for example, confabulation is associated with a deficit of strategic retrieval processes that result from damage in the region of the ventromedial frontal cortex. The strategic retrieval processes are involved in initiating and guiding search in both episodic and semantic memory and in monitoring and organizing the output from those memory systems. According to Moscovitch (1995a) the strongest evidence in favour of the hypothesis that confabulation reflects a retrieval deficit is that confabulation does not follow a temporal gradient, but affects remote as well as post-morbid memories equally. Furthermore, since chronological distortions in confabulation extend to premorbid memories that presumably are well consolidated, it has been argued (Moscovitch & Melo, 1997) that confabulatory phenomena also provide valuable information on consolidation and storage processes. This would suggest that memories are stored randomly, without regard to sequence except simple physical contiguity, an idea first advanced by Landauer (1975), and recently proposed in Conway's structural model of autobiographical memory (Conway, 1992).

PL is a 57-year-old right handed woman who developed an amnesic-confabulatory syndrome following a cardiac arrest. Our aim in studying the case of PL was to test the hypothesis of confabulation as a deficit of strategic retrieval, and to verify the idea that memories are randomly stored, without a temporal order. Accordingly we assessed PL's ability to recognize photographs that represented various people and events supposed to be highly familiar to PL, concerning her life-span from the early fifties to the late eighties. The aim of this experiment was twofold: on one hand we were interested to see whether PL would confabulate in a task in which strategic retrieval is expected to be less involved than in recall tasks. In fact, it seems reasonable to think that a recognition memory task that requires identifying relatives, friends and oneself in highly familiar situations does not require an active strategic search in memory as required for instance in the recall of autobiographical episodes. On the other hand, the second aim of the experiment was to verify whether the pattern of relation between good recognition and confabulation was similar across all periods of PL's life or whether, alternatively, a temporal gradient in PL's responses would emerge.

A set of photographs was selected with the help of PL's children. Photographs depicted PL and her family and friends in various situations and locations, from 1951 to 1988. For each decade, from the fifties to the eighties, ten photographs were selected so that the entire set included forty photographs. The photographs were presented to PL in a random order and she was asked to identify the people and give the more accurate and detailed description of the situation represented in the photographs. Figure 3 gives the results of this task. As can be seen clearly from the figure, confabulation was present in this task and was distributed along a temporal gradient. Confabulation was massive for the recognition of photographs representing people and events from the eighties and decreased consistently for the recognition of photographs representing people and events from earlier decades. Correct responses, in contrast, were distributed according to an opposite pattern. The percentage of correct recognition was very high for photographs from the fifties and consistently decreased for photographs from the following decades. If responses are pooled together, regardless whether they are correct or confabulatory (Figure 4) it

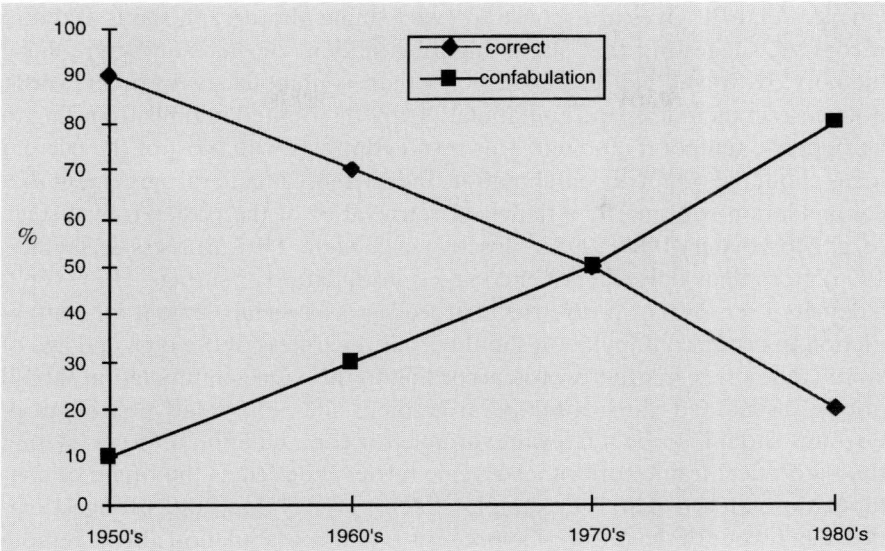

*Figure 3.* Distribution of PL's correct and confabulatory responses to familiar photographs from the fifties to the eighties.

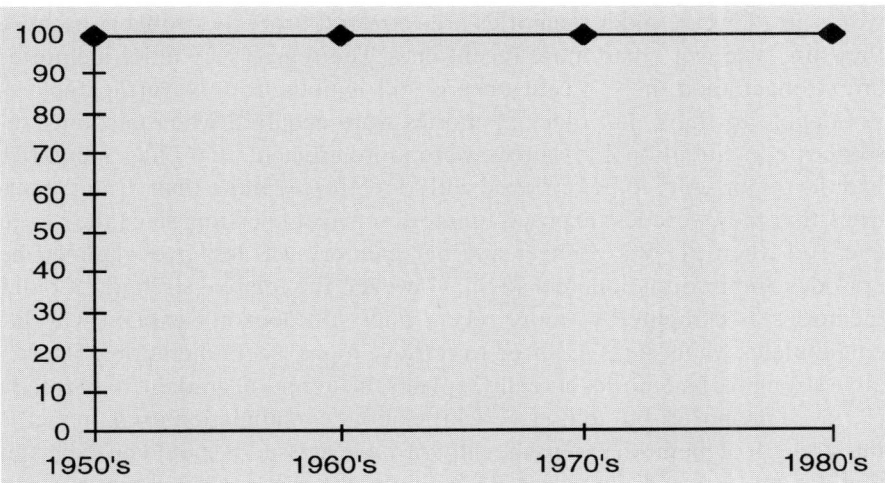

*Figure 4.* Percentage of PL's responses (correct and confabulatory) in recognition of familiar photographs.

emerges that PL gives a response to every single photograph she is asked to recognize, suggesting that she is highly confident on her autobiographical memory. However, half of her responses are confabulatory. In other words, both correct memories and confabulation are distributed in time according to an opposite temporal gradient. This result contrasts with most of the current ideas about the origin of confabulation. In fact, there is general agreement that confabulation is primarily a deficit of retrieval or of the post-retrieval stage (e. g., Moscovitch, 1989, 1995a; Moscovitch & Melo, 1997; Burgess & Shallice, 1996) more than a disorder of encoding, consolidation or storage. However, if a deficit of retrieval or postretrieval processes is a crucial element for confabulation to occur, confabulation should occur regardless of the type and age of stored memories. In other words, according to this view, confabulation should not be distributed along a temporal gradient since the relative strength of engrams should not be a relevant variable for confabulation to occur. Within the theoretical framework of a strategic retrieval deficit as the origin of confabulation, Moscovitch, for example (1995a) argues that "the strongest evidence in favour of the retrieval hypothesis is that confabulation affects remote memories as well those that were acquired post-morbidly" (p. 233). This kind of evidence does not apply to PL's case. What PL's case shows is that her confabulation, and her episodic autobiographical memory in general, is a function of the age and, presumably, strength of memories to-be-retrieved. In other words, in PL's case older memories are retrieved properly, probably because they are "stronger" than more recent ones. The reason why older memories are stronger than more recent ones is still hypothetical. Nevertheless, it is reasonable to think that older memories were acquired when encoding resources, e. g., attentional resources, were more efficient, that older memories had the opportunity to be retrieved and so reinforced more than recent memories, that they were less exposed to interference at encoding since they were encoded when PL was younger and her memory was less overwhelmed by episodes and information, and so on. However, the relative strength of older memories as compared to more recent ones still does not explain why PL confabulates when she is required to retrieve more recent memories. The relative strength of memories actually explains the temporal gradient of correctly retrieved memories, but tells us very little about confabulation itself. In fact, if the strength of memories were the only variable at issue, it should be expected that, for more recent memories, PL would make errors of omission and not confabulation. One possibility to account for PL's confabulation and its distribution along a temporal gradient is to consider that her confabulation is the result of the interaction between a pathological conscious awareness of her personal past and an impairment of retrieval of less stable or weaker memories. In other words PL's confabulation can reflect a condition in which consciousness of her personal past, or autonoetic consciousness in Tulving's terminology (Tulving, 1985), is still there but can address or become conscious only of stronger or more stable memories. This would explain why she does not confabulate when she is required to retrieve older memories, which presumably are more stable and stronger, but she does confabulate when she is required to retrieve more recent memories, which presumably are weaker and less stable. When she has to retrieve more recent memories, she retrieves or becomes conscious of memories and events that have a more stable representation in her memory so that the result is that she confabulates, mistaking habits or personal semantic information as true memories. If this reasoning is correct, a deficit of retrieval hypothesis for PL's confabulation can not be dismissed. However, such deficit is not to be considered the cause of confabulation but rather the reflection of a deeper underlying disorder, i. e., the co-occurrence and interaction of preserved autonoetic consciousness and impaired ability to access less stable memories.

As far as the organization of normal memory is concerned, it has been argued that confabulation provides insights into the way in which memories are consolidated and stored (Moscovitch & Melo, 1997). The fact that confabulation often affects remote as well as post-morbid memories has been considered (Moscovitch & Melo, 1997) an evidence supporting the idea that memories are stored randomly and not according to a temporal criteria (Landauer, 1975, Conway, 1992). The temporal gradient in PL's confabulation does not support this idea but rather suggests that memories are stored according to a temporal criteria that presumably reflects the relative strength and stability of the stored episodic memories.

## Case 2

GA is a 52-year-old right handed woman with five years of education who had a sub-arachnoid hemorrhage clipped. Clipping near the aneurysm was followed by widespread bilateral frontal ischemia and infarction. CAT, MRI and PET scans showed bilateral frontal degenerative areas extending from the orbito-frontal regions to the dorsal areas, involving the anterior cyngulum and the anterior two thirds of the Corpus Callosum. Table 1 reports GA's neuropsychological evaluation.

To further examine GA's confabulation, we submitted her to the Confabulation Battery (Dalla Barba, 1993a), including questions probing personal, general and linguistic semantic memory, episodic memory, orientation for space and time and questions to which the appropriate response would be "I don't know," both semantic (e. g., "What did Marilyn Monroe's father do?") and episodic (e. g., "Do you remember what you did on March 13, 1985?". Table 2

*Table 1.* GA's and normal controls' percentage of correct responses and confabulations on the Confabulation Battery

| | GA | | Normal Controls | |
|---|---|---|---|---|
| | correct (%) | confab. (%) | correct (%) | confab. (%) |
| Personal sem. memory | 85 | 5 | 100 | 0 |
| Episodic memory | 46 | 33 | 93 | 0 |
| Orientation time-place | 60 | 40 | 100 | 0 |
| General semantic memory | 73 | 6 | 93 | 0 |
| Linguistic sem. memory | 53 | 0 | 90 | 0 |
| "I don't know" episodic | 0 | 0 | 0 | 0 |
| "I don't know" semantic | 0 | 0 | 0 | 0 |

*Table 2.* GA's and normal controls' performance on the Crovitz Test

| | Episodic | | Semantic | |
|---|---|---|---|---|
| | Score (mean) | % of confabulation | Score (mean) | % of confabulation |
| GA | .9 | 13 | .6 | 0 |
| Normal controls | 1.9 | 0 | 1.8 | 0 |

shows GA's and 12 normal control subjects' performance on the Confabulation Battery. As it clearly emerges from Table 2, GA's confabulations were found to be restricted mainly to episodic memory and orientation in time and place. GA's confabulation appears to be independent from the availability of the correct answer since she never confabulates on "I don't know" questions or on Linguistic Semantic Memory questions were she was able to provide the correct answer only eight times out of fifteen.

## Strategic Retrieval and Confabulation

Moscovitch's (1989, 1995a; Moscovitch & Melo, 1997) hypothesis of confabulation as a consequence of a deficit of strategic retrieval is meant to be applied equally across all domains of memory. In other words, confabulation should equally affect episodic and semantic memory if both episodic and semantic memory tasks require the involvement of the strategic retrieval process. This hypothesis seems to have difficulties in accounting for the present case and for two previously described cases (Dalla Barba et al., 1990; Dalla Barba, 1993a,b) in which confabulations were confined to the domain of episodic memory. However, Moscovitch (1995) argued that Dalla Barba and co-workers' patients showed confabulation in episodic memory but not in semantic memory because the tests used to assess episodic memory made greater demands of strategic retrieval processes than those used to assess semantic memory.

*Table 3.* GA's and normal controls' performance (%) on recognition memory and source monitoring tasks

| | Recognition | | Source Monitoring | | |
| --- | --- | --- | --- | --- | --- |
| | correct | false | correct | "seen" | "imagined" |
| GA | 56 | 31 | 62 | 50 | 50 |
| Normal controls | 100 | 0 | 100 | 50 | 50 |

Accordingly, and in order to attempt to equate the strategic retrieval demands of semantic and episodic memory, Moscovitch (1995a; Moscovitch & Melo, 1997) devised a semantic, historical version of the word-cue test developed by Galton (1879) and revised by Crovitz and Schiffman (1974) to complement the traditional episodic version of the test. Using this technique Moscovitch (1995a; Moscovitch & Melo, 1997) found that patients with damage to the ventromedial portion of the frontal lobe confabulated on both the episodic and the semantic version of the test. We used Moscovitch's technique in order to ascertain whether the virtual absence of confabulation in semantic memory in GA was an artefact due to the poor involvement of strategic retrieval in answering the semantic questions of the Confabulation Battery. In the episodic version of the test, GA and 7 control subjects were presented with eight cue-words and asked to produce a specific detailed account of an autobiographical event related to that word. In the semantic version of the test the procedure was identical to that used in the episodic version, except that this time subjects in response to the cue-word had to describe in detail an historical event which occurred before they were born. Responses were scored on a 0–2 scale with two points for a detailed description of the event, one point for a less detailed description and zero points for a general statement or if nothing was provided. Table 3 shows GA's and normal controls performance on this test. GA scored poorly on both versions of the test when compared to normal subjects. Confabulations were present only in the episodic version of the test. In addition, confabulations in the episodic test were much less frequent (13%) as compared to confabulations observed in episodic memory (33%) and orientation in time and place questions (40%) of the Confabulation Battery. According to the present results the strategic retrieval hypothesis of confabulation is not confirmed.

Source Monitoring and Confabulation

It has been argued (Johnson, 1991) that confabulation might be the result of the disruption of mechanisms involved in monitoring the origin of information so that imagined events are mistaken for really experienced events. In order

*Table 4.* GA's percentage of "yes" responses to confabulatory and true memories

|                 | "Yes" responses (%) |
|-----------------|---------------------|
| Confabulations  | 86                  |
| True episodes   | 43                  |

to test this hypothesis we administered a yes/no recognition memory task to GA followed by a source monitoring task. The first task was devised in order to have a baseline control for the experimental material. In the study phase sixteen colored drawings of common objects were presented to GA and ten control subjects, one after the other, for approximately three seconds each. Immediately following the presentation of the sixteen items, the subjects were presented with a list of 32 printed words, where half of the words were names of the objects seen in the study phase and the other half were distractors, i. e., names of common objects not presented in the study phase. Subjects had to indicate the words corresponding to the objects seen in the study phase. In the study phase of the second task, following the same procedure of the previous one, the subjects were first presented with a new set of sixteen colored drawings of common objects. They were then read a list of sixteen names of common objects and for each name they were asked to imagine the corresponding object. Immediately after, they were presented with a list of thirty-two printed words, where half of the words were names of the objects seen and the other half were names of the objects they had to imagine. For each word subjects were asked to say whether that word was the name of an object they had seen or they had imagined in the study phase. Table 4 shows the results of these recognition memory and source monitoring tasks. On the recognition memory task, GA's performance was at the level of chance. However, her poor performance on this task can not be attributed to a tendency to recognize as already seen any presented item, since the rate of false recognition was only 31%. On the source monitoring task GA's performance was also very impaired, but there was no evidence of a tendency to attribute imagined events to direct perception or vice versa. In fact, regardless whether the response was correct or not, GA gave 50% of "seen" responses and 50% of "imagined" responses. These results suggest that GA's confabulation can not be attributed to the incorrect acceptance of any item as a memory nor to the tendency to consider imagined as really experienced events.

It might be suspected, however, that the low rate of false recognition, in the recognition memory task, and the lack of the tendency to attribute to visual perception what was imagined, in the monitoring task, are due to an effect of the experimental material. In fact, the items that were used, drawings and

*Table 5.* GA's and normal controls' percentage of correct and confabulatory responses to questions concerning personal past and future

| | Past Correct | Confabulation | Future Correct | Confabulation |
|---|---|---|---|---|
| GA | 20 | 60 | 10 | 60 |
| Normal Controls | 100 | 0 | 100 | 0 |

names of common objects, are "neutral events," in the sense that they are irrelevant to GA's daily-life and biography. It could be the case that GA shows a tendency to recognize as true memories only events, experienced or imagined, that concern her daily-life and biography. Would this be the case, GA should recognize as memories both really experienced episodes as well as her confabulations. In order to check this possibility we administered a yes/no recognition memory task to GA in which she was presented orally with sentences referring either to true episodes from her recent past, collected from her husband, or to confabulations she had produced in previous testing sessions. Sentences representing true episodes and sentences representing confabulatory episodes were selected and presented to her in a random order. Table 5 gives the results of this task. GA recognized as true memories 83% of her confabulations, whereas she recognized as true memories only 43% of episodes she had really experienced. From these results clearly emerges that GA does not show the tendency to accept as true any autobiographical memory candidate because of a deficit of monitoring processes. She actually seems to adhere much more to her confabulatory past that to her real past.

Confabulation and Temporality

According to the observation that confabulators often confabulate in orientation in time and place tasks, as well as when they are questioned about their personal future, it has been proposed (Dalla Barba, 1993a) that confabulation is not only a disturbance of memory but also involves all subjectively experienced temporality extending to the personal present and to the personal future. In order to test this hypothesis we administered two further tasks to GA and seven control subjects. In the first task, we selected ten episodic memory questions concerning her personal past and ten questions concerning her personal future. Episodic memory questions and questions concerning the future were matched for proximity to the moment when the questions were asked. As it can be seen from Table 6, GA's confabulations were not confined to episodic memory questions but extended in equal amount to questions concerning her personal future.

*Table 6.* GA's and normal controls' performance on the Crovitz Test

|          | GA | | Normal Controls | |
|----------|--------------|-------------------|--------------|-------------------|
|          | Score (mean) | % of confabulation | Score (mean) | % of confabulation |
| Episodic | .9 | 13 | 1.9 | 0 |
| Semantic | .6 | 0  | 1.8 | 0 |
| Future   | .5 | 50 | 1.6 | 0 |

The second task was a "future" version of the Crovitz test. In this task the same eight cue-words used in the classic episodic version of the test were given to GA and to control subjects. For each word, subjects were asked to produce a specific, detailed account of a personal project related to that word. Subjects responses were scored on a 0–2 points scale following the procedure employed for the episodic and semantic versions of the test. The results of this task are presented on Table 7 together with the results of the episodic and semantic versions of the test for comparison. The results clearly show that GA also confabulated when in response to a cue-word she had to provide a personal project and indeed even more than when she was asked to provide an auto-biographical past event. GA's performance on these tasks, together with her confabulations on orientation in time and space tasks, provide evidence in support of the hypothesis that confabulation involves all the subjectively ex-perienced temporality in its continuity and unity. The extension of GA's con-fabulation to the three dimensions of temporality – past, present and future – seems to be something more than a fortuitous coincidence. GA confabulates when she has to answer questions like "What did you do yesterday? Where are you now? What are you going to do tomorrow?" but she never confabu-lates answering questions concerning historical events or in traditional labo-ratory learning tasks. What all these tasks have in common, and at variance with tasks where GA confabulates, is that they do not involve subjective tem-porality, in the sense that they do not require the involvement of the personal history, present situation and probable future of the subject who is performing them. In contrast, GA confabulates when subjective temporality, in its conti-nuity and unity, is involved, i.e., when she has to address her personal past, present and future. When GA confabulates, she acts like somebody who is aware of his past present and future. The problem, however, is that she is aware of a past, a present, and a future that are "false," in the sense that they do not represent a past, present and future coherent with her actual situation. So, what is she aware of, when she is confabulating about her past, her present and her future? GA's confabulation is typically plausible, or semantically appropriate (Dalla Barba, 1993a) in the sense that an hypothetical observer not familiar with GA's history, background and present situation could hardly tell whether

GA's reports are confabulatory or not. She would claim, for example, that the day before she went shopping or that after the testing session she will prepare a meal for her family – which are acts consistent with her life before her illness. So this pattern of behavior suggests that, at difference with classic amnesic patients that are "lost in the present," in the sense that they are no longer aware of a personal past and of a personal future (see for example Tulving, 1989; Tulving, Schacter, McLachlan & Moscovitch, 1988), GA is perfectly aware of her personal temporality, but she mistakes her habits or personal semantics for her real past, present and future. In this sense GA is remembering "another" past and planning "another" future.

## A Hypothesis on Memory, Consciousness, and Temporality

To summarize, the results of the two studies we have described show that a retrieval deficit and, in particular, a strategic retrieval deficit account of confabulation is rather restrictive. The pattern of temporal distribution of PL's correct and confabulatory memories does not support this hypothesis. Furthermore, GA's confabulation did not manifest itself in the semantic version of the Crovitz test where strategic retrieval is assumed to be largely involved (Moscovitch, 1995a; Moscovitch & Melo, 1997). Moreover, not only did GA not confabulate on the Cognitive Estimates (Shallice & Evans, 1978) but she performed normally. This test requires that the subject answer questions which do not have a readily available correct answer (e. g., "How many camels are there in Holland?"), and the subject, in order to provide a plausible answer, is constrained to make a judgment involving the activation, coordination and control of several kinds of semantic information. Thus, strategic retrieval is expected to be prominently involved in the production of a plausible answer in this test.

We have seen in the first part of the chapter that the dysfunction of control and monitoring processes as the cognitive deficit underlying confabulation presents many difficulties at a theoretical level because it is difficult to conceive these processes either as operating on a conscious or an unconscious basis. Evidence from the case of GA shows that this hypothesis also poses experimental difficulties because GA, although showing source amnesia, does not show a tendency to systematically attribute to visual perception what was imagined or vice versa. In addition she recognizes her confabulations as true memories, whereas she is at the level of chance in recognizing really experienced episodes. If a deficit of control and monitoring processes were present in GA and responsible for her confabulation, one would expect that both confabulations and true memories would have been recognized as true. Furthermore a control deficit hypothesis does not explain why PL was perfectly able to monitor her older memories but not more recent ones.

The other theoretical problem we described in the first part of the chapter concerned the possibility of an episodic memory trace. We have seen that if we accept the idea that episodes are stored in memory with their characteristic of "pastness," that is of being past, we fall in the paradox of creating the past in a sort of magic way from elements borrowed from the present and so doing the past and, ultimately, episodic memories are presupposed and not explained. So how can we explain that we do have episodic memories if these memories cannot be stored somewhere as they are? And where do confabulations come from since they can not be the result of the retrieval of a wrong episodic memory trace? The case of patient GA helps us to sketch an answer to these questions. As we have seen GA's confabulations did not involve only the retrieval of personal past episodes but were also present when she had to project her personal future (the future version of the Crovitz test and the interview) and make sense of her personal present (orientation tasks). This seems to be something more than a fortuitous coincidence. Actually what GA's case shows is that confabulation involves all the subjectively experienced temporality in its continuity and unity extending from the past through the present to the future. If this is the case, we no longer need an episodic memory trace to explain confabulation and normal retrieval. Rather we need to explain what

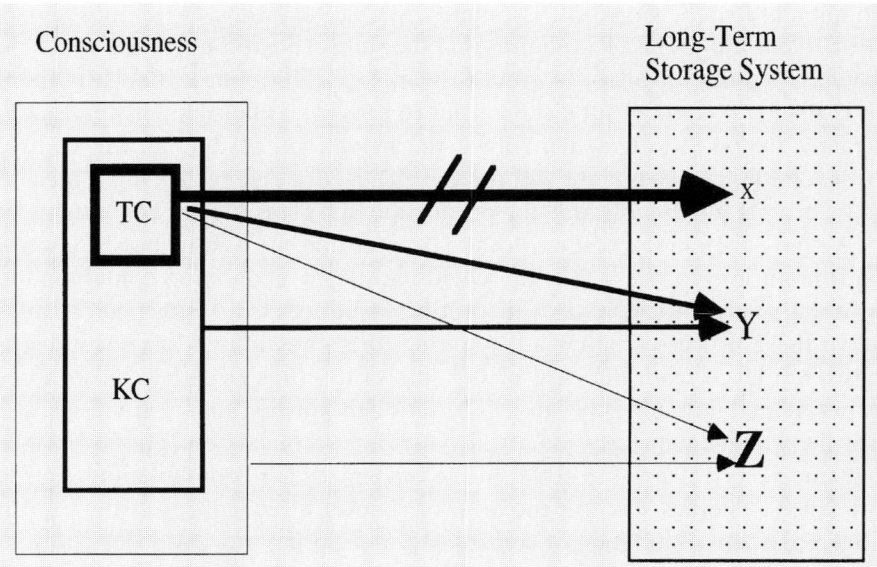

Figure 5.

subjectively experienced temporality is. One way to attempt to answer this question is to make a set of assumptions that are schematized in the model represented in Figure 5:

1. Events produce atemporal and aspecific modifications in the Long-Term storage system (LTSS). These modifications, represented in Figure 5 as X, Y, and Z, are atemporal in the sense that they do not contain any information concerning time. They do not represent the past, the present or the future, nor are they organized according to the order of succession, i. e., there is nothing in Y, for example, that tells that Y comes before Z and after X. They are aspecific in the sense that they do not contain any information specifying that they are representing episodes, meanings, rules, procedures, algorithms, etc.

2. The modifications in the LTSS can be more or less stable and more or less vulnerable depending on a number of variables. These variables act at the encoding and storage level and include, among others, attention at encoding, emotional value of encoded and stored event, depth of encoding, rehearsal and repeated experience of the same event or similar events.

3. Consciousness means to be conscious *of something in a specific way*. That means that consciousness is not an aspecific dimension that passively receives and becomes aware of different types of already specified information, but rather that different types of consciousness exist, each representing an original and unreducible way of addressing the world. Different types of consciousness include, among others, temporal consciousness (TC) and knowing consciousness (KC). TC means to become aware of something as part of a personal past, present or future. KC means to become aware of something as a meaning or as an element of impersonal knowledge or information.

4. TC is phylogenetically and ontogenetically a more evolved form of consciousness compared to KC. TC presupposes and is based on KC and therefore its integrity depends on the integrity of KC.

5. As the more evolved form of consciousness, TC uses less stable and more vulnerable modifications of the LTSS in order to remember the past, be oriented in the present and project the future.

According to this model, confabulation in episodic memory (e. g., Dalla Barba, 1993a; Dalla Barba, Cipolotti, & Denes, 1990), in orientation in time and place and in personal future planning tasks, as in GA's case, are the result of a condition in which TC is still there but can not use less stable modifications of the LTSS but only more stable ones, in order to remember the personal past, be

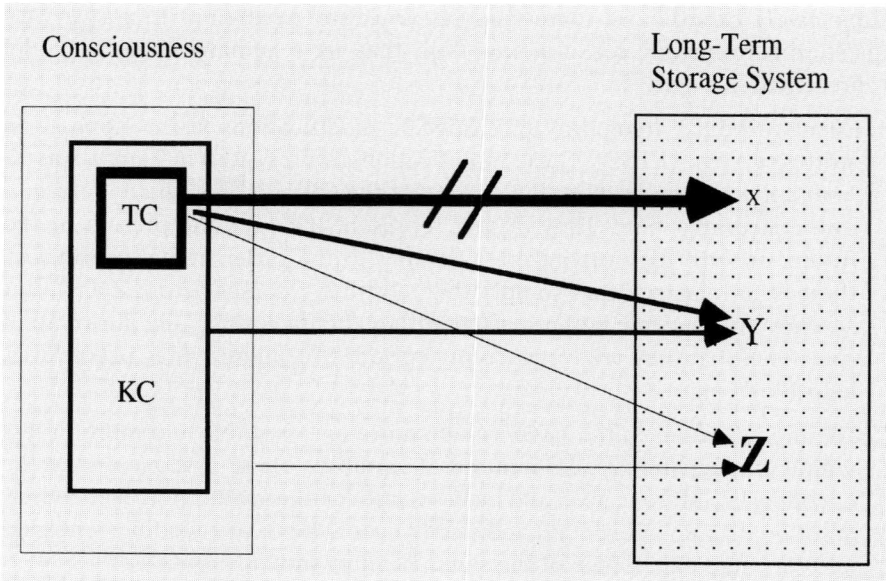

Figure 6.

oriented in the present and plan personal future. This condition is schematized in Figure 6. In other terms, this is a condition in which TC is still working but is no longer able to accomplish its usual task, i. e., to operate a sort of fine grain search in the LTSS and use less stable modifications in order to set up a personal temporal workspace. What TC does instead in this condition is to use more stable modifications of the LTSS, so that the result is that habits or personal semantic information are considered in a personal temporal framework. When asked what they have done the previous day or what they are going to do the following day, confabulating patients of this type typically answer reporting as memories and plans what they usually do in their daily life. Although admitted to the hospital, they will say, for example, that the previous day they went out shopping and that the following day will be visiting some friends, acts that presumably were part of their routine life. This situation is described clinically as anosognosia or unawareness of memory deficit. However, anosognosia is just a term that helps the clinicians to describe what they are observing, i. e., a discrepancy between an "objective" reality, the patients' past, present situation and probable future, and what is reported by the patient. The patient by itself is just conscious of a personal past, present and future, i. e., he has TC, and so, from his point of view, not only is there nothing going wrong, but there is also nothing that makes him suspect that he could be unaware of something going wrong. In this sense the patient is agnoso-anosognosic rather than anosognosic, i. e., he is unaware of his anosognosia.

It could be argued that patients that confabulate in episodic memory, orientation and planning tasks are not necessarily conscious of a confabulatory past, present and future but they just produce the more plausible answer without having a subjective experience of remembering, of being in that place at that time or of projecting their actions. If this were the case, our account of confabulation in the past, present and future would be dismissed because TC wouldn't play any role at all in confabulation. Yet there is evidence that patients who confabulate actually do become aware of their confabulatory past, present and future. Patient MB, for example, (Dalla Barba, 1993a) when asked, following the procedure described by Tulving (1985), to attribute a "remember" or a "know" judgment to his confabulation in episodic memory tasks, systematically gave "remember" judgments. Also, the same patient showed to be ready to carry out his confabulatory plans. On one occasion, for example, he said that he was looking forward to the end of the testing session because he had to go to the general store to buy some new clothes. On that occasion, he actually attempted to leave his hospital room, claiming that there was a taxi waiting for him downstairs (see also Baddeley & Wilson, 1986; Moscovitch, 1989). In addition, from a clinical point of view, confabulating patients do not look like subjects who, in answer to questions, produce their "best guess," but they seem to adhere completely to their confabulatory reports. Therefore, although more experimental evidence is suitable, it doesn't seem to be misleading to consider confabulation in episodic memory, orientation and future planning tasks as a condition in which TC can interact only with more stable modifications of the LTSS.

It is well known that patients sometime also confabulate in some semantic memory tasks (e. g., Moscovitch, 1995a; Moscovitch & Melo, 1997). According to our hypothesis, confabulation in semantic memory reflects a condition in which KC is still there but is unable to use more stable modifications of the LTSS. This kind of condition is represented in Figure 7. When this condition occurs patients confabulate in tasks tapping general semantic knowledge, such as knowledge of public and historical facts and knowledge of famous people (e. g., Moscovitch, 1995a; Moscovitch & Melo, 1997) but they do not confabulate in semantic tasks that require the use of more stable modifications of the LTSS, such as, for example word definition tasks. Some patients, however, also confabulate in word definition tasks (Dalla Barba, 1993b). They also usually produce confabulation in episodic memory tasks that are described as fantastic (Berlyne, 1972), implausible (Baddeley & Wilson, 1986), incoherent (Kopelman, 1987) or semantically anomalous (Dalla Barba, 1993a). Confabulation in word definition tasks and fantastic confabulation in episodic memory tasks

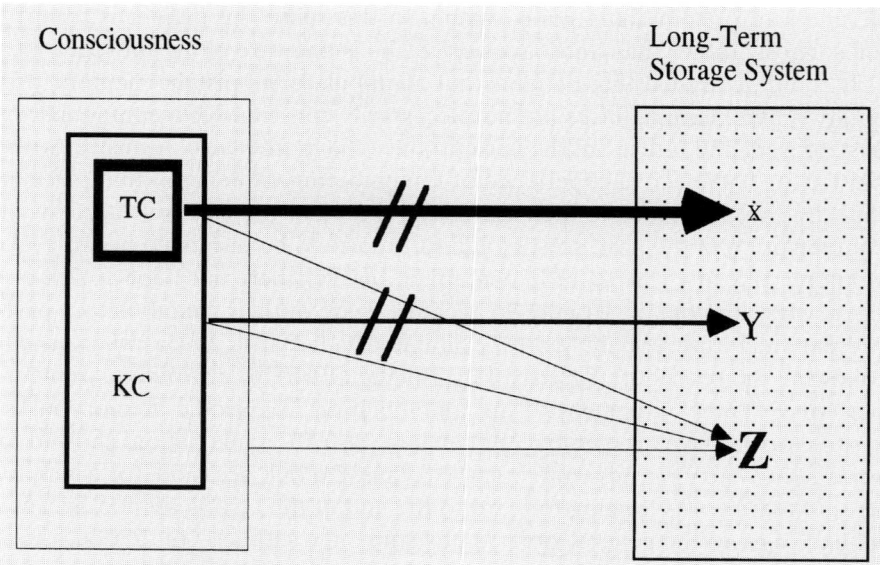

Figure 7.

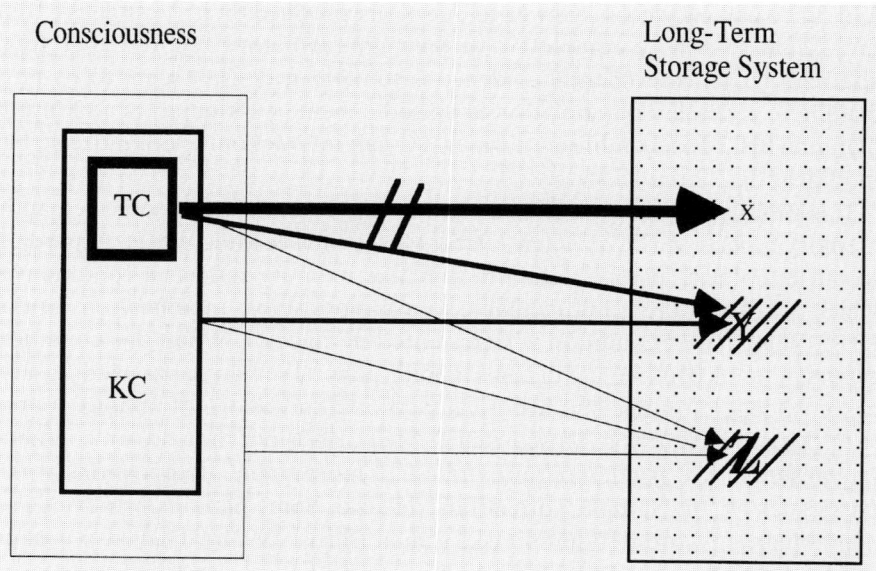

Figure 8.

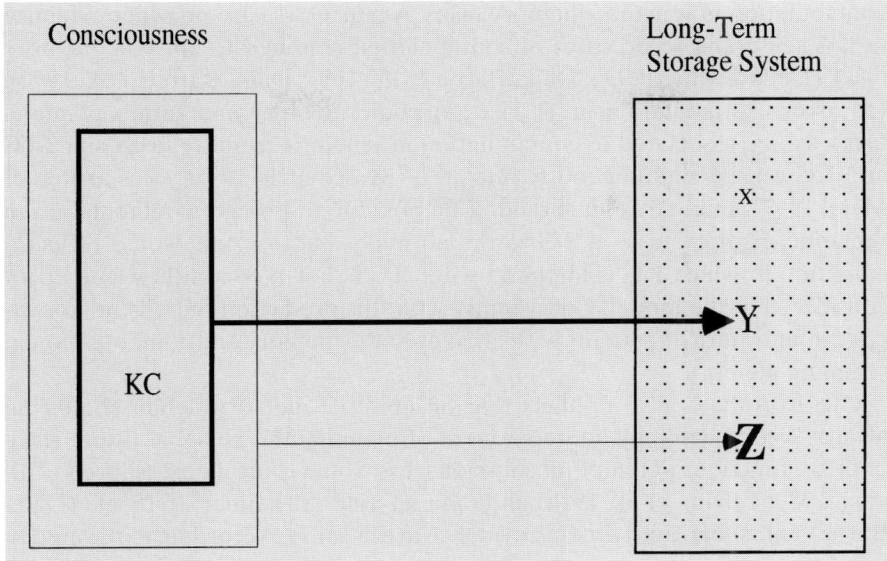

Figure 9.

reflect a condition in which the modifications in the LTSS are degraded so that the material used by TC and KC is *per se* incoherent (see Figure 8). The result is that the semantic content of confabulation in episodic memory is anomalous so that confabulation takes a fantastic and bizarre form and so does confabulation in word definition and other semantic tasks.

According to the set of assumptions schematized in our model, amnesia reflects a condition in which TC is lost so that the modifications in the LTSS can no longer be addressed in a temporal mode (see Figure 9). Classic amnesic patients not only do not remember their personal past but are usually disoriented in time and space and, according to few clinical descriptions (see, for example, Tulving, 1989; Tulving et al., 1988) and to some preliminary data from ours, they also can not plan their personal future. In other words, classic amnesic patients are lost in an instantaneous present, in the sense that they are no longer aware of a personal past, present and future.

The model we have described allows us to make some predictions. Since episodic remembering is a function of TC it shouldn't be possible to observe confabulation in episodic memory tasks without observing confabulation also in tasks that require planning the personal future. The case of GA provides the first experimental evidence in this direction. Since TC can be selectively impaired in using less stable modifications in the LTSS, it is possible to observe confabulation in episodic memory tasks and in future planning tasks without confabulation in semantic memory tasks. Again, GA's case provides evidence in this sense and so do cases of confabulation confined to episodic memory tasks (Dalla Barba, 1993a; Dalla Barba et al., 1997; Dalla Barba et al., 1990). However, confabulation in TC, i. e., episodic memory and future planning tasks, can be associated to confabulation in semantic memory tasks, since TC and KC can be simultaneously impaired (Moscovitch, 1995a; Moscovitch & Melo, 1997). In contrast, it shouldn't be possible to observe confabulation in semantic memory tasks if TC works normally, because this would reflect a condition in which KC is impaired while TC is not, a condition which is not considered in the model. Consistently with this prediction there is no knowledge in literature of patients with good episodic memory and confabulation in semantic memory.

Our hypothesis also predicts that an episodic memory deficit should be always accompanied by an impairment of planning the personal future since both are functions of temporal consciousness. Some clinical observations (Tulving, 1989; Tulving et al., 1988) and data on mild Alzheimer's patients (Dalla Barba et al., submitted) provide evidence in this sense. According to the model, a deficit of TC can be associated to a deficit of KC resulting in a deficit of episodic memory and future planning tasks as well as semantic memory tasks. More severe forms of Alzheimer's disease confirm this prediction. In contrast, it shouldn't be possible to observe deficits of semantic memory without deficits of episodic memory and future planning tasks, because this would reflect a selective deficit of KC, a condition not allowed by the model. Several authors have argued for the existence of selective impairments of semantic memory without any comparable deficits of episodic memory. However, in reported cases of selective semantic impairment, episodic memory is claimed to be normal on the basis of the observation that day-to-day memory is preserved (De Renzi, Liotti, & Nichelli, 1987; Hodges, Patterson, Oxbury, & Funnell, 1992; Hodges, Patterson, & Tyler, 1994). Typically, these patients are impaired in a variety of semantic memory tasks, but they usually remember day-to-day events including the different testing sessions and their content. These observations might lead to the conclusion that episodic memory is independent from semantic memory and that a deficit of semantic memory can occur without any comparable deficit of episodic memory. However, the comparison of patients' performance in day-to-day memory and in formal semantic memory testing can hardly lead to firm conclusions on the relation between semantic and episodic memory. In fact, day-to-day memory is observed in ecological conditions, which may be an easier situation than that of formal semantic memory testing, and variables that affect one situation might be different from variables that affect the other situation. In addition, patients with selective semantic memory deficits are usually severely impaired on learning tasks which are traditionally considered to tap episodic memory (Basso, Capitani, & Laiacona, 1988; De Renzi et al., 1987; Hodges & Patterson, 1995; Hodges et al., 1994; Pietrini et al., 1988; Warrington & Shallice, 1984; Wilkins & Moscovitch, 1978). These studies do not provide enough evidence to claim that these patients have unimpaired episodic memory, nor that semantic memory is independent from episodic memory.

The set of assumptions we have proposed and that are schematized in the model provide an account of a variety of memory disturbances, namely confabulation restricted to episodic memory, confabulation in episodic and semantic memory, confabulation described clinically as fantastic or implausible which in fact contains semantic anomalies, and amnesia. Introducing the notion of temporal consciousness, of which episodic remembering is a function, the model also helps to understand confabulation in future planning tasks and accounts for the observation that amnesics with an episodic memory deficit are also impaired in planning their personal future. Last but not least, the model has the advantage of doing all this without falling into the illusion of the homunculus and in the memory trace paradox.

## References

Anderson, J.R., & Bower, G.H. (1974). A propositional theory of recognition memory. *Memory and Cognition, 2*, 406–412.

Anderson, J.R., & Bower, G.H. (1972). Recognition and retrieval processes in free recall. *Psychological Review, 79*, 97–123.

Baddeley, A., & Wilson, B. (1986). Amnesia, autobiographical memory and confabulation. In D.C. Rubin (Ed.), *Autobiographical memory* (pp. 225–252). Cambridge, UK: Cambridge University Press.

Basso, A., Capitani, E., & Laiacona, M. (1988). Progressive language impairment without dementia: A case with isolated category specific semantic defect. *Journal of Neurology, Neurosurgery and Psychiatry., 51*, 1201–1207.

Bergson, H. (1896). *Matière et mémoire*. Paris: Alcan.

Berlyne, N. (1972). Confabulation. *British Journal of Psychiatry, 120*, 31–39.

Burgess, P.W., & Shallice, T. (1996). Confabulation and the control of recollection. *Memory, 4*, 359–411.

Claparède, E. (1911). Recognition et moïté. *Archives de Psychologie, 11*, 79–90.

Conway, M.A. (1992). A structural model of autobiographical memory. In M.A. Conway, D.C. Rubin, H. Spinnler, & W.A. Wagenaar (Eds.), *Theoretical perspectives on autobiographical memory.* (pp. 167–194). The Netherlands: Kluwer.

Crovitz, H.F., & Schiffman, H. (1974). Frequency of episodic memories as function of their ages. *Bulletin of the Psychonomic Society, 4*, 517–18.

Dalla Barba, G. (1993a). Confabulation: Knowledge and recollective experience. *Cognitive Neuropsychology, 10*, 1–20.

Dalla Barba, G. (1993b). Different patterns of confabulation. *Cortex, 29*, 567–581.

Dalla Barba, G., Boissé, M.-F., Bartolomeo, P., & Bachoud-Lévi, A.-C. (1997). Confabulation following rupture of posterior communicating artery. *Cortex, 33*, 563–570.

Dalla Barba, G., Cipolotti, L., & Denes, G. (1990). Autobiographical memory loss and confabulation in Korsakoff's syndrome: A case report. *Cortex, 26*, 525–534.

De Renzi, E., Liotti, M., & Nichelli, P. (1987). Selective semantic amnesia with preservation of autobiographical memory. *Cortex, 23*, 575–597.

Delbecq-Derouesne, J., Beauvois, M.F., & Shallice, T. (1990). Preserved recall versus impaired recognition. *Brain, 113*, 1045–154.

Galton, F. (1879). Psychometric experiments. *Brain, 2*, 149–162.

Hintzman, D.L. (1978). *The psychology of learning and memory*. San Francisco: Freeman.

Hodges, J.R., & Patterson, K. (1995). Is semantic memory consistently impaired early in the course of Alzheimer's disease? Neuroanatomical and diagnostic implications. *Neuropsychologia, 33*, 441–459.

Hodges, J.R., Patterson, K., Oxbury, S., & Funnell, E. (1992). Semantic dementia: Progressive fluent aphasia with temporal lobe atrophy. *Brain, 115*, 1783–1806.

Hodges, J.R., Patterson, K., & Tyler, L.K. (1994). Loss of semantic memory: Implications for the modularity of mind. *Cognitive Neuropsychology, 11*, 505–542.

Jacoby, L.L., Kelley, C.M., & Dywan, J. (1989). Memory attributions. In H.L. Roediger III & F.I.M. Craik (Eds.), *Varieties of memory and consciousness: Essays in honour of Endel Tulving*. Hillsdale, NJ: Erlbaum.

James, W. (1890). *Principles of psychology*. New York: Holt.

Johnson, M. (1988). Discriminating the origin of information. In F. Oltmann & B. Mahers (Eds.), *Delusional beliefs* (pp. 34–65). New York: Wiley.

Johnson, M.K. (1991). Reality Monitoring: Evidence from confabulation in organic brain disease patients. In G.P. Prigatano & D.L. Schacter (Eds.), *Awareness of deficit after brain injury* (pp. 176–197). New York: Oxford University Press.

Johnson, M.K., & Raye, C.L. (1981). Reality monitoring. *Psychological Review, 88*, 67–85.

Kopelman, M.D. (1987). Two types of confabulation. *Journal of Neurology, Neurosurgery and Psychiatry, 50*, 1482–1487.

Landauer, T.K. (1975). A multicopy storage and random access model of memory. *Cognitive Psychology, 7*, 495–531.

Mandler, G. (1980). Recognizing: The judgment of prior occurrence. *Psychological Review, 87*, 252–271.

Merleau-Ponty, M. (1945). *Phénoménologie de la perception*. Paris: Librairie Gallimard.

Morton, J., Hammersley, R.H., & Bekerian, D.A. (1985). Headed records: A model for memory and its failures. *Cognition, 20*, 1–23.

Moscovitch, M. (1989). Confabulation and the frontal system: Strategic versus associative retrieval in neuropsychological theories of memory. In H.L. Roediger & F.I. Craik (Eds.), *Varieties of memory and consciousness: Essay in honor of Endel Tulving* (pp. 133–160). Hillsdale, NJ: Erlbaum.

Moscovitch, M. (1995a). Confabulation. In D.L. Schacter (Ed.), *Memory distortion* (pp. 226–251). Cambridge, MA: Harvard University Press.

Moscovitch, M. (1995b). Recovered consciousness: An hypothesis concerning modularity and episodic memory. *Journal of Clinical and Experimental Neuropsychology, 17*, 276–290.

Moscovitch, M., & Melo, B. (1997). Strategic retrieval and the frontal lobes: Evidence from confabulation and amnesia. *Neuropsychologia, 35*, 1017–1034.

Pietrini, V., Nertempi, P., Vaglia, A., Revello, M.G., Pinna, V., & Ferro Milone, F. (1988). Recovery from herpes simplex encephalitis: Selective impairment of specific semantic categories with neuroradiological correlation. *Journal of Neurology, Neurosurgery and Psychiatry, 51*, 1284–1293.

Shallice, T., & Evans, M. (1978). The involvement of the frontal lobe in cognitive estimation. *Cortex, 14*, 294–303.

Tulving, E. (1983). *Elements of episodic memory.* Oxford: Oxford University Press.

Tulving, E. (1985). Memory and consciousness. *Canadian Psychology, 26*, 1–12.

Tulving, E. (1989). Remembering and knowing the past. *American Scientist, 77*, 361–366.

Tulving, E., Schacter, D.L., McLachlan, D.R., & Moscovitch, M. (1988). Priming of semantic autobiographical knowledge: A case study of retrograde amnesia. *Brain and Cognition, 8*, 3–20.

Warrington, E.K., & Shallice, T. (1984). Category specific semantic impairments. *Brain, 107*, 829–853.

Wilkins, A., & Moscovitch, M. (1978). Selective impairment of semantic memory after temporal lobectomy. *Neuropsychologia, 16*, 73–79.

# Stress-Related Memory Disorders

*Hans J. Markowitsch*

The interdependence between brain and behavior has a multitude of facets. Already long before the turn of the last century, Sharpey (1879) discussed to what extent the injured brain is able to re-adapt to its changed possibilities and to a confrontation with a less well decodable environment. Nevertheless, most modern brain researchers are used to thinking in straightforward and largely uni-dimensional relations between the environment and its brain correlates. Here, I will demonstrate results which show that the consequences of environmental stimulation to the brain are less fixed and may depend on previous experiences of the subject with related stimulation. These more complex and less predictable associations are found especially with respect to complex cognitive functions such as memory processing.

## Biases in Information Processing

We are used to seeing our present life and our present knowledge and behavior as caused by the experiences we have made in the past. Furthermore, we have the firm belief that we can plan our future on the basis of the knowledge and the events we have processed and stored as memories. The time-embedding of memories is one of our most basic experiences. We only rarely reflect that we possess a reliable consciousness of time which allows us to travel back in time and to order, sequence, associate, and categorize experiences. This ability to travel back in time is one of the principal features of episodic memory and distinguishes this memory system from others – the knowledge system (or semantic memory), procedural memory and the priming system (Tulving, 1995; Tulving & Markowitsch, 1998).

Patients with Korsakoff's syndrome or bilateral diencephalic or medial temporal lobe damage due to other causes have lost this basic ability. Patients with other kinds of brain damage, in particular with combined damage to temporo-polar and infero-lateral prefrontal regions (Markowitsch, 1995), may show a selective inability to retrieve information from their personal past. This inability is selective in that those patients are still able to rely on memory subsystems different from the episodic (autobiographic) one (Markowitsch, 1996). That is, they still can read, write, and calculate and are able to maintain and even develop procedural skills. The discrepancy between preservation of some forms of memory and loss of other forms has been known for a long time (Heilbronner, 1904/05; Kohnstamm, 1917; Schneider, 1912, 1928; Veraguth & Cloetta, 1907). Russell wrote in 1971 that "we must face the problem of different classes of memory system" (p. 76).

There are, however, patients without obvious brain damage who neverthe-less show widely similar amnesic disturbances, namely an inability to retrieve or ecphorize information or an inability to acquire new episodic information long term (Markowitsch, 1996). (Tulving, 1983, used the term "ecphory" to describe the process by which retrieval cues interact with stored information so that an image or a representation of the information in question appears.) Cases of this kind (i. e., without manifest brain damage) have frequently been subsumed under the heading of psychogenic amnesia. This label, however, requires an explanation as well: What are the causes leading to psychogenic amnesia? It is assumed that a labile personality and stressful life events which cannot be adequately compensated or processed may lead to a retrieval block for personal past memories. Freud (1898, 1899, 1900; 1901a, 1901b; Breuer & Freud, 1895) devoted a number of papers to psychic mechanisms of forgetting. He and others (Janet, 1894; Mai, 1995) used the term "hysterical amnesia" instead of psychogenic amnesia. Freud (1901b; Breuer & Freud, 1895) also emphasized that the forgetting may be selective (e. g., refer to only certain events or a certain time period or epoch). Furthermore, false memories may occur, that is, a subject may be of the opinion that something has happened which in fact never did occur or that something has happened in a different way than it did.

All such biases in information processing can usually be traced back to certain personality dimensions or to certain environmental events. Usually, inappropriate affective or emotional processing is a prerequisite for such mnestic blocks. As an example, a subject who had most likely been sexually abused by her relatives had lost conscious access to her life period between ages 10 and 16 (Markowitsch et al., 1997c). Specific determinants and examples for memory biases and psychogenic amnesia as well as probable neural corre-lates will be given below.

## Organic Versus Psychogenic Amnesias

The existence of a causal relationship between massive, traumatic brain dam-age and subsequent amnesia is undisputed (Fink & Markowitsch, 1999; Russell,

1971; Russell & Nathan, 1946). On the other hand, for cases with minor head concussions or other accidents, not resulting in major bodily injury, associations between memory block conditions and the previous events seemed questionable (e. g., Härtl, 1916; Kohnstamm, 1917; Müller-Suur, 1949).

Psychiatrists invented numerous labels to classify patients with specific biases in memory processing. Aside from the already mentioned "hysterical amnesia," "Wanderlust," "fugue-condition," "multiple personality," or "Ganser syndrome" were common syndrome classifications, most of which referred to a memory loss in the retrograde-autobiographic domain (Burgl, 1900; Ganser, 1898; Heilbronner, 1903, 1905; Kellner, 1898; Mörchen, 1904; Pick, 1884; Raecke, 1903, 1908; Schultze, 1903). Up to the present these syndrome constellations were painstakingly separated from cases with a known organic basis. While in organically brain damaged patients anterograde and retrograde memory disturbances are usually interwoven (Mayes, Daum, Markowitsch, & Sauter, 1997; Rempel-Clower, Zola-Morgan, Squire, & Amaral, 1996; Schmidtke & Vollmer, 1997), recently more and more cases are being described which speak for an anatomical separation of cases with an inability to acquire new information long term and cases who have lost access to their old memories (Calabrese et al., 1996; Kapur, 1993; Kapur, Ellison, Smith, McLellan, & Burrows, 1992; Kroll, Markowitsch, Knight, & von Cramon, 1997; Markowitsch, 1995; Markowitsch et al., 1993a, b; Markowitsch & Ewald, 1998; O'Connor, Butters, Miliotis, Eslinger, & Cermak, 1992)

Patients with selective or largely selective retrograde amnesia of an organic basis appear changed in their personality – primarily emotionally flattened. This makes them similar to patients with psychogenic or functional amnesia. (De Renzi, Lucchelli, Muggia, & Spinnler, 1997, introduced the term "functional amnesia" to described amnesic conditions of unknown or unclear origin.) This led to the hypothesis that there is a basic similarity between amnesias with a clear organic basis (manifest brain damage) and amnesias considered to be of principally psychic origin (Markowitsch, 1996). Furthermore, it is hypothesized that locus and extent of brain damage is not directly related to the severity of retrograde amnesia (Markowitsch, 1996, 1997a; Markowitsch, Kessler, Frölich, Schneider, & Maurer, 1999). Instead, biochemical or other changes might at least be co-factors of the amnesia.

Furthermore, the frequently involved prefrontal damage might modulate amnesia by provoking motivational changes, and changes in initiative, drive and will (Jetter et al., 1986; Markowitsch, 1997b). Results from functional neuroimaging underline the importance of the prefrontal cortex for information recall (Fink et al., 1996; Fletcher, Frith, & Rugg, 1997; Tulving, Kapur, Markowitsch, Craik, Habib, & Houle, 1994).

On the other, the often affected anterior temporal lobe region points to the importance of the emotional dimension (Damasio, 1994; Franzen & Myers, 1973). Starkstein, Fedoroff, Berthier, and Robinson (1991) found that especially patients with damage to the orbitofrontal and temporobasal cortex of the right hemisphere were easily affected by unipolar manic disturbances. Within the temporal lobe the amygdala has a special importance for the coupling of emotion and memory (Adolphs, Tranel, Damasio, & Damasio, 1994; Cahill, Babinsky, Markowitsch, & McGaugh, 1995; Fink et al., 1996; Markowitsch et al., 1994; Sarter & Markowitsch, 1985). Especially the amygdala and surrounding regions of the right hemisphere seem to be engaged in the processing of autobiographical-emotional information (Davidson & Sutton, 1995; Fink et al., 1996; Shin et al., 1997).

Of special interest is to what degree stress evoking events block the recall of old episodic information, or to what degree stress-related events have a higher chance than neutral ones to be blocked from recall (or ecphory) (Cacioppo, 1994). Southwick, Morgan, Nicolaou, and Charney (1997) found distortions and omission of trauma-related events in soldiers from the Kuwait war and Sutker, Winstead, Galina, and Allain (1991) reported cognitive deficits in prisoners of war and participants of the Korean war. Possible neural mechanisms may lie in the release of stress-related hormones (glucocorticoids) which are especially active in the anterior temporal lobe region (Lupien & McEwen, 1997; McGaugh, Cahill, & Roozendaal, 1996; Roozendaal, Portillo Marquez, & McGaugh, 1996). Furthermore, direct changes in the brain's norepinephrine level (Southwick et al., 1993) and an increased action of GABA-agonists have been postulated. Our own findings demonstrate that reactive stress can block the action of multiple brain regions (Markowitsch, Kessler, Van der Ven, Weber-Luxenburger, & Heiss, 1998).

## Examples of Cases of Others with Functional Amnesia

Several patients have been described which underline the necessity to question the dichotomy between organic and psychogenic amnesia. Table 1 lists relevant cases and gives details of the kind of mnestic deficits, possible causes and follow-up periods. Taken together, these cases indicate that even minor traumatic conditions can induce lasting amnesia.

## Our Own Cases with Functional Amnesia

In the following, our own cases manifesting retrograde or anterograde amnesia or a combination of both will be given. Table 2 gives a summary of the described cases.

*Table 1.* Cases with functional amnesia described by others

| Study | Patient | Trauma condition | Brain damage | Follow-up | Type of amnesia |
|---|---|---|---|---|---|
| Barbarotto et al. (1996) | 38 y. old woman | slipped and fell in her office | CT: normal | 1/2 year | pure RA |
| Dalla Barba et al. (1997) | 17 y. old girl | ? | EEG, CT, MRI FDG-PET: all normal | ~ 1 year | pure RA |
| De Renzi & Lucchelli (1993) | 26 y. old man | fell from tractor | MRI normal PET: hypometabolism of posterior temporal lobes | 2 years | pure RA, abnormally fast forgetting |
| De Renzi et al. (1995) | 19 y. old man | car accident w/o apparent brain damage | CT, MRI normal | 29 months | pure RA |
| De Renzi et al. (1997) | 59 y. old man | car accident | CT, MRI, SPECT: all normal | 4 years | pure RA |

Abbreviations: EEG, electroencephalography; CT, computed tomography; MRI, magnetic resonance tomography; FDG-PET, 2($^{18}$F)-fluorodeoxyglucose positron-emission-tomography; RA, retrograde amnesia; SPECT, single photon emission computed tomography.

*Case AA* (J. Kessler et al., 1997). A 29-year-old student developed within a month a complete inability to form lasting new episodic memories while his intelligence, his retrograde memory ability and his short-term memory remained preserved. In spite of major attempts to find a brain correlate for his amnesia, this could not be established: Doppler sonography, magnetic resonance imaging, 2($^{18}$F)-fluorodeoxyglucose (FDG), positron emission-tomography and electrophysiological recordings (EEG, evoked potentials) all remained with the normal range. The condition was followed up for more than a year and remained unchanged within this time period. We assumed that a complex chain of interacting variables produced the syndrome which appeared phenomenologically as anterograde amnesia. A grossly reduced drive to consolidate or ecphorize memories was probably a major determinant of his deficit.

*Case NN* (Markowitsch, Fink, Thöne, Kessler, & Heiss, 1997b). The patient came to our attention because of a persistent retrograde amnesia after a fugue condition. He rode his bicycle for several days along the river Rhine without knowing who he was or why he did it. This condition remained unchanged for more than one year. The patient had had a poor childhood. His mother would have preferred a daughter and put him into female clothes for the first five

*Table 2.* Cases with functional amnesia described by us

| Study | Patient | Trauma condition | Brain damage | Follow-up | Type of amnesia |
|---|---|---|---|---|---|
| Kessler et al. (1997) (*case AA*) | 29 y. old | ? | EEG, MRI, FDG-PET all normal | 1 year | AA |
| Markowitsch et al. (1997b) (*case NN*) | 37 y. old | Personality problems since childhood | EEG, MRI normal; $^{15}$O-PET shows abnormal autobiographical memory processing | 1 year | Episodic RA |
| Markowitsch et al. (1998) (*case AMN*) | 23 y. old | Singular childhood trauma and related trauma at present | EEG, MRI normal, FDG-PET drastically reduced in memory processing regions | 1 year | Episodic AA, episodic RA for last 6 years |
| Markowitsch et al. (1999) (*case FA*) | 46 y. old | Stressful life situations throughout life | EEG, MRI, FDG-PET normal | ~1 year | Episodic AA, reduced STM |
| Markowitsch et al. (1997a) (*case BT*) | 30 y. old | Probably stressful life situations since childhood | CT, MRI normal, past meningitis?, SPECT: right temporo-frontal hypometabolism, $^{15}$O-PET: abnormal processing of learned information | ~1 year | Episodic RA |
| Markowitsch et al. (1997c) (*case DO*) | 59 y. old | Probably multiply sexually abused as child | MRI normal, $^{15}$O-PET: temporo-polar activation during ecphory of affective memories | ~3 years | Selective RA for life period 10–16 years of age |
| Markowitsch et al. (in press) (*case TA*) | 30 y. old | Trauma due to whiplash injury (about 3 1/2 years prior to present examination) | MRI, FDG-PET, EEG, EPs normal | ~6 months | severe AA for periods > 1 hour; severe RA for events from about last 3½ years |

Abbreviations: EPs, evoked potentials; EEG, electroencephalography; CT, computed tomography; MRI, magnetic resonance tomography; FDG-PET, 2($^{18}$F)-fluorodeoxyglucose positron-emission-tomography; SPECT, single photon emission computed tomography; RA, retrograde amnesia; AA, anterograde amnesia; STM, short-term memory.

years of his life. Later, she frequently told him that he would ruin their restaurant and would be unable to lead a successful life. He had spontaneously "escaped" from his life situation before the present fugue, but had not lost his identity on those occasions. The patient was of above average intelligence and had good anterograde memory abilities. After the fugue he changed his life habits and manifested other somatic changes (e. g., he gained 15 kg of body weight within a short time, lost his allergy and asthma, changed his profession and no longer wanted to drive or ride cars because of their speed).

The patient did not reveal any brain abnormalities under (static) magnetic resonance imaging or when recording EEGs. However, an $^{15}$O-positron-emission-tomographic activation study during which his brain activity during imagery of sentences containing autobiographic events and containing biographic events from somebody else was compared, revealed that he processed both kinds of information in a similar way and different from normals (Fink et al., 1996).

*Case AMN* (Markowitsch, Kessler, Van der Ven, Weber-Luxenburger, & Heiss, 1998). A 23-year-old patient had major and persistent anterograde amnesia and six years of retrograde amnesia after a shock experience. The patient saw the outbreak of an open fire in his house and the next morning he was severely disturbed and amnesic. This condition remained unchanged for about eight months and manifested as severe verbal and nonverbal amnesia in both anterograde and retrograde directions. Four weeks after the shock condition the patient could report that he had seen a man burning to death in his car when he was four years old. As he mentioned further, since then fire meant a life-threatening situation to him. Apparently, the new fire situation had resulted in a sudden and major release of stress hormones (glucocorticoids) leading to a block of the normal mnestic information flow. After about eight months AMN somewhat improved cognitively, but even after 12 months he was severely disturbed, especially with respect to long-term memory. His FDG-PET had returned to normal glucose scores for subjects of his age and sex, his mnestic condition, however, did not allow him to return to work (Markowitsch, Kessler, Van der Ven, Weber-Luxenburger, & Heiss, submitted).

*Case FA* (Markowitsch, Kessler, Frölich, Schneider, & Maurer, 1999). A 46-year old independent engineer apparently had lost his ability to acquire new episodic information long term. Furthermore, he had a drastically reduced short-term memory, disturbances in old memories, acalculia and word finding difficulties. Otherwise, his intellectual capacity was in the normal range (that is, he was not pseudo-demented, for example). Neither neuromonitoring nor static or dynamic neuroimaging methods demonstrated any brain abnormality.

The patient was diagnosed as depressive. However, various forms of drug treatment and psychotherapy – given over a period of altogether more than a year – failed to improve his condition. The patient's personal history indicated that he had had a complicated stressful life from childhood to the present.

*Case BT* (Markowitsch et al., 1997a). A 30-year old male patient complained of having lost his personal memory for his total life time. The patient otherwise had normal intelligence and normal anterograde memory abilities. His retrograde semantic memory ("world knowledge") was within the normal range as well. He did not regain access to his autobiography over several months of follow-up. BT behaved cooperatively in neuropsychological tests. Initial computer tomography and magnetic resonance imaging revealed no brain damage. Investigation of his cerebrospinal fluid showed a slightly elevated cell count which was interpreted as a possible past meningitis. Under single photon emission computed tomography (SPECT) there was a reduction in cerebral blood flow in the anterior temporal and infero-lateral prefrontal cortex of the right hemisphere, corresponding to that seen in a patient with massive and selective retrograde amnesia due to encephalitis (Calabrese et al., 1996). Measurements of regional cerebral blood flow with PET during episodic memory retrieval revealed a pattern of activated brain structures which differed at least in part to that seen in normal subjects exposed to the same experimental design (Tulving et al., 1994). It was concluded that BT represents a case of probably psychogenic amnesia.

*Case TA* (Markowitsch, Kessler, Kalbe, & Herholz, in press). TA was a 30-year old former right-handed University student who had led an active life with multiple interests. Three and a half years prior to the present examination she was involved in a car accident with another one driving into her car. The accident provoked a whiplash injury and hearing disturbances, but no skull damage. Since this accident TA had severe and persisting anterograde amnesia which, however, occurred only after about ½ to 2 hours after information acquisition. She was disoriented with respect to time and had to learn about her situation every morning anew. Multiple CT and MRI scans remained negative. EEG was normal, showing a 10 Hz alpha EEG with vigilance changes, no signs of general or focal changes, and no hypersynchronous potentials. An FDG-PET performed 3½ years after the injury was insignificant as well compared to age and sex matched normals.

TA performed neuropsychological tests slowly but with high concentration. She gained high scores for intelligence and anterograde memory. In the revised Wechsler Memory Scale she obtained the highest possible General Memory Index for a subject of her age. In spite of this, she could not recall any acquired

information after periods of more than one or two hours. Her retrograde semantic and episodic memories were excellent until the time of the injury.
Thereafter they were practically zero. She remembered for instance events
which had happened half a year prior to her injury, but not events which had
happened two or three months thereafter.

## Personality, Stress, and Amnesia

Taken together, these cases indicate that there are basic similarities between
amnesic patients with a manifest organic basis and those lacking such a basis
(Markowitsch, 1996). Under both conditions (organic amnesia, psychic amnesia) emotional changes such as an indifference toward one's own condition
and a reduced affect in general are common. Most interestingly, our results
obtained with dynamic imaging techniques indicate that affective mnestic processing is accompanied by a right hemispheric temporo-frontal activation
(Fink et al., 1996; Markowitsch, 1997b; Markowitsch et al., 1997c), while vice
versa a reduced affective state and retrograde amnesia for autobiographic
events are followed by a reduced right hemispheric temporo-frontal activation
(Markowitsch et al., 1997a,b). This reduced affective condition can be observed
in both patients with a manifest neural basis for their amnesia (Markowitsch
et al., 1993a,b; Markowitsch & Ewald, 1998) and in patients with a psychogenic
diagnosis for their amnesia. Interestingly, Iidaka and co-workers (1997) similarly found with dynamic imaging a reduced right-hemispheric temporo-
frontal activation in patients with mood disorders.

Due to the likely overlap of behavioral manifestations in patients with a
proven and a non-proven neural basis for their amnesia, De Renzi, Lucchelli,
Muggia, and Spinnler (1997) suggested using the term *functional amnesia*. Such
patients manifest as the principal syndrome a disproportionally heavy amnesic
condition, but may show other cognitive deviations as well (Barbarotto, Laiacona, & Cocchini, 1996; De Renzi, Luccelli, Muggia, & Spinnler, 1995; De Renzi
et al., 1997; J. Kessler et al., 1997; Markowitsch, 1995; Markowitsch et al., 1999;
Mattioli et al., 1996).

In some cases, psychiatric symptoms may be manifest which are a further
correlate for the usually rapidly occurring cognitive defects. As an example, a
patient with massive anterograde and retrograde amnesia had had a major
depression since his early adulthood which had been (unsuccessfully) treated
with drugs and electroconvulsive therapy. Four of his relatives, including his
mother, had committed suicide due to depressive conditions (Markowitsch,
1997a). This patient had shown a symmetrical degeneration of his medial temporal lobe region, whose etiology was obscure. It can be speculated that his

brain damage had a relation to his depression and amnesia. Recently Gurvits et al. (1996) reported that combat veterans (who had been subjected to life threatening and consequently quite stressful situations) manifested a – compared to control subjects – significant reduction (up to 25%) in their hippocampal volumes. Most likely these reductions are due to a shrunken hippocampal neuropil (Magariños, McEwen, Flügge, & Fuchs, 1996; Magariños, Verdugo, & McEwen, 1997).

There are a number of studies which demonstrate that massive stress conditions increase the release of glucocorticoids to such a degree that they finally change the neuronal metabolism (Bremner, Krystal, Southwick, & Charney, 1995a; Bremner et al., 1993, 1995b,c, 1997a,b; Sapolsky, 1994, 1996a,b; Sapolsky, Uno, Rebert, & Finch, 1990). As a consequence, neural tissue degenerations may occur, especially in regions with a high glucocorticoid receptor density – the anterior temporal lobe with amygdaloid complex and hippocampal formation (Haas & Schauenstein, 1997; Joëls & de Kloet, 1992; Lupien & McEwen, 1997; Majewska, 1992; O'Brien, 1997; Vidal, Jordan, & Zieglgänsberger, 1986).

Effects of massive stress conditions on cognitive performance and brain function have been frequently documented (aside from the work of Bremner and of Sapolsky and their coworkers the following examples may be listed: Barrett, Green, Morris, Giles, & Croft, 1996; Carlier, Lamberts, Fouwels, & Gersons, 1996; Elder, Shanahan, & Clipp, 1997; King, 1997; Layton & Wardi-Zonna, 1995; Skodol et al., 1996; van der Kolk, 1994). The reductions in cognitive performance were attributed to reduced capacities in information processing and information evaluating neuronal nets (Brewin, Dalgleish, & Joseph, 1996; Layton & Wardi-Zonna, 1995; Markowitsch, 1996; Pitman, 1988).

A number of reports propose that a predisposition for the development of stress-related cognitive changes in adulthood is enforced by mechanisms present in childhood (Aldenhoff, 1997; Kuyken & Brewin, 1995; Liotti, 1992; Parks & Balon, 1995; Schacter, Koutstall, & Norman, 1996; Teicher, Glod, Surrey, & Swett, 1993). Teicher et al. (1993) for instance showed, highly significantly, that early physical or sexual abuse hinders the development of the limbic system. The case history of our patient AMN who had seen the outbreak of an open fire as an adult and had seen a person burning to death at age four is another example (Markowitsch et al., 1998).

The central importance of the hypothalamic-hypophyseal-adrenocortical axis (Herman & Cullinan, 1997; Holsboer, 1989) has been repeatedly emphasized for these mechanisms, and ineffective coping strategies (Heim, 1988) may foster the outbreak of the illness. (Stress conditions have even been proposed to be related to the manifestation of Creutzfeldt-Jakob disease: Brandel & Delasnerie-Laupretre, 1997.)

Depressive conditions are also known to change the glucocorticoid feedback on the brain level (Young, Haskett, Murphy-Weinberg, Watson, & Akil, 1991) with the consequence of changes in the cellular immune response (Dorian & Garfinkel, 1989; Herbert & Cohen, 1993; O'Leary 1990). Aldenhoff (1997) emphasized relations between glucocorticoids and depression. As a cautious note he pointed out that there are nevertheless some not easily explainable differences: In depression there is an overdrive of the cortisol response while in posttraumatic stress disorder a suppression follows. He concluded that the time point of the stress reaction and the state of the organism apparently determine the form of reaction and that it still has to be determined which factors cause the various differentiations of the disease conditions. He assumed that an early trauma and a (re-)activation by psychological mechanisms or biological events will after a phase of latency lead to a "vegetative-emotional cognitive dissociation," or to a "psychobiological stress reaction" or to "depression."

Presently results from a considerable number of studies indicate a close association between stress and depression and show a heightened risk for posttraumatic stress disorder patients to develop depression (Breslau, Davis, Peterson, & Schultz, 1997; Fawzi et al., 1997; Kessler, 1997; Peck, Robertson, & Zeffert, 1996; Silove, Sinnerbrink, Field, Manicavasagar, & Steel, 1997).

Relations and differences between post traumatic stress disorder and depression were also highlighted by Yehuda, Giller, and Mason (1993) and by Bleich, Koslowsky, Dolev, and Lerer (1997). Yehuda et al. pointed to similarities between the two disease conditions, namely insomnia, disturbances in concentration, social retreat, loss of interests, but discussed the opposite activity changes in the activity in the hypothalamic-hypophyseal-adrenocortical axis as well. Bleich et al. stressed the high co-morbidity between both illnesses, but mentioned some possible differences as well. Future research will have to find out in what way depressive conditions and stress-related neural and behavioral changes might be explainable.

## The Mnestic Block Syndrome

It is a common place to say that memory disturbances which lead to a general (or selective) inability to encode or recall (ecphorize) information, are determined by a corresponding brain activity. For a number of cases specific brain damage can be traced as the cause, though both the selectivity of disturbances (e. g., confined to episodic memories) and their generality (e. g., the total autobiographical old memories across the whole past life) are astonishing and call into question a complete "organic" attribution (Markowitsch, 1996). In other cases, evidence for "organicity" is obtained only indirectly or even not at all. Nevertheless, a changed brain metabolism is also assumed to be the cause for the memory block. To what degree this changed metabolism is the consequence of inner body conditions or is induced by the environment (and may then later manifest itself independent of environmental conditions), has been recognized only very rudimentarily up to now. It can, however, be assumed that there are more cases with a "mnestic block syndrome" (Markowitsch et al., 1999) than described up to now. This mnestic block syndrome can be visualized as a kind of disconnection which undermines the access to the engrams or storage places. As long as there are no clearer or more straightforward possibilities to explain the multitude of suddenly occurring and globally acting amnesias without manifest brain tissue damage, the assumption of a mnestic block condition can be taken as a preliminary model to attack the multitude of manifestations of functional amnesia.

## Acknowledgments

My sincere thanks to all my coworkers without whom this report would not have appeared. Similarly, without the kind cooperation of the patients this paper could not have appeared. My work was supported by grants from the Deutsche Forschungsgemeinschaft (German Research Council).

## References

Adolphs, R., Tranel, D., Damasio, H., & Damasio, A. (1994). Impaired recognition of emotion in facial expressions following bilateral damage to the human amygdala. *Nature, 372,* 669–672.

Aldenhoff, J. (1997). Überlegungen zur Psychobiologie der Depression. *Nervenarzt, 68,* 379–389.

Barbarotto, R., Laiacona, M., & Cocchini, G. (1996). A case of simulated, psychogenic or focal pure retrograde amnesia: Did an entire life become unconscious? *Neuropsychologia, 34,* 575–585.

Barrett, D.H., Green, M.L., Morris, R., Giles, W.H., & Croft, J.B. (1996). Cognitive functioning and posttraumatic stress disorder. *American Journal of Psychiatry, 153,* 1492–1494.

Bleich, A., Koslowsky, M., Dolev, A., & Lerer, B. (1997). Post-traumatic stress disorder and depression. *British Journal of Psychiatry, 170,* 479–482.

Brandel, J.-P., & Delasnerie-Laupretre, N. (1997). Creutzfeld-Jakob disease and stress. *Journal of Neurology, Neurosurgery, and Psychiatry, 62,* 541–548.

Bremner, J.D., Innis, R.B., Ng, C.K., Staib, L.H., Salomon, R.M., Bronen, R.A., Duncan, J., Southwick, S.M., Krystal, J.H., Rich, D., Zubal, G., Dey, H., Soufer, R., & Charney, D.S. (1997a). Positron emission tomography measurement of cerebral metabolic correlates of yohimbine administration in combat-related posttraumatic stress disorder. *Archives of General Psychiatry, 54,* 246–254.

Bremner, J.D., Krystal, J.H., Southwick, S.M., & Charney, D.S. (1995a). Functional neuroanatomical correlates of the effects of stress on memory. *Journal of Traumatic Stress, 8*, 527–553.

Bremner, J.D., Randall, P., Scott, T.M., Bronen, R.A., Seibyl, J.P., Southwick, S.M., Delaney, R.C., McCarthy, G., Charney, D.S., & Innis, R.B. (1995b). MRI-based measurement of hippocampal volume in patients with combat-related posttraumatic stress disorder. *American Journal of Psychiatry, 152*, 973–981.

Bremner, J.D., Randall, P., Scott, T.M., Capelli, S., Delaney, R., McCarthy, G., & Charney, D.S. (1995c). Deficits in short-term memory in adult survivors of childhood abuse. *Psychiatry Research, 59*, 97–107.

Bremner, J.D., Randall, P., Vermetten, E., Staib, L., Bronen, R.A., Mazure, C., Capelli, S., McCarthy, G., Innis, R.B., & Charney, D.S. (1997b). Magnetic resonance imaging-based measurement of hippocampal volume in posttraumatic stress disorder related to childhood physical and sexual abuse – a preliminary report. *Biological Psychiatry, 41*, 23–32.

Bremner, J.D., Scott, T.M., Delaney, R.C., Southwick, S.M., Mason, J.W., Johnson, D.R., Innis, R.B., McCarthy, G., & Charney, D.S. (1993). Deficits in short-term memory in posttraumatic stress disorder. *American Journal of Psychiatry, 150*, 1015–1019.

Breslau, N., Davis, G.C., Peterson, E.L., & Schultz, L. (1997). Psychiatric sequelae of posttraumatic stress disorder in women. *Archives of General Psychiatry, 54*, 81–87.

Breuer, J., & Freud, S. (1895). *Studien über Hysterie*. Wien: Deuticke.

Brewin, C.R., Dalgleish, T., & Joseph, S. (1996). A dual representation theory of posttraumatic stress disorder. *Psychological Review, 103*, 670–686.

Burgl, G. (1900). Eine Reise in die Schweiz im epileptischen Dämmerzustande und die transitorischen Bewusstseinsstörungen der Epileptiker vor dem Strafrichter. *Münchener medizinische Wochenschrift, 37*, 1270–1273.

Cacioppo, J.T. (1994). Social neuroscience: Autonomic, neuroendocrine, and immune responses to stress. *Psychophysiology, 31*, 113–128.

Cahill, L., Babinsky, R., Markowitsch, H.J., & McGaugh, J.L. (1995). Involvement of the amygdaloid complex in emotional memory. *Nature, 377*, 295–296.

Calabrese, P., Markowitsch, H.J., Durwen, H.F., Widlitzek, B., Haupts, M., Holinka, B., & Gehlen, W. (1996). Right temporofrontal cortex as critical locus for the ecphory of old episodic memories. *Journal of Neurology, Neurosurgery, and Psychiatry, 61*, 304–310.

Carlier, I.V.E., Lamberts, R.D., Fouwels, A.J., & Gersons, B.P.R. (1996). PTSD in relation to dissociation in traumatized police officers. *American Journal of Psychiatry, 153*, 1325–1328.

Damasio, A.R. (1994). *Descartes' Error. Emotion, reason and the human brain*. New York: Putnam's Son.

Davidson, R.J., & Sutton, S.K. (1995). Affective neuroscience: The emergence of a discipline. *Current Opinion in Neurobiology, 6*, 217–224.

De Renzi, E., & Lucchelli, F. (1993). Dense retrograde amnesia, intact learning capability and abnormal forgetting rate: A consolidation deficit? *Cortex, 29*, 449–466.

De Renzi, E., Lucchelli, F., Muggia, S., & Spinnler, H. (1995). Persistent retrograde amnesia following a minor head trauma. *Cortex, 31*, 531–542.

De Renzi, E., Lucchelli, F., Muggia, S., & Spinnler, H. (1997). Is memory without anatomical damage tantamount to a psychogenic deficit? The case of pure retrograde amnesia. *Neuropsychologia, 35*, 781–794.

Dorian, B., & Garfinkel, P.E. (1989). Stress, immunity and illness – a review. *Psychological Medicine, 17*, 393–407.

Elder, G.H., Shanahan, M.J., & Clipp, E.C. (1997). Linking combat and physical health: The legacy of World War II in men's lives. *American Journal of Psychiatry, 154*, 330–336.

Fawzi, M.C.S., Murphy, E., Pham, T., Lin, L., Poole, C., & Mollica, R.F. (1997). The validity of screening for post-traumatic stress disorder and major depression among Vietnamese former political prisoners. *Acta Psychiatrica Scandinavica, 95*, 87–93.

Fink, G.R., & Markowitsch, H.J. (1999). Hirntraumata. In H. Förstl (Ed.), *Klinische Neuro-Psychiatrie: Hirnerkrankungen und psychische Störungen* (in press). Stuttgart: Enke.

Fink, G.R., Markowitsch, H.J., Reinkemeier, M., Bruckbauer, T., Kessler, J., & Heiss, W.-D. (1996). Cerebral representation of one's own past: Neural networks involved in autobiographical memory. *Journal of Neuroscience, 16*, 4275–4282.

Fletcher, P.C., Frith, C.D., & Rugg, M.D. (1997). The functional neuroanatomy of episodic memory. *Trends in Neurosciences, 20*, 213–218.

Franzen, E.A., & Myers, R.E. (1973). Neural control of social behavior: Prefrontal and anterior temporal cortex. *Neuropsychologia, 11*, 141–157.

Freud, S. (1898). Zum psychischen Mechanismus der Vergesslichkeit. *Monatsschrift für Psychiatrie und Neurologie, 1*, 436–443.

Freud, S. (1899). Ueber Deckerinnerungen. *Monatsschrift für Psychiatrie und Neurologie, 2*, 215–230.

Freud, S. (1900). *Die Traumdeutung*. Leipzig: Franz Deuticke.

Freud, S. (1901a). Zum psychischen Mechanismus der Vergesslichkeit. *Monatsschrift für Psychiatrie und Neurologie, 4/5*, 436–443.

Freud, S. (1901b). Zur Psychopathologie des Alltagslebens (Vergessen, Versprechen, Vergreifen) nebst Bemerkungen über eine Wurzel des Aberglaubens. *Monatsschrift für Psychiatrie und Neurologie, 10*, 95–143.

Ganser, S.J. (1898). Ueber einen eigenartigen hysterischen Dämmerzustand. *Archiv für Psychiatrie und Nervenkrankheiten, 30*, 633–640.

Gurvits, T.V., Shenton, M.E., Hokama, H., Ohta, H., Lasko, N.B., Gilbertson, M.W., Orr, S.P., Kikinis, R., Jolesz, F.A., McCarley, R.W., & Pitman, R.K. (1996). Magnetic resonance imanging study of hippocampal volume in chronic, combat-related posttraumatic stress disorder. *Biological Psychiatry, 40*, 1091–1099.

Haas, H.S., & Schauenstein, K. (1997). Neuroimmunomodulation via limbic structures – the neuroanatomy of psychoimmunology. *Progress in Neurobiology, 51*, 195–222.

Härtl, J. (1916). Fehlende Erinnerung des Verletzten für einen Schädelschuss. Verkannter Mordversuch. *Deutsche Medizinische Wochenschrift, 42*, 1352–1353.

Heilbronner, K. (1903). Ueber Fugues und fugue-ähnliche Zustände. *Jahrbücher für Psychiatrie und Neurologie, 23*, 107–206.

Heilbronner, K. (1904/05). Zur klinisch-psychologischen Untersuchungstechnik. *Monatsschrift für Psychiatrie und Neurologie, 17*, 115–132.

Heilbronner, K. (1905). Studien über eine eklamptische Psychose. *Monatschrift für Psychologie, 17*, 277–287 und 367–460.

Heim, E. (1988). Coping und Adaptivität: Gibt es geeignetes oder ungeeignetes Coping? *Psychotherapie und medizinische Psychologie, 38*, 8–18.

Herbert, T.B., & Cohen, S. (1993). Depression and immunity: A meta-analytic review. *Psychological Bulletin, 113*, 472–486.

Herman, J.P., & Cullinan, W.E. (1997). Neurocircuitry of stress: Central control of the hypothalamo-pituitary-adrenocortical axis. *Trends in Neurosciences, 20*, 78–84.

Holsboer, F. (1989). Psychiatric implications of altered limbic-hypothalamic-pituitary-adrenocortical activity. *European Archives of Psychiatry and Neurological Sciences, 238*, 302–322.

Iidaka, T., Nakajima, T., Suzuki, Y., Okazaki, A., Maehara, T., & Shiraishi, H. (1997). Quantitative regional cerebral blood flow measured by Tc-99 m HMPAO SPECT in mood disorder. *Psychiatry Research: Neuroimaging Section, 68*, 143–154.

Janet, P. (1894). *Der Geisteszustand der Hysteriker (Die psychischen Stigmata)*. Leipzig: Deuticke.

Jetter, J., Poser, U., Freeman, R.B., Jr., & Markowitsch, H.J. (1986). A verbal long-term memory deficit in frontal lobe damaged patients. *Cortex, 22*, 229–242.

Joëls, M., & de Kloet, E.R. (1992). Control of neuronal excitability by corticosteroid hormones. *Trends in Neurosciences, 15*, 25–30.

Kapur, N. (1993). Focal retrograde amnesia in neurological disease: A critical review. *Cortex, 29*, 217–234.

Kapur, N., Ellison, D., Smith, M.P., McLellan, D.L., & Burrows, E.H. (1992). Focal retrograde amnesia following bilateral temporal lobe pathology. *Brain, 115*, 73–85.

Kellner (1898). Ueber transitorische postepileptische Geistesstörungen. *Allgemeine Zeitschrift für Psychiatrie und ihre Grenzgebiete, 58*, 863–870.

Kessler, J., Markowitsch, H.J., Huber, R., Kalbe, E., Weber-Luxenburger, G., & Kolk, P. (1997). Massive and persistent anterograde amnesia in the absence of detectable brain damage – anterograde psychogenic amnesia or gross reduction in sustained effort? *Journal of Clinical and Experimental Neuropsychology, 19*, 604–614.

Kessler, R.C. (1997). The effects of stressful life events on depression. *Annual Review of Psychology, 48*, 191–214.

King, N.S. (1997). Post-traumatic stress disorder and head injury as a dual diagnosis: "Islands" of memory as a mechanism. *Journal of Neurology, Neurosurgery and Psychiatry, 62*, 82–84.

Kohnstamm, O. (1917). Über das Krankheitsbild der retro-anterograden Amnesie und die Unterscheidung des spontanen und lernenden Merkens. *Monatsschrift für Psychiatrie und Neurologie, 41*, 373–382.

Kolk, B.A. van der (1994). The body keeps the score: Memory and the evolving psychobiology of posttraumatic stress. *Harvard Review of Psychiatry, 1*, 253–265.

Kroll, N., Markowitsch, H.J., Knight, R., & Cramon, D.Y. von (1997). Retrieval of old memories – the temporo-frontal hypothesis. *Brain, 120*, 1377–1399.

Kuyken, W., & Brewin, C.R. (1995). Autobiographical memory functioning in depression and reports of early abuse. *Journal of Abnormal Psychology, 104*, 585–591.

Layton, B.S., & Wardi-Zonna, K. (1995). Posttraumatic stress disorder with neurogenic amnesia for the traumatic event. *Clinical Neuropsychologist, 9*, 2–10.

Liotti, G. (1992). Disorganized/disoriented attachment in the etiology of the dissociative disorders. *Dissociation, V*, 196–204.

Lupien, S.J., & McEwen, B.S. (1997). The acute effects of corticosteroids on cognition: Integration of animal and human model studies. *Brain Research Reviews, 24*, 1–27.

Magariños, A.M., McEwen, B.S., Flügge, G., & Fuchs, E. (1996). Chronic psychosocial stress causes apical dendritic atrophy of hippocampal CA3 pyramidal neurons in subordinate tree shrews. *Journal of Neuroscience, 16*, 3534–3540.

Magariños, A.M., Verdugo, J.M.G., & McEwen, B.S. (1997). Chronic stress alters synaptic terminal structure in hippocampus. *Proceedings of the National Academy of Sciences USA, 94*, 14002–14008.

Mai, F.M. (1995). "Hysteria" in clinical neurology. *Canadian Journal of Neurological Sciences, 22,* 101–110.

Majewska, M.D. (1992). Neurosteroids: Endogenous bimodal modulators of the GABAA receptor. Mechanism of action and physiological significance. *Progress in Neurobiology, 38,* 379–395.

Markowitsch, H.J. (1995). Which brain regions are critically involved in the retrieval of old episodic memory? *Brain Research Reviews, 21,* 117–127.

Markowitsch, H.J. (1996). Organic and psychogenic retrograde amnesia: Two sides of the same coin? *Neurocase, 2,* 357–371.

Markowitsch, H.J. (1997a). Varieties of memory: Systems, structures, mechanisms of disturbance. *Neurology, Psychiatry and Brain Sciences, 5,* 37–56.

Markowitsch, H.J. (1997b). The functional neuroanatomy of episodic memory retrieval. *Trends in Neurosciences, 20,* 557–558.

Markowitsch, H.J., Calabrese, P., Fink, G.R., Durwen, H.F., Kessler, J., Härting, C., König, M., Mirzaian, E.B., Heiss, W.-D., Heuser, L., & Gehlen, W. (1997a). Impaired episodic memory retrieval in a case of probable psychogenic amnesia. *Psychiatry Research: Neuroimaging Section, 74,* 119–126.

Markowitsch, H.J., Calabrese, P., Haupts, M., Durwen, H.F., Liess, J., & Gehlen, W. (1993a). Searching for the anatomical basis of retrograde amnesia. *Journal of Clinical and Experimental Neuropsychology, 15,* 947–967.

Markowitsch, H.J., Calabrese, P., Liess, J., Haupts, M., Durwen, H.F., & Gehlen, W. (1993b). Retrograde amnesia after traumatic injury of the temporo-frontal cortex. *Journal of Neurology, Neurosurgery and Psychiatry, 56,* 988–992.

Markowitsch, H.J., Calabrese, P., Würker, M., Durwen, H.F., Kessler, J., Babinsky, R., Brechtelsbauer, D., Heuser, L., & Gehlen, W. (1994). The amygdala's contribution to memory – A PET-study on two patients with Urbach-Wiethe disease. *NeuroReport, 5,* 1349–1352.

Markowitsch, H.J., & Ewald, K. (1998). Right-hemispheric fronto-temporal injury leading to severe autobiographical retrograde and moderate anterograde episodic amnesia. *Neurology, Psychiatry and Brain Sciences, 5,* 71–78.

Markowitsch, H.J., Fink, G.R., Thöne, A.I.M., Kessler, J., & Heiss, W.-D. (1997b). Persistent psychogenic amnesia with a PET-proven organic basis. *Cognitive Neuropsychiatry, 2,* 135–158.

Markowitsch, H.J., Kessler, J., Frölich, L., Schneider, B., & Maurer, K. (1999). Mnestic block syndrome. *Cortex.*

Markowitsch, H.J., Kessler, J., Van der Ven, C., Weber-Luxenburger, G., & Heiss, W.-D. (1998). Psychic trauma causing grossly reduced brain metabolism and cognitive deterioration. *Neuropsychologia, 36,* 77–82.

Markowitsch, H.J., Kessler, J., Kalbe, E., Herholz, K. (in press). Functional amnesia and memory consolidation: A case of persistent anterograde amnesia with rapid forgetting following whiplash injury. *Neurocase* (in press).

Markowitsch, H.J., Kessler, J., Van der Ven, C., Weber-Luxenburger, G., & Heiss, W.-D. (submitted b). *Neuroimaging and behavioral correlates of recovery from "mnestic block syndrome".* Manuscript submitted for publication.

Markowitsch, H.J., Thiel, A., Kessler, J., & Heiss, W.-D. (1997c). Ecphorizing semi-conscious episodic information via the right temporopolar cortex – A PET study. *Neurocase, 3,* 445–449.

Mattioli, F., Grassi, F., Perani, D., Cappa, S.F., Miozzo, A., & Fazio, F. (1996). Persistent post-traumatic retrograde amnesia: A neuropsychological and ($^{18}$F)FDG PET study. *Cortex, 32*, 121–129.

Mayes, A.R., Daum, I., Markowitsch, H.J., & Sauter, B. (1997). The relationship between retrograde and anterograde amnesia in patients with typical global amnesia. *Cortex, 33*, 197–217.

McGaugh, J.L., Cahill, L., & Roozendaal, B. (1996). Involvement of the amygdala in memory storage: Interaction with other brain systems. *Proceedings of the National Academy of Sciences USA, 93*, 13508–13514.

Mörchen, F. (1904). Epileptische Bewusstseinsveränderungen von ungewöhnlicher Dauer und forensischen Folgen. *Monatsschrift für Psychiatrie und Neurologie, 17*, 15–28.

Müller-Suur, H. (1949). Beitrag zur Frage des Korsakow-Syndroms und zur Analyse der amnestisch-strukturellen Demenz. *Archiv für Psychiatrie und Nervenkrankheiten, 181*, 683–711.

O'Brien, J.T. (1997). The "glucocorticoid cascade" hypothesis in man. *British Journal of Psychiatry, 170*, 199–201.

O'Connor, M., Butters, N., Miliotis, P., Eslinger, P., & Cermak, L.S. (1992). The dissociation of anterograde and retrograde amnesia in a patient with herpes encephalitis. *Journal of Clinical and Experimental Neuropsychology, 14*, 159–178.

O'Leary, A. (1990). Stress, emotion, and human immune function. *Psychological Bulletin, 108*, 363–382.

Parks, E.D., & Balon, R. (1995). Autobiographical memory for childhood events: Patterns of recall in psychiatric patients with a history of alleged trauma. *Psychiatry, 58*, 199–208.

Peck, D.F., Robertson, A., & Zeffert, S. (1996). Psychological sequelae of mountain accidents: A preliminary study. *Journal of Psychosomatic Research, 41*, 55–63.

Pick, A. (1884). Vom Bewusstsein in Zuständen sogenannter Bewusstlosigkeit. *Archiv für Psychiatrie und Nervenkrankheiten, 15*, 202–223.

Pitman, R.K. (1988). Post-traumatic stress disorder, conditioning, and network theory. *Psychiatric Annals, 18*, 182–189.

Raecke, J. (1903). *Die transitorischen Bewusstseinsstörungen der Epileptiker*. Halle: Carl Marhold.

Raecke, J. (1908). Ueber epileptische Wanderzustände (Fugues, Poriomanie). *Archiv für Psychiatrie und Nervenkrankheiten, 43*, 398–423.

Rempel-Clower, N.L., Zola-Morgan, S., Squire, L.R., & Amaral, D.G. (1996) Three cases of enduring memory impairment after bilateral damage limited to the hippocampal formation. *Journal of Neurosciences, 16*, 5233–5255.

Roozendaal, B., Portillo Marquez, G., & McGaugh, J.L. (1996). Basolateral amygdala lesions block glucocorticoid-induced modulation of memory for spatial learning. *Behavioral Neurosciences, 110*, 1074–1083.

Russell, W.R. (1971). *The traumatic amnesias*. Oxford: Oxford University Press.

Russell, W.R., & Nathan, P.W. (1946). Traumatic amnesia. *Brain, 69*, 280–300.

Sapolsky, R.M. (1994). *Why zebras don't get ulcers*. New York: Freeman.

Sapolsky, R.M. (1996a). Why stress is bad for your brain. *Science, 273*, 749–750.

Sapolsky, R.M. (1996b). Stress, glucocorticoids, and damage to the nervous system: The current state of confusion. *Stress, 1*, 1–19.

Sapolsky, R.M., Uno, H., Rebert, C.S., & Finch, C.E. (1990). Hippocampal damage associated with prolonged glucocorticoid exposure in primates. *Journal of Neuroscience, 10*, 2897–2902.

Sarter, M., & Markowitsch, H.J. (1985). The amydala's role in human mnemonic processing. *Cortex, 21*, 7–24.

Schacter, D.L., Koutstaal, W., & Norman, K.A. (1996). Can cognitive neuroscience illuminate the nature of traumatic childhood memories? *Current Opinion in Neurobiology, 6*, 207–214.

Schmidtke, K., & Vollmer, H. (1997). Retrograde amnesia: A study of its relation to antero-grade amnesia and semantic memory deficits. *Neuropsychologia, 35*, 505–518.

Schneider, K. (1912) Über einige klinisch-psychologische Untersuchungsmethoden und ihre Ergebnisse. Zugleich ein Beitrag zur Psychopathologie der Korsakowschen Psychose. *Zeitschrift für die gesamte Neurologie und Psychiatrie, 8*, 553–615.

Schneider, K. (1928). Die Störungen des Gedächtnisses. In O. Bumke (Ed.), *Handbuch der Geisteskrankheiten* (Bd. 1) (pp. 508–529). Berlin: Springer.

Schultze, E. (1903). Ueber krankhaften Wandertrieb. *Allgemeine Zeitschrift für Psychologie, 60*, 795–814.

Sharpey, W. (1879). The re-education of the adult brain. *Brain, 2*, 1–9.

Shin, L.M., Kosslyn, S.M., McNally, R.J., Alpert, N.M., Thompson, W.L., Rauch, S.L., Macklin, M.L., & Pitman, R.K. (1997). Visual imagery and perception in posttraumatic stress disorder. *Archives of General Psychiatry, 54*, 233–241.

Silove, D., Sinnerbrink, I., Field, A., Manicavasagar, V., & Steel, Z. (1997). Anxiety, depression and PTSD in asylum-seekers: Association with pre-migration trauma and post-migration stressors. *British Journal of Psychiatry, 170*, 351–357.

Skodol, A.E., Schwartz, S., Dohrenwend, B.P., Levav, I., Shrout, P.E., & Reiff, M. (1996). PTSD symptoms and comorbid mental disorders in Israeli war veterans. *British Journal of Psychiatry, 169*, 717–725.

Southwick, S.M., Krystal, J.H., Morgan, C.A., Johnson, D., Nagy, L.M., Nicolaou, A., Heninger, G.R., & Charney, D.S. (1993). Abnormal noradrenergic function in posttraumatic stress disorder. *Archives of General Psychiatry, 50*, 266–274.

Southwick, S.M., Morgan III, A., Nicolaou, A.L., & Charney D.S. (1997). Consistency of memory for combat-related traumatic events in veterans of operation desert storm. *American Journal of Psychiatry, 154*, 173–177.

Starkstein, S.E., Fedoroff, P., Berthier, M.L., & Robinson, R.G. (1991). Manic-depressive and pure manic states after brain lesions. *Biological Psychiatry, 29*, 149–158.

Sutker, P.B., Winstead, D.K., Galina, Z.H., & Allain, A.N. (1991). Cognitive deficits and psychopathology among former prisoners of war and combat veterans of the Korean conflict. *American Journal of Psychiatry, 148*, 67–72.

Teicher, M.H., Glod, C.A., Surrey, J., & Swett, C. (1993). Early childhood abuse and limbic system ratings in adult psychiatric outpatients. *Journal of Neuropsychiatry and Clinical Neurosciences, 5*, 301–306.

Tulving, E. (1983). *Elements of episodic memory*. Oxford: Clarendon.

Tulving, E. (1995). Organization of memory: Quo vadis. In M.S. Gazzaniga (Ed.), *The cognitive neurosciences* (pp. 839–847). Cambridge, MA: MIT Press.

Tulving, E., Kapur, S., Markowitsch, H.J., Craik, G., Habib, R., & Houle, S. (1994). Neuroanatomical correlates of retrieval in episodic memory: Auditory sentence recognition. *Proceedings of the National Academy of Sciences USA, 91*, 2012–2015.

Tulving, E., & Markowitsch, H.J. (1998). Episodic and declarative memory: Role of the hippocampus. *Hippocampus, 8*, 198–204.

Veraguth, O., & Cloetta, G. (1907). Klinische und experimentelle Beobachtungen an einem

Fall von traumatischer Läsion des rechten Stirnhirns. *Deutsche Zeitschrift für Nerven-heilkunde, 32,* 407–476.

Vidal, C., Jordan, W., & Zieglgänsberger, W. (1986). Corticosterone reduces the excitability of hippocampal pyramidal cells in vitro. *Brain Research, 383,* 54–59.

Yehuda, R., Giller, E.L., & Mason, J.W. (1993). Psychoneuroendocrine assessment of post-traumatic stress disorder. *Progress in Neuro-Psychopharmacology and Biological Psychiatry, 17,* 541–550.

Young, E.A., Haskett, R.F., Murphy-Weinberg, V., Watson, S.J., & Akil, H. (1991). Loss of glucocorticoid fast feedback in depression. *Archives of General Psychiatry, 48,* 693–699.

# Perceptual and Conceptual Components of Repetition Priming in Anterograde Amnesia

*Giovanni A. Carlesimo*

An impairment in the deliberate recollection of previously experienced facts or information (as revealed by traditional memory tests of free recall or recognition) is the cognitive hallmark of the amnesic syndrome. As early as the 1960s, however, it had become evident that not all aspects of long-term memory (LTM) are deteriorated in amnesic patients. It has been repeatedly demonstrated, in fact, that both hippocampal amnesics (such as the famous patient H. M.) and diencephalic amnesics (e. g., Korsakoff's disease) learn a number of visuo-motor (e. g., the *Pursuit Rotor Learning Task*; Corkin, 1968), visuo-perceptual (e. g., *Puzzle Assembly*; Brooks, 1976) and cognitive (e. g., *Mirror Reading*; Cohen & Squire, 1980) procedures at a normal rate. Moreover, in the very early 1980s, a critical advancement in the neuropsychological characterization of the amnesic syndrome was the discovery that patients with a selective disorder of LTM are normally primed by previous exposure to visuo-verbal or visuo-perceptual stimuli. In particular, it was demonstrated that when the identification of words or pictures presented in a perceptually degraded format or completion of fragments from these same stimuli is investigated implicitly, that is, without any explicit reference to their previous presentation, the *repetition priming effect* (a measure of bias in performance accuracy or speed in favor of previously encountered stimuli) is as large in amnesics as it is in normal age-matched subjects. In one of the very first demonstrations of this phenomenon, Graf, Squire, and Mandler (1984) presented lists of words to be studied to a group of mixed etiology amnesics and a group of normal controls. In the subsequent test phase, patients were requested to complete a list of stems (i. e., the first three letters) to form a word. Half of the stems could be completed with previously studied words, the remaining half with words from an unstudied list. Amnesics' performance compared to normal controls' critically changed as a function of test instructions. When the examiner required to complete stems with words from the previously studied list (explicit memory condition), amnesic patients demonstrated the usual poor LTM, completing significantly less stems with studied words then controls did. In contrast, when the instruction was to complete stems with the first word that came to mind (implicit memory condition), both normal and amnesic subjects completed more stems with words from the studied than from the unstudied list and the extent of this priming effect was comparable in the two groups.

Starting from this first observation of *stem completion*, an impressive amount of data was subsequently provided documenting comparable repetition priming in amnesics and age-matched normals in a variety of procedures, such as *identification of tachistoscopically presented words* (Cermak et al., 1985), *free association* (Shimamura & Squire, 1984), *lexical decision* about words and nonwords (Smith & Oscar-Berman, 1990), *identification of fragmented pictures* (Wilson et al., 1996), etc. Although statistical support for this assertion is lacking, there is no doubt that in the last 15 years the number of scientific reports dealing with the different aspects of repetition priming has surpassed every other topic of interest in the field of neuropsychology of human amnesia.

I believe that the outstanding interest of neuropsychologists in repetition priming in amnesic patients has two different aspects. First, the fact that the critical variable in determining normal or deficient memory performance in amnesics is the intentionality of stimulus recollection strongly suggests that what is lost in amnesia is not the ability to form new memory representations but, rather, the deliberate access to memory representations. Accordingly, if repetition priming is able to demonstrate implicit retention of previously experienced stimuli in memory disordered patients, then it may be possible to rely on this preserved ability to teach amnesics new information or procedures in order to somewhat improve their social adjustment (e. g., Glisky & Schacter, 1987). A second reason for the interest prompted by the finding of normal repetition priming in amnesics is that it provided insights about the role of hippocampi and diencephalic nuclei in LTM processes. The suggestion that these structures are implicated in the deliberate recollection of previous experiences but that they do not play any role in the repetition priming effect was further qualified by the discovery that patients affected by Alzheimer's dementia (AD), who show memory impairment in the explicit domain similar in severity to that exhibited by pure amnesic patients, differ from amnesics in that they frequently show less than normal repetition priming (e. g., Shimamura et al., 1987; Carlesimo et al., 1995). The association of neocortical to hippocampal damage in AD patients suggests that associative neocortex may play a role in the genesis of the priming effect.

The aim of this chapter is to review and critically discuss data from literature and personal acquisitions about repetition priming in memory disordered patients (both pure amnesics and degenerative demented) in an attempt to better characterize the nature of this effect and to underline its potential contribution to the comprehension of basic mechanisms of human amnesia.

## One Memory, One System: The Multiple Memory System Approach

*Prevalent Perceptual Nature of Repetition Priming*

The enthusiastic assumption that what is lost in amnesia is only the deliberate recollection of normally stored information (which can be proficiently recollected when implicit strategies of retrieval are implemented) was precociously mitigated by the discovery of experimental dissociations suggesting basically distinct cognitive processes operating in episodic memory and repetition priming tests.

One aspect in which the two forms of memory have demonstrated to strikingly differ is the forgetting curve as a function of time. While episodic memory (e. g., word-list recall or recognition) decays according to a smooth temporal gradient and significant retrieval is still observable hours or days after stimulus acquisition, the repetition priming effect elicited by tests such as stem completion (Graf et al., 1984; Squire et al., 1987) or free association (Shimamura & Squire, 1984) is generally no longer detectable two hours after stimulus exposure.

Perhaps the most persuasive evidence of distinct cognitive operations underlying episodic memory and repetition priming is the demonstration that the two kinds of procedures are differently affected by manipulations of the perceptual and conceptual aspects of the information. Since the early 1970s, the prevalent contribution of conceptual processes to the encoding of episodic memories has been a central assumption in memory theories. This view was strongly supported by the evidence that performance on free recall or recognition tests is much better following semantic than phonological or perceptual processing of material during the study phase (Craik & Lockhart, 1972) and, in contrast, is largely the same if the perceptual format of stimulus presentation during the study and test phases matches (e. g., words studied and tested in the visual modality) or mismatches (e. g., words studied auditorily and tested visually) (Graf et al., 1985).

In contrast, it was soon evident that repetition priming in tests such as stem completion (Graf et al., 1985), word identification (Clarke & Morton, 1983) or lexical decision (Kirsner et al., 1983) is mainly based on a perceptual level of stimulus analysis. In fact, performance on these tasks is strikingly reduced if a change in the presentation modality of stimuli from study to test occurs, but it is scarcely or not at all affected by the phonological or semantic level of stimulus processing during the study phase (Graf et al., 1982; Jacoby & Dallas, 1981; Kirsner et al., 1983).

Based on this kind of evidence, Tulving and Schacter (1990; Schacter, 1990) advanced the hypothesis that different memory stores sustain episodic memory and repetition priming. In particular, a memory system storing the perceptual characteristics of the stimulus (likely articulated into a variety of subsystems depending on the modality of representation of the stimulus) would mediate repetition priming and a memory system based on the conceptual analysis of meaning would support episodic memory. The neural substrate of the two systems differs. The mesio-temporal and diencephalic structures damaged in amnesia support the episodic memory system but do not play any role in the functioning of the perceptual representation system(s).

In 1994, my research group and I described a dyslexic patient (AM) who provided a clear confirmation of the prevalent perceptual nature of the priming effect in tests such as stem completion and word identification (Carlesimo et al., 1994). Following an ischemic stroke in the territory supplied by the left posterior cerebral artery, AM's reading became laborious and very slow, characterized by frequent hesitations and phonological errors. Otherwise, AM did not demonstrate any other language deficit. He was not agraphic, had fluent and informative speech and, most importantly, showed intact auditory language comprehension. Based on his chance performance level on a test requiring visual discrimination of homophone words, we argued for AM's prevalent or absolute reliance on the sublexical reading route. In other words, due to the degradation or inaccessibility of the memory store for the visual aspect of words (*visual input lexicon*, according to Ellis & Young, 1988), AM converted single graphemes into phonemes in order to attain the overall word sound. We reasoned that the pure reading disorder exhibited by AM provided a good case for evaluating a dissociation between normal repetition priming for auditorily presented words and deficient repetition priming for visually presented ones. In fact, by virtue of its characteristics (i. e., being presemantic and modality specific), the visual input lexicon (inaccessible in AM) is the most likely candidate as the site of activation of stored representations mediating the repetition priming effect for visual words. For analogous reasons, the auditory input lexicon (normal in AM) presumably represents the perceptual representation system mediating repetition priming for auditorily presented words. Results of exp. 2 were particularly clear in confirming this prediction. Compared to a group of age- and education-matched normal controls, AM revealed a high range priming effect in the auditory stem completion test but a null priming effect in visual stem completion (Figure 1).

Data consistent with a critical role of the visual input lexicon in the genesis of visuo-verbal repetition priming have also been reported by Schacter et al. (1990). Analogously, Schacter et al. (1993) described the case of a patient (JP) who, based on deficient comprehension of spoken words in the presence of relatively intact repetition and writing to dictation, was diagnosed as suffering from word-meaning deafness. In other words, JP had difficulty in comprehend-

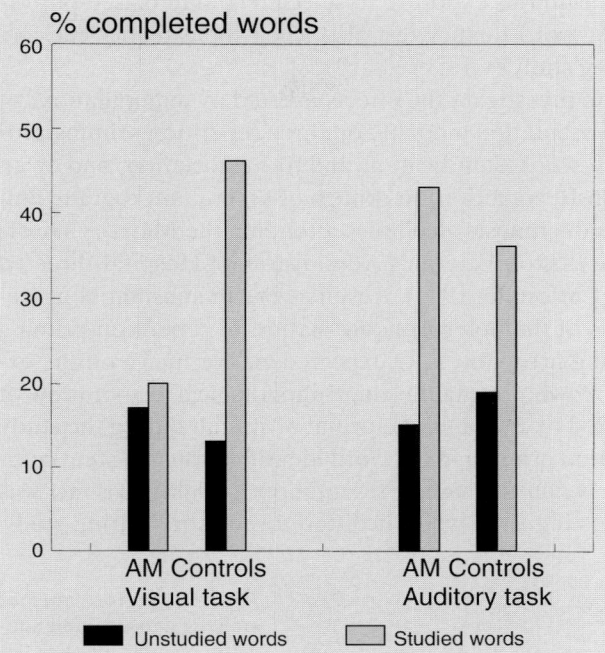

*Figure 1.* Visual and auditory stem completion in the dyslexic patient A.M. and in a group of age-matched controls. The priming effect is measured as the difference between completion of studied over unstudied words.

ing the meaning of words due to a deficit of auditorily processed words accessing the semantic system. Consistent with the hypothesis that the auditory input lexicon mediates the auditory priming for words, JP was normally primed on a test requiring auditory identification of perceptually degraded words, despite impaired comprehension of the meaning of the same words.

## Conceptual Processes and Repetition Priming

Although the claim that a perceptual level of stimulus analysis is the only source of repetition priming was attractive due to its simplicity and ability to gather a substantial number of experimental results into a coherent framework, it was soon demonstrated to be untenable. In fact, experimental evidence was provided documenting sensitivity of the repetition priming effect elicited by some procedures to the semantic elaboration of verbal material (e. g., *stem completion for new associations*; Schacter & Graf, 1985). Moreover, a significant priming effect was frequently observed also when no physical match existed between stimulus presentation during study and retrieval cue during test [e. g., free association when the cue word had not been presented during the study phase (Shimamura & Squire, 1984; exp. 4) or the *category exemplar production task* in which previous exposure to selected stimuli biased performance on the subsequent word fluency test also when the category cue had not been presented during study (Graf et al., 1985)].

I had the opportunity to investigate the effects exerted by manipulations of level of processing and presentation modality on three repetition priming procedures (stem completion, word identification, and free association) and on an explicit memory task (y/n Recognition) in groups of severe anterograde amnesics and age-matched nonamnesic alcoholics attending the Memory Disorders Research Unit of the Boston Veteran's Administration Hospital, directed by Prof. Laird Cermak (Carlesimo, 1994). Results were in substantial agreement with the hypothesis of the heterogeneous nature of repetition priming elicited by different testing procedures. As expected, performance on the explicit task was better following semantic than phonological elaboration of words but it was unaffected by the physical format of stimuli during the study phase. In contrast, repetition priming in the word identification and stem completion tests was greater when the same presentation modality (visual) was used during study and testing than when it differed (auditory during study,

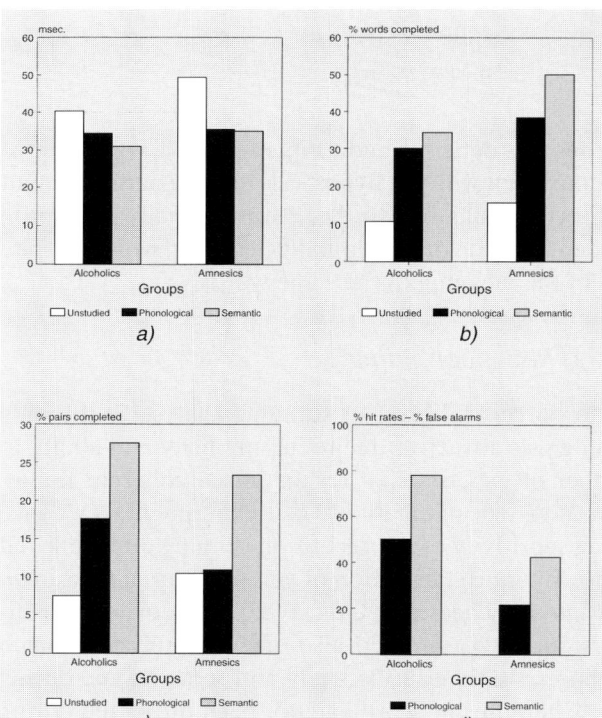

*Figure 2.* Performance of amnesic and alcoholic subjects on the implicit *a)* word identification, *b)* stem completion, *c)* free association and explicit *d)* y/n recognition tests as a function of level of processing during study. (Reproduced with permission from Carlesimo, 1994).

visual during testing) and was scarcely (stem completion) or not at all (word identification) affected by quality of stimulus processing during the study phase. Results of the free association test, instead, documented the contribution of conceptual and perceptual processes in the genesis of repetition priming elicited by this procedure. In fact, priming effect was significantly larger following semantic than phonological processing, but it was also increased (at least in the control group) if physical formats were matched during study and test phases (Figures 2 and 3).

In an attempt to reconcile the contrasting evidence in the literature, Schacter (1994) formulated a new version of the multiple memory system theory that comprehended the distinction between a perceptually-based and a conceptually-based form of repetition priming. He proposed a fractionation of the *perceptual representation system* into a class of domain-specific subsystems, each one specialized to process a particular class of perceptual material (i. e., *a visual word form system*, an *auditory word form system* and a *structural-description system* for the form of objects). These different perceptual subsystems have in common their involvement in nonconscious expressions of memory and

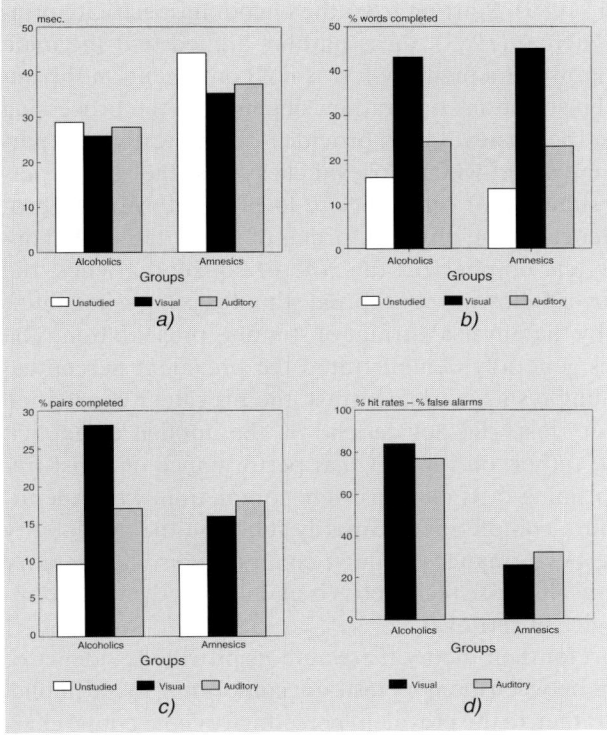

*Figure 3.* Performance of amnesic and alcoholic subjects on the implicit *a)* word identification, *b)* stem completion, *c)* free association and explicit *d)* y/n recognition tests as a function of modality of presentation during study. (Reproduced with permission from Carlesimo, 1994).

processing of domain-specific material at a presemantic level. Conceptual priming shares with perceptual priming the unconscious access to information content, but it differs in that it is based on a semantic level of stimulus elaboration. Accordingly, it would not be mediated by some modality-specific perceptual subsystem, but rather by the operations of a modality independent *semantic system*. Finally, an *episodic memory system* underlies the explicit retrieval of events and information. Consistent with previous positions, human amnesia is explained as resulting from damage to the neural substrate supporting the episodic memory system but leaving neural circuits underlying the perceptual representation and semantic systems unaffected.

## Not Systems But Processes: Transfer-Appropriate Procedures Approach

Around the same time Schacter (1990) first developed his theory of perceptual and episodic memory systems respectively mediating repetition priming and episodic memory, a strong criticism of this theoretical framework was voiced by Roediger and coworkers (Blaxton, 1989; Roediger, 1990; Roediger et al., 1989; Weldon et al., 1989). Starting from the encoding specificity principle first theorized by Tulving (1983), these authors argued that the main perceptual or semantic nature of a memory test is not contingent on the implicit or explicit retrieval instructions but, rather, depends on the processing characteristics implied in the retrieval cues provided during testing. In particular, these authors claimed that when retrieval cues stress the role of perceptual factors, the test shows poor sensitivity to level of information processing but close dependence on the physical format of presentation. In contrast, when the memory test emphasizes the role of conceptual cues, the quality of retrieval improves following conceptual stimulus processing, but is substantially unaffected by the physical format of stimulus presentation. The fact that previous studies generally demonstrated the prevalent perceptual nature of repetition priming tests and, in contrast, the prevalent conceptual nature of episodic memory tests did not depend on the implicit or explicit retrieval instructions but, rather, on the fact that performance on most frequently used repetition priming tests (such as stem completion, word identification, fragmented picture completion) primarily relies on the availability of perceptual cues while performance on most common episodic memory tests (e. g., word-list free recall, prose recall, etc.) is mainly based on the adoption of conceptual strategies of retrieval.

   As experimental support for their theory, these authors provided evidence of experimental dissociations between memory tests not conforming to the implicit-explicit dichotomy but, rather, to the prevalent perceptual or conceptual characteristics of retrieval cues. Blaxton (1989), for example, varied the conditions in which verbal material was studied, requesting subjects to read or to generate words. Results showed an interaction between levels of retrieval and modality of study which did not conform to the distinction between explicit and implicit forms of memory. In this study, in fact, a modality effect (higher retrieval for words which had been read than for words which had been generated) was observed in a word fragment completion (an implicit task) and in a graphemic cued recall (an explicit task) while the reverse pattern (better retrieval for generated words) was observed in a semantic cued recall test (explicit) and in an implicit task which involved answering general knowledge questions.

## Systems or Processes? Neuropsychology and the Episodic Memory-Repetition Priming Dichotomy

### Pure Amnesic Patients

Once it has been demonstrated that the perceptual or conceptual nature of a memory task does not depend on awareness of retrieval but, rather, on the interaction between level of information processing during study and quality of retrieval cues during testing, a further step toward reducing the heuristic value of the explicit-implicit dichotomy as a useful framework for theorizing memory systems consisted of questioning the reliability of previous findings documenting normal repetition priming and deficient episodic memory in amnesic patients. If, as described above, most frequently used repetition priming tests rely on a perceptual stage of information processing while episodic memory tests most commonly demand conceptual analysis of stimulus meaning, then it is possible that the implicit-explicit dissociation in amnesic patients is a sort of epiphenomenon, actually reflecting the more basic dissociation between intact learning of data-driven information and deficient formation of conceptually-driven memory representations.

Blaxton (1992) directly addressed this question by giving the same four memory tests previously utilized in normal subjects (Blaxton, 1989) to a group of left temporal lobe epileptic patients with memory disorder. Since intentionality of retrieval and effectiveness of semantic or perceptual cues interact orthogonally in these tests, the authors were able to directly contrast alternative predictions regarding basic mechanisms of human amnesia. According to the multiple memory system theory, amnesics were expected to be normal on the implicit tasks, regardless of their main perceptual (word fragment completion) or conceptual (answering general knowledge questions) nature, and impaired on the explicit tasks, once again regardless of their main perceptual (graphemic cued recall) or conceptual (semantic cued recall) level of stimulus analysis. In contrast, the hypothesis that amnesic patients are impaired when the memory task calls for a conceptual analysis of information but normal on perceptually-based memory tests predicts normal performance on word fragment completion (implicit) and graphemic cued recall (explicit) tests and poor memory on the answering general knowledge questions (implicit) and the semantic cued recall (explicit) tests in the amnesia group. Results of the study conformed to this second position, thus supporting the theoretical position that the critical neuropsychological dissociation in human amnesia is not between implicit and explicit memory tests but, rather, between perceptually-driven and conceptually-driven tests.

Although Blaxton's data (1992) are very fascinating since they provide a radically new explanation for basic mechanisms of human amnesia, they suffer of two important shortcomings. First, they have never been replicated. Schwartz et al. (1993) gave the same tests used by Blaxton (1992) to a group of amnesic patients and obtained results that conformed to the classical implicit-explicit dichotomy. In fact, their patients performed poorly on both data-driven (graphemic cued recall) and conceptually-driven (semantic cued recall) explicit tasks, but displayed normal priming on both the data-driven (word fragment completion) and conceptually-driven (answering general knowledge questions) implicit tasks.

A second point of concern with Blaxton's data (1992) is a methodological one. Although the multiple memory system explanation of the explicit/implicit dichotomy has been criticized mostly because its conclusions are based on the comparison of very different memory tasks, experimental data used to support the transfer-appropriate procedure approach actually suffer from the same shortcoming. In fact, if the experimental design involves the comparison of memory tasks that differ in many other respects beside the awareness of retrieval, then we can not be sure whether possible dissociations arising from this comparison are actually the effect of retrieval instructions or cuing conditions, or whether they simply reflect the adoption of different cognitive strategies applied to solve different memory tasks. In our opinion, studies investigating the alternative interpretations of memory dissociations should compare the sensitivity of the explicit and implicit versions of the same memory task to parallel experimental manipulations of encoding or modality. In this way, other variables possibly producing inter-task dissociations (e. g., perceptual format of stimulus presentation, congruence between stimulus encoding and retrieval cues, most convenient cognitive strategy for task solution) would be eliminated and possible functional and/or neuropsychological dissociations arising from this comparison would actually be the expression of the experimental variable of interest (awareness of retrieval).

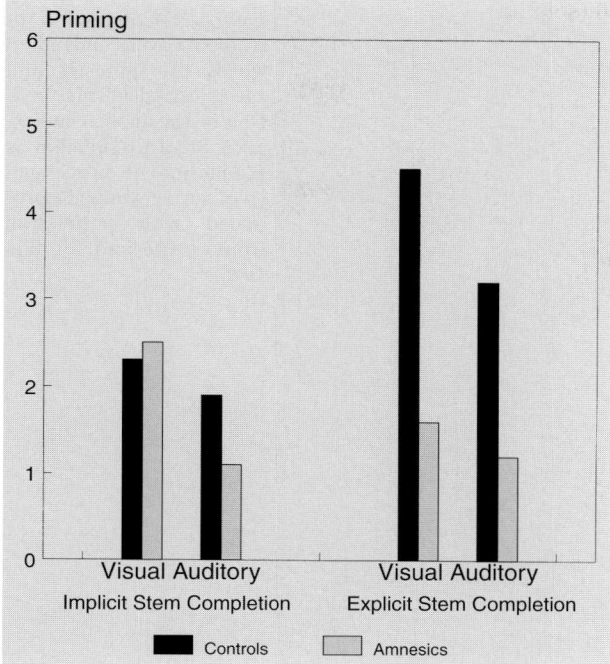

*Figure 4.* Completion of studied over unstudied words by amnesics and age-matched normal controls on the implicit and explicit stem completion as a function of presentation modality during study. (Reproduced with permission from Carlesimo et al., 1996).

We approached this problem by contrasting stem completion performance in a group of amnesic patients and a group of age-matched controls following implicit or explicit retrieval instructions (Carlesimo et al., 1996). The perceptual and conceptual components of stimulus analysis were varied by manipulating presentation modality (experiment 1) and level of elaboration (experiment 2). In the first experiment, half of the words were studied auditorily and half visually. During testing, all stems were presented visually, thus giving rise to an intramodal memory condition (both words during study and stems during testing presented visually) and an intermodal condition (auditorily studied words, visual stems during testing). Overall, the intramodal condition produced better memory than the intermodal one, regardless of explicit or implicit retrieval instructions. Amnesics demonstrated a repetition priming effect that was comparable to that exhibited by normal controls both in the intramodal and intermodal conditions of the stem completion test. In contrast, they were very poor on the explicit task for both visually and auditorily studied words (Figure 4). In the study phase of experiment 2, half of the words were analyzed according to their phonological structure (counting vowels) and half were processed at a semantic level (explaining meaning). In this case, a significant semantic effect (more stems completed with semantically than phonologically

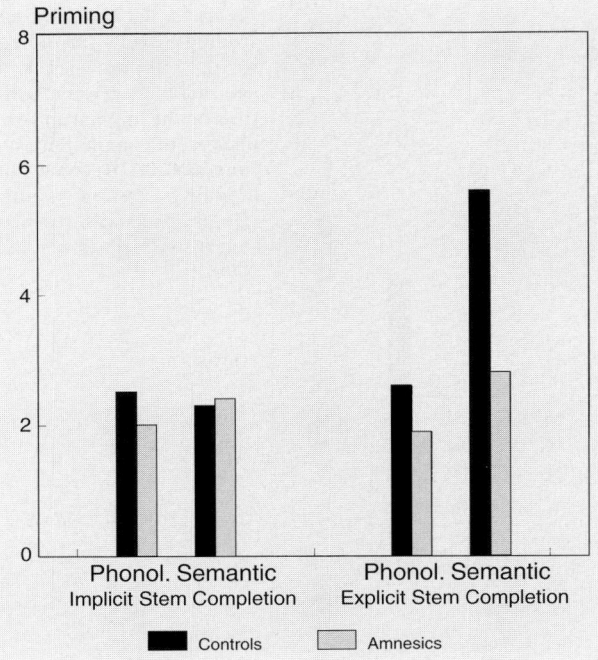

*Figure 5.* Completion of studied over unstudied words by amnesics and age-matched normal controls on the implicit and explicit Stem Completion as a function of processing level during study. (Reproduced with permission from Carlesimo et al., 1996).

processed words) emerged only in the explicit task and only for the control group. Indeed, an inspection of Figure 5 shows that amnesics were undistinguishable from controls in three out of four testing conditions (namely, implicit stem completion of phonologically and semantically studied words and explicit stem completion of phonologically processed words) but were extremely poor in the explicit completion of words that had been processed semantically.

The finding that both implicit and explicit stem completions were larger when presentation modality during study and testing matched than when they mismatched was consistent with the view that sensitivity of a task to level of information analysis is not a matter of implicit or explicit retrieval instructions but, rather, is contingent on the main perceptual or semantic nature of the retrieval cues. On the other side, the fact that only the explicit task took advantage of the semantic level of information analysis to improve completion was in contrast with this view. It should be noted that the sensitivity of implicit stem completion to semantic elaboration of stimuli is highly debatable. As pointed out by a recent meta-analysis of the relevant literature (Brown & Mitchell, 1994), about the same number of studies documenting an advantage of the semantic over the nonsemantic encoding condition (e. g., Bowers & Schacter, 1990; Graf & Mandler, 1984) or the same level of priming irrespective of the level of processing (e. g., Chiarello & Hoyer, 1988; Java & Gardiner, 1991) in the stem completion task have been reported in the literature. In any case, even when a memory advantage is observed in the elaborative encoding condition, this is consistently smaller than that observed in the explicit stem completion. In nine studies investigating the level of the processing effect in normal subjects, the advantage of the semantic over the nonsemantic encoding condition ranged from –6% to +10% (mean 0.8) in the implicit task and from +19% to +43% (mean 26.7) in the explicit task. On the other side, based on the evidence of larger implicit stem completion following semantic than phonological stimulus elaboration in normal controls but not in a mixed group of amnesic patients, Hamman and Squire (1996) concluded that the finding of a significant level of processing effect in the implicit stem completion likely results from a contamination of the implicit task by explicit retrieval strategies.

As for the amnesic group, in experiment 1 they disclosed the classical dissociation between normal implicit and deficient explicit stem completion, regardless of the intramodal or intermodal stimulus condition. In experiment 2, instead, the performance pattern was somewhat more complex. In fact, controls and amnesics correctly completed about the same number of words in the implicit task and in the phonological condition of the explicit task, with controls significantly surpassing amnesics only on the explicit completion of the semantically studied words.

In light of these data, we concluded that:

1. Both the strong modality effect in experiment 1 and the lack of a level of processing effect in experiment 2 demonstrate that repetition priming on stem completion is mainly based on a perceptual, presemantic level of stimulus elaboration.

2. Explicit stem completion is actually based on the contribution of both perceptual (as demonstrated by the modality effect of experiment 1) and conceptual (as evidenced by the striking elaborative effect disclosed by the control group in experiment 2) level of stimulus analysis.

3. It is not clear from our results whether the memory disorder in amnesic patients actually arises when explicit strategies of retrieval are required to solve the task or when a semantic level of stimulus analysis is needed to encode or retrieve information. The lack of a level of processing effect in the implicit stem completion prevented us from evaluating whether the deficient explicit stem completion of semantically processed words in amnesics is actually the expression of a deficient memory access to the product of conceptual analysis of information or whether it arises from an interaction between retrieval conditions and level of information analysis.

In order to directly address this question, we selected a memory task which, in a previous study (Carlesimo, 1994), seemed to be favored by a semantic processing of stimuli also when tested implicitly. We administered the implicit and explicit versions of the free association task to ten amnesics and age-matched controls, varying the level of information processing during study. Results (Figure 6) confirmed that both implicit and explicit completion of the word-pairs took advantage of the semantic elaboration of the pair during study. Amnesics completed a number of pairs comparable to that of normal controls in both the phonological and semantic conditions of the implicit task and in the phonological condition of the explicit task. Exactly as in the previous study involving stem completion, they differed from normals only in the explicit completion of semantically processed word-pairs.

The fact that amnesics demonstrated normal sensitivity to the level of information analysis in repetition priming militates against the hypothesis that human amnesia consists of a specific deficit of access to the product of semantic elaboration. On the other side, the fact they were normal in the explicit completion of phonologically processed words (stem completion) and word-pairs (free association) suggests that the specific locus of impairment in amnesia actually arises from an interaction between awareness of retrieval and level

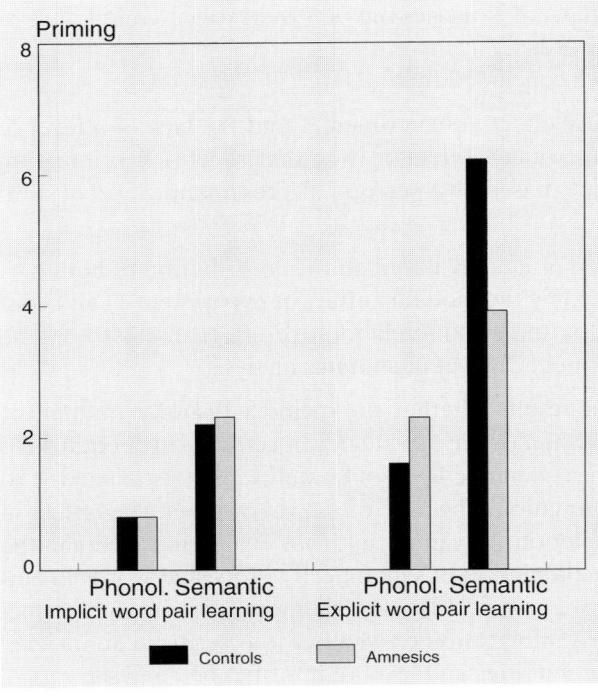

*Figure 6.* Completion of studied over unstudied word-pairs by amnesics and age-matched normal controls on the implicit and explicit word pair learning as a function of processing level during study.

of stimulus processing, with deliberate access to the product of conceptual processing being specifically affected.

## Degenerative Demented Patients

As described above, a further reason for neuropsychologists' interest in repetition priming was the discovery that it represented a possible point of qualitative distinction in the memory deficit exhibited by pure amnesics and AD patients. In 1987, Shimamura and coworkers administered tests of implicit stem completion and explicit word-list learning to groups of AD, Korsakoff's syndrome and Huntington's disease patients. Results demonstrated that while all groups were deficient in both the free recall and y/n recognition of the word-list, only AD patients exhibited reduced priming in the stem completion relative to a group of age-matched controls. In subsequent years, the finding of deficient stem completion priming in AD patients was confirmed, with only few exceptions (e. g., Grosse et al., 1990), by numerous authors (e. g., Carlesimo et al., 1995; Salmon et al., 1988) and subsequently extended to other repetition priming procedures such as free association (Carlesimo et al., 1995; Huff et al., 1988; Salmon et al., 1988). In light of this evidence, a neurobiological account of the repetition priming-explicit memory dichotomy has been proposed based on the different involvement of the mesio-temporal and associative neocortical structures in pure amnesia and degenerative dementia. The involvement of mesio-temporal regions, shared by AD and "hippocampal" forms of pure amnesia, could underlie the deficient explicit memory common to the two conditions. In contrast, the extension of histopathological changes to associative parietal and temporal neocortex in AD patients could be at the basis of the impaired repetition priming characterizing this condition.

However, the general conclusion of deficient repetition priming in AD patients was premature. In 1991, Keane et al. provided data suggesting a dissociation in degenerative demented patients between perceptual and conceptual forms of repetition priming. As a purely perceptual repetition priming task, these authors selected the word identification which, in previous studies, was shown to be closely related to modality of presentation (Jacoby & Dallas, 1981) but unaffected by processing level during study (Kirsner et al., 1983). On this task, AD patients demonstrated a facilitation effect produced by the previous exposure to stimulus words as large as that exhibited by normal controls. In this same study, Keane et al. (1991) used the stem completion as a conceptual task and replicated previous results of abnormal repetition priming elicited by this procedure in AD patients. Results consistent with those obtained by Keane et al. (1991) were successively reported by Gabrieli et al. (1994) who described normal priming in AD patients in a task involving identification of fragmented pictures (considered as perceptual task) and deficient priming in a stem completion task. In an attempt to account for the proposed perceptual-conceptual dissociation in the repetition priming showed by AD patients, these authors assumed there is a different neurobiological substrate for the two different forms of priming. In particular, the neural substrate of the representation subsystems mediating perceptual priming for words (visual word form) and pictures (structural description system) would be located in the extra-striate cortical regions of the occipital lobes. In contrast, the neural circuits sustaining the semantic system, assumed to mediate conceptual priming, could be located in more anterior regions of the temporal and parietal lobes. The relative paucity of degenerative changes in the neocortex of occipital lobes in AD patients compared to diffuse involvement of associative temporo-parietal neocortex (Morrison et al., 1990) could account for the efficient perceptual and deficient conceptual priming in these patients.

The most obvious objection to this view has to do with the nature of repetition priming in the stem completion task. As demonstrated by the consistency of modality effect, repetition priming in stem completion certainly has a strong perceptual component. In contrast, the contribution of a conceptual component is far less sure. The advantage of the semantic over the phonological processing condition in implicit stem completion is scarcely consistent (Brown & Mitchell, 1994) and there is suggestion that when occurs it actually reflects the adoption of explicit strategies of retrieval by normal subjects (Hamman & Squire, 1996).

To disentangle the relative contribution of perceptual and conceptual factors in the repetition priming elicited by stem completion in degenerative demented patients, we recently applied the same procedure previously used in amnesic patients to a group of AD patients. In experiment 1 (Figure 7), in which we manipulated level of stimulus processing during study, age-matched normal controls displayed a significant advantage of the semantic over the non-semantic condition in both the implicit and explicit versions of the test, different from what we observed in the previous study. AD patients did not significantly differ from normal controls in the implicit stem completion of phonologically processed words but were poorer in all the other conditions (implicit completion of semantically processed words, phonological and semantic conditions of the explicit task). Overall, these data seem to confirm Keane et al.'s (1991) and Gabrieli et al.'s (1994) claim of normal perceptual and deficient conceptual repetition priming in AD patients. However, in the second experiment (Figure 8), in which we varied presentation modality of words during study in order to obtain intramodal and intermodal stem completion priming, AD patients were poorer than normal controls in all four

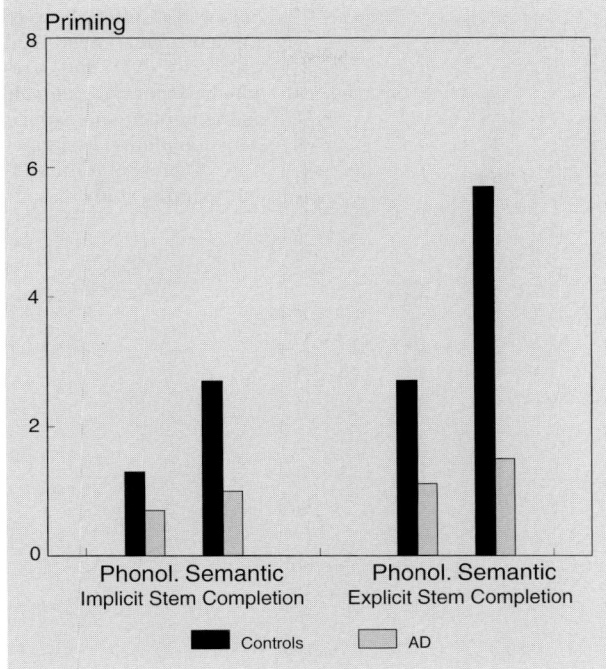

*Figure 7.* Completion of studied over unstudied words by AD and age-matched normal controls on the implicit and explicit stem completion as a function of processing level during study.

experimental conditions (intra- and intermodal conditions of both the implicit and explicit tasks). The lack of any modality effect in the stem completion of AD patients hardly support a theoretical position assuming normal repetition priming based on the perceptual analysis of stimuli and deficient priming when it relies on a conceptual level of information processing. Rather, these results seem to indicate a more pervasive impairment of AD patients in constructing memory representations able to support the priming effect on the implicit stem completion.

If the dissociation between normal perceptual and deficient conceptual repetition priming is insufficient to account for the abnormal priming effect displayed by AD patients on the stem completion test, it remains to explain why these patients show normal priming in procedures such as identification of tachistoscopically presented words (Keane et al., 1991) and fragmented picture identification (Gabrieli et al., 1994).

It is interesting to note that Keane et al. (1994) demonstrated normal facilitation in AD patients also when the tachistoscopic identification of verbal material involved three-letter non-words. In effect, the ability of memory disordered patients to be primed by exposure to verbal or figurative stimuli

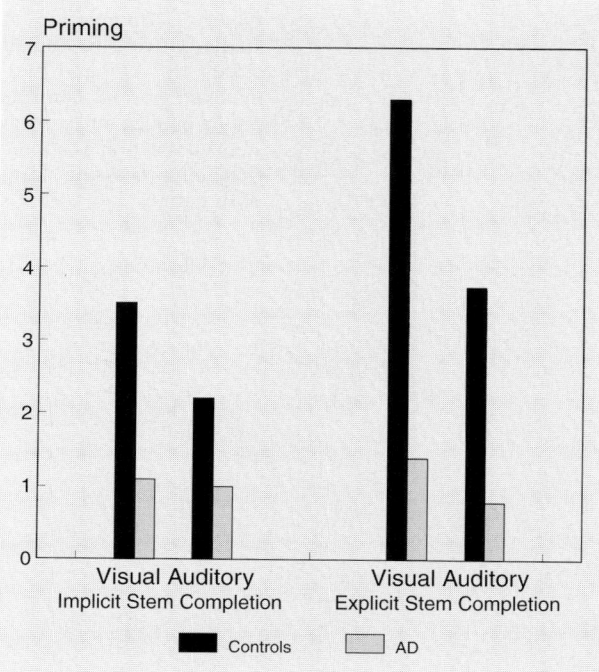

*Figure 8.* Completion of studied over unstudied words by AD and age-matched normal controls on the implicit and explicit stem completion as a function of presentation modality during study.

not previously represented in the memory system has been long debated. There are both theoretical and experimental problems in addressing this question. From a theoretical point of view, the emergence of a significant priming for novel information contrasts with one of the most popular explanations of the repetition priming effect. According to the so-called "hot-tube" theory (Rozin, 1976), when a subject is exposed to a given stimulus the previous memory representation of the same stimulus is converted to a state of "functional activation." As a consequence, the successive presentation of the same stimulus (or a fragment of it) results in faster processing or higher likelihood of completion. However, if repetition priming relies on the activation of pre-existing memory representations, then it is difficult to explain why the exposure to novel verbal (e. g., non-words or new associations between words) or visuo-perceptual (e. g., abstract figures or dot patterns) material is able to facilitate the subsequent processing of these same stimuli. A possible solution to this puzzle is that the very first exposure to a stimulus is sufficient for constructing a memory representation able to sustain explicit recollection and, at the same time, for maintaining this representation in an activated condition for a period of time sufficient for supporting the repetition priming effect.

However, if this is the case, then memory disordered patients who are expected to have difficulties in storing new memory representations are also expected to be poor in the priming effect for novel information.

Investigation of repetition priming for novel stimuli in memory disordered populations has provided very inconsistent results. For example, pure amnesics have shown abnormal repetition priming in the stem completion for new associations (Shimamura & Squire, 1989) and Identification of tachistoscopically presented non-words (Cermak et al., 1985). However, they demonstrated a fully normal facilitation in rereading novel prose passages (Musen et al., 1990), identification of novel objects (Schacter et al., 1991) and pattern completion of novel abstract shapes (Gooding et al., 1993).

As for AD patients, research dealing with repetition priming evoked by the presentation of novel stimuli has provided results that parallel the dissociation previously observed for preexisting memory representations between abnormal priming in the stem completion and normal priming in a word identification task. Demented patients, in fact, demonstrated a null priming effect in stem completion involving new associations between words (Christensen & Birrell, 1991) and normal facilitation in a non-word identification test (Keane et al., 1994).

In 1994, Monti et al. provided evidence for fully normal repetition priming in AD patients in a task involving rereading novel prose passages. The procedure, previously investigated with analogous results in pure amnesics (Musen et al., 1990), consists of requesting subjects to read a short prose passage three times in a row. Following the third reading of the first passage, a second passage is proposed for three consecutive readings. The priming effect, as measured by the progressive reduction of reading times, was specific for the passage and did not generalize between passages (as revealed by the progressive speeding up in passing from the first to the third reading of the first passage and the return to the previous performance level at the first reading of the second passage). On this task, AD patients revealed a priming effect as large as that displayed by age-matched normal controls, despite being very poor in a successive Recognition test involving explicit remembering of the content of prose passages.

Processing components involved in the facilitation induced by rereading have been a subject of debate. Also in this case, the participation of perceptual factors (a sort of augmented perceptual fluency in rereading the same text) and conceptual factors (i. e., based on reprocessing the meaning of the same passage) were invoked (Levy, 1993). In order to disentangle the relative contribution of perceptual and conceptual factors in the rereading facilitation disclosed by degenerative demented patients, in a recent experiment we varied perceptual consistency across different exposures to the same prose passage. A first condition closely replicated Monti et al.'s (1994) procedure requesting

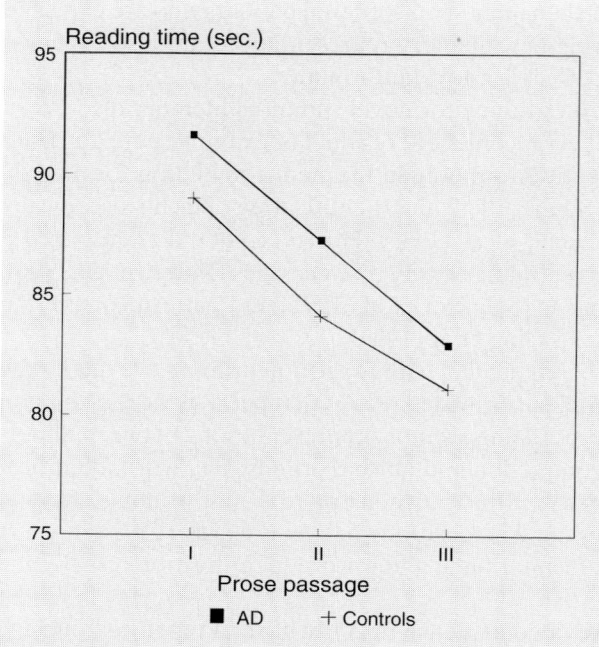

*Figure 9.* Performance of AD and age-matched normal controls on the rereading test (I = unique reading of a prose passage never heard before; II = unique reading of a prose passage previously read by the examiner; III = third rereading of a prose passage).

subjects to reread the same passage three times in a row. In a second condition, the subject listened to the examiner read a different prose passage twice before reading it just once himself. Figure 9 reports average times of the third reading of the first passage (intramodal priming), of the unique reading of the passage previously read by the examiner (intermodal priming) and of the unique reading of a third passage never heard before (baseline condition). These data clearly show better priming in the intramodal than in the intermodal condition in both the age-matched normal and AD groups. However, the intermodal condition also produced a facilitation relative to the baseline condition, thus revealing that a reduction of reading times can also result from the contribution of processing factors (likely conceptual) other than perceptual ones. Levels of both intramodal and intermodal facilitations were perfectly comparable in AD and age-matched controls, thus confirming that also in the domain of novel information, the perceptual-conceptual dichotomy is of little value in predicting normal or abnormal repetition priming in AD patients.

Monti et al. (1994) proposed a number of other dimensions along which repetition priming tests can be distinguished, possibly providing a better theoretical basis for explaining dissociations between normal and abnormal priming in demented patients. Based on the above reported experimental data, neither the perceptual-conceptual dichotomy nor a distinction based on the preexistence or novelty of memory representations supporting the priming effect are able to capture the basic mechanism determining normal or abnormal priming in AD patients. In our opinion, the dichotomy which actually provides the strongest explicative value is that between repetition priming tests requiring the generation of the target starting from a fragment of the whole stimulus (e. g., stem completion or free association) and procedures simply requiring identification of the target stimulus (e. g., rereading prose passages), possibly presented in a perceptually degraded format (e. g., word or picture identification). Tests based on generation procedures (such as Stem completion or free association) evoke deficient repetition priming in AD patients. In contrast, tests that simply require reading (e. g., word identification or rereading prose passages) or recognizing pictures (fragmented picture identification) generally elicit a normal facilitation in demented patients. Although a strong theoretical explanation of this kind of dissociation is lacking, we can temporarily conclude that repetition priming in AD patients is impaired at a level that significantly reduces the advantage of previously studied stimuli being generated in response to a fragment cue over unstudied stimuli. However, the residual priming in these patients is still able to support a speeding up or an increased accuracy in the identification of previously processed material.

## Synthesis of Data and Conclusions

In this chapter, we have dealt with functional and neuropsychological dissociations in repetition priming. The very first assumption of a pure perceptual genesis of the repetition priming effect has been successively reconsidered in the light of experimental evidence demonstrating robust priming effects sustained by conceptual processes. Two alternative theoretical explanations have been proposed for the observed dissociation between episodic memory and repetition priming and between different forms of repetition priming. The multiple-memory-system approach suggests the reliance of these different forms of memory on distinct systems, mediated by distinct neural substrates. In contrast, authors supporting the transfer-appropriate-procedure approach underestimate the theoretical relevance of the implicit-explicit dichotomy and suggest classifying memory tests according to their prevalent reliance on perceptual or conceptual level of stimulus analysis, regardless of awareness of stimulus retrieval.

Parallel to the investigation of functional dissociations in normal subjects, a great deal of experimental work has been concerned with neuropsychological dissociations in brain damaged patients. Also in this case, the distinction between perceptual and conceptual components of repetition priming has been relevant for better characterizing the boundaries between what is lost and what is preserved in the memory of pure amnesic and degenerative demented patients. We have provided experimental data suggesting that the critical locus of impairment in purely amnesic patients is actually at the interaction between the implicit-explicit and perceptual-conceptual dichotomies. In tests such as stem completion and free association, these patients were selectively impaired in the explicit retrieval of semantically processed stimuli.

In degenerative demented patients, instead, the perceptual-conceptual dichotomy does not seem to have relevant explicative value for predicting normal or abnormal memory performance. In fact, AD patients were deficient in the perceptual as well as conceptual components of both implicit and explicit stem completion. However, these patients demonstrated normal priming in procedures calling for the identification of perceptually degraded words, non-words and pictures or involving reading a prose passage previously read or listened to. We hypothesized that repetition priming in AD patients is not sufficiently strong to sustain completion of previously studied stimuli, but is strong enough to facilitate successive identification of previously experienced material.

Further research is needed to evaluate whether the above suggested theoretical explanation of the memory impairment in both pure amnesic and AD patients are confirmed on experimental grounds or whether alternative explanations are better able to predict lost and preserved components of the memory function in anterograde amnesic populations.

## References

Blaxton, T.A. (1989). Investigating dissociations among memory measures: Support for a transfer-appropriate processing framework. *Journal of Experimental Psychology: Learning, Memory, and Cognition, 15,* 657–668.

Blaxton, T.A. (1992). Dissociations among memory measures in memory-impaired subjects: Evidence for a processing account of memory. *Memory and Cognition 20,* 549–562.

Brooks, D.N. (1976). Wechsler memory scale performance and its relationship to brain damage after severe closed head injury. *Journal of Neurology, Neurosurgery and Psychiatry, 39,* 593–601.

Brown, A.S., & Mitchell, D.B. (1994). A reevaluation of semantic versus nonsemantic processing in implicit memory. *Memory and Cognition, 22,* 533–541.

Bowers, J.S., & Schacter, D.L. (1990). Implicit memory and test awareness. *Journal of Experimental Psychology: Learning, Memory, and Cognition, 16,* 404–416.

Carlesimo, G.A. (1994). Perceptual and conceptual priming in amnesic and alcoholic patients. *Neuropsychologia, 32,* 903–921.

Carlesimo, G.A., Fadda L., Marfia G., & Caltagirone C. (1995). Explicit memory and repetition priming in dementia: Evidence for a common basic mechanism underlying conscious and unconscious retrieval deficits. *Journal of Clinical and Experimental Neuropsychology, 17,* 44–57.

Carlesimo, G.A, Fadda L., Sabbadini, M., & Caltagirone C. (1994). Visual repetition priming for words relies on access to the visual input lexicon: Evidence from a dyslexic patient. *Neuropsychologia, 32,* 1089–1110.

Carlesimo, G.A., Marfia, G.A., Loasses, A., & Caltagirone, C. (1996). Perceptual and conceptual components in implicit and explicit Stem completion: A neuropsychological investigation. *Neuropsychologia, 34,* 785–792.

Cermak, L.S., Talbot, N., Chandler, K., & Wolbarst, L.R. (1985). The perceptual priming phenomenon in amnesia. *Neuropsychologia, 23,* 615–622.

Chiarello, C., & Hoyer, W.J. (1988). Adult age differences in implicit and explicit memory: Time course and encoding effects. *Psychology and Aging, 3,* 358–366.

Christensen, H., & Birrell, P. (1991). Explicit and implicit memory in dementia and normal aging. *Psychological Research, 53,* 149–161.

Clarke, R., & Morton, J. (1983). Cross modality facilitation in tachistoscopic word recognition. *Quarterly Journal of Experimental Psychology, 35A,* 79–96.

Cohen, N.J., & Squire, L.R. (1980). Preserved learning and retention of pattern-analyzing skill in amnesia: Dissociation of knowing how and knowing that. *Science, 210,* 207–210.

Corkin, S. (1968). Acquisition of motor skill after bilateral medical temporal-lobe excision. *Neuropsychologia, 6,* 255–265.

Craik, F.I.M., & Lockhart, R.S. (1972). Levels of processing: A framework for memory research. *Journal of Verbal Learning and Verbal Behavior, 11,* 671–684.

Ellis, A.W., & Young, A.W. (1988). *Human cognitive neuropsychology.* Hove: Erlbaum.

Gabrieli, J.D.E., Keane, M.M., Stanger, B.Z., Kjelgaard, M.M., & Growdon, J.H. (1994). Dissociations among structural-perceptual, lexical-semantic, and event-fact memory systems in amnesic, Alzheimer's, and normal subjects. *Cortex, 30,* 75–103.

Glisky, E.L., & Schacter, D.L. (1987). Acquisition of domain-specific knowledge in organic amnesia: Training for computer-related work. *Neuropsychologia, 25,* 893–906.

Gooding, P.A., Eijk, R. van, Mayes, A.R., & Meudell, P. (1993). Preserved pattern completion priming for novel, abstract geometric shapes in amnesics of several etiologies. *Neuropsychologia, 31,* 789–810.

Graf, P., & Mandler, G. (1984). Activation makes words more accessible, but not necessarily more retrievable. *Journal of Verbal Learning and Verbal Behavior, 23,* 553–568.

Graf, P., Mandler, G., & Haden, P.E. (1982). Simulating amnesic symptoms in normal subjects. *Science, 218,* 1243–1244.

Graf, P., Shimamura, A.P., & Squire, L.R. (1985). Priming across modalities and priming across category levels: Extending the domain of preserved function in amnesia. *Journal of Experimental Psychology: Learning, Memory, and Cognition, 11,* 386–396.

Graf, P., Squire, L.R., & Mandler, G. (1984). The information that amnesic patients do not forget. *Journal of Experimental Psychology: Learning, Memory and Cognition, 10,* 164–178.

Grosse, D.A., Wilson, R.S., & Fox, J.H. (1990). Preserved word-stem-completion priming of semantically encoded information in Alzheimer's disease. *Psychology and Aging, 5,* 304–306.

Hamman, S.B., & Squire, L.R. (1996). Level-of-processing effects in word-completion priming: A neuropsychological study. *Journal of Experimental Psychology: Learning, Memory and Cognition, 22,* 933–947.

Huff, F.J., Mack, L., Mahlmann, J., & Greenberg, S. (1988). A comparison of lexical-semantic impairments in left hemisphere stroke and Alzheimer's disease. *Brain and Language, 34,* 262–278.

Jacoby, L.L., & Dallas, M. (1981). On the relationship between autobiographical memory and perceptual learning. *Journal of Experimental Psychology: General, 110,* 306–340.

Java, R.I., & Gardiner, J.M. (1991). Priming and aging: Further evidence of preserved memory function. *American Journal of Psychology, 104*, 89–100.

Keane, M.M., Gabrieli, J.D.E., Fennema, A.C., Growdon, J.H., & Corkin, S. (1991). Evidence for a dissociation between perceptual and conceptual priming in Alzheimer's disease. *Behavioral Neuroscience, 105*, 326–342.

Keane, M.M., Gabrieli, J.D.E., Growdon, J.H., & Corkin, S. (1994). Priming in perceptual identification of pseudowords is normal in Alzheimer's disease. *Neuropsychologia, 32*, 343–356.

Kirsner, K., Milech, D., & Stander, P. (1983). Common and modality-specific processes in the mental lexicon. *Memory and Cognition, 11*, 621–630.

Levy, B.A. (1993). Fluent rereading: An implicit indicator of reading skill development. In P. Graf & M.E.J. Masson (Eds.), *Implicit memory. New directions in cognition, development and neuropsychology* (pp. 49–74). Hillsdale, NJ: Erlbaum.

Monti, L.A., Gabrieli, J.D.E., Wilson, R.S., & Reminger, S.L. (1994). Intact text-specific implicit memory in patients with Alzheimer's disease. *Psychology an Aging, 9*, 64–71.

Morrison, J.H., Hof, P., Campbell, M.J., De Lima A.D., Voigt, T., Bouras, C., Cox, K., & Young, W.G. (1990). Cellular pathology in Alzheimer's disease: Implications for corticocortical disconnection and differential vulnerability. In S.I. Rapoport, H. Petit, D. Leys, & Y. Christen (Eds.), *Imaging, cerebral topography and Alzheimer's disease* (pp. 19–40). Berlin: Springer.

Musen, G., Shimamura, A.P., & Squire, L.R. (1990). Intact text-specific reading skill in amnesia. *Journal of Experimental Psychology: Learning, Memory, and Cognition, 16*, 1068–1076.

Roediger, H.L. (1990). Implicit memory. Retention without remembering. *American Psychologist, 45*, 1043–1056.

Roediger, H.L., Weldon, M.S., & Challis, B.H. (1989). Explaining dissociations between implicit and explicit measures of retention: A processing account. In H.L. Roediger & F.I.M. Craik (Eds.), *Varieties of memory and consciousness: Essays in honor of Endel Tulving* (pp. 3–41). Hillsdale, NJ: Erlbaum.

Rozin, P.A. (1976). The psychobiological approach to human memory. In M.R. Rosenzweig & E.L. Bennett (Eds.), *Neural mechanisms of memory and learning* (pp. 3–48). Cambridge, MA: MIT Press.

Salmon, D.P., Shimamura, A.P., Butters, N., & Smith, S. (1988). Lexical and semantic priming deficits in patients with Alzheimer's disease. *Journal of Clinical and Experimental Neuropsychology, 10*, 477–494.

Schacter, D.L. (1990). Perceptual representation systems and implicit memory: Toward a resolution of the multiple memory systems debate. *Annals of the New York Academy of Sciences, 608*, 543–571.

Schacter, D.L. (1994). Priming and multiple memory systems: Perceptual mechanisms of implicit memory. In D.L. Schacter & E. Tulving (Eds.), *Memory systems 1994* (pp. 233–268). Cambridge, MA: MIT Press.

Schacter, D.L., Coper, L.A., Tharan, M., & Rubens, A.B. (1991). Preserved priming of novel objects in patients with memory disorders. *Journal of Cognitive Neuroscience, 3*, 118–131.

Schacter, D.L., & Graf, P. (1986). Effects of elaborative processing on implicit and explicit memory for new associations. *Journal of Experimental Psychology: Learning, Memory, and Cognition, 12*, 432–444.

Schacter, D.L., McGlynn, S.M., Milberg, W.P., & Church, B.A. (1993). Spared priming despite impaired comprehension: Implicit memory in a case of word-meaning deafness. *Neuropsychology, 7*, 107–118.

Schacter, D.L., Rapscack, S.Z., Rubens, A.B., Tharan, M., & Laguna, J. (1990). Priming effects in a letter-by-letter reader depend upon access to the word form system. *Neuropsychologia, 28,* 1079–1094.

Schwartz, B.L., Rosse, R.B., & Deutsch, S.I. (1993). Limits of processing view in accounting for dissociations among memory measures in a clinical population. *Memory and Cognition, 21,* 63–72.

Shimamura, A.P., Salmon, D.P., Squire, L.R., & Butters, N. (1987). Memory dysfunction and word priming in dementia and amnesia. *Behavioral Neuroscience, 101,* 347–351.

Shimamura, A.P., & Squire, L.R. (1984). Paired-associate learning and priming effects in amnesia: A neuropsychological study. *Journal of Experimental Psychology: General, 113,* 556–570.

Shimamura, A.P., & Squire, L.R. (1989). Impaired priming of new associations in amnesia. *Journal of Experimental Psychology: Learning, Memory, and Cognition 14,* 763–769.

Smith, M.E., & Oscar-Berman, M. (1990). Repetition priming of words and pseudowords in divided attention and in amnesia. *Journal of Experimental Psychology: Learning, Memory, and Cognition, 6,* 1033–1042.

Squire, L.R., Shimamura, A.P., & Graf, P. (1987). Strength and duration of priming effects in normal subjects and amnesic patients. *Neuropsychologia, 25,* 195–210.

Tulving, E. (1983). *Elements of episodic memory.* Oxford: Oxford University Press.

Tulving, E., & Schacter, D.L. (1990). Priming and human memory systems. *Science, 247,* 301–306.

Weldon, M.S., Roediger, H.L., & Challis, B.H. (1989). The properties of retrieval cues constrain the picture superiority effect. *Memory and Cognition, 17,* 95–105.

Wilson, B.A., Green, R., Teasdale, T., Beckers, K., Della Sala, S., Kaschel, R., Schuri, U., Van der Linden, M., & Weber, E. (1996). Implicit learning in amnesic subjects: A comparison with a large group of normal control subjects. *The Clinical Neuropsychologist, 10,* 279–292.

# The Memory System and Brain Organization: From Animal to Human Studies

*Jean Delacour*

During the last decade, the neurobiology of learning and memory (LM) has made impressive advances at the cellular and molecular level (Bailey et al., 1996; Feany & Quinn, 1995; Greenspan, 1995; Linden, 1994; Lisman, 1994; Martin & Kandel, 1996): at these levels, several phenomena of neural plasticity have been studied in great detail. However, the accumulation of results obtained – for precision's sake – under artificial conditions is not sufficient in itself to achieve the aim of the neurobiology of LM: to identify the mechanisms which really operate in the intact nervous system of behaving organisms.

Among all the possible mechanisms discovered under artificial conditions, only those brought into play by the intact brain under normal conditions are real. For example, in spite of the enormous amount of experimental work devoted to the study of long-term potentiation (LTP), the role of this form of synaptic plasticity in LM remains controversial (Barnes, 1995; Bliss & Collingridge, 1993; Hölscher, 1997; Rioux & Robinson, 1995). Consequently, the phenomena studied by the cellular and molecular neurobiology must be reintegrated in their normal environment, which is the living nervous system functioning under normal conditions. This integration is not only necessary from the neurobiological point of view but also for psychological reasons, because, as stressed by many psychologists (Craik, 1983; Glenberg, 1997; Neisser, 1997), LM do not constitute a separate faculty. Under real world conditions, LM are indissociable from all the other components of behavior, including perception, computation of plans, anticipation of outcomes, attention, motivation, etc.; they collaborate with the other abilities of the organism towards the fulfillment of a common objective: survival and gene diffusion. Finally, this integration of cellular and molecular mechanisms in the overall organization of the brain is also necessary for practical purposes: for example, it is recognized that memory deficits due to aging or dementia have multiple molecular origins and are consequences of the deterioration of several interacting sets of neurons (Albert, 1997; Amenta et al., 1991; Francis et al., 1992; Gabrieli, 1996; Heiss et al., 1992; Sharp & Ross, 1996; Wallin & Gottfries, 1990) and not the deterioration of a single class of molecules or cells. An efficient therapy should be based on a synthetic view of the cerebral bases of cognitive processes.

## A Model of the Brain

Consequently a prerequisite for a realistic neurobiology of LM is a model of the whole brain*, and this is perhaps the main obstacle to the progress of research. Presently, only metaphors and block diagrams are available. They reflect either philosophical views or prevailing technology (Daugman, 1990), such as the computer-brain. The inadequacy of this metaphor is now well established (Churchland et al., 1990; Churchland, 1995; Edelman, 1989; Rumelhart & McClelland, 1987; Young, 1987).

This lack of scientific models is mainly due to the computational difficulty of simulating large-scale neural networks, and the technical difficulty of obtaining synthetic views of the real brain. These obstacles will certainly be overcome, thanks in particular to the progress of brain imaging and the theory of dynamical systems (Haken, 1994; Kelso, 1995; McKenna et al., 1994). However, in the meantime, only preliminary representations are possible. I have therefore adopted an empirical and eclectic course: the framework of my model is based on the functional anatomy of the brain, as outlined by cerebral neurophysiology, and by clinical and experimental neuropsychology. According to this model, the brain consists of three systems (Table 1, columns I and II).

The first is made up of the neurons which code, i. e., represent, sensory information or motor programs with the greatest precision. We will call this system "C," for coding. Its delimitation is fairly simple. C comprises the primary sensory and motor structures as well as the sets of neurons which code high level sensory and motor information: the association cortex and on the efferent side, the premotor cortex, the supplementary motor area, the striatum, and the cerebellum. In humans, the cortical areas involved in the precise coding of linguistic activity should also be included in C. This system is distributed among modules, for instance, the visual or motor structures as well as certain parts of the language neural bases (Ojemann, 1991). The concept of module here is to great extent inspired by Fodor (1983). It is a device with the following properties: it is (1) domain-specific, (2) mandatory (automatic obligatory processing), (3) inaccessible to consciousness, (4) fast, (5) informationally encapsulated (impenetrable from an outside module), and possesses (6) specific breakdown patterns, as in apraxia and agnosia. At least some modules have a topographic organization. Even at the highest level, C is characterized by a

---

* For a similar point of view, see Edelman (1989).

*Table 1.* Memory functions of the three systems of the brain.

| System | Neural Bases | General Function | Memory function |
|---|---|---|---|
| C | Modular/topographic organization. Primary sensory/motor structures; higher order sensory and motor cortex; striatum, cerebellum. | High precision coding of sensory information, motor programs, language. Typical behavioral correlates: perception, motor activity, linguistic routines. | *Critical dimension:* the type of information learned. Relative autonomy in perceptual priming, procedural/sensori-motor tasks at late stages. |
| A | Integrative organization. Reticular formation, raphé, locus coeruleus, nucleus basalis of Meynert, some thalamic & hypothalamic nuclei, hippocampus, cingulate, amygdala and other limbic structures. | Modulation of excitability and coherence of populations of neurons; role in the formation and activation of neural assemblies. Typical behavioral correlates: arousal/motivation states such as consciousness, emotion. | *Critical dimension:* for the structures involved in "global" amnestic syndromes: the type of cognitive process. Specific role in consciousness dependent (declarative) memory. The short-term vs long-term dimension is also important. |
| S | Anatomical delimitation and organization? Prefrontal cortex and related structures. | Supervision of goal-directed behavior. Typical behavioral correlate: human "voluntary" act. | Critical dimension: the type of cognitive process. Special involvement in working memory, metacognition, as basic components of "strategic memory." |

modular organization; for instance, thirty two distinct cortical areas associated with visual processing have been described in the primate brain (Van Essen et al., 1992).

The second system is made up of neurons whose activity has no precise relationship with sensory inputs or motor outputs. These neurons are involved in arousal, attentional or motivational states*. We will call this system "A," for activation. This concept is currently used and illustrated by cerebral neurobiology (Kinomura et al., 1996; Mesulam, 1995; Steriade, 1991, 1995). An increase in central activation is characterized by:
– Higher levels of glucose utilization (Braun et al., 1997; Kennedy et al., 1982),
– An enhanced responsiveness and signal-to-noise ratio of sensory systems (Livingstone & Hubel, 1981; Steriade, 1991),

---

\* Neurons from structures belonging to system A such as the amygdala and the orbitofrontal cortex, respond to specific stimuli but their responses essentially reflect the motivation state of the organism and/or the biological value of the stimulus. Before these stimuli have an effect on system A, they are precisely coded by the sensory modules of C (LeDoux, 1996; Rolls, 1996a).

- The predominance of depolarization in thalamocortical neurons, which causes the passage from a bursting mode of discharge to a "single spike" mode – that is, a mode characterized by the stochastic independence of inter-spike intervals,
- A decrease in the contribution of low frequencies to the cortical EEG, and increase in the contribution of high frequencies (> 20 Hz)*.

The main anatomical structures which make up A are the reticular formation, the raphe and the locus ceruleus, certain thalamic and hypothalamic nuclei, the nucleus basalis of the telencephalon, and the limbic system, including the cingulate, hippocampus, amygdala, septal nuclei, etc. Experimental and clinical data clearly show that some of these structures are directly involved in the control of arousal, sleep-wakefulness cycles and/or motivation**. Their central projections modulate the spontaneous and evoked activity of large populations of the brain. Their lesion disturbs the sleep-wakefulness cycle, food intake, fear reactions or sexual activity. The role of other A structures is more complex, but their lesion has the remarkable effect of causing the global amnestic syndromes. Unlike the organization of C, that of A is neither modular nor topographic; it is, to a great extent, integrative. Information is not analyzed by separate, "encapsulated," specialized modules; typically, A neurons receive convergent afferents from heterogeneous sources and project onto different targets through highly divergent efferents. In addition, the different subsystems of A are densely interconnected (for a typical example of this kind of organization, see the description of the networks of cholinergic neurons of the A system by Woolf, 1991).

   The third system is certainly the most difficult to define and delimit. Nevertheless, it is an essential component of any description of the brain because some neural entity should account for the goal-directed character of behavior. The best illustration of its functions is the human "voluntary act"; this involves a representation of a goal and of the appropriate strategies for its achievement, the evaluation of results and the correction of errors. Time is an important dimension of the role of this entity, especially the representation and organization of the future. We will call this system "S," for supervision; as stated above, it is much harder to delimit than systems C and A. S is perhaps only a dynamic reality, a certain emergent mode of the cooperative activity of the

---

* Globally desynchronized low-amplitude cortical EEG is also a characteristic of high activation states, but local synchronizations of short duration of high frequency EEG waves also occur in these states (Steriade, 1995).
** Several limbic structures, classically involved in motivation, are also involved in sleep: orbito-frontal cortex and anterior cingulate (slow wave sleep) and amygdala (REM sleep) (Maquet et al., 1997).

whole brain. However, the effects of lesions to the prefrontal cortex in humans mostly reflect a defect in the S functions (Damasio, 1996; Duncan, 1996; Luria, 1973; Mesulam, 1986; Robin & Holyak, 1996; Shallice, 1988; Shallice & Burgess, 1996; Stuss, 1991). Data from electrophysiology (Deecke, 1996) neuroimaging in normal humans (Frith et al., 1991; Ingvar, 1985, 1994; Pardo et al., 1991) and neurophysiology and experimental neuropsychology in monkeys (Fuster, 1993; Goldman-Rakic, 1987, 1996; Watanabe, 1996) also suggest that at least the frontal cortex might be a part of S.

After this preliminary sketch, a word of warning. The framework of our model is anatomy, which remains the basis of all macro-descriptions of the brain. However, this representation has some drawbacks. The anatomical structure is a coarse division of the brain, in most cases consisting of different populations of neurons in terms of neurotransmitters, patterns of connections, intrinsic membrane properties, etc ... More fine grain divisions, such as the cortical column, should also be considered as frameworks for cellular and molecular data. In addition, the anatomical representation favors a priori localizationist and static conceptions, but C, A, and S are not solely characterized by anatomical delimitations as they have dynamic aspects which transcend anatomical limits. A task may bring different structures into play and conversely, a single structure may be involved in different tasks. Therefore, even at the anatomical level, the organization of the brain is, to a great extent, parallel and distributed (Goldman-Rakic, 1988; Mesulam, 1990).

The three systems interact and are, in varying degrees, brought into play by all types of behavior. Some states of A are a necessary condition for S functions: for instance, a certain state of arousal is necessary for the voluntary act. Reciprocally, S allocates resources of attention, which implies control over A. Likewise, the arousal/motivation level (A) affects sensory reception and motor activity (C). Again reciprocally, certain sensory stimuli, due to their novelty or biological value, have an arousal/motivational effect. S depends on the sensory/motor capacities of C but, reciprocally, S controls the functioning of C modules by focusing attention on certain targets, by correcting the motor output, etc.

These interactions are not hypothetical; their anatomophysiological bases have to a great extent been clarified, such as the control of the neocortex – the cortical stage of C modules and the prefrontal cortex (S) – by the activating systems of the brain stem and basal telencephalon (McCormick et al., 1993; Mesulam, 1995; Steriade, 1991, 1995). Likewise, anatomophysiological data show reciprocal relationships between the prefrontal cortex (S), sensory and motor modules of C and some of the main structures of A, especially the limbic structures. Note, however, that the prefrontal cortex is not a homogeneous entity but comprises several subsystems. The dorsal regions are preferentially connected with the association cortex, and the ventral regions, with limbic

structures (Barbas, 1992; Nauta, 1971; Pandya & Yeterian, 1996). Finally, thanks
to brain imaging techniques, the dynamical aspects of these interactions may
be studied in line, and even, formalized and quantified (McIntosh & Gonzales-
Lima, 1994).

## Outline of the Memory System

In spite of its imperfections, the above model of the brain allows the clear
formulation of an important question: does a separate anatomically-delimited
memory system exist? In its naive form, as the "center of memory," the "localizationist" thesis is rejected by most scientists but it still predominates in
more sophisticated forms (Mishkin et al., 1984; Squire & Zola-Morgan, 1991,
1996). According to the recent evolution of this thesis, there are several anatomically distinct memory systems. Clinical and experimental evidence seems
compelling because it has been shown that brain lesions in a specific location
produce memory deficits, while sparing other components of cognition; furthermore, even in global amnestic syndromes, only some forms of memory are
impaired. However, it should be noted that the main arguments in favor of one
or several centers of memory are based on the effects of lesions, i. e., pathologic
and a priori localizationist data. A rather different representation of the cerebral bases of memory is now emerging from the synthetic and dynamic views
of brain imaging in normal subjects, especially as regards the role of the hippocampus and frontal regions (see Section III). In addition, although global
amnestic syndromes are not associated with gross disturbances of behavior,
memory disturbances may be associated with less easily detectable changes in
other cognitive capacities. This is well established at least for Korsakoff patients as their attentional capacity is impaired (Jacoby, 1982; McEntee & Mair,
1984; Talland, 1965) as well as their metacognition abilities (Janowsky et al.,
1989a,c)*

Holistic views are the opposite of the localizationist concept as according
to this views, the memory system is the whole brain, which has a diffuse, fully

---

*   The analyses of the amnestic syndromes and the study of the normal memory in the laboratory
    were dominated for a long time and still are by the notion of a separate faculty of memory
    which can be completely dissociated from the other components of cognitive activity; on the
    neural side, a "center of memory" would correspond to this faculty. However, as already
    stressed, a different conception is possible: it is that memory is normally indissociable from the
    whole of cognitive activity. This conception is predominant in a growing trend of research
    centered on studies of memory in every-day life, natural conditions (Glenberg, 1997; Koriat &
    Goldsmith, 1996; Neisser, 1997); observation of amnestic patients under these conditions would
    be of special interest. Such an approach has already proved fruitful for analysis of the frontal
    syndrome (Damasio, 1996, Lhermitte, 1986; Lhermitte et al., 1986).

distributed organization. This is hardly tenable because the neural bases of memory, like those of any other function, possess a significant degree of local organization, as shown by clinical and experimental data. Our thesis is intermediate between the localizationist and holistic concepts: as shown by experimental data, plastic neurons, i. e., neurons whose properties are modified by experience, are found in all parts of the memory system (see section III) and this system is the whole brain. However, the whole brain does not possess a diffuse, fully distributed organization at all levels; at high levels of organization (such as the anatomical circuit) it is made up of the three anatomically distinct systems, C, A, and S. Thus at the cellular and molecular levels, the memory system may be distributed but, at the circuit level, it possesses a significant degree of local specialization. Different subsystems, having different locations in the brain, may consist of molecular and cellular elements with comparable plastic properties. However, due to different patterns or densities of intrinsic connections, and different patterns, sources or targets of afferent and efferent extrinsic connections, the emergent properties of these different subsystems may greatly differ, which results in a local organization of the memory system.

Thus, according to our model, the memory system at brain level consists of an interaction between C, A, and S, in which these component systems have different but complementary roles that reflect their respective functions in the overall organization of the brain. C is involved in LM through the fine-grain representation of sensory data and motor programs, A, through the control of the excitability and activity coherence of large populations of neurons, especially at cortical levels, and the role of S is to use past experiences and learning abilities for the benefit of the action in progress and plans for the future.

Depending on the task, learning and memory set in motion different types of interaction between C, A, and S, as defined by the pattern of activity of each system and the special involvement of certain subsystems. The relative importance of C, A, and S and the type of their interaction also depends on the stage of the task. For instance, the role of the activating systems of the brain may be much more important at the initial and intermediate stages than when the task has been perfectly mastered.

This conception of the memory system has at least two advantages: first, it accounts economically for the neural bases of the great diversity of learning and memory phenomena, without the ad hoc creation of separate memory systems. Second, it accounts for the interaction of learning and memory with the other components of behavior, i. e., perception, arousal/motivation states, goal-directed activity and, on the neural side, for the integration of the memory system into the whole brain. Memory is an aspect of whole behavior and, similarly, the memory system is a certain mode of functioning of the whole brain.

## Experimental and Clinical Evidence

Our model must be supported by experimental and clinical data on three main points:
A.　All three systems must be involved in LM.
B.　Their role in LM must reflect their respective function in the overall organization of the brain.
C.　The three systems must cooperate in all forms of LM at least at some stage.

### A. All Three Systems Are Involved in LM

Data on Behaving Animals, Patients, or Normal Humans

An enormous amount of data, based on lesion, stimulation, electrophysiological, and pharmacological experiments, shows that each of the three systems is involved at least in the expression of LM.

We will not review all these data here (see Delacour, 1988, 1994) but only stress a few points:

1. The role of C modules in LM has long been neglected for two reasons: a) the predominance of the notion of a separate, specialized "center of memory" with the exclusive privilege of plastic capacities, and b) the fact that, until recently, the neuropsychology in humans was, solely based on the effects of lesion, which confound learning with performance.

From unit recording in chronic animals, it appears that the functioning of the sensory and motor neurons can be modified by experience, even in the adults. Thus, it is possible to modify the receptive fields of the neurons of the auditory, somesthetic and visual cortices through conditioning procedures or other forms of sensory experience (Bakin & Weinberger, 1990; Delacour et al., 1987, 1990a; Fregnac et al., 1992; Merzenich et al., 1990; see review in Kaas, 1996; Kossut, 1992; Weinberger, 1995). Data from brain imaging in normal humans also strongly suggest that system C has a role in LM as they show that sensory and motor cortical areas are involved in mental representations of visual objects or motor acts (Decety, 1996; Kosslyn et al., 1995; Le Bihan et al., 1993; Rao et al., 1993; Roland, 1987).

2. There are some discrepancies between brain imaging in normal subjects and the classical neuropsychology of amnestic syndromes. For example, the role of the hippocampus seems to be negligible in many LM tasks whereas the frontal regions are almost always involved (see review in Buckner & Tulving, 1995; Grafton, 1995; Ungerleider, 1995).

3. Data on behaving animals, patients or normal humans show that C, A, and

S are at least involved in the expression of LM, and these data delimit their respective functions in the memory system. However, they do not make it possible to define precise cellular and molecular mechanisms or even to prove that neurons belonging to a given system are primarily involved in a LM task. The effects of lesions of these neurons confound learning with performance, and changes in their electrophysiological activity might only reflect changes in distant neurons. For example, changes during a learning task in the unit activity of a neuron recorded through an extracellular micro-electrode do not prove that this neuron is itself "plastic" and belongs to the primary basis for the learning of that task; the changes of that unit's activity may reflect modifications in presynaptic neurons properties. The same problem is encountered in the interpretation of EEG and evoked potentials data. For technical reasons, a complete demonstration of the cellular and molecular mechanisms involving identified neurons is not possible in behaving, intact organisms but can only be achieved in simpler preparations such as brain slices *in vitro*.

Simpler Preparations

Even though most of the research has been devoted to the hippocampus, it is now well established that the main forms of synaptic plasticity, Long-Term Potentiation (LTP) and Long-Term Depression (LTD), do exist in all three systems.

LTP (Bliss & Collingridge, 1993; Voronin, 1994) is not a property exclusive to the hippocampus; within system A, it also occurs in the amygdala (LeDoux, 1996), and outside system A, in the sensory and motor cortex (Castro-Alamancos & Connors, 1996; Iriki et al., 1989; Kirkwood et al., 1993; Tsumoto, 1994) which are part of system C, and the prefrontal cortex, part of system S (Bindman et al., 1988; Hirsch & Crepel, 1992; Sutor & Hablitz, 1989). It has also been observed in the vestibular nucleus and the interpositus nucleus of the cerebellum (Racine et al., 1986). Likewise, LTD occurs in the hippocampus, sensory and motor cortex, the prefrontal cortex, cerebellum, and striatum (Artola & Singer, 1993; Castro-Alamancos & Connors, 1996; Linden, 1994; Tsumoto, 1994). In addition, LTP and LTD are not confined to the brain: both exist in the spinal cord (Pockett & Figurov, 1993) and at peripheral synapses (Dolphin, 1985).

These data do not support the notion of one or several centers of memory which are anatomically delimited and have the exclusive privilege of neural plasticity as this plasticity seems to be widely distributed in the brain and is found in all three systems. Thus the data obtained in behaving animals, the effects of lesions on LM tasks, or changes in electrophysiological activity during these tasks, probably reflect, at least partly, some primary involvement of all three systems in LM, and not only a role in performance.

This does not rule out any possibility of differences between the systems at the level of cellular and molecular mechanisms. For example, neural plasticity may depend on hormonal factors (Bohus, 1994) whose the importance may vary from one cerebral system to the other. Steroid hormones are of special interest, due to their double action, firstly on genome expression and protein synthesis, and secondly, their much faster action on the membrane (Joels & De Kloet, 1992). In this connection, the study of a class of steroids, termed neuro-steroids, is very promising: they are synthesized in the brain, where they exert powerful neuromodulatory actions and are involved in neural plasticity (Schu-macher et al., 1996); according to recent data, they might have promnesic effects (Flood et al., 1992). Note that the density of steroid receptors is partic-ularly high in some structures of system A, such as the hippocampus (Kawata, 1995). A most important model is provided by song learning in birds which greatly depends on the sexual hormones that control the growth of the neurons involved in that learning (Nordeen & Nordeen, 1990; Nottebohm, 1991). Sex-ual hormones and glucocorticoids also modulate LTP in mammals (Pavlides et al., 1993; Warren et al., 1995).

## B. The Respective Roles of C, A, and S in LM

According to our model, even if all three systems have comparable plastic capacities at the cellular and molecular levels, their emergent properties at network level endow them different roles with in LM.

The Dimensions of Memory

Let us first introduce some basic concepts on learning and memory phenom-ena at the behavioral level. These phenomena may differ according to three dimensions (Table 2): (1) duration of retention of the learned information, (2) the nature of the learned information, i. e., visual vs. auditory, verbal vs. spatial, etc., and (3) the type of cognitive processing. This last dimension is less easily defined than the other two; however, the amnestic syndromes well illustrate its importance.

*Table 2.* Dimensions of memory.

1. Short-term vs. long-term
2. Type of information learned: auditory vs. visual, spatial vs. verbal, etc.
3. Type of cognitive processes:
    – Explicit (consciousness-dependent) vs. implicit memory
    – Strategic vs. non-strategic memory

"Global" amnestic syndromes dissociate two types of memory in terms of cognitive processing: one which is dramatically impaired (type I or explicit memory) and the other which is not (type II or implicit memory). Although there is controversy over the precise definitions of these two types of memory, there does seem to be growing agreement (Eichenbaum, Otto, & Cohen, 1992; Squire & Zola-Morgan, 1996; Tulving, 1996) that type I is characterized by conscious, explicit, deliberate forms of memory; the contents of this type of memory are relational as they are connected to, in continuity with, accessible from all conscious knowledge; furthermore, type I memories are flexible: they can be manipulated and used flexibly under a wide range of conditions, including those differing significantly from the circumstances of original learning. Type II is characterized by automatic, implicit, and unconscious forms of memory. Storage and evocation of their contents are strictly dependent on the processing modules that were engaged during the initial learning. Type II memories are not related to the other contents of the cognitive activity but are only accessible within the restrictive range of the stimuli and context in which they were originally acquired; therefore their use is much less flexible than that of Type I memories.

A typical example of a Type I memory is the recall of an autobiographical event, for instance, the meeting of a friend in a certain place, two months previously. A typical example of type II is the acquisition of a conditioned eye-blink in response to a tone through a classical conditioning procedure. These examples raise an important problem. It is relatively easy to create experimental forms of type II memory in animals but it is much more difficult for type I forms. This problem is presently one of the limiting factors of experimental research in the field.

Other amnestic syndromes also dissociate forms of memory according to the cognitive process involved. Frontal lesions impair "strategic memory" fairly selectively, that is, memory based on metacognition and internally generated strategy, as opposed to more "passive" forms of memory, which essentially depend on the environmental stimuli (Gabrieli, 1996).

System C

The critical dimension of the role of system C is the type of information. A typical example is the inferotemporal cortex (IFT) in the monkey. This area is a visual association cortex. Its neurons only respond to visual stimuli, especially to complex visual objects such as a hand or a primate face (Gross, 1992; Tanaka et al., 1991). Lesion or stimulation of the IFT only produces deficits in visual learning and memory tasks; tasks based on other sensory modalities are spared; the unit activity of the IFT is significantly correlated with behavior in visual memory tasks (Delacour, 1977a,b; Fuster & Jervey, 1981; Gross, 1973;

Lueschow et al., 1994; Mishkin, 1972; Miyashita, 1993; Ridley & Ettlinger, 1973; Tanaka, 1996).

On the other hand, the cognitive process dimension is not critical for system C. Lesion of the IFT impairs trial-unique delayed non match-to-sample tasks (generally considered as measuring type I memory in monkeys, Mishkin & Delacour, 1975) as well as pattern or object discriminations based on the repeated association of a cue and a reward (generally considered as measuring type II memory). Likewise the role of the IFT does not depend on the duration of retention: short-term as well as long-term visual memory tasks are impaired by IFT lesions. Similar data show that in monkeys, lesions of other unimodal association cortices produce memory deficits which are specific for a particular sensory modality (Pribram, 1984): gustative (anterior temporal), auditory (middle temporal), somesthesic (parieto-occipital).

Comparable data have been obtained in humans. Brain imaging shows that sensory or motor structures, including the cerebellum, are brought into play by both forms I and II of memory, by conscious, deliberate evocation of mental images (see references p. 246) as well as priming or the learning of motor skills (Buckner & Tulving, 1995; Grafton, 1995; Ungerleider, 1995); likewise, system C is involved in both short-term and long-term memory. The notion that C modules store specific information such as individual faces, is also supported by lesions limited to association cortex areas (Damasio, 1990; Damasio et al., 1990).

The modular organization of memory in system C is not limited to sensory or motor information. Memory of words bring into play different association cortex areas depending on the meaning of the words: for instance, the naming of color selectively activates a region in the ventral temporal lobe just anterior to the area involved in the perception of color whereas the naming of action activates a region in the middle temporal gyrus just anterior to the area involved in the perception of motion; naming animals selectively activates the left medial occipital lobe whereas naming tools selectively activates both a left premotor area which is also activated by imagined hand movements, and the area involved in the naming of words describing action (Martin et al., 1995, 1996).

However, it should be stressed that at least in conscious subjects, the cerebral basis of LM tasks is not limited to one or several C modules: synthetic views from brain imaging show that structures belonging to the A and S systems are also involved. In addition, LM tasks which bring into play different C modules often have identical bases in systems A and S. Almost all the tasks* involve frontal regions either bilaterally or unilaterally.

---

* In all the experiments based on brain imaging, the tasks were performed by fully conscious subjects. A most important experiment, which may, however, be impractical, would be to compare the cerebral bases of the same task during different states of vigilance.

System A

Contrarily to system C, dimension 2 (i. e., type of information) is not critical for the definition of the role of system A. Due to its anatomo-physiological properties, this system cannot encode and store precise sensorimotor or central information. On the other hand, the type of cognitive processing, insofar as it depends on activation levels, is a relevant feature of the role of system A. This is well illustrated by the distinction between forms I and II of memory (see above). A set of activation states R may be required by certain LM tasks. The psychological counterpart of R states are conscious states. R is a necessary condition for reflexive consciousness, for an explicit representation of the self and the world, the voluntary act, and more generally, for certain cognitive activities. Consequently, R is a necessary condition for some forms of encoding, storage and retrieval. It is only during R that "deep" semantic encoding is possible, that perceptual data are represented in the framework of an autobiography, i. e., experienced by a permanent self and located in a spatiotemporal context and more generally, in a world. It is only by reference to that context that a non-repeated event may be coded as unique. Likewise, it is only in R (or, on the subjective side, in a certain state of consciousness) that certain forms of retrieval are possible such as retrieval through active search, based on cognitive strategies when the information to be remembered is ambiguous, subject to interference or episodic, i. e., when it refers to a self and a world. R may also affect storage, since the quality of encoding probably affects the lifespan of a piece of information, its resistance to interference and to the deterioration of its neural basis. Therefore dimension 1 (the duration of retention of the material learned) may be also critical for the role of system A.

The irrelevance of dimension 2 (the type of information learned) to the role of some structures of system A is well illustrated by the "global" amnestic syndromes produced by lesions of these structures. As already stressed, these syndromes are not specific for a type of information, but for the type of cognitive processes set into motion by LM, since whatever the type of information, they selectively affect type I forms of memory and spare type II forms.

The interpretation of the "global" amnestic syndromes as resulting from a deficit in certain forms of cerebral activation is in general well accepted in the case of diencephalic lesions. In patients with Korsakoff's syndrome, amnesia, produced in most cases by degenerative lesions of mammillary bodies and medial thalamus, is associated with attention disturbances reflecting a deficit in central activation (Jacoby, 1982; McEntee & Mair, 1984; Talland, 1965). The amnestic syndrome produced by limited thalamic lesions (Rousseaux, 1994) or lesions of the nucleus basalis of Meynert (NBM) (Damasio et al., 1985; Morris et al., 1992) may be interpreted in the same way, since the medial thalamus and the NBM are important parts of the activating systems of the brain and control cortical arousal (see section I). According to experimental data, the NBM is involved in LM in rats and monkeys through its role in attention (Dekker et al., 1991; Muir, Everitt, & Robbins, 1994; Richardson & DeLong, 1990). In rats, unit activity during a classical conditioning shows that the intralaminar thalamus is involved in the arousal responses which characterize the early stages of the conditioning (Delacour, 1980, 1984).

In the case of the temporal lobe structures, the interpretations of the clinical and experimental data are much less concordant. The dominant interpretation of the clinical data (Squire & Zola-Morgan, 1991) is in good agreement with the anatomophysiology and with our model as the temporal amnestic syndrome, like the diencephalic syndrome, is not specific for a type of information but for the type of cognitive process brought into play by type I, explicit memory; the condition necessary for this form of memory to function is consciousness (Delacour, 1997; Tulving, 1987; Wheeler et al., 1997), that is, a certain state of cerebral activation.

However, there is an influential interpretation of the experimental data which is very different. The role of hippocampus would be to form a map of the spatial environment (O'Keefe & Nadel, 1978); in which case its role would be specific for a certain type of information, just like the role of a C module. For a detailed discussion of this "spatial" theory, I refer the reader to two recent papers (Delacour, 1994, 1995). Here, I will only stress the fact that this theory is hardly compatible with the anatomophysiology of hippocampus and that it is not supported the clinical data because the temporal amnestic syndrome is not specific for spatial information or any other type of information (Squire, 1992, 1993). It should be also stressed that the "spatial" theory, though very popular, is not the only current interpretation of the experimental data. Thus it was long ago suggested that the hippocampus has a role in attention (Bennett, 1971; Grastyan et al., 1959), and this hypothesis, which entirely agrees with the anatomophysiology and our model, still has many supporters (Buhusi & Schmajuk, 1996; Hobson & Schmajuk, 1988; Carpenter & Grossberg, 1993; Vinogradova, 1995).

Note that the "spatial" theory, which is hardly justified in its strict form, is tending to evolve toward a more general conception that the hippocampus would be involved in the formation of "flexible," "relational" representations of any kind of information and not exclusively of spatial data (Bunsey & Eichenbaum, 1996; Eichenbaum et al., 1992; Eichenbaum, 1996; Gluck & Myers, 1997; Rolls, 1996b; Rudy & Sutherland, 1995). The departure from the strict "spatial theory" is important: for instance, according to the new version, the unit activity of the hippocampus is not characterized by pure "place" cells but codes a large variety of information (Eichenbaum, 1996; Rolls, 1996b; Wiener, 1996).

This new version is compatible with the clinical data: it postulates that the role of the hippocampus would specific, not for a type of information but for a cognitive process, which is set into motion by the formation of flexible and relational representations. Such representations are characteristic of the declarative memory (Eichenbaum et al., 1992). However, to be acceptable, this version calls for the solution of two problems: (1) the definition of memory tests for animals, based on flexible and relational representations, and (2) identification of the neurophysiological mechanisms involved in these representations; these mechanisms may bring into play cortico-hippocampo-cortical loops (Delacour, 1995; Bibbig et al., 1995).

However, theories on the role of the hippocampus are perhaps still premature, as the part of this structure in the temporal syndrome is still controversial (Corkin et al., 1997; Horel, 1978, 1994; Squire & Zola-Morgan, 1991). Moreover, brain imaging in normal subjects does not confirm that the hippocampus has an exceptional importance, whatever be the type of memory (Buckner & Tulving, 1995; Grafton, 1995; Ungerleider, 1995). In contrast, the anterior cingulate, a limbic structure involved in attention, is activated by a wide variety of tasks. Some of the few positive data concerning the hippocampus suggest that it is involved in reactions to novelty (Haxby et al., 1996; Ungerleider, 1995). This is confirmed by the fact that event-related potentials and vegetative responses evoked by novel stimuli are reduced in hippocampal patients (Knight, 1996). In this respect it should be stressed that according to one of the main theories anterior to the "spatial" theory, the role of hippocampus is to detect and record novelty (Vinogradova, 1975). This hypothesis, obviously related to "attentional" interpretations, is based on convincing experimental data such as the rapid habituation of hippocampal unit responses to repeated sensory stimuli, and the regular induction of the theta rhythm by novel stimuli. It has been shown that during a classical conditioning. a population of hippocampal neurons is especially involved in the initial stage of the conditioning, characterized by orientation reactions and increases in arousal elicited by the CS (Delacour, 1980, 1984). Like the stimulation of the reticular formation, that of the hippocampus modulates the field and unit responses of the sensory cortices to peripheral stimuli (see references in Delacour, 1994); when that stimulation is applied at theta frequency, it increases the signal-to-noise ratio of the unit responses to clicks in the auditory cortex (Parmeggiani et al., 1982). More precisely, during spontaneous theta episodes in chronic rats, there is an increase in the signal-to-noise ratio of the unit responses evoked in the somatic cortex by vibrissa stimulation (Delacour et al., 1990b). Participation in arousal responses, novelty detection and control of the signal-to-noise ratio of sensory responses are obviously typical functions of a system A structure.

In conclusion, even in the case of the hippocampus, an interpretation in terms of activation seems to fit best the anatomo-physiology and neuropsychological data for animals and humans.

As already stressed, although each of the three brain systems is characterized by a general type of organization and function, it is not a homogeneous entity but it is divided into subsystems which may have specific properties. Thus, certain structures of system A may be involved in LM through peculiar states of activation or motivation. For example, one subsystem is specially involved in fear conditioning (LeDoux, 1996; Rolls, 1996a) – one of its main components being the amygdala (Bechara et al., 1995; Cahill et al., 1995; Maren & Fanselow, 1996; Markowitsch, 1994).

## System S

The role of S in learning and memory is more difficult to determine, due to the complexity of its functions and the lack of precise data on its neural implementation. However, if we assume that the prefrontal cortex is at least part of the anatomical basis of S, the clinical and experimental data fit the model fairly well.

In spite of their diversity (Stuss & Benton, 1984), the clinical data give a fairly coherent view of the memory function of the frontal cortex. Frontal lesions in humans produce memory deficits but these deficits differ from those produced by lesions to the C or A systems; they do not produce either amnesia with respect to any special type of information, or a global syndrome of the temporal or diencephalic type. Patients with frontal lobe lesions often perform well in some memory tests, like recognition tests of word lists and other materials, which require little reasoning, but they fail in tests of "strategic" memory, which require the subject to work with or reason about memories, in tasks involving metamemory and an internally generated strategy for guiding memory performance, such as free recall, recency or temporal order judgments, temporal dating of public events, frequency judgments, self-ordered pointing, and recollection of the source or the context of information (Gabrieli, 1996; Janowsky et al., 1989a, Janowsky et al., 1989b; Shimamura et al., 1990). In addition, working memory is impaired in frontal-lobe patients (Kimberg & Farah, 1993).

In normal man, brain imaging shows frontal activation in a wide variety of tasks (Buckner & Tulving, 1995; Grafton, 1995; Roland & Friberg, 1985; Roland & Seitz, 1988; Roland et al., 1989; Ungerleider, 1995). This activation does not depend on the type of information but all these tasks have the common feature of bringing into play conscious, voluntary activity. In agreement with the clinical data, brain imaging in normal subjects show that frontal regions are always involved, at least unilaterally, in working memory tasks (Buckner & Tulving, 1995; Coull et al., 1996; Courtney et al., 1996; D'Esposito et al., 1995; Grafton, 1995; McCarthy et al., 1996; McIntosh et al., 1996; Petrides et al., 1993; Smith et al., 1995; Ungerleider, 1995)

Despite the limitations of animal studies (e. g., the problem of evaluating metamemory in animals), their findings (Fuster, 1993; Goldman-Rakic, 1995, 1996) are in good agreement with those for humans. One of the most robust results of experimental neurology is the deficit produced in working memory tests by lesions to the prefrontal cortex in monkeys (Rosvold & Szwarcbart, 1964); the involvement of this cortex in these tasks was confirmed by unit recording in chronic monkeys (Funuashi et al., 1989; Fuster, 1973; Miller et al., 1996; Niki, 1974; Sakai & Hamada, 1981; Watanabe, 1990, 1996) and by data based on the 2-DG-technique (Friedman & Goldman-Rakic, 1994).

There is remarkable agreement between these data and the role in memory which our model ascribes to S. This role is one aspect of the general function of S: the control of goal-directed behavior. Within the framework of this function, S actively extracts from past experience, by different cognitive processes, the information relevant to the action in progress and to plans for the future. Working memory, which is *par excellence* the form of memory which underlies the action in progress, is a key component of this strategic memory; its time domain is not limited to the short term, because it is involved in the use of long term knowledge (Ericsson & Kintsch, 1995).

Within the framework of this general memory function, subsystems of S may have some specific role. According to Goldman-Rakic (1996), the dorsolateral region would be involved in spatial information processing, and the inferior convexity, in the processing of features or attributes of objects. Thus, at subsystem level, the dimension "type of information" would be relevant. However, according to Petrides (1995), the differences between these two regions concern the type of cognitive process and not the type of information processed.

In conclusion, the respective roles of C, A, and S may be characterized using the three dimensions of learning and memory defined above (Table 1, third column). For the sake of simplicity, we will first consider dimensions 2 and 3, i. e., the nature of the information learned and the type of cognitive process. In these dimensions, there is a clear distinction between the roles of C and A. As regards that of C, the nature of information learned is important in the sense that a specific module of C is involved in the encoding, retrieval and storage of that information depending on its sensory modality or its verbal or non-verbal character; on the other hand, the type of cognitive process is not relevant to the role of C. Conversely, for the role of A, at least for that of the subsystems involved in global amnestic syndromes, the information learned is irrelevant whereas the type of cognitive process is of critical importance because deficits in amnestic patients depend on the type of cognitive process but not on the nature of information learned: only the conscious, explicit form of memory (type I) is impaired. The role of S (insofar as it is represented by frontal regions) is also critically dependent on the type of cognitive process (dimension 3) and not on the type of information learned (dimension 2) (except perhaps at subsystem level). The short-term vs. long-term dimension only seems to be important for the role of the diencephalic and temporal lobe structures involved in global amnestic syndromes.

## C. Cooperation of the Three Systems

The respective parts of the three systems in LM may be isolated under certain normal conditions or by disease*, but under the usual normal conditions, the three systems cooperate. This has already been shown by synthetic views from brain imaging which allow direct observations of the dynamics of the interactions between all three systems, their evolution and their specificities according to the stage and nature of the task; these interactions may be studied in line and even formalized and quantified (McIntosh et al., 1996).

In animals, for technical reasons, such synthetic views are still not available, and the interactions of the three systems have to be reconstructed from the combined results of different approaches: anatomophysiology, unit recording in chronic animals, effects of lesions or pharmacological agents. For instance, the cooperation between C, A, and S has been well established in monkeys for spatial working memory tasks – delayed response (DR) and delayed alternation (DA) tests – in monkeys. The data (Diamond & Goldman-Rakic, 1989; Friedman & Goldman-Rakic, 1994; Goldman-Rakic, 1987) may be summarized as follows. DR and DA tests bring into play:

1. A certain level of attention which depends on an interaction between the prefrontal cortex and subsystems of A comprising monoaminergic structures of the brain stem, hippocampus and mediodorsal thalamus;

2. The use by the prefrontal cortex of the visuospatial information coded by the posterior parietal cortex, a module of system C;

---

*   In normal subjects, the part of the A and/or S systems in fully-mastered, overtrained tasks may be much less important than in the early stages of a novel task. In patients, brain lesions may produce double dissociations between forms of memory characteristic of different systems. For instance, patients with Parkinson's disease (lesions to the striatum) failed to learn a procedural task, but had intact memory of the training episode, while patients with "global" amnesia (limbic-diencephalic lesions) exhibited normal learning of the task but had severely impaired declarative memory of the training episode (Knowlton et al., 1996).

3. The programming of the correct motor responses and the inhibition of the incorrect ones, through an interaction between the frontal cortex and motor structures of C, i. e., the striatum and motor and premotor cortex.

There is a particularly clear-cut example of the influence exerted over C by the hypothalamic lateral area, a "motivation" structure of A. This area plays an important role in food intake and self-stimulation. Its stimulation was found to facilitate the acquisition of a classical conditioning and, concomitantly, to increase conditioned modifications of unit activity in the cat sensori-motor cortex (Aou et al., 1988; Kim et al., 1983; Woody et al., 1983). Likewise, stimulation of the NBM, one of the main components of the activating systems of the brain, was observed to facilitate conditioned changes in the unit activity of the frontal cortex (Rigdon & Pirch, 1986) as well as of the auditory cortex (Bakin & Weinberger, 1996).

Though less precise than data from animal experimentation, the clinical data also strongly suggest that interactions between C, A, and S are critical in some forms of memory: thus, certain features of the Korsakoff syndrome are "frontal" (Janowsky et al., 1989b,c; Kopelman, 1991; Shimamura et al., 1990) such as the lack of metamemory (Janowsky et al., 1989a,c); this might be because diencephalic lesions, especially those of the mediodorsal nucleus of the thalamus, which are the main causes of the Korsakoff's syndrome, may induce anterograde and retrograde degeneration in the frontal cortex. Likewise, memory deficits in Parkinson's disease have a "frontal" origin (Gabrieli, 1996). The cholinergic projections from the NBM to the cortex are particularly deteriorated in the elderly and Alzheimer patients (Amenta et al., 1991; Collerton, 1986; Decker, 1988), and these patients have deficits in both their working and long-term strategic memory; this suggests that the role of the frontal cortex in these forms of memory is critically dependent on the NBM. As the projections of this A structure facilitate the responses of the sensory cortex to natural stimuli, these projections may also be involved in type II forms of memory such as priming, classical conditioning (Bakin & Weinberger, 1996).

As indicated at the beginning of this section, brain imaging clearly shows that the three systems cooperate, in spite of the fact that in most cases, the experiments were not devised to show this co-operation but to study a few structures involved in a specific function. This restricted scope is one the reasons why the role of system A, which is by definition non specific, has been somewhat neglected. Another reason is that the activation level during the memory task and the level during the control task were probably very similar; thus, the activation measures of system A structures were greatly reduced by the subtraction method. In spite of these biases, the role of the A structures was clear in many experiments. As already stressed, the anterior cingulate is activated by a wide variety of tasks. The thalamus is also frequently involved, but in most cases the respective parts of the specific and non specific nuclei in the activation of that structure were not studied. However, recent data (Kinomura et al., 1996) clearly show the involvement of the intralaminar thalamic nuclei and activating structures of the brain stem in a visuomotor task. The prefrontal cortex and the relevant C modules (the visual and premotor cortices) were are also activated in this task.

Cooperation between the three systems has also been demonstrated in humans in a completely different task, the recall of words (Andreasen et al., 1995a,b). The data of these experiments and those from other studies suggest that "the human brain may contain a distributed multinodal general memory system." Nodes of this network include the frontal, association parietal and temporal cortices, the thalamus, the anterior and posterior cingulate, the precuneus and the cerebellum. There appears to be a commonality of components across tasks (e. g., retrieval and encoding) that is independent of the type of learned information, as well as differentiation of some components that may be information-specific or task-specific. Note that all three systems are represented in that general view on the memory system: S, by the prefrontal cortex; C, by the temporal and parietal association cortices; A, by the cingulate and also the thalamus with the restriction stressed above.

The roles of the precuneus and cerebellum are still difficult to define. However, the fact that the cerebellum is involved in a wide variety of memory tasks (Leiner et al., 1995) and not only in motor learning may be explained within the framework of an integrative and evolutionary view of the brain. Just as there is no a separate memory faculty, all cognitive functions, even the most sophisticated, probably have some relationships with the sensorimotor repertoire (Piaget, 1967); they may be derived from this repertoire through evolutionary mechanisms such as re-affectation. This has already been suggested for language in which the syntactic processes may be an extension of the ability of certain motor cortical structures to program complex manipulative acts (Greenfield, 1991; Wilkins & Wakefield, 1995). In this connection, the remarkable sensorimotor capacities of the cerebellum may be a rich source of cognitive processes. A similar explanation could be proposed for the involvement of the striatum in some forms of cognition, as suggested by the dementia frequently produced by its lesion in Parkinson

The contribution of each system to the co-operation between C, A, and S varies in importance depending on the relationships between the critical dimension of the system's function and the nature of the task. It also depends on the stage of the task. For example, in most tasks, the part played by the activating structures of the brain and/or S may be much more important in the initial and intermediate stages, i. e., as long as the situation is novel, the outcomes of the learning in progress, not fully predictable, and different strategies still in competition, than when the task is fully mastered: at this stage, the C modules brought into play may function quasi-autonomously.

## Conclusion

In conclusion, the main feature of our model is that the memory system does not have a single anatomical location but is constituted by the interaction of the three components of the brain – C, which codes information with the greatest precision, A, which controls the arousal/motivation states, and S, which pilots goal oriented behaviors. Depending on the type and stage of learning and memory, different sub-systems of C, A, and S, as well as different interaction modes, are brought into play.

This model is at least compatible with most experimental and clinical data, and it is directly supported by many of them. It has the advantage of accounting economically for the diversity of learning and memory phenomena, their integration in the behavior as a whole, and their intricate relationships with other aspects of cognitive activity, including perception, attention and metacognition.

In this integrative point of view, it emerges that any model of the memory system should be placed within the framework of evolutionary biology. Since learning and memory phenomena depend on a world which is structured by sensory and motor repertoires as well as on the computational capacities of the organism as shaped by evolution, data derived from neuroethology and ecology are necessary for a comprehensive view on the memory system.

## *Acknowledgments*

The preparation of this manuscript was supported by a grant from the US Army Research Institute's European Research Office (N68171–96-M-6141).

## References

Albert, M.S. (1997). The ageing brain: Normal and abnormal memory. *Philosophical Transactions of the Royal Society of London B, 352,* 1703–1709.

Amenta, F., Zaccheo, D., & Collier, W.L. (1991). Neurotransmitters, neuroreceptors and ageing. *Mechanisms of Ageing and Development, 61,* 249–273.

Andreasen, N.C., O'Leary, D.S., Cizadlo, T., Arndt, S., Rezai, K., Watkins, G.L., Ponto, L.L.B., & Hichwa, R.D. (1995a). I. PET studies of memory: Novel and practiced free recall of complex narratives. *Neuroimage, 2,* 284–295.

Andreasen, N.C., O'Leary, D.S., Cizadlo, T., Arndt, S., Rezai, K., Watkins, G.L., Ponto, L.L.B., & Hichwa, R.D. (1995b). II. PET studies of memory: Novel and practiced free recall of word lists. *Neuroimage, 2,* 296–305.

Aou, S., Oomura, Y., Woody, C.D., & Nishino, H. (1988). Effects of behaviorally rewarding hypothalamic electrical stimulation on intracellularly recorded neuronal activity in the motor cortex of awake monkeys. *Brain Research., 439,* 31–38.

Artola, A., & Singer, W. (1993). Long-term depression of excitatory synaptic transmission and its relationship to long-term potentiation. *Trends in Neurosciences., 16,* 480–487.

Bailey, C.H., Bartsch, D., & Kandel, E.C. (1996). Toward a molecular definition of long-term memory storage. *Proceedings of the National Academy of Sciences USA, 93,* 13445–13452.

Bakin, J.S., & Weinberger, N.M. (1990). Classical conditioning induces CS-specific receptive field plasticity in the auditory cortex of the guinea pig. *Brain Research, 536,* 271–286.

Bakin, J.S., & Weinberger, N.M. (1996). Induction of a physiological memory in the cerebral cortex by stimulation of the nucleus basalis. *Proceedings of the National Academy of Sciences USA 93,* 11219–11221.

Barbas, H. (1992). Architecture and cortical connections of the prefrontal cortex. *Advances in Neurology, 57,* 91–115.

Barnes, C.A. (1995). Involvement of LTP in memory: Are we "searching under the street light." *Neuron, 15,* 751–754.

Bechara, A., Tranel, D., Damasio, H., Adolphs, R., Rockland, C., & Damasio, A.R. (1995). Double dissociation of conditioning and declarative knowledge relative to the amygdala and hippocampus in humans. *Science, 269,* 1115–1118.

Bennett, T.L. (1971). Hippocampal theta activity and behavior. A review. *Communications in Behavioral Biology, 6,* 37–48.

Bibbig, A., Wennekers, T., & Palm, G. (1995). A neural network model of the cortico-hippocampal interplay and the representation of contexts. *Behavioral Brain Research, 66,* 169–175.

Bindman, L.J., Murphy, K., & Pockett, S. (1988). Post-synaptic control of the induction of long-term changes in efficacy of transmission in neocortical synapses in slices of rat brain. *Journal of Neurophysiology, 60,* 1053–1065.

Bliss, T.V.P., & Collingridge, G.L. (1993). A synaptic model of memory: Long-term potentiation in the hippocampus. *Nature, 361,* 31–39.

Bohus, B. (1994). Humoral modulation of learning and memory processes: Physiological significance of brain and peripheral mechanisms. In J. Delacour (Ed.), *The memory system of the brain* (pp. 337–364). Singapore: World Scientific Publishing.

Braun, A.R., Balkin, T.J., Wesensten, N.J., Carson, R.E., Varga, M., Baldwin, P., Selbie, S., Belenky, G., & Herkovitch, P. (1997). Regional cerebral blood flow throughout the sleep-wake cycle. An H₂O PET study. *Brain, 120,* 1173–1197.

Buckner, R.L., & Tulving, E. (1995). Neuroimaging studies of memory: Theory and recent PET results. In F. Boller & J. Grafman (Eds.), *Handbook of neuropsychology* (Vol. 10, pp. 439–466). Amsterdam: Elsevier.

Buhusi, C.V., & Schmajuk, N.A. (1996). Attention, configuration, and hippocampal function. *Hippocampus, 6,* 621–642.

Bunsey, M., & Eichenbaum, H. (1996). Conservation of hippocampal memory function in rats and humans. *Nature, 379,* 255–257.

Cahill, L., Babinsky, R., Markowitsch, H.J., & McGaugh, J.L. (1995). Amygdala and emotional memory. *Nature, 377,* 295–296.

Carpenter, G.A., & Grossberg, S. (1993). Normal and amnesic learning, recognition and memory by a neural model of cortico-hippocampal interactions. *Trends in Neurosciences., 16*, 131–137.

Castro-Alamancos, M.A., & Connors, B.W. (1995). Short-term synaptic enhancement and long-term potentiation in neocortex. *Proceedings of the National Academy of Sciences USA, 93*, 1335–1339.

Churchland, P.M. (1995). *The engine of reason, the seat of the soul.* Cambridge, MA: MIT Press.

Churchland, P.S., Koch, C., & Sejnowski, T.J. (1990). What is computational neuroscience? In E.L. Schwartz (Ed.), *Computational neuroscience* (pp. 46–55). Cambridge, MA: MIT Press.

Collerton, D. (1986). Cholinergic function and intellectual decline in Alzheimer's disease. *Neuroscience, 19*, 1–28.

Corkin, S., Amaral, G., Gonzales, R.G., Johnson, K.A., & Hyman, B.T. (1997). H.M.'s medial temporal lobe lesion: Findings from magnetic resonance imaging. *Journal of Neuroscience, 17*, 3964–3979.

Coull, J.T., Frith, C.D., Frackowiak, R.S.J., & Grasby, P.M. (1996). A fronto-parietal network for rapid visual information processing: A PET study of sustained attention and working memory. *Neuropsychologia, 34*, 1085–1095.

Courtney, S.M., Ungerleider, L.G., Keil, K., & Haxby, J.V. (1996). Object and spatial visual working memory activate separate neural systems in human cortex. *Cerebral Cortex, 6*, 39–49.

Craik, F.I.M. (1983). On the transfer of information from temporary to permanent memory. *Philosophical Transactions of the Royal Society of London B, 302*, 341–359.

Damasio, A. (1990). Category-related recognition defects as a clue to the neural substrate of knowledge. *Trends in Neurosciences, 13*, 95–98.

Damasio, A. (1996). The somatic marker hypothesis and the possible functions of the prefrontal cortex. *Philosophical Transactions of the Royal Society of London B, 351*, 1413–1420.

Damasio, A.C., Eslinger, P.J., Damasio, H., Hoesen, G.W. van, & Cornell, S. (1985). Multimodal amnesic syndrome following bilateral temporal and basal forebrain damage. *Archives of Neurology, 42*, 252–259.

Damasio, A., Tranel, D., & Damasio, H. (1990). Face agnosia and the neural substrate of memory. *Annual Review of Neuroscience, 13*, 89–109.

Daugman, J.G. (1990). Brain metaphor and brain theory. In E.L. Schwartz (Ed.), *Computational neuroscience* (pp.9–18). Cambridge, MA: MIT Press.

Decety, J. (1996). Do imagined and executed actions share the same neural substrate. *Cognitive Brain Research, 3*, 87–93.

Decker, M.W. (1988). The effects of aging on hippocampal and cortical projections of the forebrain cholinergic system. *Brain Research Reviews, 12*, 423–438.

Deecke, L. (1996). Planning, preparation, execution and imagery of volitional action. *Cognitive Brain Research, 3*, 59–64.

Dekker, J.A.M., Connor, D.J., & Thal, L.J. (1991). The role of cholinergic projections from the nucleus basalis in memory. *Neuroscience and Biobehavioral Reviews, 15*, 299–317.

Delacour, J. (1977a). Role of temporal lobe structures in visual short-term memory, using a new test. *Neuropsychologia, 15*, 681–684.

Delacour, J. (1977b). Cortex inférotemporal et mémoire visuelle à court terme chez le singe. Nouvelles données. *Experimental Brain Research, 28*, 301–310.

Delacour, J. (1980). Conditioned modifications of arousal and unit activity in the rat hippocampus. *Experimental Brain Research, 38,* 95–101.

Delacour, J. (1984). Two neuronal systems are involved in a classical conditioning in the rat. *Neuroscience, 13,* 705–715.

Delacour, J. (1988). A view on the memory system of the mammalian brain. In J. Delacour & J.C. Levy (Eds.), *Systems with learning and memory abilities* (pp. 83–104). Amsterdam: Elsevier.

Delacour, J. (1994). The memory system of the brain. In J. Delacour (Ed.), *The memory system of the brain* (pp. 1–65). Singapore: World Scientific Publishing.

Delacour, J. (1995). A central activation role for the hippocampus. *Neuroscience Research Communications, 16,* 1–10.

Delacour, J. (1997). Neurobiology of consciousness: An overview. *Behavioral Brain Research, 85,* 127–141.

Delacour, J., Houcine, O., & Costa, J.C. (1990a). Evidence for a cholinergic mechanism of "learned" changes in the responses of the barrel field neurons of the awake and undrugged rat. *Neuroscience, 34,* 1–8.

Delacour, J., Houcine, O., & Costa, J.C. (1990b). Modifications of the responses of barrel field neurons to vibrissal stimulation during theta in the awake and undrugged rat. *Neuroscience, 37,* 237–243.

Delacour, J., Houcine, O., & Talbi, B. (1987). "Learned" changes in the responses of the rat barrel field neurons. *Neuroscience, 23,* 63–71.

D'Esposito, M., Detre, J.A., Alsop, D.C., Shin, R.K., Atlas, S., & Grossman, M. (1995). The neural basis of the central executive system of working memory. *Nature, 378,* 279–281.

Diamond, A., & Goldman-Rakic, P.S. (1989). Comparison of human infants and rhesus monkeys on Piaget's AB task: Evidence for dependence on dorsolateral prefrontal cortex. *Experimental Brain Research, 74,* 24–40.

Dolphin, A.C. (1985). Long-term potentiation at peripheral synapses. *Trends in Neurosciences., 8,* 376–378.

Duncan, J. (1996). Attention, intelligence, and the frontal lobe. In M.S. Gazzaniga (Ed.), *The cognitive neurosciences* (pp. 721–733). Cambridge, MA: MIT Press.

Edelman, G.M. (1989). *The remembered present. A biological theory of consciousness.* New York: Basic Books.

Eichenbaum, H. (1996). Is the rodent hippocampus just for place? *Current Opinion in Neurobiology, 6,* 187–195.

Eichenbaum, H., Otto, T., & Cohen, N.J. (1992). The hippocampus – What does it do? *Behavioral and Neural Biology, 57,* 2–36.

Ericsson, K.A., & Kintsch, W. (1995). Long-term working memory. *Psychological Review, 102,* 211–245.

Essen, D.C. van, Anderson, C.H., & Felleman, D.J. (1992). Information processing in the primate visual system: An integrated systems perspective. *Science, 255,* 419–423.

Feany, M.B., & Quinn, W.G. (1995). A neuropeptide gene defined by the Drosophila memory mutant amnesiac. *Science, 268,* 869–873.

Flood, J.F., Morley, J.E., & Roberts, E. (1992). Memory-enhancing effects in male mice of pregnenolone and steroids metabolically derived from it. *Proceedings of the National Academy of Sciences USA, 89,* 1567–1571.

Fodor, J.D. (1983). *The modularity of the mind.* Cambridge, MA: MIT Press.

Francis, P.T., Pangalos, M.N., & Bowen, D.M. (1992). Animal and drug modelling for Alzheimer synaptic pathology. *Progress in Neurobiology, 39,* 517–545.

Fregnac, Y., Shulz, D., Thorpe, S., & Bienenstok, E. (1992). Cellular analogs of visual cortical epigenesis. I. Plasticity of orientation selectivity. *Journal of Neuroscience, 12,* 1280–1300.

Friedman, H.R., & Goldman-Rakic, P.S. (1994). Co-activation of prefrontal cortex and inferior parietal cortex in working memory taszs revealed by 2DG functional mapping in the rhesus monkey. *Journal of Neuroscience, 14,* 2775–2788.

Frith, C.D., Friston, K., Liddle, P.F., & Frackowiak, C.S.J. (1991). Willed action and the prefrontal cortex in man: A study with PET. *Proceedings of the Royal Society, London B, 244,* 241–246.

Funuashi, S., Bruce C.J., & Goldman-Rakic, P.S. (1989). Mnemonic coding of visual space in the monkey's dorsolateral prefrontal cortex. *Journal of Neurophysiology, 61,* 331–349.

Fuster, J.M. (1973). Unit activity in prefrontal cortex during delayed-response performance: Neuronal correlates of transient memory. *Journal of Neurophysiology, 35,* 61–78.

Fuster, J. (1993). Frontal lobes. *Current Opinion in Neurobiology, 3,* 160–165.

Fuster, J.M., & Jervey, J.P. (1981) Inferotemporal neurons distinguish and retain behaviorally relevant features of visual stimuli. *Science, 212,* 952–955.

Gabrieli, J.D.E. (1996). Memory systems analyses of mnemonic disorders in aging and age-related diseases. *Proceedings of the National Academy of Sciences USA, 93,* 13534–13540.

Glenberg, A.M. (1997). What memory is for. *Behavioral and Brain Sciences, 20,* 1–55.

Gluck, M.A., & Myers, C.E. (1997). Psychobiological models of hippocampal function in learning and memory. *Annual Review of Psychology, 48,* 481–514.

Goldman-Rakic, P.S. (1987). Circuitry of primate prefrontal cortex and regulation of behavior by representational memory. In V. Mountcastle (Ed.), *Handbook of physiology, the nervous system* (Vol. 5, pp. 373–417). Bethesda, MD: American Physiological Society.

Goldman-Rakic, P.S. (1988). Topography of cognition: Parallel distributed networks in primate association cortex. *Annual Review of Neuroscience, 11,* 137–156.

Goldman-Rakic, P.S. (1995). Cellular basis of working memory. *Neuron, 14,* 477–485.

Goldman-Rakic, P.S. (1996). The prefrontal landscape: Implications of functional architecture for understanding human mentation and the central executive. *Philosophical Transactions of the Royal Society of London B, 351,* 1445–1453.

Grafton, S.T. (1995). Mapping memory systems in the human brain. *Seminars in the Neurosciences, 7,* 157–163.

Grastyan, E., Lissak, I., Madarasz, I., & Donhoffer, H. (1959). Hippocampal electrical activity during the development of conditioned reflexes. *Electroencephalography and Clinical Neurophysiology, 11,* 409–430.

Greenfield, P.M. (1991). Language, tools and the brain: The ontogeny and phylogeny of hierarchically organized sequential behavior. *Behavioral and Brain Sciences, 14,* 531–595.

Greenspan, R.J. (1995). Flies, genes, learning and memory. *Neuron, 15,* 747–750.

Gross, C.G. (1973). Inferotemporal cortex and vision. In E. Stellar & J.M. Sprague (Eds.), *Progress in physiological psychology* (Vol. 5, pp. 77–123). New York: Academic Press.

Gross, C.G. (1992). Representation of visual stimuli in inferior temporal cortex. *Philosophical Transactions of the Royal Society of London B, 335,* 3–10.

Haken, H. (1994). A brain model in terms of synergetics. *Journal of Theoretical Biology, 171* (special issue on "Matter and Mind"), 75–85.

Haxby, J.V., Ungerleider, L.G., Horwitz B., Maisog, J.M., Rapoport, S.I., & Grady, C.L.

(1996). Face encoding and recognition in the human brain. *Proceedings of the National Academy of Sciences USA, 93,* 922–927.

Heiss, W.D., Pawlik, G., Holthoff, V., Kessler, J., & Szelies, B. (1992). PET correlates of normal and impaired memory functions. *Cerebrovascular and Brain Metabolism Reviews, 4,* 1–27.

Hirsch, J.C., & Crepel, F. (1992). Post synaptic $Ca^{2+}$ is necessary for the induction of LTP and LTD of monosynaptic EPSPs in rat prefrontal cortex in vitro. *Synapse 10,* 173–175.

Hobson, J.A., & Schmajuk, N.A. (1988). Brain state and plasticity: An integration of the reciprocal interaction model of sleep cycle oscillation with attentional models of hippo-campal function. *Archives Italiennes de Biologie, 126,* 209–224.

Hölscher, C. (1997). Long-term potentiation: A good model for learning and memory? *Progress in Neuro-Psychopharmacology, & Biological Psychiatry, 21,* 47–68.

Horel, J.A. (1978). The neuroanatomy of amnesia: A critique of the hippocampal memory hypothesis. *Brain, 101,* 403–445.

Horel, J.A. (1994). Some comments on the special, cognitive functions claimed for the hip-pocampus. *Cortex, 30,* 269–280.

Ingvar, D.H. (1985). Memory of the future. An essay on the temporal organization of con-scious awareness. *Human Neurobiology, 4,* 127–136.

Ingvar, D.H. (1994). The will of the brain: Cerebral correlates of willful acts. *Journal of Theoretical Biology, 171,* 7–12.

Iriki, A., Pavlides, C., Keller, A., & Asanuma, H. (1989). Long-term potentiation in the motor cortex. *Science, 245,* 1385–1387.

Jacoby, L.L. (1982). Knowing and remembering: Some parallels in the behavior of Korsa-koff patients and normals. In L.S. Cermak (Ed.), *Human memory and amnesia* (pp. 97–122). Hillsdale: Erlbaum.

Janowsky, J.S., Shimamura, A.P., Kritchevsky, M., & Squire, L.C. (1989a). Cognitive im-pairment following frontal lobe damage and its relevance to human amnesia. *Behavioral Neuroscience, 103,* 548–560.

Janowsky, J.S., Shimamura, A.P., & Squire, L.C. (1989b). Source memory impairment in patients with frontal lobe lesions. *Neuropsychologia, 27,* 1043–1046.

Janowsky, J.S., Shimamura, A.P., & Squire, L.C. (1989c). Memory and metamemory: Com-parisons between patients with frontal lobe lesions and amnesic patients. *Psychobiology, 17,* 3–11.

Joels, M., & De Kloet, E.R. (1992). Control of neuronal excitability by corticosteroid hor-mones. *Trends in Neurosciences, 15,* 25–30.

Kaas, J.H. (1996). The reorganization of sensory and motor maps in adult mammals. In M.S. Gazzaniga (Ed.), *The cognitive neurosciences* (pp. 51–71). Cambridge, MA: MIT Press.

Kawata, M. (1995). Role of steroid hormones and their receptors in structural organization in the nervous system. *Neuroscience Research, 24,* 1–46.

Kelso, J.A.S. (1995). *Dynamic patterns. The self-organization of brain and behavior.* Cam-bridge, MA: MIT Press.

Kennedy, C., Gillin, J.C., Mendelson, W., Suda, S., Miyaoka, M., Ito, M., Nakamura, C.K., Storch, F.I., Pettigrew, K., Mishkin, M., & Sokoloff, M. (1982). Local cerebral glucose utilization in non-rapid eye movement sleep. *Nature, 297,* 325–327.

Kim, E.H.J., Woody, C.D., & Bertier, N.E. (1983). Rapid acquisition of conditioned blink responses in cats following pairing of an auditory CS with glabella tap US and hypotha-lamic stimulation. *Journal of Neurophysiology, 49,* 767–779.

Kimberg, D.Y., & Farah, M.J. (1993). A unified account of cognitive impairments following frontal lobe damage: The role of working memory in complex, organized behavior. *Journal of Experimental Psychology: General, 122*, 411–428.

Kinomura, S., Larsson, J., Gulyas, B., & Roland, P. (1996). Activation by attention of the human reticular formation and thalamic intralaminar nuclei. *Science, 271*, 512–515.

Kirkwood, A., Dudek, S.M., Gold, J.T., Aizenman, C.D., & Bear, M.F. (1993). Common forms of synaptic plasticity in the hippocampus and the neocortex in vitro. *Science, 260*, 1518–1521.

Knight, R.T. (1996). Contribution of human hippocampal region to novelty detection. *Nature, 383*, 256–259.

Knowlton, B.J., Mangels, J.A., & Squire, L.R. (1996). A neostriatal habit learning system in humans. *Science, 273*, 1399–1402.

Kopelman, M.D. (1991). Frontal dysfunction and memory deficits in the alcoholic Korsakoff syndrome and Alzheimer-type dementia. *Brain, 114* (part 1), 117–137.

Koriat, A., & Goldsmith, M. (1996). Memory metaphors and the real life/laboratory controversy: Correspondence versus storehouse conceptions of memory. *Behavioral and Brain Sciences, 19*, 167–228.

Kosslyn, S.M., Behrmann, M., & Jeannerod, M. (1995) The cognitive neuroscience of mental imagery. *Neuropsychologia, 33*, 1335–1344.

Kossut, M. (1992). Plasticity of the barrel cortex. *Progress in Neurobiology, 39*, 389–422.

Le Bihan, D., Turner, R., Zeffiro, T.A., Cuenod, C.A., Jezzard, P., & Bonnerot, V. (1993) Activation of primary human visual cortex during visual recall: A magnetic resonance imaging study. *Proceedings of the National Academy of Sciences USA, 90*, 11802–11805.

LeDoux, J.E. (1996). In search of an emotional system in the brain: Leaping from fear to emotion and consciousness. In M.S. Gazzaniga (Ed.), *The cognitive neurosciences* (pp. 1049–1061). Cambridge, MA: MIT Press.

Leiner, H.C., Leiner, A.L., & Dow, R.S. (1995). The underestimated cerebellum. *Human Brain Mapping, 2*, 244–254.

Lhermitte, F. (1986). Human autonomy and the frontal lobes. Part II: Patient behavior in complex and social situations: The "Environmental Dependency Syndrome." *Archives of Neurology, 19*, 335–343.

Lhermitte, F., Pillon, B., & Serdaru, M. (1986). Human autonomy and the frontal lobes. Part I: Imitation and utilization behavior: A neuropsychological study of 75 patients. *Archives of Neurology, 19*, 326–334.

Linden, D.J. (1994). Long-term synaptic depression in the mammalian brain. *Neuron, 12*, 457–472.

Lisman, J. (1994). The CaM kinase II hypothesis for the storage of synaptic memory. *Trends in Neurosciences, 17*, 406–412.

Livingstone, M.S., & Hubel, D.H. (1981). Effects of sleep and arousal on the processing of visual information in the cat. *Nature, 291*, 554–561.

Lueschow, A., Miller, E.K., & Desimone, R. (1994). Inferior temporal mechanisms for invariant object recognition. *Cerebral Cortex, 4*, 523–531.

Luria, A.C. (1973). *The working brain. An introduction to neuropsychology*. New York: Basic Books.

Maquet, P., Degueldre, C., Delfiore, G., Aerts, J., Peters, J.M., Luxen, A., & Franck, G. (1997). Functional neuroanatomy of human slow wave sleep. *Journal of Neuroscience, 17*, 2807–2812.

Maquet, P., Peters, J.M., Aerts, J., Delfiore, G., Degueldre, C., Luxen, A., & Franck, G.

(1996). Functional neuroanatomy of human rapid-eye-movement sleep and dreaming. *Nature, 383*, 163–166.

Maren, S., & Fanselow, M.S. (1996). The amygdala and fear conditioning: Has the nut been cracked? *Neuron, 16*, 237–240.

Markowitsch, H.J. (1994). Effects of emotion and arousal on memory processing by the brain. In J. Delacour (Ed.), *The memory system of the brain* (pp. 210–240). Singapore: World Scientific Publishing.

Martin, A.H., Haxby, J.V., Lalonde, F.M., Wiggs, C.L., & Ungerleider, L. (1995). Discrete cortical regions associated with knowledge of color and knowledge of action. *Science, 270*, 102–105.

Martin, A.H., Wiggs, C.L., Ungerleider, L., & Haxby, J.V. (1996). Neural correlates of category specific knowledge. *Nature, 379*, 649–652.

Martin, K.C., & Kandel, E.C. (1996). Cell adhesion molecules, CREB and the formation of new synaptic. *Neuron, 17*, 567–570.

McCarthy, G., Puce, A., Constable, R.T., Krystal, J.H., Gore, J.C., & Goldman-Rakic, P.S. (1996). Activation of human prefrontal cortex during spatial and non-spatial working memory tasks measured by functional MRI. *Cerebral Cortex, 6*, 600–611.

McCormick, D.A., Wang, Z., & Huguenard, J. (1993). Neurotransmitter control of neocortical neurons activity and excitability. *Cerebral Cortex, 3*, 387–398.

McEntee, W.J., & Mair, C.G. (1984). Some behavioral consequences of neurochemical deficits in Korsakoff psychosis. In L. Squire & N. Butters (Eds.), *Neuropsychology of memory* (pp. 224–235). New York: Guilford.

McIntosh, A.R., & Gonzales-Lima, F. (1994). Structural equation modeling and its application to network analysis in functional brain imaging. *Human Brain Mapping, 2*, 2–22.

McIntosh, A.R., Grady, C.L., Haxby, J.V., Ungerleider, L.G., & Horwitz, B. (1996). Changes in limbic and prefrontal functional interactions in a working memory task for faces. *Cerebral Cortex, 6*, 571–584.

McKenna, T.M., McMullen, T.A., & Shlesinger, M.F. (1994). The brain as a dynamical physical system. *Neuroscience, 60*, 587–605.

Merzenich, M.M., Recanzone, G.H., Jenkins, W.M., & Grajski, K.A. (1990). Adaptive mechanisms in cortical networks underlying cortical contributions to learning and non declarative memory. *Cold Spring Harbor Symposia on Quantitative Biology, 55*, 873–887.

Mesulam, M. (1986). Frontal cortex and behavior. *Archives of Neurology, 19*, 320–325.

Mesulam, M. (1990). Large-scale neurocognitive networks and distributed processing for attention, language, and memory. *Archives of Neurology, 28*, 597–613.

Mesulam, M. (1995). The cholinergic contribution to neuromodulation in the cerebral cortex. *Seminars in the Neurosciences, 7*, 297–307.

Miyashita, Y. (1993). Inferior temporal cortex: Where visual perception meets memory. *Annual Review of Neuroscience, 16*, 245–263.

Miller, E.K., Erickson, C.A., & Desimone, R. (1996). Neural mechanisms of visual working memory in prefrontal cortex of the macaque. *Journal of Neuroscience, 16*, 5154–5167.

Mishkin, M. (1972). Cortical visual areas and their interaction (1972). In A.G. Karczmar & J.C. Eccles (Eds.), *The brain and human behavior* (pp. 187–208). Berlin: Springer.

Mishkin, M., & Delacour, J. (1975). An analysis of short-term visual memory in the monkey. *Journal of Experimental Psychology: Animal Behavior Processes, 1*, 326–334.

Mishkin, M., Malamut, B., & Bachevalier, J. (1984). Memories and habits: Two neural systems. In G. Lynch, J.L. McGaugh, & N.M. Weinberger (Eds.), *The neurobiology of learning and memory* (pp. 65–88). New York: Guilford.

Morris, M.K., Bowers, D., Chatterjee, A., & Heilman, K.M. (1992). Amnesia following a discrete basal forebrain lesion. *Brain, 115,* 1827–1847.

Muir, J.L., Everitt, B.J., & Robbins, T.W. (1994). AMPA-induced excitotoxic lesions of the basal forebrain: A significant role of the cortical cholinergic system in attentional function. *Journal of Neuroscience, 14,* 2313–2325.

Nauta, W.J.H. (1971). The problem of the frontal lobe: A reinterpretation. *Journal of Psychiatric Research, 8,* 167–187.

Neisser, U. (1997) The ecological study of memory. *Philosophical Transactions of the Royal Society of London B, 352,* 1697–1701.

Niki, H. (1974). Prefrontal activity during delayed alternation in the monkey: 1. Relation to direction of the response. *Brain Research, 68,* 185–196.

Nordeen, E.J., & Nordeen, K.W. (1990). Neurogenesis and sensitive periods in avian song learning. *Trends in Neurosciences., 13,* 31–36.

Nottebohm, F. (1991). Reassessing the mechanisms and origins of vocal learning in birds. *Trends in Neurosciences, 14,* 206–211.

Ojemann, G.A. (1991). Cortical organization of language. *Journal of Neuroscience, 11,* 2281–2287.

O'Keefe, J., & Nadel, L. (1978). *The hippocampus as a cognitive map.* Oxford: Clarendon.

Pandya, D.N., & Yeterian, D.H. (1996). Comparison of prefrontal architecture and connections. *Philosophical Transactions of the Royal Society of London B,351,* 1423–1432.

Pardo, J.V., Fox, P.T., & Raichle, M.E. (1991). Localization of a human system for sustained attention by positron emission tomography. *Nature, 349,* 61–64.

Parmeggiani, P.L., Lenzi, L., Azzaroni, A., & d'Alessandro, R. (1982). Hippocampal influence on unit responses elicited in the cat's auditory cortex by acoustic stimulation. *Experimental Neurology, 78,* 259–274.

Pavlides, C., Watanabe, Y., & McEwen, B.S. (1993). Effects of glucocorticoids on hippocampal long-term potentiation. *Hippocampus, 3,* 183–192.

Petrides, M. (1995). Functional organization of the human frontal cortex for mnemonic processing: Evidence from neuro-imaging studies. *Annals of the New York Academy of Sciences, 769,* 85–96.

Petrides, M., Alivasitos, B., Meyer, E., & Evans, A. (1993). Functional activation of the human frontal cortex during the performance of verbal working memory tasks. *Proceedings of the National Academy of Sciences USA, 90,* 878–882.

Piaget, J. (1967). *Biologie et connaissance.* Paris: Gallimard.

Pockett, S., & Figurov, A. (1993). Long-term potentiation and depression in the ventral horn of rat spinal cord in vitro. *NeuroReport, 4,* 97–99.

Pribram, K.H. (1984). The organization of memory in nonhuman primate model system. In L. Squire & N. Butters (Eds.), *Neuropsychology of memory* (pp. 340–363). New York: Guilford.

Racine, R.J., Wilson, D.A., Gingell, R., & Sunderland, D. (1986). Long-term potentiation in the interpositus and vestibular nuclei in the cat. *Experimental Brain Research, 63,* 158–162.

Rao, S.M., Binder, J.R., Bandettini, P.A., Hammeke, T.A., Yetkin, F.Z., Jasmanowicz, A., Lisk, L.M., Morris, G.L., Mueller, W.M., Estkowski, L.D., Wong, E.C., Haugh, V.M., & Hyde, J.S. (1993). Functional magnetic resonance imaging of complex human movements. *Neurology, 43,* 2311–2318.

Richardson, C.T., & DeLong, M.C. (1990). Context-dependent responses in primate nucleus basalis in a go/no go task. *Journal of Neuroscience, 10,* 2528–2540.

Ridley, C.M., & Ettlinger, G. (1973). Visual discrimination performance in the monkey: The activity of single cells in inferotemporal cortex. *Brain Research, 55,* 179–182.

Rigdon, G.C., & Pirch, G.H. (1986). Nucleus basalis involvement in conditioned neuronal responses in the rat frontal cortex. *Journal of Neuroscience, 6,* 2535–2542.

Rioux, G.F., & Robinson, G.B. (1995). Hippocampal long-term potentiation does not affect either discrimination learning or reversal learning of the rabbit nictating membrane response. *Hippocampus, 5,* 165–170.

Robin, N., & Holyak, K.J. (1996). Relational complexity and the function of the prefrontal cortex. In M.S. Gazzaniga (Ed.), *Cognitive neurosciences* (pp.9 89–997). Cambridge, MA: MIT Press.

Roland, P.E. (1987). Changes in brain blood flow and oxidative metabolism during mental activity. *News in Physiological Sciences, 2,* 120–124.

Roland, P.E., Eriksson, L., Widen, L., & Stone-Elander, S. (1989). Changes in regional cerebral oxidative metabolism induced by tactile learning and recognition in man. *European Journal of Neuroscience, 1,* 3–18.

Roland, P.E., & Friberg, L. (1985). Localization of cortical area activated by thinking. *Journal of Neurophysiology, 53,* 1219–1243.

Roland, P.E., & Seitz, R.J. (1988). Mapping of learning and memory functions in the human brain. In D. Ottoson (Ed.), *Visualization of brain function* (pp.141–151). London: MacMillan.

Rolls, E.T. (1996a). A theory of emotion and consciousness, and its application to understanding the neural basis of emotion. In M.S. Gazzaniga (Ed.), *The cognitive neurosciences* (pp.1091–1106). Cambridge, MA: MIT Press.

Rolls, E.T. (1996b). A theory of hippocampal function in memory. *Hippocampus, 6,* 601–620.

Rosvold, H.E., & Szwarcbart, M.K. (1964). Neural structures involved in delayed-response performance. In J.M. Warren & K. Akert (Eds.), *The frontal granular cortex and behavior* (pp. 1–15). New York: McGraw-Hill.

Rousseaux, M. (1994). Amnesia following limited thalamic lesions. In J. Delacour (Ed.), *The memory system of the brain* (pp. 241–277). New York: World Scientific Publishing.

Rudy, J.W., & Sutherland, R.J. (1995). Configural association theory and the hippocampal formation: An appraisal and reconfiguration. *Hippocampus, 5,* 375–389.

Rumelhart, D.E., & McClelland, J.L. (1987). *Parallel distributed processing.* Cambridge, MA: MIT Press.

Sakai, M., & Hamada, I. (1981). Intracellular activity and morphology of the prefrontal neurons related to visual attention task in behaving monkeys. *Experimental Brain Research, 41,* 195–198.

Schumacher, M., Robel, P., & Baulieu, E.E. (1996). Development and regeneration of the nervous systems: A role for neurosteroids. *Developmental Neuroscience, 18,* 6–21.

Shallice, T. (1988). *From neuropsychology to mental structure.* Cambridge: Cambridge University Press.

Shallice, T., & Burgess, P. (1996). The domain of supervisory processes and temporal organization of behavior. *Philosophical Transactions of the Royal Society of London B, 351,* 1405–1412.

Sharp, A.H., & Ros, C.A. (1996). Neurobiology of Huntington's disease. *Neurobiology of Disease, 3,* 3–15.

Shimamura, A.P., Janowsky, J.S., & Squire, L. (1990). Memory for the temporal order of events in patients with frontal lobe lesions and amnesic patients. *Neuropsychologia, 28,* 803–813.

Smith, E.E., Jonides, J., Koeppe, R.A., Awh, E., Schumacher, E.H., & Minoshima, S. (1995). Spatial versus object working memory: PET investigations. *Journal of Cognitive Neuroscience, 7,* 337–356.

Squire, L. (1992). Memory and the hippocampus – a synthesis from findings with rats, monkeys, and humans. *Psychological Review, 99,* 195–231.

Squire, L. (1993). The hippocampus and spatial memory. *Trends in Neurosciences, 16,* 56–57.

Squire, L., & Zola-Morgan, S. (1991). The medial temporal lobe memory system. *Science, 253,* 1380–1386.

Squire, L., & Zola-Morgan, S. (1996). Structure and function of declarative and non declarative memory. *Proceedings of the National Academy of Sciences USA, 93,* 13515–13522.

Steriade, M. (1991). Alertness, quiet sleep, dreaming. In A. Peters (Ed.), *Cerebral cortex* (Vol. 9, pp. 279–356). New York: Plenum.

Steriade, M. (1995). Neuromodulatory systems of thalamus and neocortex. *Seminars in the Neurosciences, 7,* 361–370.

Stuss, D.T. (1991). Self, awareness, and the frontal lobes: A neuropsychological perspective. In J. Strauss & G.C. Goethals (Eds.), *The self: Interdisciplinary approaches* (pp. 254–278). Berlin: Springer.

Stuss, D.T., & Benton, D.F. (1984). Neuropsychological studies of the frontal lobes. *Psychological Bulletin, 95,* 3–28.

Sutor, B., & Hablitz, J.J. (1989). Long-term potentiation in frontal cortex: Role of NMDA-modulated polysynaptic excitatory pathways. *Neuroscience Letters, 97,* 111–117.

Talland, G.A. (1965). *Deranged memory.* New York: Academic Press.

Tanaka, K. (1996). Inferotemporal cortex and object vision. *Annual Review of Neurosciences, 19,* 109–139.

Tanaka, K., Saito, H., Fukada, Y., & Poryia, M. (1991). Coding visual images of objects in the inferotemporal cortex of the macaque monkey. *Journal of Neurophysiology, 66,* 170–189.

Tsumoto, T. (1994). Long-term potentiation and depression in visual cortex.: Functional significance and molecular basis. In J. Delacour (Ed.), *The memory system of the brain* (pp. 493–523). Singapore: World Scientific Publishing.

Tulving, E. (1987). Multiple memory systems and consciousness. *Human Neurobiology, 6,* 67–80.

Tulving, E. (1996). Organization of memory: Quo vadis? In M.S. Gazzaniga (Ed.), *The cognitive neurosciences* (pp. 839–847). Cambridge, MA: MIT Press.

Ungerleider, L. (1995). Functional brain imaging studies of cortical mechanisms for memory. *Science, 270,* 769–775.

Vinogradova, O. (1975). Functional organization of the limbic system in the process of registration of information: Facts and hypotheses. In R.L. Isaacson & K. Pribram (Eds.), *The hippocampus* (Vol. 2, pp. 3–69). New York: Plenum.

Vinogradova, O.S. (1995). Expression, control, and probable functional significance of the neuronal theta-rhythm. *Progress in Neurobiology, 45,* 523–583.

Voronin, L. (1994). Mechanisms of long-term potentiation. In J. Delacour (Ed.), *The memory system of the brain* (pp. 524–589). Singapore: World Scientific Publishing.

Wallin, A., & Gottfries, C.G. (1990). Biochemical substrates in normal aging and Alzheimer's disease. *Pharmacopsychiatry, 23,* 37–43.

Warren, S.G., Humphreys, A.G., Juraska, J.M., & Greenough, W.T. (1995). LTP varies across the estrous cycle: Enhanced synaptic plasticity in proestrus rats. *Brain Research, 703,* 26–30.

Watanabe, M. (1990). Prefrontal unit activity during associative learning in the monkey. *Experimental Brain Research, 80,* 296–309.

Watanabe, M. (1996). Reward expectancy in primate prefrontal neurons. *Nature, 382,* 629–632.

Weinberger, N.M. (1995). Dynamic regulation of receptive fields and maps in the adult sensory cortex. *Annual Review of Neuroscience, 18,* 129–158.

Wheeler, M.A., Stuss, D.T., & Tulving, E. (1997). Toward a theory of episodic memory: The frontal lobes and autonoetic consciousness. *Psychological Bulletin, 121,* 331–354.

Wiener, S.I. (1996). Spatial, behavioral and sensory correlates of hippocampal CA1 complex spike cell activity: Implications for information processing functions. *Progress in Neurobiology, 49,* 355–361.

Wilkins, W.K., & Wakefield, J. (1995). Brain evolution and neurolinguistics preconditions. *Behavioral and Brain Sciences, 18,* 161–226.

Woody, C.D., Kim, E.H.J., & Berthier, N.E. (1983). Effect of hypothalamic stimulation on unit responses recorded from neurons of sensorimotor cortex of awake cats during conditioning. *Journal of Neurophysiology, 49,* 780–791.

Woolf, N.J. (1991). Cholinergic systems in mammalian brain and spinal cord. *Progress in Neurobiology, 37,* 475–524.

Young, J.Z. (1987). *Philosophy and the Brain.* Oxford: Oxford University Press.

# Memory and Brain: Unresolved Issues

*Hans J. Markowitsch and Lars-Göran Nilsson*

The previous chapters shed light on many of the main issues of brain–behavior interrelationships with respect to memory processing. The chapters demonstrated that there is already a quite sophisticated level in study designs and methods, and also much integration on the theoretical level.

We can speculate on why individuals – both human and non-human ones – have memory and how information processing is organized by the brain. Memory is found all over the animal kingdom, and there are some scientists who even speculate about memory mechanisms in plants such as mimosas. In evolutionary terms, the roots of memory may lie in its value for the survival of the individual and the species. An individual which could memorize which meal is delicious, which snake is dangerous and which place contains food most reliably, would likely have a safer and longer life. Survival of the species was promoted by memorizing, for example, the particular smell of companions eager or prepared for sexual engagement.

Both the search for food and that for sexual partners largely depend on the sense of smell, on emotions, and on spatial orientation – features which in the animal kingdom are controlled by the limbic system, originally called the smell brain (rhinencephalon) (Herz & Engen, 1996; Markowitsch, 1999). No wonder that in humans smell-related memories largely resists on verbalization, but are quite resistant to extinction as well: Under appropriate recognition conditions, when for instance a smell to which one had been exposed years ago reoccurs, the whole constellation of the event may easily be revived. (Recognition memory furthermore is the most typical paradigm in animal memory research.)

That an emotional engagement grossly facilitates information acquisition and preservation is omniscience. It was, however, a considerable way from Papez' (1937) "proposed circuit of emotion" – constituted by limbic system structures – to their implication in memory, and an even longer way to recognize the interdependence of emotion and memory processing (Markowitsch, 1994) which became particularly obvious in patients with damage to limbic structures such as the amygdala (Cahill et al., 1995; Markowitsch et al., 1994), and the septum (Cramon, Markowitsch, & Schuri, 1993) and manifested grossly impaired memories due to their emotional disorganization.

Phylogenetically explainable are also subdivisions of memory. The more complex the social behavior and the longer offsprings were dependent on their parents, the more important became learning and memorizing of flexible acts and individualized stimuli. Orangutan children, which stay with their mother for eight years and learn advantages and disadvantages of numerous tropical plants and how to survive in their environment, are good examples for the development of generalizations, concept formations, imitating, and insightful learning.

We have, however, much less idea about how information is consolidated and how it is represented by the brain. These puzzles can only be solved by combining results from all available relevant sources. They require a strong interdisciplinary approach with individual scientists having at least a basic level of background knowledge of the neighboring fields. On the other hand, they allow not only to formulate relevant approachable questions, but also to work interactively on solutions. As mentioned in Chapter 1, and as is evident from several of the other chapters, functional neuroimaging is a research tool which demonstrates particularly clearly the interaction among neuroscientists from different disciplines and the new and in part unexpected results obtainable by a theory-guided, technically sophisticated application.

In spite of this promising framework there are still more unresolved than resolved problems in the field of cognitive neuroscience of memory. Most remote from a satisfying answer is the question of memory representation in the brain. Theories and hypotheses range from modifications of the "grandmother cell" concept via cell assemblies (Sakurai, 1998) and networks (Mesulam, 1998) to holographic ideas (Pribram, 1971, 1986). For some scientists all the conventional ideas for searching for a representation of memory in the brain have failed, so that more radical views should be adopted (Hameroff, 1998; Romijn, 1997). Romijn (1997), for example, proposed that only procedural memories (i. e., episodic and semantic or knowledge-based information) are represented outside the brain in what he termed the "submanifest order of being."

The controversy over the issue of memory consolidation is represented by the articles of Knowlton and Fanselow (1998) and Moscovitch and Nadel (1998). Simplified, Knowlton and Fanselow assume an in principal time-limited phase of memory consolidation which is dependent on the hippocampal complex, while Moscovitch and Nadel proposed that (at least some) memories are dependent life-long on the hippocampal system.

A further unresolved question is to what degree similar structures are engaged in encoding and retrieval of information. As is frequently the case in the field of neuroscience, there are both similarities and dissimilarities or overlap and divergence in structures.

As an example, results based on functional neuroimaging have shown that similar regions – namely portions of the prefrontal cortex – are engaged in information acquisition and retrieval (Fletcher, Frith, & Rugg, 1997; Shallice et al., 1994; Tulving et al., 1994). On the other hand, there is some dissimilarity in that for episodic information prefrontal regions of the left hemisphere are engaged in encoding, and prefrontal regions of the right hemisphere in the stage of information retrieval: the HERA-model of Tulving et al. (1994).

When it comes to more time remote and affect-laden forms of information retrieval, the situation becomes even more complex (Fink et al., 1996; Markowitsch, 1997). Then, in addition, (anterior) temporal regions of mainly the right hemisphere are engaged. Both neuroimaging data and results from brain-damaged patients (Kroll et al., 1997; Markowitsch, 1995) are difficult to interpret as they are more of a graduated than of an all-or-none character: There might be some involvement of medial temporal lobe structures (hippocampal and amygdaloid complex) as well, but clearly less so than for information encoding.

Even more confusing and surprising are results from patients with very similar degrees of memory impairments – both in anterograde and retrograde directions – and very minor or no measurable brain damage at all (see Chapter 9).

Findings of this kind may reinforce some extreme views of memory representation (Romijn, 1997), while they might also be interpretable more conventionally, namely by a changed brain metabolism, in particular with respect to neurotransmitters, neuromodulators, and neurohormones (Kaufer, Friedman, Seldman, & Soreq, 1998; Sapolsky, 1998). The probably positive message from these findings is the need of a stronger convergence of disciplines, which in the beginning of brain research were once unified anyway: Brodmann, known widely for his cytoarchitectonical brain descriptions (Brodmann, 1909), had worked neuropsychologically as well (Brodmann, 1902, 1904). Similarly, Hering, who is most well-known for his color-theory, wrote about memory (Hering, 1921). Similar parallels could be listed for Hitzig, Freud, Munk, Pick, Nissl, von Monakow and many other outstanding scientists from the turn of the century (Markowitsch, 1992). While the present-day sophistication in techniques hinders an individual to be competent in various disciplines, the methodological broadness leads to a very fruitful and promising convergence, especially in the field of memory research, which undoubtedly in the near future will provide significant insights into the neural control of our conscious being.

# References

Brodmann, K. (1902). Experimenteller und klinischer Beitrag zur Psychopathologie der polyneuritischen Psychose [Experimental and clinical contribution to the psychopathology of the polyneuritic psychoses]. *Journal für Psychologie und Neurologie, 1*, 225–246.

Brodmann, K. (1904). Experimenteller und klinischer Beitrag zur Psychopathologie der polyneuritischen Psychose. B. Experimenteller Teil. [Experimental and clinical contribution to the psychopathology of the polyneuritic psychoses. B. Experimental part.]. *Journal für Psychologie und Neurologie, 3*, 1–48.

Brodmann, K. (1909). *Vergleichende Lokalisationslehre der Grosshirnrinde in ihren Prinzipien dargestellt auf Grund des Zellenbaues* [Comparative study of the localization in the cerebral cortex, demonstrated in its principles on the basis of cytoarchitecture]. Leipzig: Barth.

Cahill, L., Babinsky, R., Markowitsch, H.J., & McGaugh, J.L. (1995). Involvement of the amygdaloid complex in emotional memory. *Nature, 377*, 295–296.

Cramon, D.Y. von, Markowitsch, H.J., & Schuri, U. (1993). The possible contribution of the septal region to memory. *Neuropsychologia, 31*, 1159–1180.

Fink, G.R., Markowitsch, H.J., Reinkemeier, M., Bruckbauer, T., Kessler, J., & Heiss, W.-D. (1996). Cerebral representation of one's own past: Neural networks involved in autobiographical memory. *Journal of Neuroscience, 16*, 4275–4282.

Fletcher, P.C., Frith, C.D., & Rugg, M.D. (1997). The functional neuroanatomy of episodic memory. *Trends in Neurosciences, 20*, 213–218.

Hameroff, S.R. (1998). "Funda-Mentality": Is the conscious mind subtly linked to a basic level of the universe? *Trends in Cognitive Sciences, 2*, 119–124.

Hering, E. (1921). Ueber das Gedächtnis als eine allgemeine Funktion der organisierten Materie. *Vortrag gehalten in der feierlichen Sitzung der Kaiserlichen Akademie der Wissenschaften in Wien am XXX. Mai MDCCCLXX* [On memory as a general function of organized matter. Lecture given in the high session of the Imperial Academy of Sciences in Vienna on the 30th of May in 1870] (3rd ed.). Leipzig: Akademische Verlagsgesellschaft.

Herz, R.S., & Engen, T. (1996). Odor memory: Review and analysis. *Psychonomic Bulletin and Reviews, 3*, 300–313.

Kaufer, D., Friedman, A., Seldman, S., & Soreq, H. (1998). Acute stress facilitates long-lasting changes in cholinergic gene expression. *Nature, 393*, 373–377.

Knowlton, B.J., & Fanselow, M.S. (1998). The hippocampus, consolidation and on-line memory. *Current Opinion in Neurobiology, 8*, 293–296.

Kroll, N.E.A., Markowitsch, H.J., Knight, R., & Cramon, D.Y. von (1997). Retrieval of old memories – The temporo-frontal hypothesis. *Brain, 120*, 1377–1399.

Markowitsch, H.J. (1992). *Intellectual functions and the brain. An historical perspective.* Toronto: Hogrefe & Huber.

Markowitsch, H.J. (1994). Effects of emotion and arousal on memory processing by the brain. In J. Delacour (Ed.), *Memory, learning and the brain* (pp. 210–240). Singapore: World Scientific Publ.

Markowitsch, H.J. (1995). Which brain regions are critically involved in the retrieval of old episodic memory? *Brain Research Reviews, 21*, 117–127.

Markowitsch, H.J. (1997). The functional neuroanatomy of episodic memory retrieval. *Trends in Neurosciences, 20*, 557–558.

Markowitsch, H.J. (in press). The limbic system. In R. Wilson, & F. Keil (Eds.), *The MIT encyclopedia of cognitive science.* Cambridge, MA: MIT Press.

Markowitsch, H.J., Calabrese, P., Würker, M., Durwen, H.F., Kessler, J., Babinsky, R., Brechtelsbauer, D., Heuser, L., & Gehlen, W. (1994). The amygdala's contribution to memory – a PET-study on two patients with Urbach-Wiethe disease. *NeuroReport, 5,* 1349–1352.

Mesulam, M.-M. (1998). From sensation to cognition. *Brain, 121,* 1013–1052.

Moscovitch, M., & Nadel, L. (1998). Consolidation and the hippocampal complex revisited: In defense of the multiple-trace model. *Current Opinion in Neurobiology, 8,* 297–300.

Papez, J.W. (1937). A proposed mechanism of emotion. *Archives of Neurology and Psychiatry, 38,* 725–743.

Pribram, K.H. (1971). *Languages of the brain. Experimental paradoxes and principles in neuropsychology.* Englewood Cliffs, NJ: Prentice-Hall.

Pribram, K.H. (1986). Nonlocality and localization in the primate forebrain. In S.B. Filskov & T.J. Boll (Eds.), *Handbook of clinical neuropsychology* (Vol. 2, pp. 606–651). New York: Wiley.

Romijn, H. (1997). About the origin of consciousness. A new, multidisciplinary perspective on the relationship between brain and mind. *Proceedings van de Koninklijke Nederlandse Akademie van Wetenschappen, 100,* 181–267.

Sakurai, Y. (1998). The search for cell assemblies in the working brain. *Behavioural Brain Research, 91,* 1–13.

Shallice, T., Fletcher, P., Frith, C.D., Grasby, P., Frackowiak, R.S.J., & Dolan, R.J. (1994). Brain regions associated with acquisition and retrieval of verbal episodic memory. *Nature, 368,* 633–635.

Tulving, E., Kapur, S., Craik, F.I.M., Moscovitch, M., & Houle, S. (1994). Hemispheric encoding/retrieval asymmetry in episodic memory: Positron emission tomography findings. *Proceedings of the National Academy of Sciences of the USA, 91,* 2016–2020.

# Author Index

**A**

Abdi, H. 135, 146
Ackell, A.B. 100
Adams, R.D. 56, 78
Adolfsson, R. 40, 160, 161
Adolphs, R. 196, 204, 260
Aerts, J. 265
Aggen, S.H. 109
Aguirre, G.K. 64, 78
Aizenman, C.D. 265
Akert, K. 268
Akil, H. 203, 211
Alberoni, M. 41, 73, 76
Albert, M.S. 41, 45, 54, 65, 75, 77, 86, 101, 239, 259
Albright, T.D. 95, 101
Aldenhoff, J. 202, 203, 204
Alexander, M.P. 56, 72
Alivisatos, B. 63, 77, 267
Alkire, M.T. 52
Allain, A.N. 196, 210
Alpert, N.M. 41, 45, 54, 65, 77, 86, 101, 210
Alsop, D.C. 73, 262
Alvarez, P. 4, 9, 87, 88, 98, 101
Amaral, D.G. 56, 58, 72, 77, 82, 99, 101, 102, 195, 209
Amaral, G. 261
Amenta, F. 239, 257, 259
Andermann, F. 100
Anderson, C.H. 262
Anderson, J.A. 115, 139
Anderson, J.R. 171, 189
Andreasen, N.C. 25, 37, 86, 96, 98, 258, 259
Andreasson, L.A. 162
Andrews, S. 138, 145
Anzini, A. 76
Aou, S. 257, 260
Arbib, M.A. 67, 74
Arndt, S. 37, 98, 259
Arnett, P.A. 59, 72
Arnsten, A.F.T. 117, 139

arrett, D.H. 204
Artola, A. 247, 260
Asanuma, H. 264
Ashby, F.G. 127, 140
Atlas, S. 73, 262
Austin, E.J. 141
Awh, E. 75, 269
Azzaroni, A. 267

**B**

Babcock, R.L. 107, 140
Babinsky, R. 196, 205, 208, 260, 274, 275
Bachevalier, J. 82, 100, 266
Bachoud-Lévi, A.-C. 165, 190
Backer Cave, C. 87, 98
Backhovens, H. 160
Bäckman, L. 16, 37, 39, 40, 153, 154, 155, 160, 161, 162
Baddeley, A. 39, 58, 62, 68, 73, 76, 144, 163, 164, 171, 185, 189
Baer, R.A. 138, 140
Bailey, C.H. 239, 260
Baker, J.R. 77, 101
Baker, S.C. 47, 52
Bakin, J.S. 246, 257, 260
Baldi, P. 121, 140
Baldwin, P. 260
Balinsky, B. 106, 140
Balkin, T.J 260
Balon, R. 202, 209
Balota, D.A. 74
Baltes, P.B. 5, 8, 103, 104, 106, 107, 109, 110, 126, 137, 139, 140, 143, 144
Bandettini, P.A. 267
Barbarotto, R. 197, 201, 204
Barbas, H. 244, 260
Barkhof, F. 75
Barnes, C.A. 239, 260
Barnes, J.M. 121, 140
Baron, J.C. 38, 52, 58, 74
Barrett, D.H. 202

Bartolomeo, P. 165, 190
Bartsch, D. 260
Basso, A. 189
Baulieu, E.E. 268
Bear, M.F. 265
Beauvois, M.F. 164, 190
Bechara, A. 254, 260
Bechtel, W. 104, 140
Bechterew, W. von 79, 98
Becker, J.T. 151, 160
Beckers, K. 237
Behniea, H. 99
Behrmann, M. 265
Beiser, D.G. 104, 141, 142
Bekerian, D.A. 190
Belenky, G. 260
Bell, B.D. 72, 73
Benali, K. 38
Benbow, C. 160
Bench, C. 47, 53, 75
Bennett, E.L. 236
Bennett, T.L. 252, 260
Benson, D.F. 35, 41
Bental, E. 102
Benton, D.F. 254, 269
Bergson, H. 168, 170, 189
Berlyne, N. 185, 189
Bernardin, L. 72
Berns, G.S. 104, 140
Berthier, M.L. 196, 210
Berthier, N.E. 270
Bertier, N.E. 264
Bettinardi, V. 73, 76, 77
Bhatia, S. 56, 73
Bibbig, A. 253, 260
Bienenstok, E. 263
Binder, J.R. 267
Bindman, L.J. 247, 260
Birrell, P. 231, 235
Birren, J.E. 111, 135, 140, 146
Bjork, E.L. 41
Bjork, R.A. 41
Bjorklund, D.F. 138, 140
Black, S.E. 40
Blair, R.C. 61, 75
Blaxton, T.A. 47, 52, 220, 221, 222, 234
Bleich, A. 203, 204
Blennow, K. 147, 161
Bliss, T.V.P. 239, 247, 260
Bloom, F.E. 116, 145

Bly, B.M. 68, 73
Bohus, B. 248, 260
Boissé, M.-F. 165, 190
Boles Ponto, L.L. 37, 98
Boll, T.J. 275
Boller, F. 37, 42, 73, 260
Bonda, E. 71, 73
Bonnerot, V. 265
Bookheimer, S.Y. 56, 73
Bookstein, F.L. 40, 52, 53
Bouras, C. 236
Boutelle, W. 58, 78
Bowen, D.M. 263
Bower, G.H. 171, 189
Bowers, D. 267
Bowers, J.S. 224, 234
Brand, C.R. 141
Brandel, J.-P. 202, 204
Brandt, J.P. 56, 74
Braun, A.R. 241, 260
Brayne, C. 161
Brechtelsbauer, D. 208, 275
Bremner, J.D. 202, 204
Breslau, N. 203, 205
Bressi, S. 41, 73, 76
Breteler, M.M. 161
Breuer, J. 194, 205
Brewer, J.B. 86, 99
Brewin, C.R. 202, 205, 207
Brodeur, D. 104, 138, 144
Brodmann, K. 273, 274
Broeckhoven, C. Van 148, 159, 160, 161
Broekhooven, C. Van 161
Bronen, R.A. 204
Brooks, D.N. 213, 234
Brown, A.S. 224, 228, 234
Brown, G.M. 39, 44, 53, 75, 100
Brown, G.W. 100
Brown, H.D. 51, 52
Brown, J. 9
Brown, M.W. 88, 98
Bruce C.J. 263
Bruckbauer, T. 38, 48, 52, 206, 274
Bryan, A.I. 137, 141
Bucht, G. 40, 161
Buck, A. 4, 8, 79, 92, 93, 94, 99
Buckner, R.L. 24, 25, 26, 27, 29, 33, 37, 40,
    46, 52, 246, 250, 253, 254, 255, 260
Buhusi, C.V. 252, 260
Bumke, O. 210

Bunsey, M. 252, 260
Burgess, P. 243, 268
Burgess, P.W. 163, 164, 171, 174, 189
Burgl, G. 195, 205
Burke, D.M. 117, 143
Burrows, E.H. 195, 207
Burt, C. 106, 137, 140
Butters, N. 57, 58, 73, 77, 195, 209, 236, 237, 266, 267

**C**

Cabeza, R. 22, 23, 29, 34, 37, 38, 39, 40, 45, 50, 51, 52, 53, 65, 67, 73, 75, 101
Cacioppo, J.T. 196, 205
Cahill, L. 46, 52, 196, 205, 209, 254, 260, 271, 274
Cahusac, P.M.B. 88, 101
Calabrese, P. 35, 38, 40, 195, 200, 205, 208, 275
Caltagirone, C. 41, 76, 234
Campbell, M.J. 236
Canal, N. 76
Capelli, S. 205
Capitani, E. 189
Cappa, S.F. 41, 58, 60, 69, 73, 76, 77, 208
Cardon, L.R. 154, 160
Carlesimo, G.A. 214, 216, 218, 223, 226, 227, 234
Carlier, I.V.E. 202, 205
Carpenter, G.A. 252, 261
Carr, C.A. 77, 101
Carson, R.E. 142, 260
Case, R. 138, 140
Castro-Alamancos, M.A. 247, 261
Catts, S.V. 138, 145
Ceballos-Baumann, A.O. 77
Cendes, F. 100
Cerella, J. 113, 140
Cermak, L.S. 195, 209, 214, 218, 231, 235, 264
Challis, B.H. 236, 237
Chandler, K. 235
Charness, M.E. 56, 73
Charney, D.S. 196, 202, 204, 210
Chatterjee, A. 267
Chauvin, Y. 121, 140
Chelune, G.J. 138, 140
Chen, X. 162
Chermak, G.D. 137, 140
Chiarello, C. 225, 235

Chorney, K. 160
Chorney, M.J. 148, 160
Christen, Y. 236
Christensen, H. 109, 140, 231, 235
Chronister, R.B. 116, 141
Church, B.A. 236
Churchland, P.M. 240, 261
Churchland, P.S. 103, 104, 140, 143, 240, 261
Cipollotti, L. 76
Cipolotti, L. 41, 183, 190
Cizadlo, T. 37, 98, 259
Claparède, E. 170, 189
Clark, C.R. 116, 141
Clarke, M. 161
Clarke, R. 215, 235
Clipp, E.C. 202, 206
Cloetta, G. 194, 210
Cocchini, G. 201, 204
Cohen, J.D. 104, 145
Cohen, L. 76
Cohen, N.J. 4, 8, 87, 89, 90, 95, 96, 98, 213, 235, 249, 262
Cohen, S. 203, 206
Collerton, D. 257, 261
Collier, W.L. 259
Collingridge, G.L. 239, 247, 260
Collins, A.F. 39
Collins, G.H. 56, 78
Collins, L.M. 144
Colombo, F. 73
Comalli, P.E. 138, 141
Comar, D. 75
Comi, G. 76
Connelly, A. 42, 102
Connor, D.J. 261
Connors, B.W. 247, 261
Constable, R.T. 266
Conway, M. 39
Conway, M.A. 172, 175, 189
Cooper, B. 161
Cooper, L.A. 41
Copeland, J.R. 161
Coper, L.A. 236
Corballis, M.C. 16, 42
Corkin, S. 77, 101, 213, 235, 236, 253, 261
Cornelius, S.W. 106, 140
Cornell, S. 261
Corvelli, A. 118, 144
Corwin, J.V. 117, 141
Costa, J.C. 262

Costes, N. 73
Coull, J.T. 255, 261
Courtney, S.M. 255, 261
Cowan, W.M. 58, 72
Cox, K. 236
Craik, F.I.M. 3, 4, 9, 20, 35, 37, 38, 39, 42,
    44, 51, 53, 54, 75, 78, 95, 100, 102, 123,
    144, 190, 215, 235, 236, 239, 261, 275
Craik, G. 195, 210
Cramon, D.Y. von 56, 73, 195, 207, 271, 274
Crepel, F. 247, 264
Croft, J.B. 202, 204
Cronbach, L.J. 103, 141
Crossman, E.R.F.W. 108, 112, 114, 141
Crott, H.W. 106, 143
Crovitz, H.F. 177, 189
Crow, C.D. 137, 146
Crowder, R.G. 12, 38
Cruts, M. 158, 160, 161
Cuénod, C.A. 57, 73, 265
Cullinan, W.E. 202, 206
Cummings, J.L. 39, 53
Cunningham, W.R. 106, 141

D
Dale, A.M. 37
d'Alessandro, R. 267
Dalgleish, T. 202, 205
Dalla Barba, G. 16, 38, 164, 165, 175, 176,
    179, 180, 183, 185, 188, 189, 190, 197
Dallas, M. 215, 227, 235
Dalmaz, Y. 138, 141
Damasio, A. 196, 204, 243, 244, 250, 261
Damasio, A.C. 250, 251, 261
Damasio, A.R. 56, 73, 196, 205, 260
Damasio, H. 56, 60, 68, 69, 73, 196, 204,
    260, 261
Daniel, M.H. 134, 141
Daniels, J. 160
Dannefer, D. 109, 144
Dartigues, J.F. 161
Dary, M. 52
da Silva-Droux, A. 161
Daugman, J.G. 240, 261
Daum, I. 195, 209
Davidson, R.J. 196, 205
Davies, P. 148, 160
Davis, G.C. 203, 205
Davis, J.L. 104, 141, 142
Deary, I.J. 134, 141

Decety, J. 67, 71, 73, 246, 261
Decker, M.W. 257, 261
Deecke, L. 243, 261
DeFrance, J.F. 116, 141
DeFries, J.C. 154, 160
Degueldre, C. 265
Dehaene, S. 76
Dekker, J.A.M. 252, 261
de Kloet, E.R. 202, 207, 248, 264
de Knijff, P. 161
DeKosky, S.T. 160, 161
Delacour, 269
Delacour, J. 246, 249, 250, 252, 253, 260,
    261, 262, 266, 268, 269, 274
Delaney, R.C. 205
De La Paz, R.L. 56, 73
de la Sayette, V. 38
Delasnerie-Laupretre, N. 202, 204
Delbecq-Derouesne, J. 164, 190
Delfiore, G. 265
De Lima A.D. 236
Della Sala, S. 237
DeLong, M.C. 252, 267
Dempster, F.N. 138, 141
Denes, G. 38, 183, 190
Denys, A. 73
De Renzi, E. 188, 189, 190, 195, 197, 201,
    205
Desgranges, B. 16, 38, 46, 52
Desimone, R. 95, 101, 265, 266
Desmond, J.E. 42, 86, 99
D'Esposito, M. 62, 64, 73, 78, 255, 262
DeTeresa, R. 162
Detre, J.A. 73, 262
Detterman, D.K. 134, 141, 160
Deutsch, S.I. 237
Dey, H. 204
Diamond, A. 256, 262
Dinse, H.R. 108, 145
Di Piero, V. 76
Dohrenwend, B.P. 210
Dolan, R. 64, 65, 67, 73
Dolan, R.J. 38, 39, 41, 45, 46, 47, 48, 51, 52,
    53, 54, 74, 75, 77, 86, 97, 98, 99, 101, 275
Dolev, A. 203, 204
Dolphin, A.C. 247, 262
Donaldson, W. 9, 42, 78, 102, 162
Donhoffer, H. 263
Dorian, B. 203, 205
Dostrovsky, J. 87, 101

Dow, R.S. 265
Downs, J.H. 76
Downs, R.M. 144
Doyon, J. 63, 76
Dreifus, F.E. 102
Dudek, S.M. 265
Duffy, L. 16, 38
Duijn, C. Van 148, 160
Duncan, J. 204, 243, 262
Dupoux, E. 76
Durwen, H.F. 38, 40, 205, 208, 275
Dutruge, J. 138, 141
Düzel, E. 16, 33, 38
Dywan, J. 190

**E**

Earles, J.L. 138, 144, 151, 160
Ebbinghaus, H. vii, viii
Eccles, J.C. 266
Edelman, G.M. 240, 262
Edvardsson, H. 161
Egan, V. 141
Eich, J.E. 44, 54
Eichenbaum, H. 4, 8, 87, 89, 90, 95, 96, 98,
    249, 252, 253, 260, 262
Eijk, R. van 235
Elder, G.H. 202, 206
Eley, T. 160
Ellis, A.W. 216, 235
Ellis, S. 115, 145
Ellison, D. 195, 207
Engen, T. 271, 274
Enns, J.T. 104, 138, 144
Erickson, C.A. 266
Ericsson, K.A. 255, 262
Eriksson, L. 268
Erngrund, K. 40, 153, 154, 160, 161
Eskes, G.A. 35, 41
Eslinger, P. 195, 209
Eslinger, P.J. 56, 73, 261
Essen, D.C. van 241, 262
Estkowski, L.D. 267
Ettlinger, G. 250, 268
Eustache, F. 38, 46, 52
Evans, A.C. 40, 63, 73, 76, 77, 87, 101, 267
Evans, J. 16, 38
Evans, M. 181, 191
Everitt, B.J. 252, 267
Ewald, K. 195, 201, 208
Eysenck, H.J. 112, 113, 115, 120, 141, 142

**F**

Fabisch, G.M. 83, 99
Fadda L. 234
Fadiga, L. 67, 71, 74, 77
Fahy, F.L. 88, 98
Fallon, J. 46, 52
Fanselow, M.S. 254, 266, 272, 274
Farah, M.J. 64, 78, 254, 264
Faulkner, D.W. 154, 160
Fawzi, M.C.S. 203, 206
Fazio, F. 41, 58, 69, 73, 75, 76, 77, 208
Feany, M.B. 239, 262
Fedoroff, P. 196, 210
Feeney, D.M. 58, 74
Feigenbaum, J.D. 88, 101
Felleman, D.J. 262
Fennema, A.C. 236
Ferrell, R.E. 160, 161
Ferro Milone, F. 191
Ferruzza, E. 38
Field, A. 203, 210
Field, D. 151, 161
Field, H.L. 78
Fieschi, C. 76
Fiez, J.A. 62, 74
Figurov, A. 247, 267
Filippi, M. 76
Filskov, S.B. 275
Finch, C.E. 145, 202, 209
Fink, G.R. 35, 38, 48, 50, 51, 52, 77, 194,
    195, 196, 197, 199, 201, 206, 208, 273, 274
Fiske, D.W. 112, 141
Flanigin, H.F. 100
Fletcher, P. 39, 41, 64, 65, 67, 73, 77, 275
Fletcher, P.C. 17, 24, 29, 38, 41, 45, 47, 48,
    51, 52, 53, 54, 64, 67, 74, 86, 96, 97, 98,
    99, 101, 195, 206, 273, 274
Flood, J.F. 248, 262
Flügge, G. 202, 207
Fodor, J.D. 240, 262
Fogassi, L. 71, 74
Ford, I. 61, 75
Forette, F. 73
Forsell, Y. 16, 39
Förstl, H. 206
Foster, J.K. 13, 35, 38, 41, 42
Fouwels, A.J. 202, 205
Fox, J.H. 235
Fox, P.T. 21, 38, 60, 74, 76, 267
Fozard, J.L. 109, 141

Frackowiak, C.S.J. 263
Frackowiak, R.S.J. 21, 38, 39, 41, 45, 46, 47,
　48, 52, 53, 54, 60, 62, 67, 74, 75, 76, 77,
　78, 86, 87, 96, 98, 99, 100, 101, 261, 275
Franceschi, M. 41, 73, 76
Francis, P.T. 239, 263
Franck, G. 75, 265
Franzen, E.A. 196, 206
Freedman, M. 56, 72
Freeman, R.B., Jr. 207
Fregnac, Y. 246, 263
Frensch, P. 115, 143
Freud, S. 194, 205, 206
Friberg, L. 254, 268
Friedman, A. 273, 274
Friedman, H.R. 255, 256, 263
Friston, K.J. 21, 26, 38, 39, 46, 47, 53, 60, 61,
　67, 74, 75, 86, 96, 99, 100, 263
Frith C.D. 77
Frith, C.D. 17, 38, 39, 41, 45, 46, 47, 48, 52,
　53, 54, 60, 62, 64, 67, 74, 75, 76, 77, 86,
　87, 96, 98, 99, 100, 101, 195, 206, 243,
　261, 263, 273, 274, 275
Frölich, L. 195, 199, 208
Fuchs, E. 202, 207
Fukada, Y. 269
Funnell, E. 60, 75, 188, 190
Funuashi, S. 255, 263
Fuster, J.M. 243, 249, 255, 263

**G**
Gabrieli, J. 105, 116, 141
Gabrieli, J.D.E. 42, 86, 96, 99, 227, 228, 229,
　235, 236, 239, 249, 254, 257, 263
Gadian, D.G. 42, 102
Gaffan, D. 82, 99
Gaillard, W.D. 56, 73
Gainotti, G. 72, 74
Galina, Z.H. 196, 210
Gallese, V. 71, 74
Galton, F. 177, 190
Ganser, S.J. 195, 206
Gardiner, J.M. 16, 39, 225, 236
Garfinkel, P.E. 203, 205
Garrett, H.E. 106, 137, 141
Garry, P.J. 138, 142
Gathercole, M.A. 39
Gazzaniga, M.S. 52, 54, 99, 210, 262, 264,
　265, 268, 269
Geffen, G.M. 116, 141

Geffen, I.B. 116, 141
Gehlen, W. 38, 40, 205, 208, 275
Gersons, B.P.R. 202, 205
Gerundini, P. 76
Gibson, E.J. 17, 39
Gibson, G.J. 141
Gigerenzer, G. 103, 141
Gilardi, M.C. 73, 76
Gilbertson, M.W. 206
Giles, W.H. 202, 204
Giller, E.L. 203, 211
Gillin, J.C. 264
Gillund, G. 123, 142
Gingell, R. 267
Glass, T. 76
Glees, P. 79, 99
Glenberg, A.M. 239, 244, 263
Glisky, E.L. 214, 235
Glod, C.A. 202, 210
Glover, G.H. 42, 86, 99
Glowinski, J. 138, 142
Gluck, M.A. 252, 263
Godde, B. 108, 145
Goebel, R.P. 122, 142
Goel, A.K. 121, 143
Goethals, G.C. 269
Gol, A. 83, 99
Gold, J.T. 265
Goldman-Rakic, P. 63, 74
Goldman-Rakic, P.S. 117, 139, 145, 243, 255,
　256, 262, 263, 266
Goldsmith, M. 244, 265
Gonzales, C. 77
Gonzales, R.G. 261
Gonzales-Lima, F. 244, 266
Gonzalez, R.G. 77, 101
Goodglass, H. 72, 74
Gooding, P.A. 231, 235
Goodwin, J.S. 138, 142
Gordon, E. 110, 143
Gore, J.C. 266
Gorno Tempini, M.L., 76
Gorno-Tempini, M. 77
Gott, R.E. 127, 140
Gottfries, C.G. 239, 269
Goulding, P.J. 60, 77
Goulet, L.R. 144
Grabowski, T.J. 73
Grady, C.L. 25, 29, 30, 39, 50, 52, 53, 64, 73,
　74, 75, 99, 100, 108, 142, 264, 266

Graf, P. 213, 215, 217, 218, 224, 235, 236, 237
Graff-Radford, N.R. 56, 73, 74
Grafman, J. 37, 42, 58, 72, 78, 260
Grafton, S.T. 67, 74, 246, 250, 253, 254, 255, 263
Grajski, K.A. 266
Granick, S. 107, 142
Grant, M. 117, 145
Grasby, P. 41, 54, 77, 275
Grasby, P.M. 38, 46, 47, 53, 64, 65, 74, 75, 86, 96, 98, 99, 101, 261
Grassi, F. 41, 69, 73, 76, 208
Grastyan, E. 252, 263
Green, M.L. 202, 204
Green, R. 237
Greenberg, S. 235
Greene, J.D. 16, 39
Greenfield, P.M. 258, 263
Greenough, W.T. 270
Greenspan, R.J. 239, 263
Gregory, E. 162
Grèzes, J. 73
Griffith, H.B. 79, 99
Gross, C.G. 95, 101, 249, 263
Grossberg, S. 252, 261
Grosse, D.A. 227, 235
Grossman, M. 262
Grossmann, M. 73
Growdon, J.H. 235, 236
Grünthal, E. 79, 99
Guimaraes, A.R. 77, 101
Gulyas, B. 47, 53, 265
Gurvits, T.V. 202, 206
Guynn, M.J. 20, 41

**H**
Haaland, K.Y. 138, 142
Haas, H.S. 202, 206
Habib, R. 4, 9, 26, 38, 40, 42, 45, 50, 51, 53, 54, 78, 101, 102, 195, 210
Hablitz, J.J. 247, 269
Haden, P.E. 235
Haenninen, T. 77
Hagnell, O. 147, 148, 161
Haier, R.J. 46, 52
Hajek, M. 84, 99
Haken, H. 240, 263
Hale, S. 109, 111, 112, 136, 142
Halgren, E. 88, 99
Hallikaininen, M. 77

Hamada, I. 255, 268
Hambrick, D.Z. 107, 145
Hameroff, S.R. 272, 274
Hamman, S.B. 225, 228, 235
Hammeke, T.A. 267
Hammer, M. 151, 161
Hammersley, R.H. 190
Hancock, H.E. 107, 145
Hanno, D.J. 115, 142
Hansen, L.A. 162
Harnishfeger, K.K. 138, 140
Härting, C. 208
Härtl, J. 195, 206
Hashimoto, A. 117, 141
Haskett, R.F. 203, 211
Hasselhorn, M. 138, 142
Haugh, V.M. 267
Haupts, M. 38, 40, 205, 208
Haxby, J.V. 17, 25, 39, 50, 53, 60, 65, 74, 75, 86, 88, 94, 95, 96, 99, 100, 142, 253, 261, 263, 266
Hayslip, B., Jr. 106, 142
Heather, J.D. 74
Hebel, N. 56, 73
Heilbronner, K. 194, 195, 206
Heilman, K.M. 56, 73, 75, 117, 141, 267
Heim, E. 202, 206
Heinze, H.-J. 38
Heiss, W.D. 38, 48, 52, 75, 196, 197, 199, 206, 208, 239, 264, 274
Henderson, A.S. 109, 140
Hendrickson, A.E. 112, 113, 114, 115, 120, 142
Hendrickson, D.E. 142
Heninger, G.R. 210
Henke, K. 4, 8, 79, 85, 86, 87, 91, 92, 93, 94, 99
Herbert, T.B. 203, 206
Herholz, K. 59, 75, 200, 208
Hering, E. 273, 274
Herkovitch, P. 260
Herlitz, A. 16, 39, 153, 155, 161
Herman, J.P. 202, 206
Herscovitch, P. 142
Herz, R.S. 271, 274
Heuser, L. 208, 275
Hichwa, R.D. 37, 73, 98, 259
Hicks, R.E. 110, 142
Hintzman, D.L. 171, 190
Hirsch, J.C. 247, 264

Hirsch, T.B. 76
Hitty, C.W.M. 78
Hobson, J. 116, 143
Hobson, J.A. 252, 264
Hockley, W.E. 142
Hodges, J.R. 38, 39, 60, 75, 188, 189, 190
Hoesen, G.W. van 261
Hof, P. 236
Hof, P.R. 105, 144
Hofman, A. 147, 160, 161
Hofstetter, C.R. 162
Hokama, H. 206
Holinka, B. 38, 205
Holmberg, B. 161
Holmes, A.P. 38, 61, 74, 75
Holmgren, G. 161
Holsboer, F. 202, 206
Hölscher, C. 239, 264
Holthoff, V. 264
Holyak, K.J. 243, 268
Horel, J.A. 81, 100, 253, 264
Horn, J.L. 144
Horwitz, B. 39, 50, 74, 75, 99, 100, 142, 263, 266
Houcine, O 262
Houk, J.C. 104, 141, 142
Houle, S 53
Houle, S. 3, 4, 9, 37, 38, 39, 40, 42, 44, 45, 46, 50, 51, 53, 54, 75, 76, 78, 94, 100, 101, 102, 195, 210, 275
Hoyer, W.J. 115, 142, 225, 235
Hubel, D.H. 241, 265
Huber, R. 207
Huff, F.J. 227, 235
Huguenard, J. 266
Hultsch, D.F. 151, 161
Humphreys, A.G. 270
Hurtig, R. 37, 98
Hutton, J.T. 148, 161
Hutton, M. 160, 162
Hyde, J.S. 267
Hyman, B.T. 261

**I**

Iacoboni, M. 43, 53
Iidaka, T. 201, 207
Ikeda, K. 162
iller, E.K. 266
Ingvar, D.H. 39, 243, 264
Innis, R.B. 204, 205

Iriki, A. 247, 264
Isaacson, R.L. 269
Isler, P. 86, 102
Ito, M. 264
Iwai, A. 162

**J**

Jacoby, L.L. 190, 215, 227, 235, 244, 251, 264
James, W. 11, 12, 39, 170, 190
Janet, P. 194, 207
Janowsky, J.S. 244, 254, 257, 264, 268
Jasmanowicz, A. 267
Java, R.I. 16, 39, 225, 236
Jay, T.M. 138, 142
Jeannerod, M. 73, 265
Jehenson, P. 73
Jelicic, M. 13, 38, 42
Jenkins, W.M. 266
Jennings, J.M. 21, 26, 39
Jennings, P.J. 77, 101
Jensen, A.R. 111, 113, 115, 142, 144
Jerabek, P.A. 76
Jervey, J.P. 249, 263
Jetter, J. 195, 207
Jezzard, P. 265
Joëls, M. 202, 207, 248, 264
Johnson, D. 210
Johnson, D.R. 205
Johnson, K.A. 261
Johnson, M. 163, 164, 166, 190
Johnson, M.K. 164, 166, 171, 177, 190
Jolesz, F. 75
Jolesz, F.A. 206
Jones, C. 39, 44, 53, 75, 100
Jones, E.G. 101
Jones-Gotman, M. 83, 100
Jonides, J. 62, 75, 269
Jonker, C. 75
Jordan, W. 202, 211
Jorm, A.F. 109, 140
Joseph, S. 202, 205
Josephs, O. 78
Juraska, J.M. 270

**K**

Kaas, J.H. 246, 264
Kail, R. 138, 142
Kalbe, E. 200, 207, 208
Kamboh, M.I. 160, 161
Kammer, Th. 117, 143

Kandel, E.C. 239, 260, 266
Kanter, S. 117, 141
Kanwisher, N. 43, 53
Kaplan, D. 73
Kaplan, E. 72, 74
Kapur, N. 30, 39, 86, 96, 100, 195, 207
Kapur, S. 3, 4, 9, 17, 22, 24, 29, 30, 33, 37,
    39, 40, 42, 44, 45, 47, 48, 51, 53, 54, 64,
    65, 67, 75, 78, 86, 94, 95, 96, 100, 102,
    195, 210, 275
Karczmar, A.G. 266
Karlsson, S. 40, 161
Karlsson, T. 160
Kartsounis, L.D. 82, 100
Kaschel, R. 237
Kassel, N. 56, 73
Katzman, R. 162
Kaufer, D. 273, 274
Kausler, D.H. 151, 162
Kawata, M. 248, 264
Kaye, W. 58, 78
Keane, M.M. 227, 228, 229, 231, 235, 236
Keator, D. 52
Keil, F. 275
Keil, K. 261
Kellaghan, T. 141
Keller, A. 264
Kelley, C.M. 190
Kellner 195
Kelso, J.A.S. 240, 264
Kempf, E. 118, 142
Kennedy, C. 241, 264
Kenny, A.D. 161
Kessler, J. 38, 48, 52, 196, 197, 199, 200,
    201, 206, 207, 208, 264, 274, 275
Kessler, K. 195, 198
Kessler, R.C. 203, 207
Khan, N. 84, 99
Kikinis, R. 206
Killiany, R.J. 57, 75
Kim, E.H.J. 257, 264, 270
Kimberg, D.Y. 254, 264
King, N.S. 202, 207
Kinomura, S. 241, 258, 265
Kinsbourne, M. 110, 142
Kintsch, W. 255, 262
Kirkwood, A. 247, 265
Kirsner, K. 215, 227, 236
Kischka, U. 117, 143
Kjelgaard, M.M. 235

Kleban, M.H. 107, 142
Knight, R. 195, 207, 274
Knight, R.T. 4, 8, 72, 77, 88, 91, 96, 100, 253,
    265
Knobler, R. 77
Knowlton, B.J. 16, 39, 256, 265, 272, 274
Koch, C. 261
Koeppe, R.A. 75, 269
Köhler, S. 25, 40, 94, 100
Kohnstamm, O. 79, 100, 194, 195, 207
Koivisto, K. 77
Kolen, J.F. 121, 143
Kolk, B.A. van der 202, 207
Kolk, P. 207
König, M. 208
Kopelman, M.D. 185, 190, 257, 265
Koriat, A. 244, 265
Korten, A.E. 109, 140
Koslowsky, M. 203, 204
Kosslyn, S.M. 51, 52, 68, 73, 210, 246, 265
Kossut, M. 246, 265
Koutstaal, W. 37, 210
Koutstall, W. 202
Kraiuhin, C. 110, 143
Kritchevsky, M. 264
Kroll, N. 51, 54, 195, 207
Kroll, N.E.A. 21, 42, 99, 100, 273, 274
Krystal, J.H. 202, 204, 210, 266
Kugler, C.F.A. 110, 143
Kuyken, W. 202, 207

**L**
Laguna, J. 237
Laguna, K.D. 107, 140
Laiacona, M. 189, 201, 204
Lalonde, F.M. 60, 75, 266
Lamberts, R.D. 202, 205
Lammerstsma, A.A. 74
Lancaster, J.L. 76
Landahl, S. 155, 162
Landauer, T.K. 172, 175, 190
Landeau, B. 38
Landis, T. 86, 102
Lanke, J. 148
Lanke, J., 161
Larsson, J. 265
Lasko, N.B. 206
Launer, L.J. 57, 75
Lautenschlager, G. 138, 144
Laver, G.D. 117, 143

Lawley, D.N. 115, 143
Layton, B.S. 202, 207
Le Bihan, D. 246, 265
Lechevalier, B. 38, 52
LeDoux, J.E. 241, 247, 254, 265
Lee, G.P. 100
Leenders, K.L. 84, 99
Leibniz, G.W. von 103, 143
Leiner, A.L. 265
Leiner, H.C. 258, 265
Leino, E.V. 151, 161
Lemmo, M.S. 72, 74
Lenzi, G.L. 41, 73, 76
Lenzi, L. 267
Lepage, M. 26, 37, 40
Lerer, B. 203, 204
Lernfelt, B. 155, 162
Levav, I. 210
Levine, B. 35, 40
Levy, B.A. 231, 236
Levy, J.C. 262
Lewandowsky, S. 122, 142
Lewin, W. 56, 78
Leys, D. 236
Lhermitte, F. 244, 265
Li, S.-C. 109, 111, 114, 115, 116, 118, 120,
    126, 136, 137, 143
Liben, L.S. 144
Liberman, A.M. 72, 75
Liddle, P.F. 39, 60, 67, 74, 263
Lienert, G.A. 106, 143
Liess, J. 40, 208
Lin, L. 206
Lindeboom, J. 75
Linden, D.J. 239, 247, 265
Lindenberger, U. 5, 8, 103, 107, 110, 115,
    116, 126, 137, 140, 143
Liotti, G. 202, 207
Liotti, M. 188, 190
Lisk, L.M. 267
Lisman, J. 239, 265
Lissak, I. 263
Little, V. 137, 146
Livingstone, M.S. 241, 265
Llinas, R.R. 104, 143
Loasses, A. 235
Lobek, L. 72
Lockhart, R.S. 215, 235
Loeber, J.N. 102
Long, J. 144

Lopez, O.L. 151, 160
Loring, D.W. 83, 100
Lubinski, D. 160
Lublin, F. 77
Lucchelli, F. 195, 197, 201, 205
Lucignani, G. 76
Lueschow, A. 250, 265
Lupien, S.J. 196, 202, 207
Luria, A.C. 243, 265
Luxen, A. 265
Lynch, G. 266

M
Maas, H.L. van der 115, 143
Mack, L. 235
Mackinnon, A. 109, 140
Macklin, M.L. 210
Macko, K.A. 95, 100
MacLeod, A.K. 29, 40
MacRae, P.G. 117, 138, 143
Madarasz, I. 263
Maddox, W.T. 127, 140
Madigan, S.A. 12, 42
Maehara, T. 207
Magariños, A.M. 202, 207
Maguire, E.A. 86, 87, 96, 100
Mahers, B. 190
Mahlmann, J. 235
Mai, F.M. 194, 208
Maier, S. 117, 143
Mair, C.G. 244, 251, 266
Mair, W.G.P. 56, 75
Maisog, J.M. 39, 74, 75, 99, 142, 263
Majewska, M.D. 202, 208
Malamut, B. 266
Malhot, C. 160, 162
Mamelak, A.N. 116, 143
Mandel, P. 118, 142
Mandler, G. 164, 190, 213, 224, 235
Manelis, J. 102
Mangels, J. 38
Mangels, J.A. 265
Mangun, G.R. 38
Manicavasagar, V. 203, 210
Mann, D.M.A. 60, 77
Manshardt, J. 118, 143
Mantovan, M.C. 38
Mäntylä, T. 153, 154, 160, 161
Maquet, P. 242, 265
Marchal, G. 52

Marcusson, J. 147, 161
Maren, S. 254, 266
Marfia G. 234
Marinkovic, K. 88, 99
Markowitsch, H.J. 4, 6, 8, 9, 15, 26, 35, 38,
    40, 42, 48, 51, 52, 54, 78, 86, 88, 91, 95,
    96, 102, 193, 194, 195, 196, 197, 198, 199,
    200, 201, 202, 203, 204, 205, 206, 207,
    208, 209, 210, 254, 260, 266, 271, 273,
    274, 275
Marsiske, M. 110, 143
Martin, A. 60, 68, 69, 75, 88, 94, 96, 100
Martin, A.H. 239, 250, 266
Martin, C.C. 76
Martin, J.J. 160
Martin, P. 58, 78
Martin, R.C. 100
Martinelli, V. 76
Masliah, E. 162
Mason, J.W. 203, 205, 211
Masson, M.E.J. 236
Matarrese, M. 76
Matelli, M. 77
Mattingly, I.G. 72, 75
Mattioli, F. 201, 208
Maurer, K. 195, 199, 208
May, P.C. 116, 144
Mayes, A.R. 195, 209, 235
Mayfield, D. 117, 145
Mazure, C. 205
Mazziotta, J.C. 43, 53, 73
McCarley, R.W. 206
McCarthy, G. 205, 255, 266
McCarthy, R.A. 68, 78
McClelland, J.L. 104, 143, 240, 268
McCloskey, M. 133, 144
McCormick, D.A. 243, 266
McDowd, J.M. 123, 144
McEntee, W.J. 244, 251, 266
McEwen, B.S. 196, 202, 207, 267
McGaugh, J.L. 52, 196, 205, 209, 260, 266,
    274
McGlynn, S.M. 236
McGuffin, P. 160
McHugh, R.B. 107, 144
McIntosh, A.R. 35, 37, 38, 39, 40, 45, 46, 50,
    52, 53, 74, 75, 76, 94, 100, 101, 244, 255,
    256, 266
McKenna, T.M. 240, 266
McLachlan, D.R. 181

McLellan, D.L. 195, 207
McMackin, D. 100
McMullen, T.A. 266
McNally, R.J. 210
McNaughton, B.L. 104, 143
Meador, K.J. 100
Meares, R. 110, 143
Mehler, J. 76
Meinz, E.J. 107, 145
Melo, B. 163, 171, 172, 174, 175, 176, 177,
    181, 185, 188, 190
Mendelson, W. 264
Mentis, M.J. 39, 74, 142
Merleau-Ponty, M. 170, 190
Merzenich, M.M. 246, 266
Messa, C. 58, 76
Mesulam, M. 241, 243, 266
Mesulam, M.-M. 272, 275
Metcalfe, J. 96, 100
Meudell, P. 235
Meunier, M. 82, 100
Meyer, E. 63, 77, 267
Michot, J.L. 73
Miezin, F.M. 37, 40, 41, 46, 52
Milberg, W.P. 236
Milech, D. 236
Miliotis, P. 57, 73, 195, 209
Miller, B.L. 39, 52
Miller, E.K. 255, 265
Miller, M.B. 99
Milner, B. 40, 56, 76, 79, 80, 81, 82, 83, 84,
    85, 87, 97, 101
Minoshima, S. 75, 269
Mintun, M.A. 60, 74, 75
Miozzo, A. 60, 76, 208
Mirzaian, E.B. 208
Mishkin, M. 42, 81, 82, 95, 99, 100, 102, 142,
    244, 250, 264, 266
Mitchell, D.B. 224, 228, 234
Mitchell, D.R. 77
Miyaoka, M. 264
Miyashita, Y. 48, 88, 101, 250, 266
Miyasita, Y. 54
Modgil, C. 141
Modgil, S. 141
Mogenson, G.J. 116, 146
Molenaar, P.C.M. 115, 143
Mollica, R.F. 206
Monti, L.A. 231, 232, 236
Moore, C. 39

Mora, F. 138, 144
Mörchen, F. 195, 209
Morgan, A., III 196, 210
Morgan, C.A. 210
Morgan, D.G. 116, 144
Morley, J.E. 262
Moroz, T.M. 38
Morris, G.L. 267
Morris, M.K. 251, 267
Morris, P.E. 39
Morris, R. 202, 204
Morris, R.G. 58, 76
Morrison, J.H. 105, 144, 228, 236
Morse, C.K. 109, 144
Mortimer, J.A. 148, 161
Morton, J. 171, 190, 215, 235
Mos, L.P. 145
Moscovitch, M. 3, 9, 24, 25, 30, 35, 38, 40,
    42, 43, 44, 46, 47, 49, 51, 53, 54, 94, 95,
    100, 102, 163, 164, 171, 172, 174, 175,
    176, 177, 181, 185, 188, 189, 190, 191,
    272, 275
Moss, M.B. 75
Mountcastle, V. 263
Mueller, W.M. 267
Muggia, S. 195, 201, 205
Muir, J.L. 252, 267
Müller-Suur, H. 195, 209
Murphy, E. 206
Murphy, K. 260
Murphy-Weinberg, V. 203, 211
Murray, E.A. 82, 83, 99, 100, 101
Musen, G. 231, 236
Myers, C.E. 252, 263
Myers, R.E. 196, 206
Myerson, J. 109, 136, 142

N
Nadel, L. 4, 8, 47, 53, 87, 101, 252, 267, 272,
    275
Nagy, L.M. 210
Nakajima, T. 207
Nakamura, C.K. 264
Namba, Y. 160, 162
Nanko, S. 162
Nathan, P.W. 195, 209
Nauta, W.J.H. 244, 267
Neary, D. 60, 77
Nebes, R.D. 58, 76
Neisser, U. 239, 244, 267

Nelis, E. 158, 161
Nelson, E.A. 109, 144
Nertempi, P. 191
Nesselroade, J.R. 106, 109, 112, 139, 140, 144
Newell, A. 104, 144
Ng, C.K. 204
Nichelli, P. 188, 190
Nicolaou, A. 196, 210
Niki, H. 255, 267
Nilsson, L. 162
Nilsson, L.-G- 45
Nilsson, L.-G. 8, 16, 39, 40, 46, 50, 53, 76,
    149, 152, 153, 154, 155, 156, 158, 159,
    160, 161, 162
Nishino, H. 260
Nordeen, E.J. 248, 267
Nordeen, K.W. 248, 267
Norman, K.A. 202, 210
Nottebohm, F. 248, 267
Nutt, J.G. 74
Nyberg, L. 17, 23, 24, 28, 29, 33, 35, 37, 38,
    40, 45, 46, 48, 50, 51, 52, 53, 65, 73, 76,
    86, 101, 154, 161, 162
Nylander, P.-O. 161
Nyquist, L. 151, 162

O
O'Brien, J.T. 202, 209
O'Carroll, R. 16, 38
O'Connor, M. 195, 209
Oden, A. 162
Ohta, H. 206
Ojemann, G.A. 240, 267
Ojemann, J.G. 37, 41
Öjesjö, L. 148, 161
Okazaki, A. 207
O'Keefe, J. 4, 8, 87, 101, 252, 267
Okuizumi, K. 160, 162
O'Leary, A. 203, 209
O'Leary, D.S. 37, 98, 259
Oliverio, A. 118, 142
Olivier, A. 100
Olofsson, U. 154, 161, 162
Oltmann, F. 190
Onodera, O. 160, 162
Oomura, Y. 260
O'Reilly, R.C. 104, 143
Orr, S.P. 206
Oscar-Berman, M. 214, 237
Ostry, D. 73

Otto, T. 89, 98, 249, 262
Ottoson, D. 268
Owen, A. 63, 76
Owen, A.M. 25, 40, 63, 76, 77, 87, 101
Owen, M.J. 160
Owens, W.A. 107, 144
Oxbury, S. 60, 75, 188, 190

**P**
Palermo, D.S. 144
Palm, G. 260
Palmertz, B. 162
Pandya, D.N. 244, 267
Pangalos, M.N. 263
Pantano, P. 76
Papez, J.W. 271, 275
Pardo, J.V. 243, 267
Park, D.C. 138, 144
Parks, E.D. 202, 209
Parmeggiani, P.L. 253, 267
Parsons, L.M. 71, 76
Partanen, K. 77
Passafiume, D. 76
Passingham, R.E. 74, 77
Patterson, K. 60, 75, 188, 189, 190
Paulesu, E. 59, 62, 73, 76
Pavlides, C. 248, 264, 267
Pawlik, G. 264
Pearson, K. 115, 143, 144
Peck, D.F. 203, 209
Penfield, W. 79, 80, 84, 85, 97, 101
Perani, D. 13, 41, 58, 59, 60, 65, 67, 68, 69,
    73, 75, 76, 77, 208
Pericak-Vance, M.A. 162
Perl, R. 137, 141
Perlmutter, M. 151, 162
Perner, J. 16, 41
Persson, G. 162
Peters, A. 101, 269
Peters, J.M. 265
Petersen, S.E. 26, 37, 40, 41, 46, 52, 74
Peterson, E.L. 203, 205
Petit, H. 236
Petit-Taboué, M.C. 38, 52
Petrides, M. 40, 48, 53, 62, 63, 67, 73, 76, 77,
    87, 101, 255, 267
Pettigrew, K. 264
Peyrin, L. 138, 141
Pham, T. 206
Piaget, J. 258, 262, 267

Pick, A. 195, 209
Picton, T.W. 38
Pietrini, P. 39, 74, 99, 142
Pietrini, V. 189, 191
Pillemer, D.B. 16, 41
Pillon, B. 265
Pinker, S. 17, 41
Pinna, V. 191
Pirch, G.H. 257, 268
Pitkaenen, A. 77
Pitman, R.K. 202, 206, 209, 210
Platt, D. 110, 143
Plomin, R. 6, 8, 154, 160
Plude, D.J. 104, 138, 144
Pockett, S. 247, 260, 267
Poline, J.-B. 74
Poline, J.-P. 38
Polster, M.R. 41
Ponto, L.L.B. 259
Poole, C. 206
Poon, L.W. 109, 136, 140, 142
Portillo Marquez, G. 196, 209
Poryia, M. 269
Poser, U. 207
Posner, M.I. 21, 27, 41, 104, 144
Pozzilli, C. 76
Premack, D. 72, 77
Press, G.A. 56, 77
Pribram, K. 269
Pribram, K.H. 250, 267, 272, 275
Price, C. 78
Price, C.J. 39
Prigatano, G.P. 190
Printz, H.W. 104, 145
Procyk, E. 73
Puce, A. 266
Pulisi-Allegra, S. 118, 142

**Q**
Quinn, W.G. 239, 262

**R**
Rabbitt, P.M. 109, 111, 135, 144
Racine, R.J. 247, 267
Raecke, J. 195, 209
Rafal, R. 99
Raichle, M.E. 21, 27, 37, 40, 41, 46, 52, 60,
    74, 267
Raife, E.A. 74
Ramponi, C. 39

Randall, P. 205
Rao, S.M. 72, 246, 267
Rapoport, S.I. 39, 50, 53, 75, 99, 100, 142, 236, 263
Rapscack, S.Z 237
Rauch, S.L. 41, 45, 54, 65, 77, 86, 101, 210
Raye, C.L. 164, 166, 190
Rebert, C.S. 202, 209
Recanzone, G.H. 266
Reed, T.E. 113, 144
Regard, M. 86, 102
Reiff, M. 210
Reiman, E. 41
Reiman, E.M 60, 74
Reinert, G. 106, 137, 144
Reinkemeier, M. 38, 48, 52, 206, 274
Reis, D.J. 118, 144
Reminger, S.L. 236
Rempel-Clower, N.L. 82, 83, 101, 195, 209
Renella, R.R. 86, 102
Revello, M.G. 191
Rezai, K. 37, 98, 259
Ribot, T. vii, viii
Rice, L. 112, 141
Rich, D. 204
Richardson, C.T. 252, 267
Richardson-Klavehn, A. 39
Riches, I.P. 88, 98
Ridley, C.M. 250, 268
Riekkinen, P.J. 77
Rigdon, G.C. 257, 268
Rimmler, J.B. 162
Rioux, G.F. 239, 268
Rioux, P. 46, 52
Rizzolatti, G. 67, 71, 74, 77
Robbins, T.W. 252, 267
Robel, P. 268
Roberts, E. 262
Robertson, A. 203, 209
Robin, N. 243, 268
Robinson, G.B. 239, 268
Robinson, R.G. 196, 210
Rocca, W.A. 161
Rockland, C. 260
Roediger, H.L., III 20, 41, 190, 220, 236, 237
Roesch, S.C. 107, 140
Rogers, J. 116, 145
Rohan de Silva, H.A. 160, 162
Roland, P.E. 47, 53, 246, 254, 265, 268

Rolls, E.T. 88, 101, 138, 144, 241, 252, 254, 268
Romijn, H. 272, 273, 275
Romo, R. 117, 145
Rönnlund, M. 153, 161
Roos, A. 86, 102
Roozendaal, B. 196, 209
Rorsman, B. 148, 161
Ros, C.A. 268
Rose, R 39
Rosen, B.R. 37, 77, 101
Rosene, D.L. 80, 101
Rosenzweig, M.R. 236
Roses, A.D. 162
Rosi, B.L. 160, 162
Roskies, A. 24, 41
Ross, C.A. 239
Rosse, R.B. 237
Rossetti, C. 76
Rosvold, H.E. 255, 268
Rothman, R.B. 117, 145
Rotte, M. 37
Rousseaux, M. 251, 268
Rowe, J.W. 144
Royce, J.R. 104, 145
Rozin, P.A. 230, 236
Rubens, A.B. 236, 237
Rubin, D.C. 189
Rudge, P. 82, 100
Rudy, J.W. 252, 268
Ruffman, T. 16, 41
Rugg, M.D. 17, 29, 33, 38, 41, 45, 46, 47, 48, 50, 53, 64, 74, 86, 97, 101, 195, 206, 273, 274
Rumelhart, D.E. 240, 268
Rushworth, M.F.S. 63, 77
Russell, W.R. 194, 209

**S**
Sabbadini, M. 234
Saito, H. 269
Saitoh, T. 162
Sakai, K. 48, 54
Sakai, M. 255, 268
Sakurai, Y. 272, 275
Salerno, J.A. 142
Salmon, D.P. 58, 77, 227, 236, 237
Salmon, E. 75
Salomon, R.M. 204

Salthouse, T.A. 107, 109, 111, 136, 138, 142, 145, 151, 160, 162
Sandor, T. 75
Sanghera, D.K. 160, 161
Sann, L. 138, 141
Sannguinetti, A.M. 138, 144
Sapolsky, R.M. 202, 209
Sarter, M. 196, 210
Saults, J.S. 151, 162
Sauter, B. 195, 209
Savage, C.R. 41, 45, 54, 65, 77, 86, 101
Sawaguchi, T. 117, 145
Sawle, G.V. 74
Schacter, D.L. 3, 8, 13, 17, 29, 33, 37, 41, 44, 45, 46, 49, 53, 54, 65, 77, 86, 96, 97, 101, 104, 145, 158, 162, 181, 190, 202, 210, 214, 215, 216, 217, 219, 220, 224, 231, 234, 235, 236, 237
Schaie, K.W. 149, 151, 161, 162
Schaie, R.W. 140
Schallert, T. 117, 145
Schapiro, M.B. 39, 74, 99, 142
Schauenstein, K. 202, 206
Scheich, H. 38
Scheltens, P. 75
Schiess, R. 86, 102
Schiffman, H. 177, 189
Schmajuk, N.A. 252, 260, 264
Schmidtke, K. 195, 210
Schneider, B. 195, 199, 208
Schneider, E.L. 144, 145
Schneider, K. 194, 210
Schneider, W. 104, 145
Schneiderman, C.R. 137, 140
Schnur, T. 69, 73, 77
Schultz, L. 203, 205
Schultz, W. 117, 138, 145
Schultze, E. 195, 210
Schumacher, E.H. 269
Schumacher, M. 248, 268
Schuri, U. 56, 73, 237, 271, 274
Schwartz, B.L. 222, 237
Schwartz, E.L. 95, 101, 261
Schwartz, S. 210
Schwarz, J.P. 74
Scott, L.R. 109, 140
Scott, T.M. 205
Scoville, W. 79, 81, 82, 83, 84, 85, 97, 101
Sebastian Galles, N. 76
Seese, N. 160

Seibyl, J.P. 205
Seitz, R.J. 254, 268
Sejnowski, T.J. 103, 104, 140, 141, 261
Seki, K. 162
Selbie, S. 260
Seldman, S. 273, 274
Semon, R. 3, 8, 44
Serdaru, M. 265
Servan-Schreiber, D. 104, 116, 117, 118, 120, 145
Seward, J. 77
Shallice, T. 24, 35, 38, 41, 44, 47, 48, 52, 54, 64, 65, 67, 74, 77, 86, 96, 98, 101, 163, 164, 171, 174, 181, 189, 190, 191, 243, 268, 273, 275
Shanahan, M.J. 202, 206
Sharp, A.H. 239, 268
Sharpey, W. 193, 210
Shelley, A.M. 138, 145
Shenton, M.E. 206
Shepard, R.N. 104, 145
Shiffrin, R.M. 123, 142
Shimamura, A.P. 58, 77, 214, 215, 217, 227, 231, 235, 236, 237, 254, 257, 264, 268
Shin, L.M. 196, 210
Shin, R.K. 73, 262
Shiraishi, H. 207
Shlesinger, M.F. 266
Shrout, P.E. 210
Shulz, D. 263
Siegel, A.M. 100
Siegel, L.S. 138, 145
Siegler, R.S. 115, 145
Sikes, R.W. 116, 141
Sikström, C. 161
Silbersweig, D. 77
Silove, D. 203, 210
Simpson, J. 99
Sinden, M. 40
Singer, W. 247, 260
Sinnerbrink, I. 203, 210
Sirabian, G. 76
Sirota, A. 73
Skodol, A.E. 202, 210
Skoog, I. 147, 148, 155, 161, 162
Small, B.J. 16, 37, 151, 161
Smith, A.D. 138, 144
Smith, E.E. 75, 255, 269
Smith, G.A. 109, 111, 136, 142, 145
Smith, J.R. 100

Smith, M.E. 214, 237
Smith, M.P. 195, 207
Smith, S. 58, 77, 236
Snowden, J.S. 60, 77
Soardi, M. 60, 76
Soininen, H.S. 57, 77
Sokoloff, M. 264
Soreq, H. 273, 274
Soufer, R. 204
Southwick, S.M. 196, 202, 204, 210
Spearman, C.E. 106, 111, 145
Spengler, F. 108, 145
Spinnler, H. 189, 195, 201, 205
Spirduso, W.W. 117, 138, 143, 145
Spiro, A. 106, 140
Spitzer, M. 116, 146
Sprague, J.M. 263
Squire, L. 244, 249, 252, 253, 266, 267, 268,
    269
Squire, L.C. 264
Squire, L.R. 4, 8, 15, 16, 17, 24, 37, 39, 41,
    56, 77, 78, 82, 87, 88, 89, 90, 98, 101, 102,
    195, 209, 213, 214, 215, 217, 225, 228,
    231, 235, 236, 237, 265
Staats, A.W. 104, 145, 146
Staib, L. 205
Staib, L.H. 204
Stander, P. 236
Stanfield, P. 110, 143
Stanger, B.Z. 235
Stanley, G. 111, 145
Starkstein, S.E. 196, 210
Statistiska Centralbyrån 147, 152, 162
Staudinger, U.M. 103, 140
Staunton, H. 100
Steel, S. 203
Steel, Z. 210
Stellar, E. 263
Stephan, K.M. 67, 77
Steriade, M. 241, 242, 243, 269
Stern, C.E. 65, 77, 86, 94, 96, 101
Sterns, H.L. 106, 142
Stevens, J.M. 82, 100
Stone-Elander, S. 268
Storch, F.I. 264
Störring, G.E. 79, 99
Strauss, J. 269
Strong, E.K. 123, 146
Studer, A. 117, 145

Stuss, D.T. 35, 38, 39, 40, 41, 42, 43, 54, 243,
    254, 269, 270
Suda, S. 264
Suddendorf, T. 16, 42
Sugiura, R.M. 77, 101
Sunderland, D. 267
Sundsmo, M. 162
Sundstrom, E. 145
Surrey, J. 202, 210
Sutherland, R.J. 252, 268
Sutker, P.B. 196, 210
Sutor, B. 247, 269
Sutton, S.K. 196, 205
Suzuki, W.A. 82, 102
Suzuki, Y. 207
Svanborg, A. 162
Sweeney, K.F. 138, 144
Swett, C. 202, 210
Swick, D. 72, 77
Swirsky-Sacchetti, T. 59, 77
Sypert, G.W. 56, 75
Szafran, J. 108, 112, 114, 141
Szelies, B. 264
Szwarcbart, M.K. 255, 268

**T**
Tadary, B. 73
Taghavy, A. 110, 143
Takahashi, H. 162
Talairach, J. 26, 27, 29, 30, 34, 42, 48, 54, 61,
    78
Talbi, B. 262
Talbot, N. 235
Talland, G.A. 244, 251, 269
Tanaka, H. 162
Tanaka, K. 249, 250, 269
Tang, C. 52
Teasdale, T. 237
Teicher, M.H. 202, 210
Testa, H.J. 60, 77
Tettamanti, M. 77
Thal, L.J. 162, 261
Tharan, M. 236
Theodore, W.H. 56, 73
Theuns, J. 160
Thiel, A. 208
Thierry, A.M. 138, 142
Thomas, D.G. 137, 146
Thomas, J.C. 109, 141
Thomas, R.G. 162

Thompson, L.A. 160
Thompson, W.L. 210
Thompson-Schill, S. 64, 78
Thöne, A.I.M. 197, 208
Thorpe, S. 263
Tieman, J. 75
Tierney, M.C. 151, 162
Toth, J.P. 40
Tournoux, P. 26, 27, 29, 34, 42, 48, 54, 61, 78
Tranel, D. 56, 73, 74, 196, 204, 260, 261
Tsumoto, T. 247, 269
Tulving, E. 2, 3, 4, 8, 9, 12, 13, 14, 15, 16,
    20, 21, 23, 24, 26, 27, 29, 32, 33, 37, 38,
    39, 40, 41, 42, 43, 44, 45, 46, 50, 51, 52,
    53, 54, 63, 65, 67, 68, 75, 76, 78, 83, 86,
    88, 91, 95, 96, 100, 101, 102, 158, 162,
    164, 175, 181, 185, 187, 188, 193, 194,
    195, 200, 210, 215, 220, 236, 237, 246,
    249, 250, 252, 253, 254, 255, 260, 269,
    270, 273, 275
Turner, R. 265
Tyler, L.K. 188, 190

U
Uchimura, J. 79, 102
Uecker, A. 41
Ueki, A. 162
Underwood, B.J. 121, 140
Ungerleider, G.L. 50
Ungerleider, L. 246, 250, 253, 254, 255, 266,
    269
Ungerleider, L.G 142
Ungerleider, L.G. 39, 53, 60, 74, 75, 88, 95,
    99, 100, 142, 261, 263, 266
Uno, H. 202, 209

V
Vaglia, A. 191
Vainio, P. 77
Valavanis, A. 86, 102
Valenstein, E. 117, 141
Valentin, D. 135, 146
Vallar, G. 41, 58, 73, 76
Van, G. 160
Vandenberghe, R. 69, 78
Van der Linden, M. 237
Van der Ven, C. 196, 199, 208
Van Hoesen, G.W. 56, 73, 74, 80, 101
Van Paesschen, W. 42, 102
Varga, M. 260

Vargha-Khadem, F. 15, 42, 83, 102
Vedantham, V. 77, 101
Veraguth, O. 194, 210
Verdugo, J.M.G. 202, 207
Vermetten, E. 205
Victor, M. 56, 78
Vidal, C. 202, 211
Videen, T.O. 41
Vinogradova, O. 252, 253, 269
Vogt, S. 72, 78
Voigt, T. 236
Vollmer, H. 195, 210
Voronin, L. 247, 269
Vranes, L.F. 138, 142

W
Wagenaar, W.A. 189
Wagner, A.D. 33, 34, 35, 42
Wagner, E. 142
Wakefield, J. 258, 270
Walk, R.D. 17, 39
Wallin, A. 147, 161, 239, 269
Wang, S.-Y. 160
Wang, Z. 266
Wapner, S. 138, 141
Ward, P.B. 138, 145
Wardi-Zonna, K. 202, 207
Warren, J.M. 268
Warren, S.G. 248, 270
Warrington, E.K. 56, 60, 68, 72, 75, 78, 189,
    191
Watanabe, M. 243, 255, 270
Watanabe, Y. 267
Watkins, G.L. 37, 98, 259
Watkins, K.E. 42, 102
Watson, J.D.G. 61, 75
Watson, R.T. 117, 141
Watson, S.J. 203, 211
Waugh, N.C. 109, 141
Weber, B. 4, 8, 79, 92, 93, 94, 99
Weber, E. 237
Weber-Luxenburger, G. 196, 199, 207, 208
Wehnert, A. 160
Weinberger, N.M. 246, 257, 260, 266, 270
Weinbren, M. 118, 144
Weingartner, H. 58, 78
Weinstein, H.C. 75
Weisbrod, M. 117, 143
Weiskrantz, L. 56, 72, 75, 78
Weiss, A.D. 107, 142

Weldon, M.S. 220, 236, 237
Welford, A.T. 108, 111, 112, 114, 115, 135, 146
Wennekers, T. 260
Werner, H. 138, 141
Wesensten, N.J. 260
Wheeler, M.A. 15, 36, 42, 43, 54, 252, 270
Whitaker, E. 137, 146
White, S.H. 16, 41
Whitty, C.W.M. 56, 76
Widen, L. 268
Widing, M. 40, 161
Widlitzek, B. 205
Widlitzek, H. 38
Wiener, P.P. 143
Wiener, S.I. 252, 270
Wieser, H.G. 4, 8, 79, 84, 85, 86, 92, 93, 94, 99, 100, 102
Wiggs, C.L. 60, 75, 88, 100, 266
Wilcox, R.E. 117, 143
Wilkins, A. 189, 191
Wilkins, W.K. 258, 270
Williams, M.V. 111, 135, 140
Willis, S.L. 106, 140
Wilson, A.A. 39, 75, 100
Wilson, B. 38, 163, 164, 171, 185, 189
Wilson, B.A. 214, 237
Wilson, D.A. 267
Wilson, R. 275
Wilson, R.S. 235, 236
Winblad, B. 40, 161
Winocur, G. 38, 40
Winstead, D.K. 196, 210
Wise, R. 78
Wolbarst, L.R. 235
Wolf, E.S. 96, 100
Wong, E.C. 267
Woodruff, G. 72, 77
Woods, A.M. 111, 135, 140
Woods, R. 73
Woods, R.P. 43, 53
Woody, C.D. 257, 260, 264, 270

Woolf, N.J. 242, 270
Worsley, K.J. 38, 74
Wragg, M. 160, 162
Wraight, E.P. 38
Wu, J. 52
Würker, M. 208, 275
Wurtman, R.J. 118, 143

**X**
Xia, Y. 160, 162

**Y**
Yamamoto, T. 162
Yamaoka, L.H. 162
Yang, C.R. 116, 146
Yasargil, M.G. 84, 102
Yehuda, R. 203, 211
Yeterian, D.H. 244, 267
Yetkin, F.Z. 72, 267
Yonelinas, A.P. 38
Young, A. 39, 86
Young, A.W. 216, 235
Young, E.A. 203, 211
Young, J.Z. 240, 270
Young, W.G. 236
Yun, L.S. 41

**Z**
Zaccheo, D. 259
Zangwill, O.L. 76
Zatorre, R.J. 100
Zeffert, S. 203, 209
Zeffiro, T.A. 265
Zeki, S. 43, 54
Zieglgänsberger, W. 202, 211
Zimmerman, D.W. 116, 146
Zipursky, R.B. 39
Zola, S.M. 82, 101
Zola-Morgan, S. 56, 78, 82, 102, 195, 209, 244, 249, 252, 253, 269
Zola-Morgan, S.M. 82, 88, 90, 101, 102
Zubal, G. 204

# Subject Index

**A**

Ablation studies 79
Abnormal priming 231, 233
Abstract figures 230
Acalculia 199
Action 7
  memory 156
  memory tasks 157
  recognition 72
Activation 108
  level(s) 251, 257
  maps 21
  studies 60
Adulthood 202
Age 5
  cohorts 5
  deficits 151
  -induced changes 5
  -related deficits 153
  -related deterioration 152, 153
  -related diseases 159
  -related increase 136
  -related slowing 111, 136
Aging 5, 239
  deficits 108
  -induced changes 113
  -induced degeneration 4, 116
  -induced deterioration 116
Agnosia 240
Alcohol 148
Alcoholics 218
Alleles 148, 155
Alpha-1-antichymotrypsin (AACT) 160
Aluminum 148
Alzheimer's disease 1, 3, 58, 147, 148, 155,
  156, 159, 188, 214, 227, 228, 229, 231,
  232, 234, 257
Amino acid 155
Amnesia 7, 15, 56, 57, 65, 165, 171, 187,
  189, 201, 202, 216, 254
Amnesic 79

confabulatory syndrome 6, 172
  disturbances 194
  patients 3, 4, 18, 181, 244
  syndromes 81, 86, 213, 244, 246, 248
Amnesics 56, 213, 214, 223, 225, 226
Amobarbital testing 86
Amygdala 80, 196, 242, 254, 271
Amygdalohippocampectomy 83, 84
Amygdaloid complex 202, 273
Amyloid
  angiopathy 148
  precursor protein (APP) 148
Aneurysm 175
Animal 1
  experimentation 257
  memory research 271
  studies 7, 255
Anosognosia 184, 185
Anoxia 58
Answering general knowledge questions 222
Anterior
  cingulate 253, 257
  cyngulum 6
Anterograde
  amnesia 83, 196, 197, 200, 201, 218, 234
  degeneration 257
  memory 63, 64, 199, 200
Aphasics 72
ApoE 148, 155, 156, 157, 158, 159, 160
APP 159
Apraxia 240
Army Alpha Test 107
Arousal 7
  motivation level 243
  motivational effect 243
Associate memory 166
Association
  centers 113
  cortex 47, 240, 243, 250, 258
Associative
  learning 46, 86, 91, 93, 94, 95, 97, 107

retrieval 163
Attention 7, 243, 252, 259
Auditory
    cortex 246, 253, 257
    input lexicon 216
    language comprehension 216
    -verbal working memory 62
    word form system 219
Autobiographic events 199
Autobiographical
    episodes 172
    event 177, 249
    information 35
    memory 13, 63, 172, 174, 179
    past event 180
Automatic retrieval 64
Autonoetic 3
    awareness 12, 13, 15, 17, 36
    consciousness 175

**B**
Back-propagation networks 121
Balance of a system 169
Basal
    forebrain 56
    ganglia 4, 59, 116
    telencephalon 243
Behavior 245
Behavioral neurology 1
Betula
    study 154, 156, 158, 159
    test battery 156
Biographic events 199
Blood
    fat 151
    flow 95
    flow increases 93
    sample testing 151
    sugar 151
Brain
    activity 48, 199, 203
    aging 135
    damage 3
    imaging 240, 244, 246, 250, 253, 254, 256,
        257
    Brain injury 6
    maps 21
    metabolism 204, 273
    state vector 115
    stem 243, 256, 258

Broca's area 71
Brodmann 27, 28, 45
Brodmann system 26

**C**
C3 155
CA1 56
Cardiac arrest 172
Cardiovascular disease 155
CAT 6, 175, 200
Catecholamines 104, 116
Categorization
    learning 105
    tasks 5, 127
Category exemplar production task 218
Caudate nucleus 95
Cell assemblies 272
Cellular immune response 203
Center of memory 244, 246
Central activation 241, 251
Central executive 62
Central nervous system 105, 148, 159
    variability 109, 112, 114
Cerebellum 4, 59, 69, 240, 247, 258
Cerebral
    activation 251
    activity 60
    blood flow 21, 57, 200
    glucose metabolism 59
    pathways 71
Cerebrospinal fluid 200
CG 155
Child development 138
Childhood 202
Children 4
Chinese boxes game 166
Cholesterol 155
Cholinergic
    neurons 242
    projections 257
Chromosome 19 155
Cingulate 242, 258
    gyrus 3, 56, 58
Classical conditioning 18, 249, 252, 253, 257
CNS variability 109, 112, 114
Coactivations 89, 90
Coding 7
Cognitive
    abilities 4, 106
    activation studies 60

activities 249, 251, 259
aging 106, 107, 108, 114, 153
capacities 110, 244
deficit 181
estimates 181
functioning 5
map theory 87
neuroscience 1
plasticity 110
psychology 1
speed 150
strategies 222, 251
system 167
test battery 5
Color-theory 273
Common-cause hypothesis 110
Complement C3 154
Compositionality 89
Computational
capacities 259
frameworks 112
modelling 1
processing 169
Computed tomography (CT) 6, 56, 165, 175,
200
Computer-brain 240
Concept
formations 272
identification 107
Conceptual priming 220, 228
Conditional task 63
Conditioned eye-blink 249
Confabulation 6, 163, 171, 172, 174, 175,
176, 177, 179, 180, 181, 182, 185, 187,
188, 189
Confabulation Battery 175, 177
Confabulatory
episodes 179
future 185
memory 181
past 179, 185
present 185
Connectionist
modelling 68
networks 105, 132, 133
simulations 104
Conscious
awareness 12, 14, 16, 17, 36
consciousness 166
control 165

recollection 8
Consciousness 6, 11, 181, 183
Consolidation 46, 88, 174
hypothesis 87
Control processes 165, 166
Cooperative activity 242
Coping strategies 202
Corpus callosum 6, 175
Correct memory 166, 174
Cortex 95
Cortical
arousal 252
networks 104, 108
Cortico-hippocampo-cortical loops 253
Cortisol response 203
Creutzfeldt-Jakob disease 202
Critical life events 5
Crovitz test 180, 181
Crystallized intelligence 106
CT scan 6, 56, 175, 165, 200
Cued recall 47, 64, 90, 123
test 156
Cuing conditions 222
Cyngulum 175
Cytoarchitectonical brain descriptions 273

**D**
Day-to-day memory 188
Declarative
information 15
memory 4, 15, 63, 79, 82, 253
(semantic) memory 13
systems 14
task 94
Dedifferentiation 4, 5, 106
Dedifferentiation hypothesis 5
Deep encoding 64, 65
Deficit of retrieval 174
Degenerative dementia 227
Delayed
alternation (DA) 256
non-match-to-sample task 82
response (DR) 256
Dementia 57, 147, 159, 239
Demyelinating process 59
Dendritic spines 169
Dentate gyrus 79, 83
Depression 7, 148, 202, 203
Diagonal band of Broca 56
Diencephalic

amnesics 213
 lesions 251, 257
 lobe 256
 nuclei 214
 syndrome 252
Diencephalon 56
Differentiation hypothesis 137
Digit memory span 109
Disconnection 58
Diseases 5
Distinct memory systems 244
Distracting task 62
DNA 154, 158
Dopamine 5, 116
 metabolites 138
 receptors 117
Dopaminergic system 5, 117, 138
Doppler sonography 197
Dorsolateral frontal cortex 4
Dot patterns 230
Down's syndrome 148
Drug treatment 200, 201
Dual-task
 conditions 154
 interference 67

**E**
Ecphory 3, 33, 43, 44, 46, 47, 48, 49, 65, 194,
 203
EEG 197, 199, 200, 242, 247
Electroconvulsive therapy 201
Electrolytes 151
Electrophysiological
 activity 247
 recordings 197
Emotion 79, 196
Emotional disorganization 271
Encephalitis 200
Encoding 8, 14, 22, 23, 24, 27, 28, 30, 31, 36,
 46, 47, 64, 87, 88, 96, 154, 174, 183, 251,
 255, 272, 273
 activations 34
 specificity principle 33
Encoding tasks 46, 91
Engram 3, 51, 167, 174, 204
Engrams 44, 47
Entorhinal cortex 83
Environmental stimulation 193
Epicenters of retrieval 34
Epilepsy 80, 81, 83, 84

 surgery 4, 79, 83
Epinephrine 116
Episodic
 encoding 21, 25
 information 33
 learning 58
 memory 2, 5, 6, 7, 11, 12, 37, 43, 58, 59,
  63, 64, 83, 95, 105, 109, 150, 152, 153,
  155, 158, 164, 175, 176, 177, 182, 183,
  185, 188, 189, 193, 197, 201, 203, 215,
  216, 220, 221, 233
 memory deficit 188
 memory encoding 51
 memory questions 179
 memory retrieval 44, 46, 48, 50, 51, 200
 memory system 220
 memory tasks 151, 153, 157, 158, 185,
  187, 188
 memory tests 5, 220
 memory trace 169, 182
 retrieval 21, 22, 36, 44, 45, 50, 51
 semantic memory 63
 tasks 45
Event(s) 2
 memory 13
 -related potentials 50, 88, 253
Evoked potential 71, 137, 197, 247
Explicit memory 249, 252
 condition 213
 tests 222
Explicit retrieval 220, 223, 224
Extrastriate cortex 43
Extrinsic connections 245

**F**
False memory 166, 194
Family history 5
Famous people 69
Fear conditioning 254
Fluid intelligence 106, 109, 126
2(18F)-fluorodeoxyglucose (FDG) 59, 197,
 199, 200
Forebrain infarction 56
Forgetting 194
Fornix 56, 79
Fragmented picture completion 220
Fragmented picture identification 233
Fragmented pictures 214
Free association 214, 215, 217, 218, 219, 226,
 227, 233, 234

task 226
Free recall 64, 123, 213, 227, 254
test 156
Frontal
activation 254
basal cortex 3
cortex 8, 46, 58, 59, 63, 64, 65, 95, 164, 171, 243, 254, 257
gyrus 34, 71
ischemia 6, 175
lesions 44
Frontal lobe(s) 16, 24, 43, 51, 62, 163, 177
lesions 67, 254
operculum 34
pole 48
syndrome 244
Fugue condition 197
Fugue-condition 195
Functional
activation 230
amnesia 195, 196, 201, 204
brain imaging 12, 43
imaging 86
magnetic resonance (fMRI) 2, 33, 36, 55, 57, 86
neuroimaging 79, 86, 195, 272, 273
Fusiform gyri 69, 93
Fusiform gyrus 93, 95
Future planning tasks 187, 188, 189

**G**
GABA-agonists 196
Ganser syndrome 195
Gaussian input signal 120
GC 155
Gender differences 153
Gene pool 158
General
factor 6
intelligence 111
knowledge 16, 153, 221
Memory Index 200
semantic knowledge 185
Generalizations 272
Genetic(s) 1
analysis 6
markers 5, 154, 155, 158, 159
Genome expression 248
Global
amnesia 3, 86

amnestic syndromes 8, 242, 244, 249, 251, 255
syndrome 254
pure amnesia 57
Glucocorticoid feedback 203
Glucocorticoids 202, 203, 248
Glucose 151, 241
Glucose
metabolic rate 46
metabolism 57, 58
scores 199
Grandmother cell 272
Graphemic cued recall 221, 222
Grey matter 59

**H**
$H_2^{15}O$ PET studies 86, 91
Haptoglobin (HP) 154
Head trauma 57, 148
Health 5
care 5
Hearing disturbances 200
Hemisphere 84
Hemispheric asymmetry 23, 25, 31
Hemoglobin 151
HERA 24, 26, 27, 28, 29, 30, 31, 32, 36, 51, 273
Heritability 6
Heterozygotes 155
High recall 45
High-cued recall 46
HIPER model 26
Hippocampal
activation 65, 86, 87, 94, 95, 96
amnesics 213
blood flow 86
complex 272, 273
damage 56, 82, 214
formation 202
memory hypothesis 79, 83
metabolism 46
neurons 253
regions 3
volume 56, 202
Hippocampectomy 83
Hippocampi 214
Hippocampus 4, 44, 47, 49, 56, 65, 79, 81, 82, 242, 246, 248, 252, 253, 256
Hippocampus proper 79, 82
Historical event 177

Holographic 272
Homunculus 6
Hormonal factors 248
Hormones 151
Hot-tube theory 230
HP 155
Human(s) 7
    faces 25
    studies 7
Huntington's disease 227
Hypometabolism 59
Hypothalamic-hypophyseal-adrenocortical
    axis 202, 203
Hypothesis of confabulation 176
Hysterical amnesia 194, 195

**I**

Identification of fragmented pictures 228
Illusion of the homunculus 163, 166, 189
Imagination 166
Imitating 272
Imitation 68
Immune response factors 155
Implicit memory 18, 57, 58, 59, 150, 249
    condition 214
    tests 222
Implicit retrieval 220, 223, 224
Incidental
    learning 25
    retrieval 45
Indirect priming 117
Infarction 6, 175
Inferotemporal cortex 249
Information
    processing system 12
    recall 195
Input-output mapping 122, 133
Insightful learning 272
Insomnia 203
Instincts 17
Instrumental conditioning 18
Intelligence 4, 6, 106, 111, 158, 159, 197
    tests 106
Intentional
    learning 25
    retrieval 43, 45
Intentionality 166
Interindividual variability 109, 135
Intermodal priming 232
Internal noise 5

Inter-network variability 126, 132
Inter-spike intervals 242
Intersystemic link 114
Intra-network variability 118
Intracranial electrodes 88
Intraindividual variability 109
    hypothesis 136
Intralaminar thalamic nuclei 258
Intramodal priming 232
Intrinsic connections 245
Intrinsic membrane 243
IQ 113
    tests 111
Ischemic
    damage 82, 83
    lesions 82

**J**
Judgment task 62

**K**
Know judgment 185
Knowing consciousness (KC) 183, 187, 188
Knowledge 165
    memory 13
    of the world 17, 22
    system 193
Korsakoff syndrome 257
Korsakoff's disease 56
Korsakoff's syndrome 58, 193, 227, 251

**L**
L-dopa 117
Labile personality 194
Language
    areas 59
    comprehension 84
    deficit 216
Lasting amnesia 196
Lateral temporal areas 3
Laterality of activations 50
Learning 2, 17, 56, 79, 245, 246, 248, 250,
    254, 255, 259
    list 34
    rate 133
    task 180, 247
Left hemisphere 23, 31, 51, 273
Letter-matching task 62
Leukocytes 151
Lexical

decision 214
  retrieval 69
  semantic processes 60
Life span 4
Lifespan 106
Limbic structure 253
Limbic structures 243, 244, 271
Limbic system 46, 242, 271
Limbic-diencephalic lesions 256
Limited-capacity store 61
Lingual gyrus 79, 93, 95
Linguistic activity 240
Linguistic Semantic Memory questions 176
Lipids 155
Lipoprotein(s) 155
  receptor (VLDL-R) 160
List learning 64
  tasks 12
Living organisms 1
Lobectomy 80, 84
Localizationist thesis 244
Locus ceruleus 242
Long-term depression 1, 247
  episodic memory 57
  knowledge 255
  memory 4, 21, 46, 57, 58, 88, 163213, 214
  memory tasks 250
  potentiation (LTP) 1, 89, 239, 247
  retention 64
  storage 88
  storage system 168, 183, 185, 187
Loss of knowledge 60
Lost in the present 181
Low recall 45
Low-cued recall 47
LTM 4, 21, 46, 57, 58, 88, 163, 213, 214

**M**

Magnetic resonance imaging (MRI) 6, 56, 58,
  59, 84, 175, 197, 200
Major depression 201
Mammillary bodies 56, 251
Mammillo-thalamic tracts 56
Manifest brain damage 195
Marker
  property 157
  systems 155
Massive stress conditions 202
Match-to-sample tasks 250
Medial

diencephalon 8
  parietal neocortical areas 3
Medication 5, 152
Meeness 170
Memory 1, 2, 3, 5, 6
  block 204
  block conditions 195
  consolidation 272
  decline 1
  deficits 59, 117, 184, 244
  disorders 1, 147
  disturbances 244
  errors 90
  for context 13
  functions 1
  impairment 57
  loss 81, 195
  performance 152, 154
  processing 193, 195
  space 90
  span 138
  store 15
  subsystems 13, 194
Memory system(s) 3, 4, 7, 8, 13, 20, 171,
  193, 194, 244, 247, 259
  tasks 13, 222, 249, 258
  testing 150
  tests 57, 254
  trace hypothesis 170
  trace paradox 6, 163, 167, 169
  traces 44, 95
Meningitis 200
Mental
  activity 79
  illness 148
  lexicon 63
  representations 246
  set 43
  time travel 15, 16, 19, 32
Metabolic activities 112
Metabolism 58
Metacognition 244, 249, 259
Metamemory 254
Micro-electrode 247
Middle networks 121
Minerals 151
Mirror reading 213
Mnesic activity 167
Mnestic block syndrome 7, 203, 204
Mnestic blocks 194

Models of memory 168
Modular 7
Monitoring processes 166, 179
Monkeys 8
Monte Carlo simulations 115
Motivation 7
Motor
    actions 71
    activity 243
    area 240
    cortex 247
    neurons 246
    output 241, 243
    skills 250
    theory of perception 72
MRI 6, 56, 58, 84, 175, 197, 200
MTL 16
Multi-component system 57
Multifactorial diseases 160
Multiple
    memory system 13, 61, 55, 215, 222
    memory system theory 219, 221, 233
    personality 195
Multiple sclerosis (MS) 3, 59

N
Neocortex 89, 214, 227, 228, 243
Neocortical
    damage 214
    structures 227
Neocorticectomy 83
Nerve conduction velocity (NCV) 113
Nervous system 112, 169, 239
Network 5, 58, 90, 98, 134, 258
Networks 242
Neural
    circuitry 104
    circuits 33
    coding 112
    connectivity 113
    imaging 104
    models 104
    networks 240
    noise 108, 112, 138
    noise hypothesis 114, 117
    plasticity 239, 247
    signal 112
    transmission 112
Neuroanatomy 1
Neurobiology of learning and memory 7

Neurocognitive system 13
Neurodegenerative disease 148
Neurofibrillary tangles 148
Neurohormonal levels 7
Neurohormones 273
Neuroimaging 2, 55, 57, 243
    field 64
    studies 47
Neurological disease states 3
Neuromodulator 7, 273
Neuronal
    activation 90
    activity 88
    loss 148
    metabolism 202
    nets 202
Neurophysiology 1
Neuropsychology 1
Neurosteroids 248
Neurotransmitter(s) 104, 116, 243, 273
    receptor studies 151
    systems 4
Neutral events 179
New associations 231
Noetic awareness 14, 16
Non-amyloid precursor protein (NACP) 160
Non-matching-to-sample task 18
Nonsemantic encoding condition 224
Nonverbal
    amnesia 199
    learning 83
    memory 84
Non-words 229
    identification 231
Norepinephrine 116, 196
Normal priming 222, 227, 231, 233, 234
Novelty 4
Novelty
    assessment 51, 88
    detection 88, 96
    encoding hypothesis 51
Nucleus basalis 242
Nucleus basalis of Meynert 251

O
Object discriminations 250
Occipital
    cortex 93
    lobe 228, 250
Old

age 1, 105, 106, 147
  episodic information 196
  memory 174, 182, 195, 199, 203
  networks 121
  people 4
Olfaction 79
Orbito-frontal
  cortex 196
  regions 6
Organic amnesia 196, 201
Organic amnesias 194
Organicity 203
Organization of the brain 246
Orientation tasks 182, 185
Orosomucoid (ORM1) 154
Overlapping network 69

**P**

P300 110
Paired associate(s) 47
  learning 64, 97
  recall 121
  tasks 126
  word learning 86
Palinscopic memory 19
Pantomime recognition 72
Papez's circuit 4, 56, 58
Parahippocampal
  activation 87
  gyrus 56, 79, 80, 93, 94
Parietal
  cortex 59, 108, 256
  lobes 29, 228
Parkinson's disease 256, 257
Parkinson's diseaseand Huntington's
  diseaseÄ& 258
Past event 49, 168
Pastness 11, 19, 168, 170, 182
  of experiences 12
Past time regions 34
Pathological
  conscious awareness 174
  memory 164
Pattern completion 231
Perception 169, 245, 259
  of motion 250
Perceptual
  priming 16, 220
  representation system(s) 5, 219, 216
  task 92, 93, 94, 96

Peripheral synapses 247
Perisylvian language areas 4
Permanent
  memory 89
  storage 89
Persistent
  amnesia 56
  anterograde amnesia 199
  retrograde amnesia 197
Personal
  future 179, 180, 184, 187, 188, 189
  future planning tasks 183
  memory 13, 200
  past 43, 174, 180, 183, 187, 193
  past memory 194
  present 179, 180, 187
Personality 201
PET activation studies 60
  $^{15}$O-positron-emission-tomographic
    activation study 199
Phonological loop 62
Phosphorylation 156
Physical abuse 202
Picture
  discrimination task 69
  identification 233
  matching task 68
  naming tasks 68
Planning tasks 185
Plastic neurons 245
PMP-22 158
Positron emission tomography (PET) 2, 3, 4,
    6, 20, 21, 22, 24, 26, 27, 29, 33, 34, 35, 36,
    44, 45, 46, 47, 48, 49, 50, 52, 55, 57, 58,
    59, 60, 61, 62, 65, 67, 69, 71, 72, 79, 86,
    92, 95, 175, 197, 199, 200
Post-anoxic amnesia 56
Post-encephalitic amnesia 56
Post-morbid memory 172, 175
Postoperative
  amnesia 84
  memory deficits 82
Post-retrieval
  processing 49
  stage 174
Posttraumatic stress disorder 203
Precentral gyrus 34
Precuneus 47, 64, 258
Prefrontal
  activation 3, 71

activations 50
activity 49
cortex 24, 31, 45, 46, 48, 51, 67, 88, 108,
    138, 195, 200, 243, 247, 254, 255, 256,
    273
damage 195
region 3
Premorbid memory 172
Premotor
    area 250
    cortex 240, 257
Presenilin-1 (PS-1) 148
    gene 160
Presenilin-2 (PS-2) 148
Present event 169
Presynaptic neurons 247
Primary memory 5, 16, 150, 153
Primate brain 241
Priming 18, 152, 153, 250
    conditioning 257
    effect 214, 223, 229, 231
    system 193
    task 94
Principles of encoding specificity 14
Procedural
    learning 59
    memory 5, 15, 59, 150, 193, 272
Processing speed 134, 138
Progressive brain diseases 1
Properdin factor B (BF) 154
Proposed circuit of emotion 271
Proscopic 18
    memory 19
Prose recall 220
Prospective memory 63
    task 154
Protein(s) 151, 169
    level 155
    synthesis 248
Psychic amnesia 201
Psychobiological stress reaction 203
Psychogenic 6
    amnesia 194, 195, 196, 200
Psychopharmacology 1
Psychotherapy 200
Psychotic disorders 81
Pure amnesics 7, 214, 221, 227, 231, 234
    place cells 252
Pursuit Rotor Learning Task 213
Putamen 95

Puzzle assembly 213

**R**
R/K paradigm 16
Random state vector 115
Raphe 242
rCBF 95
Reality monitoring 164
Recall 64
    tasks 83, 172
Recent memory 80, 174, 175, 182
Receptive fields 108, 246
Recognition 22, 47, 123, 213, 215
    memory 271
    memory task 172, 178, 179
    strategy 68
    test 231, 254
Recollective experience 3, 44, 49
Recovery 49
Reduced blood flow 58
Reflexive consciousness 251
Regional cerebral blood flow (rCBF) 95, 108
Rehearsal 62
Remember judgment 185
Repetition priming 7, 214, 216, 217, 218, 219,
    220, 221, 227, 228, 229, 232, 233
Repetition priming effect 213, 230
Repetition priming tests 215, 220, 232
Representational flexibility 89
Representational systems 14
Rereading 231, 233
Response
    generation 67
    109, 111, 113
    speed 117
    time (RT) 109
Retention 56
Reticular formation 242
Retrieval 3, 4, 8, 14, 15, 20, 21, 22, 23, 24,
    27, 28, 29, 30, 31, 32, 33, 36, 43, 47, 48,
    50, 55, 65, 86, 87, 88, 96, 154, 163, 169,
    182, 217, 222, 251, 255, 272, 273
    activations 25, 34
    attempt 33
    block 194
    circuit 35
    conditions 45
    cues 220, 221
    deficit 171, 181
    hypothesis 174

mode 3, 43, 46
new 91, 95
old 91, 95
processes 171, 176
task 49, 91
Retrograde
amnesia 83, 88, 195, 196, 199, 200, 201
degeneration 257
memory 63, 197
semantic memory 200
Rhinal cortex 82
Right hemisphere 23, 31, 50, 51, 196, 200, 273
Risk factors 148

**S**
Selective
attention 138
autobiographic amnesia 6
semantic memory deficits 188
Self-awareness 35
Semantic
cued recall 222
dementia 60
encoding 251
encoding condition 224
knowledge 14, 22, 68
memory 3, 4, 51, 57, 58, 68, 82, 83, 94,
150, 153, 158, 164, 175, 176, 177, 188,
189, 193, 201
memory retrieval 22, 36
memory tasks 152, 157, 158, 185, 188
memory tests 5
priming 117
retrieval 21
system 220, 228
tasks 187
Senile plaques 148
Sensorimotor cortex 108, 257
Sensory
cortex 247
functioning 5
inputs 241
/motor capacities 243
neurons 246
Separate memory systems 245
Septal nuclei 56, 242
Septum 271
Serum protein polymorphisms 154, 155
Severe amnesia 82
Sex difference 155

Sexual
abuse 202
engagement 271
hormones 248
Sexually abused 194
Shock experience 199
Short term knowledge 255
Short-term memory 3, 4, 57, 58, 59, 64, 88,
117, 197, 199
Short-term memory (STM) 61, 62
Short-term memory tasks 250
Sigmoid activation function 105
Signal coding 104
Signal-to-noise ratio 104, 116, 241, 253
Single
item learning 91, 92, 93, 94, 95, 96
neuron recording studies 88
photon emission computed tomography
(SPECT) 57, 200
spike mode 242
task conditions 154
word learning 86
Smell brain (rhinencephalon) 271
Smoking 148
Smoothing 61
Social
retreat 203
variables 5
Somatic cortex 253
Somesthetic cortices 246
Source
amnesia 153, 181
memory 13, 153
monitoring 177
monitoring tasks 178
recall test 156
Spatial
cognition 150
information 4
learning 87
theory 252
working memory tasks 256
Statistical Parametric Mapping (SPM) 60, 61
Stem completion 214, 215, 216, 218, 219,
220, 223, 224, 225, 226, 227, 228, 229,
231, 233, 234, 235
for new associations 217
priming 228
Stereotactic normalization 61
Steroid

hormones 248
  receptors 248
Stimulus
  response mapping 134
  retrieval 233
Storage 8, 104, 174, 251, 255
  capacity 89
  level 183
Strategic memory 249, 254
Strategic retrieval 6, 44, 163, 164, 172, 176, 177
  deficit 181
  hypothesis 177
Stress 6, 201, 203
Stress
  evoking events 196
  related hormones (glucocorticoids) 196, 199
Stressful life 200
Striatum 116, 240, 247, 257, 258
Stroop test 138
Structural-description system 219
Sub-arachnoid hemorrhage 175
Subarachnoid hemorrhage 6
Subiculum 79, 83
Substantia innominata 56
Subtraction
  analysis 93
  method 21, 26, 257
Successful retrieval 167
Suicide 201
Supervision 7
Supraspan 46
Symmetrical asymmetry 28
Synapses 113
Synaptic
  connectivity 89
  efficacy 89
  networks 169
  plasticity 239, 247

T
Tachistoscopic identification 229
Telencephalon 242
Temporal
  activations 96
  amnestic syndrome 252
  associative cortex 59
  consciousness (TC) 183, 184, 185, 187, 188, 189

cortex 58, 200
  gradient 174, 175
  gyrus 48, 96, 250
  lobe 8, 56, 79, 195, 196, 201, 202, 250, 256, 273
  lobe damage 193
  lobe epileptics 221
  order 6
  pole 60, 69
  stem 81
  syndrome 253
Temporality 6, 163, 171, 179, 180, 181, 182
Temporary memory 89
Temporobasal cortex 196
Temporo-frontal activation 201
TF 155
Thalamic
  lesions 56, 251
  nucleus 56
Thalamus 3, 56, 58, 95, 251, 256, 257, 258
Theta
  episodes 253
  frequency 253
  rhythm 253
Thyroid gland disease 148
Time
  and place tasks 179
  travel 13
Tone discrimination task 110
Topographic 7
Tower of London test 63
Trait 6
Transferrin C (TF) 155
Transmission 104
Transmitter 6
Trauma 203
Travel back in time 193
True episodes 179
True memory 164, 165, 175, 179, 181

U
Unconscious consciousness 166, 167
Uncus 80
Unsuccessful retrieval 167
Urine 151

V
Vascular
  dementia 155
  disease 148

disorders 155
lesion 79
Vegetative
 emotional cognitive dissociation 203
 responses 253
Verbal
 amnesia 199
 fluency 153
 information 14
 learning 12, 83
 memory 84
 semantic information 35
 tasks 63
 working memory 62
Vestibular nucleus 247
Vibrissa stimulation 253
Visual
 area 108
 association cortex 249
 cliff 17
 cortex 113
 cortices 246
 imagery 47
 input lexicon 216
 landmark 87
 learning 249
 memory 95
 memory tasks 249
 recognition memory 82
 scenes 14
 striatum 95
 tract 113
 word form system 219
 word recognition 44
 working memory 62
Visuomotor task 258
Visuospatial
 sketchpad 62
 task 153
Vitamin(s) 151
 B12 148
Vocabulary tests 153
Voluntary act 7, 242

**W**
Wanderlust 195
Warmth and intimacy 170
Wechsler Memory Scale, revised 200
Wechsler's 106
Wechsler's Intelligence Scale 107
Whiplash injury 200
White cells 151
White-matter 35
Wisconsin Card Sorting Test (WCST) 138
Woodcock-Johnson Tests 138
Word
 comprehension 153
 cue test 177
 definition tasks 185
 finding difficulties 199
 fluency tests 157
 fragment completion 221, 222
 generation task 69
 identification 215, 216, 218, 219, 220,
  227, 231, 233
 knowledge 16
 lists 65
 pairs 65
 recognition 48
 stems 45
Word-lists 215
 free recall 220
 learning 227
Word-stem completion 58
Working
 conditions 5
 memory 4, 61, 107, 117, 254
 memory model 62
 tasks 255
World knowledge 200

**Y**
Yes/no recognition 32, 156, 218, 227
 memory task 178
Young networks 121